tterns in Crime

Paul and Patricia Brantingham
Simon Fraser University

Macmillan Publishing Company
New York
Collier Macmillan Publishers
London

..ATION

our son Jeff

Copyright © 1984, Macmillan Publishing Company, a division of
Macmillan, Inc.

Printed in the United States of America

Macmillan Publishing Company
866 Third Avenue, New York, New York 10022

Collier Macmillan Canada, Inc.

Library of Congress Cataloging in Publication Data

Brantingham, Paul J.
  Patterns in crime.

  Bibliography: p.
  Includes index.
  1. Crime and criminals. 2. Crime and criminals—
History. I. Brantingham, Patricia L. II. Title.
HV6025.B69 1983   364'.042   82-14928
ISBN 0-02-313520-4

Printing: 1 2 3 4 5 6 7 8   Year: 4 5 6 7 8 9 0

ISBN   0-02-313520-4

Patterns in Crime

Paul and Patricia Brantingham
Simon Fraser University

Macmillan Publishing Company
New York
Collier Macmillan Publishers
London

DEDICATION

To our son Jeff

Macmillan Publishing Company
866 Third Avenue, New York, New York 10022

Collier Macmillan Canada, Inc.

Library of Congress Cataloging in Publication Data

Brantingham, Paul J.
    Patterns in crime.

    Bibliography: p.
    Includes index.
    1. Crime and criminals.   2. Crime and criminals—
History.   I. Brantingham, Patricia L.   II. Title.
HV6025.B69   1983   364'.042   82-14928
ISBN 0-02-313520-4

Printing: 1 2 3 4 5 6 7 8   Year: 4 5 6 7 8 9 0

Preface

This book presents a broad range of advanced-level information about the spatial and temporal patterns of crime in the United States, in England and Wales, and in Canada. We have assumed that students using this book have previously completed an introductory course in methods of social science research. Within the context of that assumption, the book provides detailed comparative information about crime patterns and should prove useful in courses on crime analysis or criminal justice planning. In a more general fashion, the book should be useful in courses on the history of crime and the geography of crime and might also supplement an upper-division survey course on criminology.

Chapter 1 provides a general introduction to the fields of criminology and criminal justice and distinguishes between them. *Criminology* is defined as the empirical science of crime and criminal events, studied in a manner basically consistent with Ernst Nagel's views on the structure of science. *Criminal Justice* is defined as the policy science of crime control. The subject of *Patterns in Crime* is criminology.

Chapters 2, 3, 4, and 5 comprise a major division of the book. These chapters are committed to a discussion of the sources of information about crime. Chapter 2 describes memoirs and other first-person accounts of criminal events. Chapter 3 describes data provided by the criminal justice system. Chapter 4 describes survey sources of information about criminal events: self-report studies and victimization studies. Chapter 5 provides a strategy for using multiple information sources in criminological research.

The second major division of the book might be titled "The Temporal Harmonics of Crime." This division—Chapters 6, 7, and 8—explores the temporal patterns of criminal events. Chapter 6 provides a brief introduction to temporal analysis in criminological research, moving from a very simple visual inspection of graphed, temporally arrayed data to fairly sophisticated time-series analysis. Chapter 7 traces trends in American, English, and Canadian crime since 1960, examines the major correlates of these modern trends, and considers a number of the major explanations for the crime trends and their correlates. Chapter 8 traces historical trends over very long periods of time: 800 years for England; 350 years for the United States; a century for Canada. Social, economic, demographic, and institutional changes are examined.

The third major division of the book examines the spatial dynamics of crime. Chapter 9 provides a brief introduction to the geographic imagination and to spatial analysis. Chapter 10 examines macrogeographic patterns in crime at the international, intranational, and intercity levels. Chapter 11 traces patterns of crime within the city. It contains much of the material traditionally considered part of the ecology of crime. Chapter 12 examines microspatial crime patterns, the recent findings of researchers working in the field known as *environmental criminology*. This chapter provides information about the patterning of criminals' target choices and how the physical and social structure of the city influences criminal events.

We would like to thank a number of people for their help with this book. Aileen Sams typed large segments of the manuscript. Professor Lee Bowker provided many helpful suggestions and comments. Our editors at Macmillan Publishing Company, especially Kenneth J. Scott, Senior Editor, and Juli Barbato, Production Editor, were supportive, flexible, and helpful throughout.

Finally, we would like to say a word about order of authorship. This book is in every respect a completely joint effort. There is no meaningful "first author/second author" distinction to be made. The requirements of Library of Congress cataloging in publication data dictated that one name should appear first. Order of authorship was selected by a coin flip.

Contents

Contents

5 Using the Sources of Information About Crime   83

6 Temporal Analysis of Crime   93

7 Modern Temporal Patterns in Crime   119

8 Long-Term Patterns in Crime   161

9 Spatial Analysis of Crime   211

1

Patterns in Crime

Introduction

The study of crime is one of the most important pursuits of the social sciences, for two very different reasons: (1) Crimes are inherently dramatic events. They cause great harm and elicit a strong social response. People find tales of mass murder more interesting than reports of an increase in coal production or a decline in the fertility ratio. People are entertained by a thief's coup in taking a jewel from a heavily guarded museum, but they are bored by the everyday heroics of sanitation workers, assembly-line supervisors, or bankers. Robin Hood is legend but the first chancellor of the Exchequer is unknown. As a result, much of social life can be studied through crime and communicated to an audience unreached by parallel studies of similarly important but less dramatic events. (2) Crime is the actual focal point of the consideration of many of the most important issues in social organization. Crime implies punishment and raises the issue of power. It relates the individual citizen to society and government. Crime reflects social decisions about the appropriate distribution of status, privilege, and wealth and about the methods people use to attain them. The patterns of crime have long been seen as a touchstone that reveals the inner composition of society.

This book is about the patterns of crime in Canada, England, and the United States. Although different in many ways, the societies of these countries are similar in several critical respects. They are industrialized societies with high standards of living. They share a dominant language. They have evolved from a single imperial source: a homeland and its North American colonies. They have similar legal systems grounded in the English common law. Most centrally, their laws have developed from a common base and have had a mutual influence even as they have moved apart and differentiated. It is possible, because of these similarities, to compare and contrast Canadian, English, and American crime patterns in illuminating ways.

Criminology and Criminal Justice

Crime is a complex social phenomenon. Every crime has a legal component (a rule that prohibits specific conduct on pain of punishment) and a behavioral component (conduct in violation of that rule). Every crime generates the possibility of social response: the enforcement of the law against its violator. The study of crime is currently organized through two principal disciplines: criminology and criminal justice.

Criminology

Criminology is the empirical[1] science of crime. That is, criminologists are concerned with such things as the origins of criminal laws, the origins of criminal motivation, the characteristics of criminal events, and, more recently, the characteristics of the criminal justice system.

In pursuing these concerns, criminologists, like other scientists, engage interactively in three activities: description and measurement, the use of formal logic, and the use of creativity.

Descriptive Science

The core of science is the constant search for and examination and testing of facts about the thing under study. Statements of fact that are substantiated by evidence, and about which most competent observers agree, can be used to construct explanations of how things happen and to state rules of relationship that permit the prediction of future events. Facts can be used to test the efficacy of suggested rules of relationship through controlled observation and experiment.

An example of descriptive activity in criminology is the history of the study of southern homicide problems in the United States. The relative distribution of deaths caused by homicide in the various American states became an issue of factual inquiry during the 1920s and 1930s as two sets of data were systematically collected for the first time: the vital statistics on causes of death listed in death certificates and crimes known to the police. Both data sets showed that the states of the Old South, states that formed the secessionist Confederacy during the period 1861–1865, had homicide rates that were far higher than the homicide rates recorded in the rest of the United States. This crime differential, measured by two independent data sets, appeared early (Brearly, 1932) and has persisted as the major feature of the American geography of crime (Shannon, 1954; Harries, 1974). This fact proved exceptionally interesting to social scientists during the 1960s, and essentially identical explanatory schemes were advanced by historians (Hackney, 1969) and sociologists (Gastil, 1971): a regional culture of violence had evolved in the South. According to this thesis, people raised in this culture were far more likely to use lethal violence than people raised outside it. Moreover, the culture was strong: it persisted among Southern emigrants and it coopted Southern immigrants. The culture of violence was held to be far more important to an understanding of Southern homi-

---

[1] The term *empirical* is used in its broad meaning denoting enquiries based on controlled observation of phenomena. (See Nagel, 1961, 450–459.) It is not used in the narrow meaning that denotes enquiries based solely on experiment.

cide rates than such things as racism, poverty, or lack of adequate emergency medical services.

The idea of a Southern culture of violence seemed particularly useful because it offered independent corroboration of an inductively developed model of the origins of individual violence advanced at about the same time by criminologists (Wolfgang and Ferracuti, 1967). But subsequent studies demonstrated that better (or at least alternative) measures of things such as poverty, race, and income variation could diminish the apparent analytic importance of culture to virtually nothing (Loftin and Hill, 1974; Brantingham, 1975b), and that Southerners approved of violent behavior no more than did non-Southerners (Erlanger, 1976). Thus, this particular explanation of Southern homicide became untenable.

In this example, a descriptive fact about American crime had been established. A question requiring understanding, or "explanation," became apparent: Why were Southern murder rates so high? Various *other* fact patterns—considered on the basis of commonly observed associations with crime or the South or both— were compared for their congruence with the pattern of homicide. Some congruencies, such as the apparent fit between homicide rates and climate, were rejected because they required unacceptable assumptions about the character of criminal motivations and criminal events. The climatic explanation, for instance, required researchers to assume that human irritability and aggressiveness—and hence proneness to lethal violence—rise with the ambient air temperature and are biologically determined. Remaining congruencies, such as the fits between homicide and patterns of economic privation, medical service, or historical traditions of violence, were examined more carefully. An explanation was suggested on the basis of the apparent relative importance of these congruencies in predicting the observed homicide rates of the various states. That is, an explanatory model for Southern homicide rates was constructed by comparison with *other* empirical facts. This model was then *tested* by other researchers using refined measurements of such facts as economic deprivation. The model failed the test and was generally abandoned.

Formal Logical Science

A second activity is the use of formal logical techniques in which statements about the relationships are put precisely, but in general form, and are then extended through the process of logical deduction to state additional or more detailed relationships and to predict additional facts or events. The validity of formally extended statements can be tested internally (against the rules of logic) or externally (against established facts, through observation or experiment).

Examples of formalization in criminology are more difficult to find than examples in physics or economics, but the works of Edwin Sutherland and Jack Gibbs can serve as cases in point. Sutherland probably did more to structure American criminology than any other writer. Gibbs is a contemporary formalist.

Sutherland is known for the development of "differential association" theory, an attempt to codify and abstract extant information about criminal behavior into a sociological theory of the origin of individual criminality. The theory contained nine propositions (Sutherland, 1947, pp. 6–9) asserted to be empirically and logically coherent. DeFleur and Quinney (1966) reduced Sutherland's propositions to

3

set theory notation and tested their formal logic. They found that the theory was internally inconsistent and proceeded to rewrite it. Reconstructed—that is, rendered logically consistent and stripped of logically unnecessary propositions—the theory of differential association could be stated in forty-six words:

> Overt criminal behavior has as its necessary and sufficient conditions a set of criminal motivations, attitudes and techniques, the learning of which takes place when there is exposure to corresponding anti-criminal norms during symbolic interaction in primary groups. (DeFleur and Quinney, 1966, p. 7)

Gibbs (1972) has been among the foremost in asserting the virtues of formalization in social science. He has used formalization procedures to define the theory of deterrence in which common-law criminal justice is grounded. The formal theory of deterrence has in turn been used to specify detailed hypotheses for factual testing through observation and experiment (Gibbs, 1975). The result has been an extremely fruitful structuring of research into the empirical validity of some basic assumptions underlying the criminal law in Canada, England, and the United States.

Creative Science

The third activity is the business of creative insight. There is no way to plan for or work toward or guarantee the occurrence of creative insight, yet it is crucial to science. Creative insight leaps beyond the data; it synthesizes facts in a new way; it fundamentally reshapes a disciplinary paradigm and dominates thinking in that area of science for long periods of time afterward. The theory of plate tectonics, which has transformed geology in recent years, is grounded in a creative insight that the shapes of the continents can be fit together like a jigsaw puzzle. From that insight came the theory of continental drift and the ordering of information about the distribution of fauna, the magnetic properties of seabed sediments, and the nature of mountains and earthquakes. Current ideas about the chemistry of inheritance are grounded in the creative insight that genes are structured in a double helix of proteins. Our understanding of the structure of time, matter, and energy is based on Einstein's insights in developing the theory of relativity.

The danger of scientific insight is that it may exercise a powerful hold over generations of scientists and take them in the wrong direction. Criminology has a well-documented example. Cesare Lombroso's sudden insight in 1866 that criminality was biological in origin, produced by a genetic atavism, dominated the field for half a century. Work on matters now held to be far more important was long disregarded as Lombroso's adherents and detractors fought over the question of biological versus sociological single causes in the making of criminal careers.

Elements of Criminology:
The Empirical Science

Empirical science, of course, is not one of these three activities, but all of them. Scientific knowledge is not gained by following the steps in a checklist guide to

4

good research. It comes from an interaction of description and formalization and insight that moves back and forth as advances in one approach make advances possible in another. Science is an iterative process, now descriptive, now intuitive, now formal. What is clear, is that an empirical science advances through constant reference back to descriptive information. This is the test for both formal models and creative insights: their fit with factual data (Kuhn, 1970; Nagel, 1961).

Descriptive Studies of Crime

As empirical scientists, criminologists have been concerned about describing the characteristics of criminal events in terms of temporal and locational patterns, the offenders' techniques, the victims' characteristics, and the like. A significant number of systematic descriptive studies of crime now exists for Canada and England and the United States. For instance, burglary has been studied in depth for Washington, D.C., and Toronto; for Sheffield (England), Tallahassee (Florida), and Portland (Oregon); for a small city in northern Ontario and a town in Massachusetts. Robbery has been described for London, Boston, and Oakland, California. Homicide has been analyzed for Philadelphia, Chicago, and Houston. The descriptive literature is now extensive, but it remains diffuse, in the form of scattered individual reports.

Criminal Law

The origins of criminal law—that is, the methods and purposes of the people who enact the laws and the social structures and social dynamics associated with lawmaking—have been studied by criminologists only lately. As recently as 1972, the English criminologist Hermann Mannheim and the American criminologist C. R. Jeffery engaged in a bitter debate over whether "criminology" properly includes what Mannheim (1972) referred to as "the sociology of criminal law."

Jeffery's position in that debate appears to have prevailed. Criminal-lawmaking is currently a major area of criminological research. The literature in this area, as is true of the descriptive analysis of criminal events, remains diffuse (Brantingham and Kress, 1979). A few attempts at synthesis have been made (Black, 1976; Chambliss and Seidman, 1971), but they have not been generally acclaimed. They have certainly not shaped a major paradigm for the field.

The Criminal Justice System

The characteristics of the criminal justice system have been studied rather more extensively than either the criminal event or the origins of criminal law. Correctional institutions such as prisons and probation services have long formed the job market for criminologists outside the universities and have been extensively described in England, in Canada, and in the United States. Police and the courts have been studied less than correctional institutions. Research into the institutions of criminal justice has increasingly been seen as falling within the province of the discipline of criminal justice.

An exception is research into the *criminogenic* characteristics of criminal justice institutions. Some students of criminal justice argue that criminal justice agencies, as bureaucratic organizations, *create* criminals in order to ensure a workload. Other students argue that the labeling process (i.e., the social stigma that attaches to the process of arrest, trial, conviction, and punishment) of criminal justice creates social circumstances that convert occasional or accidental deviants into committed, full-time criminals.

Motivation

The study of the criminal event, the origins of criminal law, and the characteristics of the criminal justice system remain smaller currents. The mainstream of research in criminology deals with the question of criminal motivation: How do people become motivated to commit crimes? The majority of criminological research over the past century or so has been focused on this single issue.

Two Perspectives on Motivation

Criminal motivation, the desire or compulsion to commit crime, has been studied from two perspectives. Some students of crime have seen criminal motivation as something inherent in criminals, the product of some internal cause. This perspective dominated thinking about crime in the latter half of the nineteenth century and during the first two decades of the twentieth century. Other students of crime have viewed criminal motivation as the product of forces external to the individual, with the pressures of the social and economic environment shaping criminal behavior in some, law-abiding behavior in others. This viewpoint has dominated thinking about crime since the early decades of the twentieth century.

Internal Perspective. The dominant approach to the study of criminal motivation during the late nineteenth and early twentieth centuries assumed that criminal behavior is the product of internal forces inherent in the individual. Researchers followed many different pathways along this route. Some looked for external indicators of internal evil in the shape of the skull, the shape of the body, or the presence of physical anomalies. Some postulated the heritability of criminality and traced the genealogies of criminals. Some researchers sought criminal motivation in organic damage in the central nervous system or in biochemical malfunctions in the body. Still other researchers attributed criminality to low intelligence. All of the researchers who followed this approach assumed that individual criminals are internally different from law-abiding people.

The internal perspective, grounded in various forms of social Darwinism, led down many paths. The most prominent path looked to external indications of internal evil. The *phrenologists,* particularly in America, tried to explain criminality in terms of skull shape, on the theory that the shape of the skull conformed to the shape of the brain within. As different parts of the brain were thought to control different aspects of emotion and thought, so the overdevelopment of some areas coupled with the underdevelopment of others could in different combinations produce human monsters: oversexed prostitutes and rapists; selfish, acquisitive thieves; incontinent drunkards; pitiless murderers. Brain development caused and controlled criminal motivation, and the expert phrenologist diagnosed criminal temperament

6

from the external manifestations of the brain, that is, the skull's protrusions (Fink, 1938).

The *criminal anthropologists,* led by Lombroso, saw criminal motivation as the product of biological atavism. Criminals were throwbacks to an earlier stage, a savage caveman stage, of human evolution. As such, they were distinguishable from humans by external biological differences. They had *stigmata,* the markings of a race apart: small stature, a small skull, a sloping forehead, close-set eyes, a protruding jaw—a long list appearing in many combinations. These born criminals were afflicted with biological predispositions to criminal behavior or with biological incapacities that forced them into crime as a means of economic survival. The stigmata predicted criminality (Lombroso, 1911; Hooton, 1939).

The *constitutionalists* held that personality type was connected to body type. People possessing specific sorts of body builds (typically, a round, fat type; a very thin type; and a muscular, athletic type) were predisposed to specific behavior patterns. Analysis of body type could predict those persons most likely to commit crimes. Extensive research on juvenile delinquents seemed to confirm this thinking during the 1950s (Sheldon et al., 1949; Glueck and Glueck, 1956), but little further has been done.

The search for external indications of criminality seems to have been abandoned. Phrenology expired in the face of neural research: the external shape of the skull does not conform to the internal shape of the brain; the functions of the brain do not conform to the rather quaint moral-sentiment charting developed by the phrenologists. Crude anthropometric criminal anthropology expired in the face of a large-scale empirical test, Goring's study of 3,000 English convicts and thousands of citizens (1913). The analysis of body type is now ignored.

Another path followed by those interested in internal, inherent sources of criminal behavior has been genetics. The assumption is that criminal motives are genetically programmed into individuals. People inherit a propensity to steal or murder from their ancestors and pass it as a legacy to their posterity. This idea was pursued through genealogical studies of criminal families by researchers who were ignorant of the elementary principles of Mendelian genetics (Dugdale, 1895; Goddard, 1931); through studies of the criminal behavior of identical twins before knowledge of the chemistry of genetics made it possible to tell whether twins were in fact monozygotic (Lange, 1930); and through studies of chromosomal abnormalities thought to create propensities toward violence (Jarvik, Klodin, and Matsuyama, 1973). This path has recently attracted a new cluster of scholars interested in biological causation (e.g., Jeffery, 1979; Mednick and Christiansen, 1977). Further developments in this area will depend on developments in behavioral genetics and sociobiology, fields of study that appear to be racked by major disputes and unresolved issues.

Some students of internal sources of criminal motivation looked to organic defect or biochemical malfunction. Organic brain damage has long been seen as a probable cause of criminal behavior. Benedikt studied brain malformation and Lombroso looked to epilepsy (Fink, 1938). More recently, researchers have tried to explain delinquency as the product of cumulative minimal brain damage (Stott, 1966; West, 1969) or as the product of brain lesions that are repairable through stereotactic brain surgery (Mark and Irvin, 1970). The biochemistry of behavior is

7

also cited as a cause of criminal motivation: abnormal endocrinal conditions have long been considered probable causes of criminality (Schlapp and Smith, 1928; Hippchen, 1978), though the linking data are sparse.

Another pathway in the study of internal sources of criminal motivation involves the study of intelligence. Criminals are held to be less intelligent than law-abiding people. This lack of intelligence creates economic and social situations in which the less intelligent must commit criminal acts to compete and survive. This pathway was followed with some diligence in the period before World War I. It was linked, on the one hand, to a broad concern about social pathology that attributed many social problems, such as crime, drunkenness, and poverty, to "fee-blemindedness" (e.g., Henderson, 1893) and, on the other hand, to the development of standardized intelligence tests, particularly the Stanford-Binet test in the United States. Early research seemed to demonstrate that prison populations had large numbers of people of very low measured intelligence (Goddard, 1914; Goring, 1913).

Improvements in both intelligence testing itself and information about the distribution of intelligence scores in the population at large forced a rethinking of the association between low intelligence and criminal motivation. Sutherland's review of 350 studies of low IQ and criminality (1931) led him to conclude that low intelligence was not importantly related to criminality. This conclusion remained largely unshaken until the 1970s, when a study of delinquency among a cohort of working-class youths in England found low measured IQ at age 14 to be a major predictor of both juvenile and adult convictions (West and Farrington, 1973, 1977); and a review of the literature in the United States concluded that convict populations did, after all, exhibit substantially lower IQ distributions than the general population, and that IQ really must be taken into account in the construction of theories of criminal motivation (Hirschi and Hindelang, 1977). Thus, this pathway appears to have been reopened, after having been closed for almost fifty years.

External Perspective. The dominant theme in twentieth-century thinking about the origins of criminal motivation assumes that forces external to the individual shape criminal behavior. Such thinking about crime has involved economists, lawyers, and political scientists, but it has been primarily and preeminently connected with sociology. Further, such thinking about crime has been, dominantly, an American sociological enterprise.

Sociologists explore crime at three of many possible levels within a social cone of resolution. The term *cone of resolution* is used more frequently by geographers than by sociologists, but it seems particularly helpful in sorting through the many different levels at which crime is studied. A cone of resolution depicts the same phenomenon within contexts of many different sizes. It permits an examination of the features, the characteristics, and relationships of that phenomenon in each particular size of context and also facilitates a comparison with the characteristics and features of the phenomenon in contexts of other sizes.

The possible levels within a cone of resolution are infinite, but they are usually divided into three levels: *micro, meso,* and *macro.* Microlevel resolution is the highest level of resolution; it is focused on the individual phenomenon. Mesoresolution is an intermediate level of resolution, focused on the phenomenon in a broader context. The characteristics of the individual are lost in the characteristics of the group. Macroresolution is the lowest level of resolution and the highest level of aggregation. In macroresolution, only the big picture is seen.

For instance, economists may be interested in the behavior of consumers faced with a tax rebate intended to stimulate spending and thereby reduce unemployment (and perhaps incidentally reduce crime rates). In such a situation, two levels in a cone of resolution are important: the microlevel and the macrolevel. At the micro-level one may ask: What will consumer Harry Smith do with his personal tax rebate? Will he spend his munificent windfall on a new soccer ball for his ten-year-old? Will he use it as a down payment on a motorcycle? Or will he put it in the bank and live off the interest? At the macrolevel, one may ask: What will millions of consumers do with their munificent tax rebates? How many will buy soccer balls, stimulating retail sales and soccer ball production and causing the hiring of extra workers by sporting goods stores and sporting equipment manufacturers throughout the land? How many will make down payments on motorcycles, stimulating mo-torcycle production? How many will put the money into the bank, making more money available for mortgages and stimulating the construction industry? At the microlevel, it is possible to study Harry Smith's decision in terms of personal eco-nomic constraints and desires. At the macrolevel, it is important to study groupings or aggregates of millions of decisions and the flow of blocks of money into different segments of the economy. A trivial amount of money handed to each individual and treated as such at the microlevel may amount to billions of dollars at the macrolevel of resolution.

Unlike this economic example, the sociological study of criminal motivation has generally been concerned with all three levels within the social cone of resolu-tion. At the macrolevel, sociologists have been concerned about analyzing, describ-ing, and accounting for large-scale patterns in the social, temporal, and spatial distributions of crime rates among very large aggregates of people, such as a nation, a province, or a city. Thus, in the nineteenth century, the cartographers of crime studied the distributions of criminal convictions across the provinces of France (Guerry, 1831) and the counties of England (Plint, 1851) in relation to the distri-butions of literacy and types of work, in terms of seasonality, and so forth. At the mesolevel, sociologists have tried to account for criminal motivation and the pat-terns of criminal organization within small groups. For example, during the 1950s and 1960s in particular, American sociologists tried to explain the development and persistence of juvenile gangs in terms of group processes (Short & Strodtbeck, 1965; Yablonsky, 1970).

At the microlevel, sociologists have tried to explain the development of indi-vidual criminal motivation through the mechanisms of social psychology. Thus, Tarde (1968), Sutherland (1947), Jeffery (1965), and Akers (1973) have all tried to explain the development of criminal motivation through individual social learning. Social interactionists such as Lemert (1951), Becker (1963), Schur (1965), Lofland (1969), and, in England, Cohen (1972) and Young (1971) have attempted to ex-plain individuals' criminal motivation as a reaction induced by social labeling.

Sociological analysts of crime have ranged up and down the levels of resolution in constructing theories of the origins of criminal motivation. Two of the major theories produced by Chicago-trained criminologists in the decade before World

9

War II exhibit this propensity overtly: Shaw and McKay's theory of cultural transmission (1942) and Sutherland's theory of differential association (1947). The cultural transmission theory tried to account for the differential distributions of delinquency across the neighborhoods of Chicago and other American cities. In essence, it held that particular neighborhoods developed traditions of delinquent behavior that were passed from one generation of juvenile residents to the next. Sutherland tried to develop an integrated theory that explained how *any* individual became motivated to commit a crime. In essence, his theory held that a person learned criminal motivation from contact with other people. Many such contacts carried implications of approval or disapproval with respect to criminal and law-abiding behavior. When the sum of procriminal contacts exceeded the sum of pro-law-abiding contacts, the individual developed criminal motivation. Shaw and McKay cited Sutherland's microlevel theory to support their macrolevel theory. Sutherland cited Shaw and McKay's macrolevel theory in support of his microlevel theory.

More recently, Wolfgang and Ferracuti (1967) have attempted to account for both the variation in murder rates from country to country (macrolevel) and the propensity of individuals to engage in murders and assaults (microlevel) in terms of a mesolevel postulate, the *subculture* of violence. Even radical criminologists range up and down the cone of resolution, explaining differential national crime rates in terms of differing systems of economic organization and explaining individual criminal motivation in terms of a rational reaction against oppression by economic power elites in some cases or in terms of brutalization by economic oppression in other cases (Taylor, Walton, and Young, 1975; McDonald, 1976).

To date, no clear agreement about the origins of criminal motivation has come out of this research. A large number of distinctive schools of thought remain vigorous, each marshalling some supportive evidence and each suffering the problem of firmly established counterevidence at most levels within the social cone of resolution. The criminological mainstream, like the smaller currents of research into criminal events (the sociology of criminal law and the criminal justice system) remains unsynthesized, and perhaps irreconcilable in the current state of knowledge. The potential for synthesis and scientific advance seems high, but it requires a return to descriptive and analytic fundamentals.

As the empirical science of crime, criminology has concentrated on criminogenic issues, that is, those things thought to cause crime by definition, by situation, or by compulsion. There is, of course, a second interesting aspect to crime, and that is its control. No society can long tolerate high levels of crime, and all societies take steps to control it. During the major revolutions in thinking about crime that occurred at the end of the eighteenth century and again at the end of the nineteenth century, the major institutions of common-law crime control were created or reshaped and articulated into what is now called the *criminal justice system:* police were invented; prisons were transformed into instruments of punishment; superior and summary courts developed most of their current functions and institutions; probation and parole were devised; and specialized institutions such as the juvenile court were created. These developments took place with little attention to the problems of operation and administration in these new institutions, and as a result, a separate area of knowledge, often called *penology,* developed. In recent years, this applied area of criminology has broken free and developed into an independent but symbiotic discipline, *criminal justice*.

Criminal Justice

Criminal justice is the policy science of crime control. That is, students of criminal justice are concerned with the statecraft of crime control and with the character and quality of those governmental courses of action intended to prevent, reduce, or control the incidence of crime.

Policy science is composed of two different sets of issues dealing with matters of process and matters of content. These issue sets are studied for the purpose of developing empirically validated theories about the processes of policymaking and policy implementation and about the quality of policy performance. They are also studied for the purpose of developing empirically tested, demonstrably effective, and socially responsive bodies of policy for accomplishing many different public tasks. Policy science describes and predicts the manner in which specific policies are adopted; it describes and predicts the sorts of distortions and modifications in policy that occur from conception to implementation; and it tests, evaluates, criticizes, and (occasionally) helps to improve the substantive contents of social policy (Scioli and Cook, 1975:5; Johnson, 1975).

Process Issues

The process issue set has dominated criminal justice research through much of the current century. Process questions have included both administrative process issues and policymaking process issues.

The Administrative Process

Policy scientists interested in the administrative process touching criminal justice have asked such questions as: What governmental agencies handle an accused person, and in what sequence? What does the law of criminal procedure specify, and what really happens?

Surprisingly, the answers to such seemingly straightforward questions have remained elusive. Criminal justice professionals tend to have a limited and specific view of the administrative processes, one that is too segmented to enable them to answer these questions. Police see a case from citizen complaint to arrest to midtrial, where they may testify as witnesses. Prosecutors and defense lawyers see a case from postarrest to formal charge to disposition and sentence. Besides the judge involved in the trial and sentence, many different judges may see a case, each considering some different aspect such as whether the accused should have bail, whether there is a *prima facie* case for the accused to answer, whether some defense motion such as a request for a change of venue should be granted, whether to accept a guilty plea, and, on appeal, whether the trial was conducted properly and the sentence imposed was appropriate. Probation officers may see a case only in the period between conviction and sentence. Prison officials will see the case only after sentence, when the judge has issued a warrant of commitment. A parole board may see the case only when the convict has served a portion of his prison term and has become eligible for parole consideration. Each criminal justice professional knows a part of the process, but not all of it.

Conversely, outside observers sometimes see the entire process but lack insight into the character and quality of the events observed.

Research designed to answer simple process questions has been conducted in all three countries under our consideration, but with limited success until recently. Most early research treated the various criminal justice agencies as discrete governmental activities to be analyzed separately (Pound and Frankfurter, 1922; National Commission on Law Observance, 1931).

Administrative process issues have been handled more usefully in recent years by means of a process model derived from the field of systems analysis. This model of process analyzes events and structures in terms of functional interdependencies and interactions. A systems model draws a boundary around such relationships and separates them from the rest of the universe. It is used to examine the *inputs* into the system from the rest of the universe, the behavior of the system's elements, and the *outputs* from the system to the rest of the universe.

Using the systems model approach, criminal-justice policy scientists have defined a variety of criminal justice systems to answer some of the questions posed by administrative process issues. The most common aspect of criminal justice scholarship in recent years has been the answer to the question: What agencies handle an individual accused of crime? Ordered sequentially, the criminal justice system is defined as *these* agencies: the police, the courts, and corrections.

Another popular model of the criminal justice system can be defined by the question: What should happen to a person accused of a crime? This model defines the system in terms of a series of process steps mandated by the law of criminal procedure rather than as a sequence of agencies. The progress of the accused through a series of decision points at which he or she can be sent out of the system or sent forward for further processing depicts the criminal justice system of most common-law countries.

Models of the criminal justice system need not be so simple, of course. They may specify detail. Agency and flow models can be merged to describe and predict processing sequences within the agencies of the criminal justice system. In fact, some of the most ambitious projects in criminal justice research over the past fifteen years or so have involved just such detailed system modeling.

The Policymaking Process

Administrative process models are only half the picture. Policy scientists are also interested in the processes by which specific courses of action are selected and implemented. Policy science draws on political science, planning theory, and decision theory. Because criminal justice systems are already in place in Canada, England, and the United States, most of the interesting decision processes studied by criminal justice scholars represent modifications to or innovations in current practices or techniques. Occasionally, such innovations may involve the creation of new agencies or institutions of criminal justice. Two principal approaches to thinking about such processes, seem to have been dominant: the rational-functional process model and the systems model.

The Rational-Functional Process Model. The rational-functional process model assumes a linear, multistep sequence of events in the choice of a specific policy to accomplish some public task. It is a widely held model of the way policy choices *ought* to be made. One version of the rational-functional process model was adopted and proselytized by the Law Enforcement Assistance Administration in America during the 1970s (Criminal Justice Planning Institute, 1976).

The rational-functional process model reduces the decision-making process to a set of seven well-defined steps: (1) initiation; (2) information gathering; (3) consideration; (4) decision; (5) implementation; (6) evaluation; and (7) program establishment or termination. This model assumes that information gathering will be comprehensive and that the consideration and decision processes will be based on fact. It further assumes that the results of evaluation will be used for further decision making.

The rational-functional process model focuses attention at points where the process fails to work according to the ideal. Thus, the collapse of diversion programs intended to protect offenders from the labeling consequences of criminal conviction might be assessed in terms of a failure at the implementation step: instead of diverting people who had already been handled by the criminal justice system, diversion programs, as implemented, widened the net of social control, extending criminal justice system controls to people previously ignored (Blomberg, 1979).

The Policy Systems Model. A different approach to the study of public policymaking processes, developed by political scientists such as Easton (1965) and Dye (1972), involves the use of systems analysis. The process model assumes a linear, logical policymaking process. The systems model looks at policymaking as a dynamic interaction of four elements in the sociopolitical environment: policy demands, policy decisions, policy outputs, and policy outcomes.

Policy demands are claims on the government for action on some specific task or problem. They can come from inside or outside government, and they often represent a coalition of many different interests. *Policy decisions* are governmental responses to policy demands. They may create new rules or new goals in support of (or in resistance to) specific policy demands. Policy decisions are frequently made by legislative bodies, though they can also be made by courts and executive agencies. *Policy output* is what the system does in pursuit of a policy decision. Policy outputs can be measured in terms of money spent, legislation enacted, regulations adopted, judgments rendered, and so forth. *Policy outcomes* or *impacts* are the consequences, both intended and unintended, resulting from policy decisions.

The policy systems model assumes that policy choices are nonlinear, with many and varied feedback loops, and with system inputs occurring at all stages in the decision-making process. Political pressures and the constraints within the system are more easily accommodated than in the rational-functional process model.

Taken together, the rational-functional process model and the systems model of policy choice can be used to develop a fairly complete understanding of the ways in which specific policy choices come to be made. Some choices are rational and are the products of deliberately planned changes. For these, the process model is a helpful descriptor, and variants of it (e.g., the synoptic and planning models) have proved useful in describing, predicting, and, occasionally, controlling innovations in the criminal justice system. Some choices are less controlled and are more shaped by politics, by organization, and by chance. The systems model has proved a very useful descriptor for these policy choices because it treats the choice process as variable and describes it flexibly within the context of the four system elements. Criminal-justice policy scientists use both models depending on the type of policy choice they are studying.

Content Issues

Content issues in policy science look to the substance of policies rather than the processes by which they are chosen or the agencies or procedures through which they are administered. Content issues in criminal justice seem to have three aspects: (1) goals; (2) knowledge bases; and (3) ideology. These three aspects of content are often intertwined and difficult to disentangle. Wilson (1975, pp. 43–63) has demonstrated how a confusion of goals, ideologies, and knowledge led American criminologists to propose crime control programs based on political preference instead of scientific knowledge during the late 1960s, with expensive but disastrous results (also see Moynihan, 1969).

Goals

Policy goals can involve broad outcomes, the desired ends of policy. They can also involve discrete, more easily measurable, system behavior goals: *Input goals* can be defined in terms of resource allocations to specific programs; *process goals* involve specific system behaviors; *output goals* are measurable products of policy activity; and *outcome goals* are broader objectives of policy. For example, where the outcome goal is "equality before the law," the process goal might be the trial or termination of all criminal cases within ninety days of arrest, and the resource goal might be the allocation of more money to the offices of the prosecutor and the public defender and to the courts to increase the number of lawyers and judges. The output goal would be reduced criminal-case backlogs.

Knowledge Bases

Knowledge bases form the core of policy content, or at least many policy scientists think that they should. In fact, much public policy seems to be made in ignorance.

Knowledge bases are diverse. They derive from four different problem sets common to criminal justice and criminology (criminality, criminal politics, the criminal event, and the criminal justice system) and from many different data sets, for example, those dealing with economic, demographic, geographic, political, ecological, and technological information, as well as information about crime and criminal justice.

Knowledge bases can be descriptive, that is, depictions of the way things are.

14

Knowledge bases can also be theoretical, that is, formal statements about systems of relationships. The best use of knowledge bases requires the fitting together of descriptive knowledge and theoretical knowledge. Theoretical knowledge is used to order and organize descriptive knowledge. Descriptive knowledge is used to test the validity of theoretical knowledge. Both ought to be used in the selection of policy content.

Ideology

Sets of general principles or ideas about behavior shape the contents of most social policy. Assumptions about human nature, about the character of "justice," about the organization of economic effort, and so forth seem to form the basis for selection among different policy contents. Ideology about the comparative social utility of competitive market economies and noncompetitive, centrally planned economies can lead to very different policy contents in penal legislation. Canada, through its anticombines legislation, and the United States, through its antitrust legislation, both place criminal sanctions on noncompetitive, collusive production and pricing schemes. By contrast, Article 153 of the criminal code of the Russian Soviet Federated Socialist Republic punishes entrepreneurial activity with a prison term of up to five years.

Two basic sets of principles dominate contemporary common-law criminal justice. Classical criminology, developed in the late eighteenth century, is the application of Enlightenment philosophy to the problem of crime control. Under its influence, the ancient methods of English criminal justice were modified and humanized, and the institutions of the police and prisons as we know them were created. Classical criminological ideology is written into the U.S. Constitution and, to a lesser extent, the Canadian Charter of Rights. Classical writers were quoted by John Adams in his defense of the British soldiers in the Boston massacre case, and the works of these writers had a major influence on the debates leading up to the Pennsylvania penal law reforms of the 1790s. Classical doctrine dominated European and North American thinking about crime for a hundred years and still dominates many, perhaps most, common-law criminal justice choices.

Positive criminology developed in the late nineteenth and early twentieth centuries as an acknowledged antithesis to classical doctrine. Positive ideology involves the application of the doctrines of positive science to the problems of crime control. A number of important contemporary criminal-justice institutions—indeterminate sentence and parole, probation, and the juvenile court—were created or brought to fruition under the positive ideological aegis. Prisons were converted—in terms of output and outcome *goals,* at any rate—from places of punishment to institutions for treatment. Positive doctrine played down the importance of criminal justice institutions and stressed the need for the discovery and eradication of the "root causes" of crime.

Classical Ideology. Classical criminological ideology can be divided into three sets of general principles: basic assumptions, legal principles, and principles of punishment.

1. Basic assumptions.
    a. Society is formed through a social contract in which people relinquish absolute freedom and agree to live according to laws made by an acknowledged central authority.
    b. People have free will in the sense that they can choose to control their own behavior.
    c. Free will is constrained by the facts of pleasure and pain. People are hedonistic: they will behave so as to maximize personal pleasure and minimize personal pain.
    d. The goal of a central authority (a government) ought to be to pursue policy choices that maximize the goods and pleasures and minimize the pains and privations experienced by both society as a whole and every individual.
2. Legal principles.
    a. The principles of *legality* prohibit *ex post facto* definitions of behavior as criminal, require that criminal laws be published prior to their coming into effect, and require the courts to interpret the criminal laws so as to give them the smallest possible reach.
    b. The principle of minimum criminalization requires that legislators make as few criminal laws as are consistent with the maintenance of an ordered society.
    c. The principle of equality before the law requires that people be treated identically for identical behavior and that nonbehavioral attributes such as sex, race, or wealth be ignored by the criminal justice system.
    d. The principle of fair criminal procedure requires the humane treatment of accused persons and fair fact-finding through an open trial.
3. Principles of punishment.
    a. The purpose of punishment is the prevention of crime through general and special deterrence. The justification for any particular form of punishment is that it can be shown, empirically, to have general and special deterrent effects.
    b. The effectiveness of a punishment depends on a balance of certainty, celerity, and severity. If certainty and celerity are high, severity need not be high. All offenders should be caught and punished immediately.
    c. The limiting principles of punishment require that only the offender be punished and that the punishment be proportional in gravity to the harm done.
    d. Imprisonment for a fixed term scaled in proportion to the harm done by the crime is the preferred form of punishment.
    e. People manifestly lacking the capacity of rational self-control—children, the insane, and the senile, for example—should not be punished.

Positive Ideology. Positive ideology can be considered in terms of basic assumptions, legal principles, and tenets of treatment:

1. Basic assumptions.
   a. People are the products of the society in which they live. Therefore, they owe a duty of obedience to the laws of that society.
   b. Human behavior is determined by forces that transcend individual control. People engage in different kinds of behavior, including criminal behavior, because social, economic, political, biological, psychological, geographic, and climatic influences compel them to do so. Free will is a myth.
   c. Society has both a right and a duty to protect itself and its members from dangerous behavior.
   d. Crime is a disease. Criminals are sick people who must be cured or quarantined.
2. Legal principles.
   a. The sole ground for the exercise of society's power of coercion over an individual is a scientific prediction that the individual will engage in dangerous behavior in the future. Social coercion should never be based on some past act. Where indications of future dangerousness are present, society need not wait for a criminal act to occur in order to exercise control over an individual.
   b. The purpose of the legal process is a scientific analysis of the offender's condition and future dangerousness.
   c. Legal niceties are not important and should be abolished whenever they interfere with the scientific efficiency of the assessment process. Such doctrines as legality, equality before the law, minimal criminalization, and strict interpretation are specifically rejected.
3. Tenets of treatment.
   a. The purpose of penal treatment is to protect society or to help the individual's condition, or both. The justification for any particular form of treatment is that one of these purposes is accomplished. Note that many things can be done in the name of treatment (e.g., the castration of sex offenders, lobotomies on political prisoners, and indeterminate periods of incarceration of burglars) that cannot be done, under classical ideology, in the name of punishment.
   b. Treatment must be individualized on the basis of the individual offender's condition. Notions of equality and proportionality are rejected as unscientific.
   c. The common forms of treatment include social engineering (e.g., the economic reorganization of society, the lighting of streets, the provision of health service and free housing to the poor, and the preemptive arrest and treatment of dangerous offenders through social screening programs); repression; and elimination.

Current Impact of Classical and Positive Ideologies. Both of these ideological systems have a strong influence on the policy contents of decisions made by and about the agencies of the criminal justice system. In generalized form, the common-

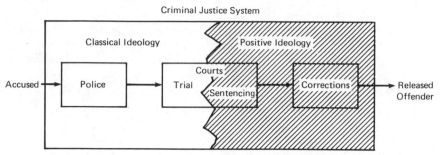

Figure 1–1. The criminal justice system against its ideological backcloth.

law criminal justice system can be arrayed against an ideological backcloth as shown in Figure 1–1.

The police are basically grounded in classical ideology. They are concerned with the essential classical questions: What happened? Was it against the law? Who did it?

Correctional agencies, such as probation services, prisons, and parole commissions, are fundamentally positive in ideology. They are concerned with essentially positive questions, such as: What is the offender like? Has the offender been rehabilitated? Will the offender be dangerous in the future?

The courts are ideologically divided. The trial function is wholly classical, concerned with the question: Did (s)he do it? The sentencing function contains the ideological interface between the classical and the positive doctrines. The sentencing judge is expected to consider the gravity of the crime committed and the condition of the offender (learned from the probation officer's presentence investigation) and to hand down a sentence that both punishes the crime and treats the offender. The sentence is supposed to provide both equality before the law and an individualization of treatment [Model Penal Code, Section 1.02(2)].

The contents of the choices in criminal justice policy in Canada, England, and the United States must be understood as products of this ideological division between the classical and the positive schools in criminal justice thinking. Policy contents often represent accommodations between the classical and the positive positions. The U.S. Supreme Court, in holding that the condition of being addicted to a narcotic drug cannot form the *actus reus* of a crime (despite legislation attempting to create such a crime), has struck a balance between classical notions of free will and positive notions of determinism (*Robinson* v. *California,* 1962). The creation of writs of assistance (general search warrants) for narcotics cases by Canada in the face of their virtually total abandonment by other common-law countries strikes a rather different balance between classical and positive ideology (Clarke et al., 1977, p. 90). The adoption by the English of parole and their socialization of juvenile justice during the late 1960s mark yet a different balance between classical and positive ideology.

Crime Patterns, Criminology, and Criminal Justice

Criminology and criminal justice, as disciplines, share four problem sets. These problem sets can be characterized as criminal politics problems, criminality problems, criminal-justice-system problems, and criminal event problems.

Criminal Politics

The criminal-politics problem set deals with the origins of criminal law. Criminal law is important to criminologists because it defines the scope of research: the contents of criminal law circumscribe the issues of criminality, criminal events, and justice system behavior. The creation of a new criminal law or the abandonment of an existing criminal law thus becomes an important event for scientific study because criminality, criminal events, and justice system behavior are tied to the legal maxim *nullem crimen sine lege* ("there is no crime without a law"). Criminal politics are important to the criminal justice scholar because they *are* the policy process and because their content outcomes largely determine the outlines of policy *within* the criminal justice system.

Criminality

The criminality problem set concerns the origins of criminal motivation in individuals and in groups of people. Explanations of criminal motivation fall into a variety of broad clusters. Moral explanations hold that some people make the conscious choice to be wicked. Biological explanations attempt to account for individual and group criminality in terms of pathologies (e.g., brain tumors or hypoglycemia) or biological imperatives (e.g., a genetic propensity toward violence or a nervous system response to the ambient air temperature). Psychological explanations hold that criminality is the product of a warped personality. There is little agreement about the sources of this warp. It is variously attributed to childhood trauma (such as maternal deprivation), to some Freudian mechanism (such as penis envy or an Oedipal complex), to poor conditioning of law-abiding behavior patterns, or to good conditioning of criminal behavior patterns. Sociological explanations of criminality locate the origins of individual and group criminality in the social structure and in social interaction patterns. People are held to be caught in social situations that impel criminal behavior. Political explanations deny the existence of criminality and assert that the criminal behavior of both individuals and groups can be understood only in terms of criminal politics.

Criminal Justice System

The criminal-justice problem set involves the structure, functions, and behaviors of the agencies of crime control. This problem set, of course, is central to the concerns of criminal justice scholars. It is very important to criminologists as well. Much of what criminologists know about criminals, and therefore about criminal motivation, is filtered through the criminal justice system. Criminologists must know a great deal about the criminal justice system in order to interpret the information it provides about the characteristics of criminals. Moreover, to the extent that criminologists seek to explain criminality in terms of the behavior of the criminal justice system itself, particularly through such notions as labeling theory, the criminal-justice problem set becomes central to the empirical study of criminality.

Criminal Events

The criminal-event problem set revolves around the dimensions of discrete criminal events. It involves the study of the temporal and spatial components of crime, for example, when murders or burglaries occur and where. It also involves the technical components of crime, for example, how burglars break into a house and what weapons murderers use. It involves the characteristics of offenders and victims and targets.

The criminal-event problem set synthesizes, to a significant degree, the issues of the criminal politics and the criminality problem sets. Criminal events occur when there is a concurrence of behavior and prohibition in time and space. Issues of criminal politics and the origins of criminal motivation can, in effect, be treated as dimensions of the criminal-event problem set.

The criminal-event problem set forms the empirical basis on which the criminal-politics and the criminal-justice problem sets are constructed and from which information about the problems of criminality can be inferred. Contemporary criminal politics builds on the basis of established law in the light of contemporary criminal events. The behavior of the criminal justice system is dependent on the occurrence of criminal events. The criminal event is the fundamental input into the contemporary criminal justice systems in Canada, England, and the United States. The study of criminality is ultimately dependent on the study of criminal events: only the occurrence of a criminal event can confirm the existence of a criminally motivated person.

The study of criminal events—that is, of crimes—forms the meeting ground for criminologists and criminal justice scholars. In it are inherent both the intellectual appeal of a search for order and pattern (i.e., for prediction and explanation) and the utilitarian policy appeal of control.

There is a very large literature about criminal events, but it is a scattered and unorganized literature. The search for patterns in crime has been among the least systematic of searches conducted by criminologists and criminal justice scholars.

Patterns in Crime

This book explores the patterns in crime found in Canada, England, and the United States. Primary emphasis is placed on the temporal and spatial dimensions of crime, and a secondary emphasis on the technical characteristics of criminal events and on the characteristics of known offenders, known victims, and known targets. Issues drawn from the criminal-politics, criminality, and criminal-justice problem sets are explored only when they can be used to inform or explain the primary problems: Are there patterns in crime? If so, what are these patterns? Do these patterns obtain in different societies?

Chapter Summary

The study of crime is organized through the disciplines of criminology and criminal justice. Criminology is the empirical science of crime. Criminologists study the origins of criminal law, the sources of criminal motivation, the characteristics of the criminal justice system, and the characteristics of criminal events. Criminal justice is the policy science of crime control. Students of criminal justice study the techniques of crime control policy formation and implementation, the content of crime control policy, and the effectiveness of criminal justice agency operations.

Criminologists, like other empirical scientists, gather and test information through a variety of strategies for controlled empirical inquiry. Such strategies involve description, formal modeling, and a certain amount of creative insight. Constant reference must be made to facts established through descriptive studies. Formal models, however pretty, that are unrelated to established facts are of little use in understanding crime. Creative insights that are not tested through the rigors of formal modeling or against established facts can be extremely misleading: Lombroso's concept of the born criminal is a well-known example of a creative insight that misled the field.

Most of the work in criminology, to date, has been descriptive. Descriptive studies of crimes such as homicide, robbery, and burglary have been conducted in England, Canada, and the United States. Descriptive studies of criminal lawmaking have become an important part of criminology in recent years. Descriptive studies of the criminal justice system play an important role in theories of crime, such as labeling theory.

Most criminological research has been directed toward description of the sources of criminal motivation. Motivation has been viewed from both an internal and an external perspective. Research taking the internal perspective has assumed that criminal motivation is the product of something inherent in the individual: defective biology, or defective personality, or defective intelligence. Research taking the external perspective has assumed that criminal motivation is the product of something outside the individual: inappropriate or defective socialization, flaws or inequities in the socioeconomic structure, political or economic oppression. No line of research currently dominates the field.

Criminal justice specialists study both administrative and policymaking processes and assess their effectiveness. Administrative processes are studied by means of systems analysis. The structure, expected and actual behavior, and effectiveness of the criminal justice system are analyzed. Policymaking processes are studied by means of formal models derived from the disciplines of planning and political science. Policy demands, decisions, outputs, and impacts are analyzed in terms of specific policymaking procedures.

Students of criminal justice also study the contents of criminal justice policies in terms of policy goals, supporting knowledge bases, and ideology. The modern common-law criminal justice system appears to be based on two conflicting ideological systems. The police and the trial courts adhere to the ideology of the Classical school of criminology. Sentencing judges and correctional agencies adhere to the ideology of the Positive school of criminology. As a result, criminal justice policies often appear inconsistent with one another.

The disciplines of criminology and criminal justice overlap in four areas of research: criminal politics, criminality, criminal justice system, and criminal events. The emphases differ. This book emphasizes the patterns in criminal events and, in doing so, explores an area of interest to both criminology and criminal justice.

2

Personal Descriptions of Crime

Introduction

Crimes are important because they cause death, injury, fear, damage, and inconvenience. Their qualitative impact is tremendous. Crime is also expensive. The U.S. President's Commission on Law Enforcement and Administration of Justice estimated, in 1967, that annual losses from crimes might exceed $14 billion (President's Commission on Law Enforcement and Administration of Justice, 1967b, pp. 42–53).

Crimes are, nevertheless, *rare* events. Compared to the frequencies with which people experience or observe such things as shopping in a grocery store, driving an automobile, attending church, or going to work, criminal events occur with striking infrequency. Homicides account for only a small percentage of the deaths that occur. Only a few homes in a thousand are apt to be burglarized in a year's time. Forged checks form an infinitesimal proportion of the billions of drafts handled by banking systems. Even drunk drivers account for only a small proportion of drivers. Few people have personal observational experience with criminal events.

The rarity of criminal events poses a significant problem: How is one to study an infrequently observed phenomenon? The answer, as it is for physicists who want to study subatomic particles, is to study crimes through the traces they leave when they occur. Such traces generally fall into two broad categories: personal accounts of criminal events given by participants and witnesses and the records of the criminal justice system.

Personal accounts of criminal events can be subdivided into firsthand descriptions and survey descriptions. Firsthand descriptions tend to be volunteered and may be offered by many different observers: offenders, victims, witnesses, police, medical examiners, and field observers. Survey descriptions are gathered by researchers using techniques developed by market researchers, political pollsters, and sociologists. Personal accounts are generally treated as logically separable from the traces of crime found in the records of the criminal justice system, whereas survey descriptions of crime are usually treated as supplements or alternatives to these records. The discussion of these sources of information about crime in this chapter and Chapters 3 and 4 will separate the two forms of personal accounts, taking up firsthand descriptions in this chapter, then turning to the records of the criminal justice systems (Chapter 3), and then returning to the survey descriptions (Chapter 4).

Personal Descriptions of Crime

A major source of information about crime is found in the personal descriptions of criminal events given by participants and observers. Such descriptions may take the form of memoirs written by retired criminals or police officers; interviews with victims, witnesses, or offenders; or, occasionally, the accounts of social scientists who have themselves witnessed actual crimes in the course of systematic field research.

Memoirs

Personal descriptions provide rich detail about events. They give texture to the patterns of crime by describing techniques and by giving an insider's view of how criminal events are carried out and what they mean.

Robert Allerton was a professional criminal: He made his living through robbery and theft and viewed his occasional prison terms as a business risk. He coldly calculated that the cost was well worth paying in exchange for the luxurious lifestyle that his illegal earnings financed when he was at liberty. Allerton's description of the smash-and-grab technique he used in and around London in the 1950s gives palpable texture to the study of commercial burglary:

> Smash-and-grab can only be done properly as a team job, and so long as everyone knows what he's doing, and does it, it's fairly easy. You need a car and a hook on a chain fastened to the back to pull away the window-grille. The car backs up, you slam the hook through the grille into the glass, the car pulls the grille away, and you thrash in what's left of the window with an iron bar, taking care to knock out any jagged pieces sticking up from the bottom, otherwise you can cut your arms reaching over it. At the same time your other men are moving in a couple of paces behind you to start hauling the stuff out. (Parker and Allerton, 1969, p. 79)

Chic Conwell, Sutherland's professional thief, outlined the forms of professional theft in America during the first quarter of the twentieth century. He provided significant information about the techniques of pickpockets, shoplifters, hotel thieves, and confidence men and talked about where thieves looked for victims:

> There are many spots where the graft is lucrative. . . . The shopping districts are the spots where moll-buzzers [pickpockets specializing in female victims] do their best work. Railroad stations, steamship docks, and similar points where transients congregate are the best spots for mobs on the short con, and hotel lobbies for mobs on the major con rackets. The boosters [shoplifters] concentrate on the better stores

24

in the central business district but sometimes get forced out of this district because it is burned out for them. They have been spotted in all the stores, are known as professional thieves, and have to get out of that territory. . . . For cannon mobs [pickpockets] every streetcar crossing is a potential field, but most of the transfer points are not lucrative, and consequently the ones which are found to be fruitful get a strong play. The get-ons [e.g., bus shelters] outside large factories or business centers get a strong play, too. (Sutherland, 1956, p. 149)

Vincent Swaggi, a contemporary American fence (dealer in stolen property) studied by Carl Klockars, provided an unromantic description of the business of theft in an account of the development of a stable flow of stolen plumbing supplies:

About six blocks from me there was this big plumbing supply company. I mean they had a half a city block which was just plumbing supplies. I got to know the guy who was the shipper. He used to come into my store. He knew what I had was hot stuff, so one day I asked him where he worked. He told me, Howard Plumbing, the big warehouse. So I kept talkin' to him and we made a little arrangement: when I put in an order for like one dozen toilets I'd get four dozen. I mean I'd pay for the one dozen but I'd get the three dozen free. He'd get the order in the warehouse and just load the extra on the truck. . . . He got twenty percent on three for one. It's like this: I order one thing, he sends me four. I pay the company full price on the one and I give him twenty percent on the other three. Say he gives me four items which cost a dollar each. I give the company a dollar and him sixty cents. Each piece, averaged out, runs me forty cents. I sell it for eighty cents and give my buyer twenty percent off dealer wholesale. (Klockars, 1974, pp. 107–108)

John Allen, a contemporary robber, pimp, and narcotics dealer who operated in Washington, D.C., as recently as 1977 (despite having been rendered a paraplegic in a 1970 shootout with police) described the casual quality of lethal violence. He and a friend had gone cruising in a stolen car and were stopped by the police:

The look that this police holding me in the car with his gun had, you couldn't tell me that this man wasn't gonna shoot me. I just felt it. Then all of a sudden a sly grin came on his face. Many times this same type of grin had come across *my* face when I was about to do something. So I recognized it in him immediately. I reach in my lap and I pull my gun out. The gun surprised him. He jumped back like he was ready to give up and threw his gun hand up. So I shot him. Bam! He hollered like a broad and fell all in the street. I just shot him in the shoulder so he couldn't use his gun, but there he was rolling around in the street.

   I couldn't get over the fact that so many police got there in so little time! (Allen, Kelly, and Heymann, 1977, p. 209)

In addition to providing a texture or feel to the study of crime, these personal accounts provide extremely useful information about how crimes are committed and where crimes are committed. They also show how different crimes can flow out of planned situations, such as Swaggi's cultivation of the plumbing-supply worker, or out of unplanned situations, such as Allen's shooting of the police officer.

   The systematic comparison of information across personal accounts of crime sets parameters to the detail of criminal events. A comparison of the four studies mentioned above, for instance, yields parameters to the use of violence by criminals. Allen, the American robber, said:

> There was a rule with me that I always have a gun at all times, 'cause sometimes you'd be out in the street and the opportunity just presents itself where you see a lot of money. Then you want to be armed. (Allen, Kelly, and Heymann, 1977, p. 179)

Allerton, the English robber, considered violence dispassionately:

> So violence is wrong, on a fundamental level, I admit that. But on a day-to-day level it just happens that it's a tool of my trade and I use it—like an engineer uses a slide rule, or a bus-driver the handbrake, or a dentist the drill. Only when necessary, and only when it can't be avoided. If I've got to whack a bloke with an iron bar to make him let go of a wages-bag he's carrying, O.K., so I'll whack him. If he lets go without any trouble, I don't. That's all. (Parker and Allerton, 1969, p. 93)

Allerton, however, disagreed with Allen's belief in the utility of the gun as weapon of choice:

> Some mug goes into a post office, waving a gun at the old woman behind the counter and what does she do? She says: "Put that away, you silly boy, don't you know it might go off and hurt somebody?"
>
> But if you use an iron bar it's different. You go into a place waving one of those over your head and with a determined look in your eye, like you're going to clout them as soon as look at them—and they know this is real, they know it's direct. They start to back away automatically, without time to start weighing the situation up. You've got the initiative, you've got them afraid. (Parker and Allerton, 1969, pp. 100–101)

Chic Conwell used violence as the major technical divide between thieves and other sorts of professional criminals:

> The professional thief has technical skills and methods that are different from those of other professional criminals. Manual skill is important in some of the rackets, but the most important thing in all the rackets is the ability to manipulate people. The thief depends on his approach, front, wits, and in many instances his talking ability. The professional burglar or stickup man (robber with a gun), on the other hand, uses violence or threat of violence even though he may on occasion use soothing language in order to quiet people. (Sutherland, 1956, p. 3)

Violence plays such a small role in the crime of dealing in stolen property that Swaggi had no occasion to discuss it. Neither *violence* nor *guns* are indexed in his account of life as a professional fence.

Comparison on other issues is possible and illuminating. Narcotics played a central role in most of Allen's crimes, whereas Conwell indicated that narcotic use is a major disadvantage to the professional thief and indulged in by only a minority. Narcotics play virtually no role in the memoirs of Allerton and Swaggi. Both Allen, the robber, and Swaggi, the fence, made good use of skilled criminal-defense lawyers, working honestly within the legal system, to protect themselves when caught. Allerton, the English robber, and Conwell, the American thief, shared a common contempt for the law and lawyers and focused instead on the fix: a bribe to some-body for cooperation in dropping charges or destroying evidence and modifying testimony. Though separated by thirty years' time and the Atlantic Ocean, Chic Conwell and Robert Allerton agreed that police could be bribed, and they described strikingly similar examples of police officers' memory lapses on the witness stand. Allerton, Allen, Conwell, and Swaggi all described criminal relationships as tran-sitory: gangs form for specific crimes or for a specific season; fences and thieves deal in an on-again, off-again fashion. All agreed that lasting partnerships or relation-ships are exceptions to the general pattern.

Clustered Personal Accounts

A second approach to using personal accounts of crime is to cluster them, frequently by interviewing several known offenders. Some of the richness of detail inherent in memoirs is inevitably lost in this form of information gathering, but data so gathered can be used to construct more generalized pictures of the patterns of crime.

Klein and Montague (1977), for instance, studied the behavior patterns of check forgers. They interviewed three different groups of forgers: imprisoned forg-ers; retired forgers; and active, uncaught forgers. They were able to cluster their interview responses in order to describe general patterns of the criminal career de-velopment, the *modus operandi,* and the criminal justice contact among writers of bad checks in Canada. They found the career patterns of most check writers to be unrelated to the archetypal pattern described by the classic literature on professional thieves. They demonstrated that the crime of check forgery depends on a knowledge of legitimate banking practice and procedure and the ability to identify and exploit the opportunities inherent in these procedures. Klein and Montague's selections of *typical* anecdotes have much the same immediacy found in memoirs, but they stand as examples of general patterns of conduct among forgers. Their well-known inter-view with a working forger illustrates both the technique of setting up a respectable front and the spatial dynamics of target selection:

> I arrived in Toronto on a Friday, a few days before the end of the month. I used the weekend to get settled into my hotel. By this I mean get known by the staff to the extent they know that I am so-and-so in Room such-and-such and that I'm some sort of engineer from Calgary whose employer is paying him to take some sort of special course at the University of Toronto. Armed with a street map, I spent Saturday and Sunday like a tourist, wandering around downtown Toronto. What I was actually doing was marking bank locations on the map so that I could work out the quickest route between them. Doing this on a weekend is preferable to me, because I hate to waste the hours when banks are open doing what I call the non-productive end of the business. Like, when they're open I want to be either in them or enroute. (Klein and Montague, 1975, p. 265)

Peter Letkemann (1973) studied forty-five bank robbers and burglars in Brit-ish Columbia. He was able to make useful cluster comparisons about the timing and techniques of safecracking and bank robbery, about the character of crime as a "moonlighting" occupation, and about the social organization of Canadian criminals. The study provides most of the information criminologists have about "casing" (target selection) and contains important information about how criminals learn criminal skills. It provides useful insights into the importance of urban design and architecture as variables in bank robbery: robbers are concerned about parking places for getaway cars (1973, p. 99) and have come to rely on the architectural uniformity of modern banks in order to make rapid hits with a minimum of planning (1973, p. 94). Letkemann was also able to sort out the reasons for the decline of safecracking as a criminal art: modern safe technology has made it almost impossible to open a safe without destroying its contents.

Systematic Observation

A third form of personal account of crime is systematic observation of criminal events by a trained social scientist who has developed rapport with criminals or delinquents in the field. This form of personal account yields systematic, often theoretically informed, descriptions of one or many crimes.

Systematic personal accounts by trained observers constitute a relatively rare form of information about crime. Such studies are time-consuming: Whyte's classic study of social organization in an American slum required four years of full-time field work and another two years to write up (1955, p. vii); Spergel's study of delinquents in three different neighborhoods in New York City took eight months' time to conduct and had been prefaced by six years as a gang social worker in those very neighborhoods (1964, p. xviii). Crimes are relatively rare events, even in the lives of people who more-or-less consistently engage in them: a participant—observer in the field may actually witness only a few such events during a long period of field study. The majority of accounts of crimes found in this literature turn out, on close examination, to be descriptions gleaned through interview with others who happened to be present at crimes that occurred in the observer's absence.

Problems with Personal Accounts of Crime

Because personal accounts of crime make interesting and frequently entertaining reading, and because they contain rich detail about the crimes, the criminals, and the social systems they describe, why not use them as the principal source of information about crime? The answer to this reasonable question is that personal accounts of crime, because they are case studies of unique events, or people, or times and places, present a number of problems that make them poor sources of information for crime analysis and crime-control policy planning if used alone.

Personal accounts of crime share, with third-person case studies of individual crimes, the problem of representativeness and comparability. They describe people or events or circumstance that may be examples of the way that things are in most places, most of the time, but that may be, on the other hand, distortions of the usual pattern.

Recent case studies of celebrated murders, for instance, reconstruct and recount the gruesome Tate—LaBianca killings by members of the Manson "family"

(Bugliosi and Gentry, 1974), the death of a police officer at the hands of petty criminals in a California onion field (Wambaugh, 1973), and a wife's murder and mutilation of a tiresome, older husband who was interfering with her pursuit of pleasure in the swinging city of Hamilton, Ontario (Campbell, 1974). The killings described occurred in two very different cities, in two similar countries, at three different times. The weapons used included knives, axes, and pistols. The motivations appear to have ranged from quasi-religious fanaticism, to panic, to the pursuit of sex and money. Of the ten killings reported in the three case studies, eight involved mutilation.

But it is not possible to use these detailed studies to construct a map of the patterns of murder in North America. The Tate–LaBianca murders are only eight of the more than fourteen thousand murders known to the police in the United States in the same year. Drawing conclusions about the character of murder from the Tate–LaBianca killings would, in fact, badly distort the patterns of relationship between murderers and victims; the places where murders occur; the choice of weapons by killers; the types of wounds inflicted on victims; the probability that the victim's behavior, itself, may have precipitated the killing; and the apparent motivations for the killings. The police killing is clearly anomalous in its execution style, for both ordinary murders and police deaths. The Canadian husband-killing is anomalous as well, as most Canadian murders are hot-blooded killings carried out in the course of a dispute.

There is a second problem besides representativeness. It is the problem of interpreting differences in a small number of cases. These killings occurred in two different places: Canada and the United States. Should differences in them be attributed to differences between the two societies, which led to different choices of technique? Again, the killings occurred in 1946, 1963, and 1969. They move from shooting with postmortem mutilation, to execution-style shooting, to killing with knives and guns and the mutilation of both living victims and dead bodies. Are these differences in circumstance, or do they represent changing trends in the behavior of killers over time? Neither set of questions can be answered from the case studies themselves.

These problems are apparent in memoirs and clustered personal accounts. Should the differences in the recruitment, training, and social organization of thieves exhibited by Sutherland's Chic Conwell, Klockars' Vincent Swaggi, and Klein and Montague's check forgers be attributed to differences in location (the American Midwest, the American East Coast, and Canada); or should they be attributed to changes over time? Conwell wrote about professional theft in the quarter century before 1925. Swaggi's memoirs cover the period from the Great Depression to the late 1960s. Klein and Montague's check forgers talked about the business of theft in the late 1970s. Should the differences in attitude toward the use of violence exhibited by Conwell, on the one hand, and the robbers Allerton and Allen, on the other, be attributed to differences in personal preference, to differences in the requirements of different sorts of criminal enterprise, to differences of place, or to changes over time? It is not possible to answer these questions from these sources of information alone.

The personal-account literature also suffers, as a source of information about crime, from two different, but important, validity problems. The first problem is common to all personal accounts of crime, including those generated by survey research: people do not always report criminal events, criminal motivations, and criminal techniques correctly. This inaccurate reporting may come from memory failure, or it may come from lack of knowledge, or it may be the product of deliberate deceit. Except for the rare situations where a systematic observer is present at the criminal event, there are only a limited number of ways that such information can be cross-checked for validity. Even in such circumstances, it is possible that the observer's informant is not naive, and that the events observed are neither a representative nor a complete sample of the criminal lifestyle under observation. Without recourse to other data sources, it is difficult to assess the validity of personal-account information.

The second validity problem touches on the ethical problems inherent in this sort of research. Informants writing memoirs or responding to interviews may well make inculpatory statements, that is, admissions of criminal behavior for which they could be prosecuted. Field researchers may well observe criminal events that their duty as citizens requires them to report to the police, along with the identities of the offenders. At the same time, most researchers feel that they owe an obligation of confidentiality to their informants. The common solution to this problem has been to fictionalize the identity of the informants, the location of the events described, and so forth. Among the memoirs considered here, Robert Allerton apparently spoke under his own name, as did John Allen, but "Chic Conwell" was the thief's underworld alias rather than his real name, and "Vincent Swaggi" was strictly a fictitious name. As Klockars forthrightly observed, he had "changed names, dates, places, and descriptions of events" in order to protect Swaggi's identity from law enforcers and merely curious people (Klockars, 1974, p. 225). Klein and Montague (1977) and Letkemann (1973) held the identities of their informants confidential, and Spergel (1964) pointed out that "all names of persons or places used in this volume are fictitious or disguised" (p. xv). George Kirkham's (1976) efforts to solve these ethical problems in writing up his participant observation of policing in the American South led to such extensive fictionalization that the book eventually passed over the line that separates sanitized sociology from autobiographical fiction and must be treated as a police procedural novel.

Fictionalization—that is, the modification of names, places, and dates—in writing up sensitive research results represents the principal, traditional, time-honored solution to the researcher's ethical dilemma within sociology. However, it creates major problems for the use of personal-account information in criminological analysis. Fictionalization violates that major canon of scientific method that requires the sources of facts and theories to be publicly accessible and therefore subject to independent verification or refutation. This is not possible when the sources of information are held confidential by the researcher. Thus, differences may be attributed to differences of place or time or to the relative competencies of the researchers themselves. This situation fosters the proliferation of theories and *ad hominem* disputes between groups of researchers, but it does not produce any resolution of factual ambiguities.

These problems—representativeness, comparability, and validity—are serious enough to render these forms of personal accounts, by themselves, insufficient sources of information about crime, criminality, criminal politics, or the criminal justice system. Both the empirical science of criminology and the policy science of criminal justice must turn to additional source data.

Chapter Summary

Firsthand personal descriptions of crime provide a rich source of information about criminal events, criminal techniques, and criminals themselves. Firsthand personal accounts of crime commonly take the form of memoirs, of clustered personal accounts of crime, or of the reports of a trained, systematic observer.

Memoirs, written by criminals or police officers, victims, or witnesses, provide detailed information about crime and criminal behavior in specific times and places. The memoirs of a robber, a thief, a fence, and a narcotics dealer and pimp are considered. These memoirs provide information about the techniques of smash-and-grab robbery, the best locations for picking pockets and shoplifting, the intricate microeconomics of dealing in stolen goods, and the criminal utility of violence. They also provide information about the use of drugs by criminals, the quality of relationships between criminals, and the character of the criminal justice system.

Clustered personal accounts of crime obtained by researchers through interviews with several criminals provide more generalized information about crime and criminals. Studies of the techniques of check forgers and the behavior of safecrackers are representative of this source of information about crime.

Systematic observations of criminal events are extremely useful, but rare. Crimes are rare events at which trained field observers are only infrequently present.

Though rich with information, firsthand personal accounts of crime are a poor source of data regarding crime patterns. The behavior described in such accounts is often unrepresentative. The accounts are often written so that valid comparisons with other accounts of similar crimes cannot be made. Further, it is often difficult to verify the information found in personal accounts of crime, either because the writer has misremembered or lied about events or because the writer has deliberately changed names, places, and dates in order to protect an information source. Firsthand personal accounts of crime should never be used as the sole source of information about crime patterns. They should always be supplemented by other sources of information.

3

Criminal Justice System Records of Crime

Introduction

The records of the criminal justice system comprise the largest extant source of information about crimes and criminals. Police, prosecuting lawyers, public defenders, courts, and correctional agencies collect and record information about the numbers and types of criminal events that occur and the characteristics of offenders (and, occasionally, victims) in the course of routine daily operations. These records, of course, also contain information about the operation of the system itself.

The amount of information contained in criminal justice records can be staggering, particularly in comparison to the amount of information contained in personal accounts of crime. Robert Allerton's account of his career as an English robber describes perhaps a dozen criminal events. Records of police departments contain data about thousands of criminal events. Allerton's account gives rich detail about motive, technique, and victim—offender interaction. Police data contain little about motive or victim—offender interaction, but they usually do contain detailed information about the time, the place, the technique, and legal-behavioral classification of each offense; the specifics of the premises where the crimes occurred, the type and value of the property lost, and whether a weapon was used and what kind; the characteristics of the complainant; and, for those crimes that have been solved, information about how they were solved and the descriptive characteristics of the persons charged.

Memoirs of judges or famous criminal trial lawyers may contain accounts of a few celebrated or interesting cases, described in detail. The short-lived Florida Case Disposition Reporting system operated by the State Court Administrator's office from 1973 through 1976 collected charge and disposition, flow, and timing information on all criminal cases dealt with by the courts of Florida during those years.

Prison memoirs by convicts and prison officials contain descriptions of the quality of prison life and accounts of some personalities and events. Prison records contain detailed information about the social and criminal histories of offenders, about their physical and tested mental characteristics, and about important behavioral incidents while the offenders are in prison.

Such data are routinely available to government officials (and are occasionally available to researchers) for tens of thousands of convicted offenders on any given day. Goring (1913), for instance, was able to tap this massive accumulation of information about English convicts in the early part of this century in his refutation of Lombroso's notion that criminals are a biologically distinct species of humanity marked by externally visible physical stigmata.

Criminal Justice System Structures

The type and quantity of information about crimes and criminals collected by the agencies of criminal justice depends, to a significant degree, on the *structure* of a particular criminal justice system. In broad outline, the criminal justice systems of Canada, England, and the United States are structured similarly because they are all derivatives of the ancient common-law system that was in effect when North America was first colonized and because the subsequent evolution of the three systems has been at least partially interactive. The American system developed the theory of degrees of criminal offense and such penal innovations as the use of prisons for punishment and the system of parole release now common to all three systems. The Canadian system can lay claim to the development of the first juvenile court (Hagan, 1977:20-23). The generalized structure of the common-law system of criminal justice, defined from both *agency* and *procedure* perspectives, is illustrated in Figure 3-1.

The *agency* perspective for defining the structure of the common-law criminal justice system asks which agents of the law deal with an accused person and in what sequence. The agencies include the police, the prosecution and defense lawyers, magistrates, juvenile courts, superior courts, appeals courts, adult and juvenile probation services, adult and juvenile custodial institutions, and parole supervision organizations. Each of these agencies can be seen as a separate organization composed of people, resources, process rules and practices, and information-recording and information storage capacities. For current purposes, it is important to note that the information-recording capacity of the system is very large indeed.

The *procedural* perspective for defining the common-law criminal justice system asks about the process through which an accused person is put for the assessment of the truth of the accusation. In simple form, this process can be visualized as a sequence of steps or stages through which the accused passes. They are arrest; initial appearance and bail hearing; formal charge screening, usually by grand jury indictment or by committal hearing before a magistrate following the filing of a charge by a prosecutor; arraignment, at which the accused is required to plead to the charges; the trial; acquittal or conviction and sentencing; possibly an appeal to an appeals court claiming that the conviction is erroneous or the sentence too harsh; and the execution of the sentence. In moving through the various stages in this

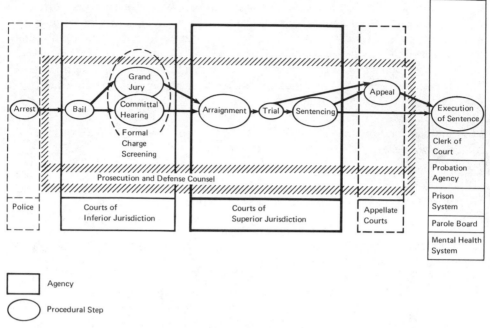

Figure 3–1. Generalized common-law criminal justice system.

process, the accused is the subject of extensive record keeping. Again, viewed from this perspective, the capacity of the system to generate records is very large indeed.

Outlines of the Criminal Justice Systems in England, Canada, and the United States

The structures of the criminal justice systems in England, Canada, and the United States are derived from the same roots in English common law and in classical criminological reform. All three systems have police forces, hierarchically ordered criminal court systems, and correctional systems organized at several levels of government. There are some significant organizational differences within these basic similarities.

Criminal Jurisdiction and Criminal Codes

Criminal jurisdiction is constitutionally located in the national government in England and Wales. Parliament has sole power to create criminal law. There is a single, national criminal law composed of many different statutes and interpretive judicial decisions. Although some unofficial consolidations of the criminal law exist, England has never adopted a single, comprehensive criminal code. Municipal gov-

34

ernments have the power to define minor penalties for the violation of municipal bylaws.

In Canada, criminal jurisdiction is shared between the federal and the provincial governments. The federal Parliament has sole power to make criminal laws. Since 1892, Canada has had a single, comprehensive criminal code that consolidates nearly all of the law of crimes. Some additional acts of federal legislation, such as the Dangerous Drugs Act or the Anti-Combines Act, impose criminal sanctions for violation. The provinces have the power to impose penal sanctions for the violation of provincial law, and municipalities may impose penal sanctions for the violation of municipal bylaws. Neither of the latter constitute "criminal law" within the meaning of the Canadian Constitution, but they can be considered equivalent to elements of English and American criminal law for comparative purposes.

In the United States, criminal jurisdiction is shared between the federal and the state governments. The federal government has sole power to make criminal laws for federal territories (such as military bases or the District of Columbia) and to impose criminal sanctions for the violation of federal laws. Each state has complete power to make criminal laws covering all conduct within its borders. The result is two separate, but completely parallel, sets of criminal law in each state. Some acts, such as the robbery of a federally insured bank, may violate both federal and state criminal law simultaneously, rendering the criminal liable to two separate prosecutions and two separate punishments. The result is that the United States has fifty-two separate criminal codes. Which criminal law applies to any given act depends on where it is done and what its specific factual context is.

Police Organization

The English system is organized at the local government level into forty-three separate police forces. The best known is the London Metropolitan Police Force, known popularly as Scotland Yard, which polices most of Greater London and is directly controlled by the Home Secretary, a cabinet minister. The other forces are controlled jointly by a local police board and a chief constable. The cost of policing is shared by the national government and the local government. The national government sets minimum standards of training, organization, and conduct as a condition of its fiscal contribution.

The Canadian police system is organized at the federal, provincial, and local governmental levels. The federal government maintains the Royal Canadian Mounted Police (RCMP), a national police force charged with enforcing the criminal code and other federal legislation, such as the Dangerous Drugs Act. Two provincial governments, Ontario and Quebec, maintain provincial police forces charged with enforcing the criminal code and provincial law in unincorporated areas. The other eight provinces contract with the RCMP for policing services in unincorporated areas. Municipalities either maintain their own municipal police forces, charged with enforcing the criminal code, provincial law, and municipal by-laws, or they contract with the RCMP for municipal policing services. RCMP contract policing is advantageous to provincial and local governments because the federal government pays a substantial share of the policing costs in the contract areas.

The American police system is extremely diverse. In the late 1970s, there

35

were nineteen thousand different police forces in the United States operating as agencies of the federal government, of state governments, of county governments, and of city governments. Policing accounted for 49 percent of federal-government criminal justice expenditures and 65 percent of local-government criminal justice expenditures. Police forces ranged in size from departments with one or two officers to New York City's force of thirty-five thousand.

Prosecution and Defense

The English system differs markedly from those of Canada and the United States. The English legal profession is divided into *solicitors,* who handle clients and legal paperwork, and *barristers,* who are litigation specialists and can be hired only by solicitors. The Canadian and American legal professions are unified: a single lawyer can handle clients and legal paperwork as well as litigation.

The Canadian and American systems both feature professional prosecution lawyers who work on salary for the government. Called *crown counsel* in Canada and usually called *district attorney* or *state's attorney* in the United States, these lawyers have the principal responsibility for filing and prosecuting criminal charges.

In England, prosecution is less formally organized. The police file criminal charges. Solicitors are hired to prosecute cases in lower courts; barristers are hired to prosecute specific cases in the high court. The same lawyer may prosecute some cases and defend in other cases in the same court on the same day.

Criminal defense is handled in essentially the same way in all three countries. The accused hires a defense lawyer (in England, a solicitor, and, if necessary, a barrister as well). The accused pays the cost of the defense out of her or his own pocket. Indigent accused may apply for legal aid; if granted, the government pays the cost of the defense. In some American and Canadian jurisdictions the defense of the indigent is handled by governmentally salaried *public defenders,* who are full-time criminal-defense specialists.

Criminal Court Organization

England and Wales have a single, integrated national court system. Magistrates' courts staffed by panels of unpaid lay justices of the peace or by single, paid, legally qualified stipendiary magistrates try summary offenses and, at the accused's election, some serious offenses. They also conduct the preliminary screening of serious cases. Crown courts try serious cases before juries. Appeals on the merits go to the criminal division of the court of appeal, and appeals on points of law only go to the divisional court of Queen's Bench. In matters of exceptional importance, a further appeal may be taken to the House of Lords.

The Canadian court system is typical of those found in federal states. The federal government maintains full criminal court systems for the two federal territories; a separate federal court system for the trial of matters involving the federal government or its officers as litigants and for the enforcement of some federal legislation; and the Supreme Court of Canada, which serves as the court of last resort for all Canadian court systems. Each province maintains a separate court system for the enforcement of provincial laws and the criminal code. Each provincial court system has four levels: magistrates' or provincial courts try minor offenses and are staffed by judges appointed and paid by the province. County or district courts try more serious matters, before juries. The superior or supreme court of general trial jurisdiction tries very serious crimes. Each province also has a paramount appellate court, typically called the supreme court or court of appeal, which exercises appellate jurisdiction over all of the courts in the province. The judges of the county, superior, and supreme courts are appointed and paid by the federal government. Final appeal from a provincial court system is to the Supreme Court of Canada.

The American court system is composed of fifty-two separate court hierarchies similar to the single, integrated system found in England: the federal court system; the court system of the District of Columbia; and one court system for each of the fifty states. Though exceptionally diverse in terminology, most systems are similar in having a magistrates' level court for the trial of minor criminal cases and the initial screening of accusations of serious crime; a superior trial court of general jurisdiction for the trial of serious criminal cases before juries; and one or two levels of appeals courts. The single unifying element is that some claims of right under federal law or the U.S. Constitution may be appealed to the U.S. Supreme Court.

The interplay of criminal jurisdiction and the organization of criminal courts mean that England has a unitary system of criminal law, that Canada has "thirteen judicial hierarchies and two different systems of law" (Cheffins and Tucker, 1976, p. 99), and that the United States has fifty-two different judicial hierarchies and systems of law, subject to only a few minimal standards imposed by the federal constitution.

Correctional Systems

The English correctional system is organized at two governmental levels. The prison department is an agency of the national government. It operates in excess of one hundred institutions for adults, young persons, and juveniles. It services both long- and short-term prisoners, provides holding facilities for accused persons in custody on remand, and holds civil prisoners committed for contempt of court. The system has a daily average population of around forty-two thousand inmates and a staff of about twenty-two thousand. Local governments are responsible for maintaining a system of community homes to accommodate juvenile delinquents. Local governmental committees in each of the eighty-two magistrates' court areas (called *petty sessional areas*) administer probation and aftercare services. The national government shares the cost of maintaining both local-level correctional services.

The Canadian Constitution gives the federal government the responsibility for penitentiaries, and the provinces are given the responsibility for maintaining jails and reformatory prisons. In practice, both levels of government maintain a variety of custodial correctional institutions. Offenders sentenced to terms of two years or longer are held in the federal prison system; offenders sentenced to prison terms of under two years are held in a provincial institution. The provincial governments maintain juvenile institutions and probation services. The federal government maintains a parole system.

The American correctional system is extremely diffuse. The federal government maintains probation, prison and juvenile institutions, and parole systems for offenders convicted in federal courts. Each state maintains a prison system. Probation and parole systems may be maintained by the state government (as in Florida) or by a local government, such as a county (as in California). Local governments (counties or municipalities) maintain jail systems for persons in custody awaiting trial and for persons sentenced to terms of imprisonment of one year or less. Juvenile institutions are maintained by federal, state, and local governments. There are also a large number of private and charitable custodial institutions for juvenile offenders.

Crime Statistics

Systematic, standardized criminal-justice records date from the mid-nineteenth century or later. The rationale for the development of criminal statistics was multifold: (1) the accumulation of data on the efficiency and effectiveness of criminal justice agencies; (2) the enumeration of crimes as an *index* of national moral health (see, e.g., Plint, 1851; Guerry, 1831); (3) the enumeration of crimes for scientific analysis in comparison with other data, both social (Plint, 1851) and physical (Quetelet, 1842), in order to understand and remove their causes; and (4) the enumeration of *criminals* for purposes of scientific study (Tobias, 1972b, pp. 82–87).

Judicial Statistics

Court records became available first. Given the sequence by which the criminal justice system was constructed, with courts long preceding both police and prisons, the order in which criminal justice statistics came to be collected is not surprising.

The French began collecting comprehensive national judicial statistics in the *Compte Général* in 1825. These statistics gave (and still give) information on the numbers of criminal charges and the numbers of criminal convictions. Data from the first five years of the *Compte Général* formed the basis for the earliest studies of the spatial and temporal distributions of crime, which, for the first time, analyzed sex, age, income, education, and occupation among criminals (Guerry, 1831; Quetelet, 1842).

The English collected judicial statistics periodically, from 1805. They collected standardized judicial statistics recording indictments and convictions for indictable offenses annually from 1834. From 1857, the English criminal statistics also included information about persons tried summarily in magistrates' courts (Gatrell and Hadden, 1972, pp. 340–345).

Canadian criminal judicial statistics date from 1876 through 1973. They were collected annually by the central statistical office (originally the Dominion Bureau of Statistics, now Statistics Canada), carrying out one of the major functions assigned the central government by the British North America Act. The judicial data give information about the number of charges, the number of indictable and summary convictions, and the number of various kinds of sentences. The judicial statistics are also stratified by detailed offense categories (Zay, 1963; Cole 1974a,b).

Disputes between the federal and the provincial governments led to a suspension in this program after 1973.

The divided governmental structure in the United States appears to have made the collection of national criminal judicial statistics impossible, at least to date. Some state series exist, though many are recent and poorly detailed. Ohio data are available from the mid-nineteenth century (Monkkonen, 1975), but many states do not yet produce reliable statistics. Federal criminal judicial data date from 1941. Even a simple case-flow count from state felony courts cannot be assembled from the published statistical series. No general count of charges or convictions by crime can be assembled (National Commission on Law Observance, 1931; Parisi et al., 1979).

Correctional Statistics

English prison statistics date from 1836 (though some earlier prison and jail returns were published from 1820) as an appendix to the report of the Home Counties Prisons Inspector and, from 1856, as a part of the composite criminal statistics. The prison returns gave information on the age, sex, education, number of previous commitments, and, from 1856, the occupation and birthplace of all offenders sentenced to prison or jail. The prison returns also indicated the number of persons committed for summary and indictable offenses (Gatrell and Hadden, 1972). These and other data on the prison establishment were published in the current century as the *Report of the Prison Commissioners* and, from 1963, as the *Report on the Work of the Prison Department* of the Home Office. Since 1962, the statistical tables have been published separately as *Prison Statistics* (Walker, 1971, p. 142).

Canadian correctional statistics have been published since 1867. Federal penitentiary statistics date from 1867, though detailed information about prisoners dates only from 1937 (Zay, 1963). Information on offenders in provincial jails and prisons, on juveniles in training schools, and on probationers must be obtained from various provincial reports.

American correctional statistics have varied over time. To the extent that they exist, data for much of the nineteenth century are to be found in the annual reports of individual prisons. Between 1850 and 1933, the U.S. Census Bureau conducted a series of nine prison-population enumerations: with the decennial censuses in 1850, 1860, 1870, 1880, and 1890, and with separate enumerations in 1904, 1910, 1923, and 1933. These enumerations covered federal, state, and local prisons; jails; workhouses; and other custodial institutions. They counted the *number* of offenders serving out sentences on the enumeration date and gathered information on sex, race, age, and length of sentence, and a variety of other information.

Beginning in 1926, first the Bureau of the Census, then the Federal Bureau of Prisons, then the Law Enforcement Assistance Administration, and, most recently, the Bureau of Justice Statistics, have conducted an annual census of sentenced prisoners in state and federal prisons and other custodial correctional institutions. The coverage has never been complete, requiring difficult annual adjustments for comparative purposes. By means of these data, a national time series spanning more than fifty years can be constructed.

There are occasional attempts to produce enumerations of jail and local prison populations, but such data must, in the main, be gathered from local agency reports or from uncompiled agency records. Probation and parole statistics are reported in a federal probation-service report, by state agencies, or by local agencies (National Commission on Law Observance, 1931; Wattenberg, 1976, pp. 407, 411).

Police Statistics

English police statistics date from 1857 and provide counts of indictable offenses known to the police, by detailed crime type. These have been published annually, along with the judicial statistics and, until fairly recently, with the prison statistics in an annual parliamentary sessional command paper titled *Criminal Statistics, England and Wales.* For the years before 1949 and for 1975 through 1979, detailed tables give crime counts for each police jurisdiction. For 1949–1975, such data are available only through unpublished "supplementary statistics," which may be made available to researchers on application to the Home Office (Gatrell and Hadden, 1972; Radzinowicz, 1945; Walker, 1971). The publication format of the *Criminal Statistics—England and Wales* was reorganized again in 1980. Data are now published in five volumes. Police data are contained in a general volume of data and commentary which is published as a Command Paper, and in a separate volume of supplementary statistical tables published by the Home Office.

Canadian police statistics date from 1920, when the Dominion Bureau of Statistics began an annual voluntary tabulation of crimes known to the police forces for municipalities of four thousand population or more. Beginning in 1962, an improved Uniform Crime Reports System tabulating crimes known to the police and crimes cleared by arrest, summons, or otherwise for all municipalities of 750 or more population has been in effect. Major revisions in the early 1970s now give comprehensive coverage in the annual *Crime and Traffic Enforcement Statistics* published by Statistics Canada.

American police statistics are the most recent of all. No national reporting system existed until 1930, when Congress assigned responsibility for the maintenance of a voluntary *Uniform Crime Reports* system (begun experimentally by the International Association of Chiefs of Police in 1929) to the Federal Bureau of Investigation. Up to that time, no state published statistics tabulating the crimes known to the police, and only one state published statewide statistics on arrests. The Wickersham Committee's survey of criminal statistics in 1931 demonstrated that only a handful of cities published annual police reports containing criminal statistics (Wolfgang, 1963; National Commission on Law Observance, 1931, Vol. 3, pp. 32–33).

The *Uniform Crime Reports* contain two categories of crime statistics. Eight offenses, originally designated "Part I offenses" and subsequently identified as the basis of a "crime index," are reported on the basis of crimes known to the police. Seven of these offenses have been reported since the beginning of the program. The eighth offense, arson, was added to the index crime category in 1979. The index offenses are reported as national aggregates and over the years since 1930, have been reported for individual police departments, for Standard Metropolitan Statistical Areas (the Census Bureau's category, which includes urban areas such as the New York metropolitan area and the Boston metropolitan area), for aggregates of cities of various sizes, and for states and regions. Numbers of arrests are reported for the seven index offenses and for twenty-two additional crime categories. Since 1970, the uniform crime reporting system has moved from a voluntary to a mandatory footing, as some states passed legislation requiring state and local police agencies to report to a central state bureau, which in turn reports state and city data to the FBI. Many states now publish state uniform crime reports annually.

Many other countries collect police statistics and publish them as national series. In addition, the International Criminal Police Organization (Interpol) collects and publishes a biannual compilation of crimes known to the police in some member countries, classified according to broad, generic categories of crimes (Normandeau, 1969).

Enumerating Crimes

The principal criminological question addressed by these criminal justice system statistics is: How much crime is there? This question is interesting and important for several reasons. First, of course, the answer to this question holds a certain morbid fascination for most of us. Counting crime seems to satisfy some fundamental urge to know the dimensions of our misery, as if knowing by itself makes things better. People want to know whether the crime rate has gone up or down recently, and people seem to want to compare *their* problems with those experienced by other people. New Yorkers want to know whether they suffer more bank robberies than Montrealers or more murders than Londoners.

More important, enumeration of crime gives us a measure of political success: it tells us whether and how well (or poorly) our crime control policies are working. Enumerating crime has practical significance. Political campaigns, governmental budget allocations, and public behavior can all be shaped by changes in the crime count. Third, the enumeration of crime has long been seen as a necessary precondition to its scientific analysis. Accurate, valid, and reliable measurement has been the keystone in the construction of physical science and engineering. The counting of crimes seems to be an important precondition of the analysis of the causes of criminal behavior.

Problems with Crime Statistics

A number of problems cause criminologists to question the usefulness of crime statistics in answering the basic enumeration question: How much crime is there? Criminologists ordinarily want to answer this question in such a way that the answer can be used comparatively, either over time or across space. Such a desire poses a series of threshold questions: How is crime defined? Where in the system was *this* count generated? What are the scope and the coverage of the counting

41

body? What sorts of counting rules and procedures have been used? Obviously, direct comparisons of two sets of crime counts are best made when the answers to these questions are identical for both sets; comparisons must be more tentative and more cautious as the answers to these questions differ.

Defining Crime

Definitions of crime vary with time and space. Crime, ultimately, depends on a *legal* definition and the proscription of a specific form of behavior. We know, empirically, that such definitions differ, at least in detail, from society to society at any given time. The crime of vagrancy, for instance, has been abolished in Canada and has been subsumed by the law of disorderly conduct in California, but it remains an offense punishable by imprisonment for up to two years in Russia.

Burglary, a generic common-law crime defined as the breaking and entering of a dwelling house in the night time with the intent to commit a felony therein, has been extended in California to cover entry of "any house, room, apartment, tenement, shop, warehouse, store, mill, barn, stable, outhouse or other building, tent, vessel, railroad car, trailer coach . . . , vehicle . . . , aircraft . . . , mine or any underground portion thereof" at any time whatsoever (Calif. Penal Code, § 459). Canada has abolished burglary, replacing it with a set of breaking-and-entering offenses protecting dwellings, other buildings and structures, railway vehicles, vessels, aircraft and trailers, and enclosures where "fur-bearing animals are kept in captivity for breeding or commercial purposes." Russia recognizes no separate offense involving breaking and entering private places but apparently subsumes these activities under such crimes as theft, robbery, or rape.

By way of contrast, Russia recognizes the crime of obstruction of exercise of equal rights of women and makes it punishable by two years of imprisonment, but neither Canada nor California defines such conduct as criminal.

Another example of variation in criminal law from jurisdiction to jurisdiction can be found in gambling laws. Nevada permits most forms of gambling, whereas neighboring California permits only poker and pari-mutuel wagering at horse-race tracks. Canada prohibits casino gambling but permits pari-mutuel wagering on horse races and runs government-sponsored lotteries.

Definitions of crime are known to change over time within the same legal jurisdiction: new crimes may be added to the criminal law or old crimes may be deleted from the criminal law. The United States created a new set of crimes through the prohibition of the manufacture, import, sale, or use of alcoholic beverages in 1920. Canada defined the new crime of public incitement to hatred in 1970. Canada, England, and the United States defined new offenses related to the use of narcotic drugs in the period between 1909 and 1925. Both the United States and Canada have recently defined new and serious crimes of electronic eavesdropping. The creation of new offenses, of course, can change the apparent number of crimes occurring, even if behavior patterns do not alter.

The United States abolished its national alcoholic beverage prohibition law in 1933. In 1967, the English abolished the crime of buggery (intercourse *per anum*) when done privately and by consent by males aged at least twenty-one. The abolition of crimes can cause an apparent reduction in aggregate crimes recorded in criminal statistics without changing the incidence of a particular behavior.

Definitional changes in the criminal law may also take the form of technical adjustments in the language of the law, so that no crime is created anew or abolished, but new behaviors are made subject to the law and added to criminal statistics, or behaviors are removed from the law and dropped from criminal statistical records. Thus, technical adjustments by the U.S. Supreme Court to the law on obscenity have, over the past two decades, had a significant impact on the apparent number of crimes in this area.

No criminal code exhausts the possible forms of behavior that *might* be criminalized. People holding strong political views might wish to criminalize adherence to different political positions. Persons objecting to specific forms of economic activities might wish to criminalize those activities. Persons objecting to specific public behavior might want those behaviors criminalized. People might seek to impose specific religious practices by means of criminal sanctions. To the extent that such possibilities are held up as reflecting some "natural law" of crime, the absence of the desired prohibition from the formal criminal code means that formal criminal statistics will fail to reflect the true state of "crime."

Case Filtration

A second problem with crime statistics as a measure of crime arises from the way in which the criminal justice system processes criminal cases sequentially. Each step in the processing sequence results in the resolution or loss of cases, in a loss of information about criminal events, and, possibly, in a distortion of information about criminal events. The criminal case statistics in British Columbia for the year 1971 nicely illustrate the problem. During that year, 395,999 offenses were reported to the police, but only 185,547—that is, about 47 percent—were cleared by a criminal charge. About 6 percent of the charges brought were against juveniles; the remainder were against adults. Among the charged juveniles, less than half ever appeared in court, though 95 percent of those who did were found delinquent. Fewer than 1.5 percent of the juveniles found delinquent were sentenced to a custodial institution. Of the adult charges that went forward, 94 percent were summary offenses. A negligible 284 cases out of 166,528 (about 0.2 percent) went to trial before a judge and jury. About 60 percent of all adult charges resulted in convictions in 1971, but only about 6 percent of those convicted were sentenced to some term in a custodial institution; that is, a penitentiary, prison, or jail.

The problem posed by criminal justice case filtration is this: What statistic best measures crime and what statistic best measures criminality? Prison statistics are clearly a poor choice for the measurement of either. Such a small proportion of convicted offenders end up in institutions that we can easily infer that they, and/or their crimes, are special and unrepresentative of most crimes and most offenders. The patterns found in the crimes and characteristics of these specially selected offenders would badly mislead us if we sought to use them to establish the characteristics of most people who commit crimes, or the characteristics of most crimes. Unless assignment to various sentences were wholly random (and whatever else it may be, neither judges nor criminologists think that sentencing is random), we would expect prison populations to exhibit a record of high-frequency commission of serious crimes.

Problems with Judicial Data

Judicial data really fall into two categories: charges and convictions. Both categories of data exist in fairly long time-series, for example, in England from 1834, in Canada from 1876, and in France from 1825. These data bases can be pushed back still further if information is gathered from individual court records. In recent years, historians have gathered charge and conviction data well back into medieval times.

The patterns and fluctuations in conviction data formed the basis for most nineteenth-century and positive criminological analyses of crime. Quetelet (1842) and Plint (1851) used conviction data to assess changes in the crime pattern over time; to analyze the geographical distributions of crime in France and England, respectively; and to compare the evidence of crime with variations in population characteristics, such as relative mixtures of age and sex, and with variations in the price of food, variations in literacy, patterns of employment in major occupational groupings, and so forth. Ferri (1917), Bonger (1916), and other major turn-of-the-century criminologists equated criminal convictions with crimes for analytic purposes.

Definitional Problems

Criticisms of judicial records as measurements of crime really flow from several different sources. One criticism is based on a definitional point, a clash of philosophies: What, properly, should be called a *crime?* For some criminologists, particularly legalists such as Tappan (1947) and labeling theorists such as Ditton (1979), crime cannot be said to have occurred until the moment of conviction. Legalists argue that allegations of crime made to police or contained in prosecutorial documents represent nothing more than speculations until a conviction confirms beyond a reasonable doubt that a crime was committed and that the accused did it. Labeling theorists argue that crime is not inherent in any behavior; rather, it is a social status conferred on a person (and his or her behavior) by a formal status-conferring agency: the court. The logic of the labeling position holds that criminal conviction is the *only* measure of crime, because no crime exists prior to the moment of conviction.

Most criminologists adhere to a different definition of *crime*, however. The majority position argues that a crime is composed of a behavior *and* a legal prohibition. A crime occurs, in this view, when a behavior is performed in violation of an extant criminal law explicitly prohibiting that behavior.

This definition of *crime* logically precludes the use of conviction data as an *enumeration* of crime. We know that criminal convictions enumerate only a small proportion of the crimes that have taken place. In the case of British Columbia in 1971, affirmed convictions accounted for only 27 percent of the *known crimes.* Put another way, almost three-fourths of the known crimes were not enumerated in the conviction data in the first place because no one was arrested, or because no prosecution took place, or because an accused was acquitted. Thus, conviction data cannot be treated as an enumeration of crime.

Information Distortion

A second major critique of conviction statistics involves a problem of information distortion. The judicial processing of a criminal charge may modify the basic content of the behavioral description inherent in the charge; that is, a person arrested and charged for one kind of offense may be convicted of some very different offense with a strikingly different behavioral content. This transformation may occur through a variance in evidence produced in court or through a process of plea negotiation in which the prosecution agrees to change the charge in order to obtain a plea of guilty and avoid the trouble, uncertainty, and expense of a trial.

The classic study of this sort of variation was conducted by David Sudnow (1965) in a California public defenders' office. He found that 80 percent of the criminal cases were settled by means of a guilty plea and that a significant proportion of these pleas were to some offense other than that initially charged. Patricia Brantingham (1977, pp. 289, 300) demonstrated that the aggregate charge–conviction switch patterns for the crimes of murder, manslaughter, rape, aggravated assault, robbery, burglary, larceny, and auto theft for the State of Florida during the middle 1970s were consistent with Sudnow's model: between 10 and 20 percent of the cases originally charged as one of these serious felonies eventually resulted in convictions for nonindex crimes.

Policy Variations

Conviction statistics can also be affected by policy differences among courts or jurisdictions, or within courts or jurisdictions over time. This problem has long been recognized. Quetelet (1842), for instance, attributed differentials in French and Belgian conviction rates in the mid-1820s to differences in judicial policy rather than to differentials in criminal incidence, because the rates at which people were committed to appear before the French and Belgian courts were virtually identical. Similarly, shifts in judicial or prosecutorial policy can significantly alter the apparent mix of crimes as measured by convictions for various offenses, although no actual difference in the underlying pattern of criminal events may occur.

Similar criticisms can be lodged against other forms of judicial statistics, particularly the records of the number of charges laid, the number of committals for trial on indictable offenses, the number of indictments, or other measures of the commencement of judicial proceedings. They are subject to systemic manipulation and they are vulnerable to policy variations. In Florida, in the mid-1970s, for instance, two separate priorities in state's attorneys' offices interacted to create large fluctuations in the number of theft offenses prosecuted from month to month. One policy held that first priority should be given to violent crimes against the person. A second policy held that deputy state's attorneys ought to keep reasonably steady case loads. Together, these policies meant that in a month when a large number of violent offenses were solved by the police, few routine theft offenses were prosecuted rigorously; in a month when fewer serious violent offenses were presented by the police, a larger proportion of simple thefts were rigorously prosecuted.

An analysis of information contained in the computerized data system called *PROMIS* (*PRO*secutor *M*anagement *I*nformation *S*ystem) for the thirteen American jurisdictions using it in 1976–1977 showed interjurisdictional differences in policy affecting the apparent crime rates reflected in criminal case filings. The pattern was very clear for burglary: the proportion of cases rejected for prosecution at screening by the prosecutor's office was inversely related to the number of burglary filings per 100,000 population. In Atlanta, prosecutors rejected none of the burglary cases that the police brought to them for prosecution: case filing statistics showed burglary prosecution rates of 97 per 100,000 population. In Salt Lake City, prosecutors rejected 22 percent of the cases police brought to them: burglary filing rates were 44 per 100,000 population. In Los Angeles, prosecutors rejected 47 percent of police burlgary cases: filing rates were 25 per 100,000 population (Brosi, 1979, pp. 139–141).

Problems with Police Data

Police data come in two basic forms of interest to criminologists: arrest records and records of crimes made known to the police. Arrest records enumerate the number of arrests made for many different categories of crime. They may also provide information about the characteristics of the people arrested. The American *Uniform Crime Reports* detail numbers of arrests for thirty categories of crime. Neither the English nor the Canadian police statistics provide information on arrests per se, though these are subsumed in a larger category that the English call "crimes cleared up" and the Canadians call "crimes cleared by charge" and "crimes cleared otherwise." Records of crimes made known to the police give the numbers of offenses discovered by the police by any means. The American *Uniform Crime Reports* provide compilations of known offenses for eight categories of crime, called *Part I* or *index offenses*. The Canadian *Crime and Traffic Enforcement Statistics* provide counts of known offenses for twenty-five categories of crime, some of which subdivide into more detailed subcategories. The *Criminal Statistics* for England and Wales provide counts of known indictable offenses for sixty-four crime categories divided into eight major groupings. Table 3–1 outlines the categories for which crimes known to the police are published in the three countries.

Selection and Categorization

Police statistics are imperfect enumerations of the total amount of crime. The most obvious enumeration problem can be seen in Table 3–1. It is the problem of selective inclusion and categorization. The American *Uniform Crime Reports* (UCR) enumerate only eight offenses. Many other sorts of offenses that are important in terms of frequency, the harm done, and frightfulness are not counted: business fraud, riot, handling stolen goods, blackmail, public drunkenness, disorderly con-

TABLE 3–1. Major Categories for Which Crimes Known to the Police Are Recorded

United States	Canada	England and Wales
Part 1: Index Offenses	Murder	Murder
	Attempted murder	Manslaughter
	Manslaughter	Infanticide
Murder	Rape	Attempted murder
Forcible rape	Other sexual offenses	Threat or conspiracy to murder
Robbery	Wounding	Child destruction
Aggravated assault	Assaults (not indecent)	Causing death by dangerous driving
Burglary	Robbery	Wounding
Larceny–theft	Breaking and entering	Endangering railway passenger
Motor vehicle theft	Theft, motor vehicle	Other wounding
Arson	Theft over $200	Assault
	Theft, $200 and under	Abandoning child under two years of age
Part II Offenses: Arrest Data Only	Have stolen goods	Child stealing
	Frauds	Procuring abortion
	Prostitution	Concealment of birth
Other assaults	Gambling and betting	Buggery
Forgery and counter- feiting	Offensive weapons	Attempt to commit buggery
	Other criminal code	Indecency between males
Fraud	Federal statute violations	Rape
Embezzlement	Addicting, opiatelike drugs	Indecent assault on female
Stolen property: Buying, receiving, possessing	Cannibis	Unlawful sexual intercourse with girl under thirteen
	Controlled drugs	
	Restricted drugs	Unlawful sexual intercourse with girl under sixteen
Vandalism	Provincial statute violations	
Weapons offenses	Municipal by-law viola- tions	Incest
Prostitution and com- mercialized vices		Procuration
		Abduction
Other sex offenses		Bigamy
Narcotic drug laws		Burglary in a dwelling
Gambling		Aggravated burglary in a dwelling
Offenses against family and children		Burglary in a building other than a dwell- ing
Driving under the in- fluence		Aggravated burglary in a building other than a dwelling
Liquor laws		Going equipped for stealing
Drunkenness		Theft from the person of another
Disorderly conduct		Theft in a dwelling
Vagrancy		Theft by employee
All other offenses		Theft from mail
Suspicion		Theft of pedal cycle
Curfew and loitering (juveniles)		Theft from vehicle
Runaway (juveniles)		Shoplifting
		Theft from automatic machine or meter
		Theft of motor vehicle
		Handling stolen goods
		Fraud by company director
		False accounting
		Other fraud
		Forgery and uttering prescription
		Other forgery and uttering
		Arson
		Criminal damage endangering life

(continued)

TABLE 3–1.   (continued)

United States	Canada	England and Wales
		Criminal damage over £20
		Other criminal damage
		Threat or possession with intent to commit criminal damage
		Blackmail
		High treason
		Riot
		Unlawful assembly
		Other offenses against state or public order
		Perjury
		Libel
		Aiding suicide
		Other indictable offenses

SOURCE: Federal Bureau of Investigation (Annual) *Crime in the United States* (Washington, D.C.: Government Printing Office [Uniform Crime Reports], 1980); Statistics Canada, *Crime and Traffic Enforcement: Statistics* (Ottawa: Queen's Printer [Catalogue 85-205 annual], 1980); Home Office (Annual), *Criminal Statistics: England and Wales* (London: HMSO, 1978 [Cmnd7670]).

duct, and drunken driving, for example. We have no way of accounting for the numbers of these offenses that occur and become known to the police even though we suspect that some of them occur in very large numbers (given their frequency of appearance in *other* data, such as judicial statistics or private insurance statistics), and even though we believe that others, such as business fraud, may be—socially, at least—as important as those included in the UCR index.

The English police statistics provide far more detail on indictable offenses than the American police statistics, but they provide no counts of summary offenses, though summary offenses account for most cases appearing in the judicial statistics. The Canadian police statistics do provide some counts of summary-level offenses, but for some offenses, they apparently commingle summary and indictable offenses under single generic categories. As Sellin (1951) observed more than thirty years ago, the problem of selection and categorization is inherent in the business of constructing any scheme of police statistics.

Canada has the advantage of a single national criminal code, but many crimes and penal offenses are defined by federal and provincial statutes, and judicial interpretations of specific code provisions have varied from province to province, actually creating different criminal laws. Beyond this consideration, the sheer number of criminal offenses defined by law make it necessary to consolidate some offenses into broader categories. The Law Reform Commission of Canada, for instance, estimates that in 1974 there were more than 41,000 statutory offenses then in force in Canada (Stuart, 1982, p. 4). Failure to cluster and categorize such a vast array of crimes would produce a set of statistics too diffuse and too cumbersome to comprehend.[1]

---

[1] The introduction of large-scale electronic data-processing should eventually resolve this problem, of course. But electronic data-processing is expensive and requires skilled specialists. In the early 1980s, the majority of police departments still find such information systems beyond their grasp.

Troublesome categorization problems persist in England because there has never been a code consolidation of the criminal law, which lies scattered through hundreds of statutes and judicial decisions. The situation in the United States is much worse. Fifty-two separate criminal codes, more than three thousand county codes, and tens of thousands of municipal bylaws define crimes, all in slightly different form. Thus, a categorization of offenses under generic definitions, which do violence to nice legal differences but capture the core meaning of the behavioral prohibitions, is a necessity. Moreover, selection of some set of offenses thought to be important and also sufficiently robust in character to survive generic classification with some comparability is also a necessity.

The Dark Figure of Criminality

Crimes known to the police are literally just that. The police can record only those offenses about which they have some knowledge. Some large number of crimes occurring each year are neither reported to the police nor discovered by the police.

It is possible to hypothesize a number of reasons that people might not report a crime to the police.

1. *A crime may be of such a subtle character that it is never known to have happened.* Suppose that while the owner was out, a person used a passkey to break into an apartment with the intent to steal the color television, then changed his mind and left, disturbing nothing. This action constitutes a burglary, but no one save the burglar would ever know it had happened.

2. *A crime might not be perceived as such.* Suppose, in the course of a championship play-off game, a defenseman for the Philadelphia Flyers were to slash a star center of the Montreal Canadiens with his hockey stick, causing a cut requiring six stitches to close. Such incidents do occur in the heat of competition in hockey games, and they are defined as major penalties within the context of the game. The incident described, of course, also constitutes a crime that might be classified as an aggravated assault under the American *Uniform Crime Reports,* or as a wounding in the Canadian *Crime Statistics.* The event is unlikely to be perceived as a crime by either player, by either team, by the referees, or by the fans, and it is unlikely to be reported to the police.[2]

3. *A crime might not be reported because the offender is a family member, a friend, or an acquaintance.*

4. *A crime might not be reported because the victim believes that it was trivial, or that the potential penalty is too grave for the harm done.*

5. *A crime might not be reported because the victim fears reprisal.*

6. *A crime might not be reported because the victim feels antipathy toward the police, or because the victim is herself or himself a criminal, or because the victim is embarassed by the circumstances under which the crime occurred.*

[2] Occasionally, an ambitious prosecuting attorney will decide to prosecute such an incident, usually when a member of the home team is injured in a losing game. The angry uproar that ensues among the sporting public is amazing to behold.

In fact, most of these reasons are now known to play some role in nonreporting.[3]

What all of this means, of course, is that police statistics do not enumerate all crimes that occur within a jurisdiction during any given time period. The difference between the number of crimes reported to the police and the total number of crimes that actually occur cannot be known, though as we shall see, two different techniques have been developed to help estimate the magnitude of this gap. The actual number of crimes that really occur, this unknown quantity, is colorfully called the *dark figure of criminality*.

The existence of the dark figure has, of course, been appreciated for a very long time. Many criminologists, particularly sociologists concerned with the broader concept of *deviance* rather than the legally bounded concept of *crime*, seem to think that the scientific assessment of causal patterns in criminality or criminal events depends on a complete enumeration of all the crimes that occur. Such a complete enumeration is no more necessary to criminology than a counting of all the stars is necessary to a viable cosmology. What is necessary is some idea of the pattern relationship between the numbers of crimes reported to the police and the numbers of crimes actually occurring in given time periods and at given locations. Because there seems to be a large pool of unreported crime at any one time, a rise in the reported crime rate might reflect a real change in the incidence of criminal events, or it might indicate a change in public reporting behavior, so that a larger part of the unknown reservoir is made known with no real change in criminal behavior.

Nineteenth-century criminologists tended to deal with the problem of the dark figure by assuming it away. Quetelet (1842, p. 82) dealt with the problem by means of a confession:

> our observations can only refer to *a certain number of known and tried offences, out of the unknown sum total of crimes committed.* Since this sum total of crimes committed will probably continue unknown, all the reasoning of which it is the basis will be more or less defective. I do not hesitate to say, that all the knowledge which we possess on the statistics of crimes and offences will be of no utility whatever, unless we admit without question that *there is a ratio, nearly and invariably the same, between known crime and the sum total of crimes committed.* (Italics in the original.)

He also argued that the ratio would vary by offense, approaching unity for homicide and being very small for thefts and "offences of smaller importance."

Bonger (1916, p. 85) addressed the problem with three arguments. First, while admitting that the number of offenses not appearing in criminal statistics is certainly large, he argued that they were "chiefly insignificant misdemeanors, such as insults, trifling assaults, petty thefts, etc." Serious crimes, in most cases, appear in the criminal statistics. Second, he argued that "the ratio of known crime to unknown crime remains relatively constant." The proof he found in the criminal statistics themselves, in the constancy of their patterns over time, and in a statistical rule that he called the "law of averages." Third, he argued that although the number of offenses reported might not reflect all the crimes that occur, it does, over time, count most criminals.

---

[3] See Table 4–3.

This particular dispute remains unresolved. Twentieth-century criminologists continue to debate the impact of the dark-figure problem on the scientific utility, for enumerative and analytic purposes, of criminal justice statistics in general and of the statistics on crimes known to the police particularly. Some argue that this problem, coupled with a second dark figure discussed in the next section, render police statistics useless as a measure of criminal behavior (Kitsuse and Cicourel, 1963).

The alternate approach has been to use police statistics with sensitivity to the interpretational limitations imposed by the dark figure and, at the same time, to seek means for the measurement—or at least the estimation—of the parameters of the problem. Two different methods have been developed, both involving surveys of first-person accounts of criminal events. The outcomes of such research are discussed in Chapter 4, but for the moment, it should be noted that they seem to support the general lines of argument advanced by Bonger (Skogan, 1977*b*).

The Dark Figure of Recording

Once a crime report has come to the attention of the police, that report must be assessed, classified, and recorded before it becomes part of the criminal statistics. Police exercise a very wide discretion in deciding whether and how to record crime reports. Variations in the exercise of this discretion over time and from place to place can have a significant impact on the numbers and types of offenses that appear in official statistics and can make comparative research among jurisdictions and within jurisdictions over time extremely difficult.

A basic problem, much discussed in the earlier criminological literature, involves standardized reporting periods. The reporting-period problem is largely important in historical studies or studies involving long time periods. For instance, the English police statistics were reported on crimes occurring in a fiscal year running from October 1 to the following September 30 for the years 1857–1892. Beginning in 1893, they were reported for calendar years. Warner's survey (1934, pp. 82–83) of crime in the Boston area prior to the introduction of the *Uniform Crime Reports* system showed a welter of different police reporting periods: Boston's statistics were reported for a fiscal year ending November 30, Cambridge reported for a year ending March 31, and most other Massachusetts police departments reported statistics for calendar years. This problem was found to be generic to American criminal statistics by the National Commission on Law Observance (1931, p. 84). Obviously, shifts in reporting periods or differences in reporting periods affect the comparability of the statistics reported. Such shifts are no longer a major problem: English, American, and Canadian statistics are now all collected and reported for calendar year periods.

A second basic problem involves the categorization and counting rules used to record the criminal offenses reported to the police. How should a set of facts be translated into categorized statistical counts? Suppose that two men go on a crime spree. They enter a convenience store, rob the proprietor and three customers, shoot dead a police officer who tries to arrest them, knock cans and bottles off shelves, curse, and set fire to the store as they leave. A prosecutor might charge sixteen crimes out of this event: one murder, four robberies, one act of vandalism, one use of obscene language, and one arson, a total of eight crimes against each of two defendants, for a total of sixteen counts. For police administrative purposes, and for criminological purposes, there are alternative counting procedures and problems. One logical method is to count transactions: because this was a single event (a single criminal transaction), it would be counted as a *single* crime. A second logical method would be to count the number of offenders involved: two offenders, two crimes.

Both of the latter approaches raise the additional problem of *what* type of crime should be counted, because four different legal categories were involved. We might score the most serious offense (murder), or the most frequent offense (robbery), or the first offense (robbery), or the last offense (arson). Another logical approach might be to count the number of victims, producing, in this case, a count of five crimes (against the police officer, the three customers, and the proprietor). Where there are multiple offenses against one victim, such as the proprietor in this case (robbery, vandalism, obscene language, and arson), the problem of *what* crime to count again occurs.

The uniform crime-reporting rules in Canada (Statistics Canada, 1979, pp. 16-7—16-18; Silverman and Teevan, 1975, pp. 72—73), England (Walker, 1971, pp. 24—25), and the United States (*Uniform Crime Reporting Handbook;* Wolfgang, 1963, pp. 720—724) have solved the problem of counting in essentially similar fashion. Crimes of violence are counted on the basis of victims: one crime is counted for each victim. Property crimes are counted by transaction. For example, when one offender assaults three people in a bar, three assaults are counted, whereas when one offender breaks into an apartment shared by three people and steals property belonging to each of them, a single offense is counted. When multiple offenses are involved in a single event or criminal transaction, as in the hypothetical case given in the prior paragraph, only the most serious crime is recorded: the hypothetical case would be recorded as *one* murder. Attempted crimes (with the exception of attempted murder) are scored as if they were completed.

These solutions obviously raise problems. They clearly overstate the relative frequency of violent crimes with respect to property crimes. At the same time, they clearly result in an understatement of the numbers of offenses known to the police. The inclusion of attempted and completed crimes within the same counting categories is a traditional ground for complaint among academic criminologists (e.g., Wolfgang, 1963; Silverman and Teevan, 1975). The logic of the complaint is not clear. An attempted crime is usually punished less severely than the completed crime would be, but both are behaviorally identical save for some intervening circumstance that frustrated the offender's effort (Smith and Hogan, 1969, p. 8).

England, Canada, and the United States have all developed handbooks to guide local police forces in categorizing and counting offenses under these countries' respective uniform crime-reporting rules. Even so, problems persist. The Canadian uniform crime-reporting system went into effect in 1962, yet for 1977, the crime statistics carried this warning about the figures for Toronto, Canada's largest metropolis:

> Because the Toronto metropolitan police force does not apply the multiple offence rule when reporting crimes, Metro Toronto crime figures cannot be compared to those

censuses, the census bureaus in the three countries make population estimates. These estimates may be reasonably accurate, or they may be much too high or much too low, depending on what is happening to the population growth rate. The problem for the agencies that collect and publish police statistics is whether to use these population estimates in calculating rates. For a time, from the mid-1930s to the late 1950s, the U.S. Federal Bureau of Investigation (FBI) elected to use the rather more certain census-year figures as the base for crime rate calculations for each year in the decade until a new census was taken. The result was the artificial inflation of the crime rates over the course of each decade, as well as the production of an automatic and dramatic drop in the calculated crime rate in each census year. Since 1957, the FBI has used annual Census Bureau midyear population estimates in calculating crime rates, removing this artificial "crime wave" from the data.

The second problem in rate calculation involves finding an *appropriate* base for use with any particular crime. As Sarah Boggs (1966) argued and demonstrated, some sorts of crime are better analyzed through rates based on something other than total population. Rape, for instance, can be more intelligently analyzed through rates based on the population at risk (females) rather than on the basis of the total population. Auto theft is more appropriately analyzed in terms of rates based on motor vehicle registrations. Burglary is more intelligently analyzed in terms of the numbers of dwelling units or the numbers of buildings than in terms of total population figures. Appropriate base rates must be calculated by the individual researcher. Moreover, there is no general agreement on what might constitute the most appropriate base for any particular crime except residential burglary and rape.

The final technical problem that we shall mention involves a change in the *format* used to collect police data. Such format shifts may take the form of a modification in the crimes for which information is sought, a modification in the method of aggregation of various offenses into categories such as "violent crimes" and "property crimes," or a modification in the temporal period for which data are collected. Any of these format shifts can cause significant problems for researchers wishing to compare levels or amounts of recorded crime from year to year.

Examples of these problems abound, and only a few illustrative examples need be mentioned. The American *Uniform Crime Reports* underwent such a transformation in 1973. Before that year, theft offenses were recorded in two categories: larceny over $50 was an index offense, for which figures on the crimes known to the police were compiled and reported; larceny under $50 was a Part II offense, for which records were reported only when an arrest was made. Beginning in 1973, the two categories were merged, to form the single index offense larceny—theft. All thefts, of whatever value, were now recorded when they became known to the police. This change caused an abrupt rise in the index larceny category. In Florida, for instance, index larceny rose from 101,221 offenses known to the police in 1972 to 234,263 offenses known in 1973.

Canadian police statistics were completely reorganized in 1962, so that the data for the period 1920–1961 and those for 1962 to the present are noncomparable. English police practice stopped making any record of thefts under the value five pounds sterling for a brief period in the early 1970s, then returned to recording all thefts reported. In 1980, the counting rules used for compilation of the Criminal Statistics—England and Wales were changed. The result is that English police statistics for 1980 and subsequent years cannot be compared with those from earlier years.

Many of the problems mentioned with respect to police data could be repeated in detail with respect to judicial and correctional statistics. The records of the criminal justice system must be used with caution as a source of information about criminal events, about crime patterns, and about criminals.

Chapter Summary

The records of the criminal justice system comprise the largest extant source of information about crimes and criminals. National judicial statistics have been collected since 1805 in England and from 1876 through 1973 in Canada but have never been collected in the United States. National police statistics date from 1857 in England, from 1920 in Canada, and from 1930 in the United States. National correctional statistics date from 1836 in England and from 1867 in Canada. In the United States, the Census Bureau conducted prison and jail censuses periodically between 1850 and 1933. Since 1926, the U.S. Department of Justice has conducted an annual census of prisons and jails.

Although the criminal justice systems that collect the vast resources of information about crimes and criminals are similar in structure, they exhibit interesting differences. England and Wales have a single national criminal code administered by a single national court system. Police are organized at the regional level. Corrections are organized at the national and local levels. Canada has a federal system of criminal justice. Criminal laws are made by the federal government, but administered by the provincial governments. There are local, provincial, and federal police forces. Courts are organized provincially, but ultimate appeal lies with the Supreme Court of Canada. There are both federal and provincial correctional systems. The United States has a more diffuse federal system of criminal justice. The federal government and all of the states maintain separate criminal codes, police forces, court systems, and correctional systems. The collection of criminal statistics began earliest and has proved easiest in England and Wales, with the most centralized criminal justice system. The collection of national criminal statistics began latest and has proved most difficult in the United States, with the least centralized criminal justice system.

Criminal justice statistics do not enumerate all crimes. They enumerate only those crimes made known to the criminal justice system. A substantial number of crimes are never reported to the police or any other agent of criminal justice. The true number of crimes, called the *dark figure of criminality* is unknown. For more than a century, criminologists have had to assume that criminal justice statistics constitute some consistent fraction of the dark figure in order to examine patterns in crime.

Criminal justice statistics present a number of problems. Criminal laws and social definitions of crime vary from place to place and from time to time so that apparently similar statistics may be based on very different forms of behavior. Many criminal cases disappear from criminal statistics as they are processed from arrest to trial to conviction to punishment. Prison statistics record only some proportion of the cases that resulted in conviction. Conviction statistics record only some proportion of the cases that went to trial. Criminal charges record only some proportion of arrests. Arrests record only some proportion of crimes known to the police. Variations in how people interpret the rules for defining, counting and recording crimes and variations of the number of criminal justice agencies participating in any particular statistical reporting program mean that criminal justice statistics must be used with caution.

Despite a number of problems, some fundamental and some merely technical, criminal justice statistics provide our largest source of information about crime and criminals. Used with due attention to their problems, criminal justice statistics provide a large quantity of useful information about the spatial and temporal patterns of crime.

4
Surveys of Crime

Introduction

Criminologists, noting the apparent imperfections of statistics gathered by the criminal justice system, have recently turned to aggregate personal accounts of crime gathered through field surveys as major sources of information about the numbers, types, and characteristics of crime found in contemporary society. Opinion survey technology, which has proved enormously useful in such diverse fields as politics and marketing, has been applied to the problem of counting crime in two slightly different ways. Self-report studies ask people to list the crimes that they, personally, have committed. Victimization studies ask people to list the crimes that they, personally, have suffered.

Self-report Studies

Self-report studies take a very straightforward approach to the enumeration of criminal behavior: they ask people to confess the crimes that they have committed. The responses people give are totaled (for a relevant jurisdiction and time period); are cross-analyzed against the fundamental demographic and socioeconomic characteristics of the respondents, such as sex, age, race, social class, and known criminal record; and are used to assess both the validity of criminal justice statistics as an enumerator or as a pattern index of crime, and the viability of criminological theories based on inferences drawn from the patterns found in criminal justice statistics.

Pioneering work with the self-report (SR) technique was done in the 1940s. The initial results of the pioneering studies were startling. They demonstrated that much more crime occurred than was discovered by, reported to, or recorded by the police; and they showed that virtually everyone asked would confess to the commission of some crime. The first finding, of course, merely confirmed the "dark figure" speculation that had been a staple topic for discussion among criminologists for a century. The second finding was startling because many criminologists, following the traditions of the positive school, apparently assumed that any given population could be sorted into two classes: the criminals, who committed crimes; and the law-abiding masses, who never committed crimes. The early self report studies demolished this assumption.

Austin Porterfield (1946) conducted the first SR study at Texas Christian University in the early 1940s. He asked college students whether they had ever engaged in any of fifty-five different types of deviant and criminal behavior. Two different groups of students, surveyed in 1940–1941 and 1942–1943, gave a 100-percent affirmative response. Every student admitted having engaged in at least one of the listed behaviors at least once. On that basis, every student could be called a deviant. A subset of male students were asked about the number of crimes and deviant acts committed during their college years: the average was 11.2 acts.

Porterfield asked about acts of varying seriousness. Some were very serious crimes. A few respondents confessed to murder. Most acts, however, were either not prohibited by the criminal law of Texas or were legally trivial. The proportion of respondents confessing to any particular form of deviant or criminal behavior varied more-or-less inversely with the seriousness of the offense. Of the male respondents, 79 percent admitted using abusive language, 77 percent admitted throwing spitwads at other people, 68 percent admitted speeding, and 69 percent admitted having stolen fruit at some time in their precollege life; only 10 percent admitted shoplifting, only 8 percent admitted burglary, and only 0.5 percent admitted auto theft. Porterfield also found a strong sex differential in self-reported involvement in deviant behavior. Far fewer female than male respondents admitted the commission of any particular act.

Wallerstein and Wyle (1947) studied the self-reported crimes of adults in New York City. They asked more than sixteen hundred people whether they had violated any of forty-nine criminal laws during their adult life. Of the people asked, 99 percent admitted having committed one or more of the named offenses. Men admitted to an average of eighteen crimes; women admitted to an average of eleven offenses. In this same sample, 64 percent of the men and 29 percent of the women admitted that they had committed some felony. As in the Porterfield study, the number of people admitting the commission of any particular offense varied inversely with the seriousness of that offense. Of the men, 89 percent admitted some form of petty larceny, 85 percent admitted disorderly conduct, and 77 percent admitted to acts of indecency; but only 17 percent admitted to burglary, only 13 percent admitted to grand larcency, and only 11 percent admitted to the commission of a robbery.

These pioneering studies developed into a major area of criminological research during the 1960s and the 1970s. A large number of scholars studied the problems of perfecting self-report methodology and analyzing and interpreting the substantive results of SR surveys (e.g., Short and Nye, 1958; Dentler and Monroe, 1961; Slocum and Stone, 1963; Akers, 1964; Christie et al., 1965; Elmhorn, 1965; Anttila and Jaakkola, 1966; Clark and Tifft, 1966; Gold, 1966; Vaz, 1966; Voss, 1968; Hardt et al., 1968; Hirschi, 1969; McDonald, 1968; LeBlanc, 1971; Tribble, 1972; Waldo and Chiricos, 1972; Belson, 1968, 1975; Elliott and Ageton, 1980).

Self-report studies have demonstrated that some people will admit to the commission of an incredible number of criminal offenses, most of which are unknown to the police. Erickson and Empey (1963), for instance, interviewed 180 boys in Provo, Utah: 50 who had never been to juvenile court, 30 who had been to court once, 50 who were repeat offenders on probation, and 50 who were incarcerated in a nearby reformatory. The boys were asked about the lifetime frequency of their commission of some twenty-two criminal and delinquent activities. The resulting count of crimes was, in the authors' words, "staggering": 123,469. The count was an average admission of 686 offenses per boy! Inciardi's recent research (1979) on 239 active male heroin users produced a similarly staggering count of self-reported offenses: 80,644 during the prior twelve months alone. This figure represents a mean admission of 337 offenses per respondent per year. Only 0.2 percent of these offenses resulted in arrest.

Self-report studies have also demonstrated that the strong sex differences found in criminal statistics for the past century and a half are reasonable reflections of confessed deviant activity. Martin Gold's self-report study (1970) among a representative sample of adolescents in Flint, Michigan, makes a finding consistent across studies in which sex differentials could be measured: "a larger proportion of girls than boys reported few or no delinquent acts; . . . girls were especially less delinquent than boys when seriousness of offenses were taken into account" (p. 61; see also, Williams and Gold, 1972, pp. 213–215).

Other self-report findings are less clear and seem embroiled in methodological disputes. The relationship between self-reported delinquency and the social class of the respondents (and the consequent critical application of the finding in assessing criminological theory) is particularly disputed (e.g., Elliott and Ageton, 1980; Johnson, 1980; Hindelang, Hirschi, and Weis, 1981; Tittle and Villemez, 1977). Two essentially different findings appear to emerge. The larger set of studies has shown *no* relationship between social class and self-confessed criminality. A smaller set of studies, which nevertheless appear to be marked by greater sophistication and sensitivity in data collection and analysis, has shown a strong relationship between social class and self-reported criminal activity: frequency and seriousness of self-reported criminal activity are inversely related to social class, as criminal justice statistics suggest (Elliott and Ageton, 1980).

Problems with Self-report Data

Noncomparability

Self-report studies of criminal and deviant behavior are extremely difficult to use for purposes of assessing the variance in the actual incidence of these behaviors from place to place and from time to time. They are difficult to compare with criminal justice statistics. They are also difficult to compare with one another. There are several reasons.

First, self-reported studies have not, until recently, been conducted in any standardized fashion. Research has been done by different researchers in different places at different times. No serious attempts have been made to repeat self-report surveys with the same populations in the same areas using the same questions in successive time frames.[1]

Second, self-report studies have not, in general, asked about comparable lists of behavior, nor have they asked about lists of behavior that can be easily translated back into the categories of criminal behavior recorded in official criminal statistics. Table 4–1 lists the behavior categories used in two classic self-report studies. These should be compared with one another and with the offense categories used for police statistics that are listed in Table 3–1. Clearly, considerable information loss must occur in any effort at comparison.

Third, self-report studies have not involved comparable areas or comparable time frames. Self-report respondents have been asked to confess the numbers of instances occurring during their entire lifetime (e.g., Porterfield, 1946), during the prior five years (e.g., Tittle and Villemez, 1977), during the prior three years (e.g., Gold, 1970), or during the prior year (Elliott and Ageton, 1980). This discrepancy, of course, creates problems in cross-comparisons between self-report studies and between self-report studies and criminal justice statistics. Jurisdictions involved in self-report studies have involved parts of cities, entire states or nations, and sometimes no spatial boundaries at all.

Comparability problems in self-report studies render them essentially useless for any assessment of the efficiency of criminal justice statistics or as an index, or consistent measure, of patterns in criminal events. They may be useful, though, for the assessment of evenhandedness in the criminal justice system's selection and handling of offender populations. There are, however, some additional problems.

Reliability, Validity, and Fair Inference

Reliability, validity, and fair inference have been explicated and assessed by Gwynn Nettler (1978) in a thorough critique of the self-report technique. Nettler holds that self-report studies are plagued by reliability problems; are of doubtful validity; and have led researchers to draw unfair and incorrect inferences because of poor research design and the use of inappropriate divisions of the data.

Reliability
The term *reliability* refers to the capacity of a measuring device to provide consistent measurements. A bathroom scale that showed you weighing three substantially different weights on three different trials over a period of ten minutes would be unreliable. One that showed you weighing exactly the same on each of several trials would be reliable.

In the context of self-report studies, reliability essentially relates to the ability

---

[1] Two exceptions can be mentioned. West and Farrington (1977) have conducted a longitudinal cohort study on boys from a specific section of London since the boys were eight years old. At various intervals, the boys have participated in a self-report interview, so that consistent data have been gathered on the same cohort at several different times. More recently, Delbert Elliott and his associates obtained support funding and conducted a five-year panel-design self-report study on a national sample of American teenagers for the years 1976, 1977, 1978, 1979, and 1980 (Elliott and Ageton, 1980).

TABLE 4–1. Self-report Categories in Two Classic Studies

Erickson and Empey (1963)	*Clark and Tifft (1966)*
1. Theft less than $2 value	1. Ran away from home
2. Theft $2–$50 value	2. Attacked someone with idea of taking his or her life
3. Theft more than $50 value	3. Attempted to take my own life
4. Auto theft	4. Used force to get money or valuables from another person
5. Forgery	5. Gotten a female other than my wife pregnant
6. Gambling	6. Bribed or attempted to bribe a police officer or another type of official
7. Smoking (habitually)	7. Visited a house of prostitution
8. Driving without license	8. Carried a razor, gun, or switchblade as a weapon
9. Other traffic violation	9. Took part in gang fights
10. Running away from home	10. Used or sold narcotic drugs
11. Skipping school	11. Took things of value (worth more than $50) that did not belong to me
12. Breaking and entering	12. Broke into and entered a home, store, or building
13. Destroying property	13. Struck my girlfriend or wife
14. Setting fires (arson)	14. Had a steady girlfriend
15. Buying beer or liquor	15. "Beat up" on someone who hadn't done anything to me
16. Drinking beer or liquor	16. Defied my parents' authority to their faces
17. Selling narcotics	17. Took a car for a ride without the owner's knowledge
18. Using narcotics	18. Attempted to force or forced a female to have intercourse with me
19. Armed robbery	19. Drove a vehicle in an unauthorized drag race
20. Fighting, assault	20. Witnessed a crime and neither reported it nor made sure someone else had
21. Defying parents	21. Had sex relations with a person of the same sex
22. Defying others	22. Started a fist fight
	23. Purposely damaged or destroyed public or private property that did not belong to me
	24. Drove a car without a driver's license or permit
	25. Falsified information while filling out an application or report
	26. Took things from someone else's desk or locker at school without permission
	27. Gambled for money or something else with persons other than my family members
	28. Had sex relations with a person of the opposite sex (other than my wife)
	29. Masturbated
	30. Bought or drank beer, wine, or liquor illegally
	31. Took things of medium value (worth be-

TABLE 4–1. (continued)

Erickson and Empey (1963)	*Clark and Tifft* (1966)
	tween $2 and $50) that did not belong to me
	32. Drove a motor vehicle at extreme speeds
	33. Had in my possession pictures, books, or other materials that were obviously obscene and prepared to arouse someone sexually
	34. Skipped school without a legitimate excuse
	35. Took little things (worth less than $2) that did not belong to me.

of the procedure used and the questions asked to produce consistent responses from the same subjects on repeated administrations. Several self-report studies have attempted to measure response reliability through a retest procedure, but with mixed results.

Dentler and Monroe (1961) put respondents through a second self-report exercise two weeks after the initial administration. They found that each of their five items received the same response from at least 92 percent of the respondents. Belson (1968) reported a rate of the same responses of 88 percent on a self-report questionnaire when he allowed a one-week interval between the first and second administrations. Kulik et al. (1968) reported a test–retest consistency rate of 98 percent for their testing instrument. Christie et al. (1965) reported on a Norwegian study that reinterviewed subjects six to nine months after the completion of a self-report questionnaire; 94 percent of the subjects insisted that they had answered honestly the first time. Such high levels of consistency would appear to establish the reliability of self-report measures; however, two additional studies cast some doubt on this general conclusion.

Clark and Tifft (1966) used a multistage questioning procedure. Volunteer college students were given a self-report questionnaire containing the thirty-five items listed in the right-hand column of Table 4–1. Subsequently, the students were interviewed and were told that they would be subjected to a polygraph (popularly called a *lie detector*) examination. They were invited to change their responses to particular items. In the third stage, they were interviewed under polygraph conditions and were invited to change responses again. The overall consistency pattern was 81.5 percent; that is, about 18.5 percent of responses were changed in the course of the second and third interviews. The change patterns, however, varied by behavioral category: confessions to attempted suicide and running away from home were not changed at all; drag racing and fist fighting had a 20 percent change rate; masturbation and intermediate theft had a 35 percent change rate; possession of pornographic materials had a 50 percent change rate; and petty theft (under $2 value) had a 67.5 percent change rate. This change rate implies remarkable possibilities for unreliability in the instrument initially used, and it also raises questions about the *validity* of the responses obtained.

Farrington (1973) administered a self-report task to a cohort of boys from an

63

inner London neighborhood at age fourteen to fifteen and two years later at age sixteen to seventeen. The boys were asked, in both procedures, to give answers about their lifetime commission of thirty-eight different offenses. What is critical for current purposes is that fully 25 percent of the behaviors admitted to at age fourteen to fifteen were denied (i.e., the respondents said that they had never committed that offense) at age sixteen to seventeen. Moreover, the rate of admission and subsequent denial rose more or less with the seriousness of the offense. Sixty percent or more of the admitted burglaries were subsquently denied. Seventy-five percent of admissions to obtaining property under false pretenses were subsequently denied. Overall, half of all the serious offenses first admitted were later denied.

The conclusion to be drawn is that self-report studies should be treated as reliable, but subject to qualifications. The qualifications are that self-report data are probably less reliable for trivial actions (e.g., theft under $2), for personally embarrassing activities (e.g., masturbation), and for very serious criminal offenses (e.g., burglary), but for different reasons. This reliability problem makes self-report data a poor substitute for criminal justice statistics.

Validity

The term *validity* refers to the capacity of a measuring instrument actually to measure the thing that one is trying to measure. The bathroom scale mentioned in our discussion of reliability may also be used in illustrating validity. Note first that reliability is usually assumed as a component of a valid measure because it is difficult to assess which of a set of unreliable measures might be correct.[2] However, if we assume that our bathroom scale gives us a consistent reading of 175 pounds on each of five successive trials, so that we are happy with its reliability, we may still have an invalid measure. The scale may, for instance, be miscalibrated, say, set 25 pounds too light. We receive a consistently invalid measure of our real weight, which, measured on a perfect scale, is actually 200 pounds.

The scale, being consistent in its error, gives an index of our actual weight, however, and although its readings of true, total weight are invalid, it can be used to measure *changes* in our weight over successive trials if we embark on a diet to get thin or a body-building program to add bulk. This consistency, of course, is precisely what criminologists (e.g., Quetelet, 1842; Bonger, 1916) assumed to be the case with criminal statistics, that is, that they consistently index changes in trends and patterns of crime even though they are an invalid measure of the totality of criminal events.

Invalidity can take a far more pernicious form, however. It can stem from the fact that we are using the wrong instrument to measure the phenomenon. Suppose our scale gives us a correct and consistent reading of 200 pounds when we are trying to measure our *height*. A scale is the wrong instrument, and its measures are invalid because it is not capable of measuring what we are trying to study, just as a steam

---

[2] Note, however, that as the measurement problem becomes difficult because the phenomenon to be measured is small or faraway or otherwise elusive, some variation in measurement is to be expected. In such circumstances, we take a set of measurements and calculate some form of average value to constitute our measure of the phenomenon.

pressure gauge will not measure how much electricity we are using and a ruler will not tell us what shutter setting to use for a good exposure with our new camera.[3]

An analysis of the validity of self-report data as a measure of crime patterns is necessary for several reasons. People are imperfect creatures. They may lie when asked about what they have done, either to protect themselves,[4] or to gain respect, or for fun, or for no very good reason at all. They may not remember things correctly, especially when asked to enumerate things done over the past three or five years, or over a lifetime.[5] They may misunderstand or misinterpret what is being asked for by the researcher and therefore give incorrect answers.

Researchers are also imperfect. They may ask questions poorly. They may misunderstand the responses. They may misrepresent answers, either deliberately or by accident.

The problem is this: What criterion should be used as validation of the self-report findings? We do not have a measure of all criminal events and who committed them; that is what self-report research is trying to provide. Essentially, three forms of validation have been used: comparisons of self-reported information with information gained from other unofficial sources; comparisons of self-reported information with official criminal-justice information; and the use of external tests for lying.

Unofficial Validation Criteria. Martin Gold (1970) provided the clearest example of the unofficial validation approach. He sought out potential informants among the Flint, Michigan, high school students not included in his sample population and asked them to describe delinquent acts committed by members of the sample. Criminal events described by the informants formed a check on the veracity of the self-reporting subjects when they were interviewed. As Gold puts it:

> A youngster was considered a "truthteller" if he confessed to what the relevant informant had told us, or if he told about more recent offenses of a similar nature, or if he told about more serious offenses. A respondent was considered a "concealer" if he did not confess to an offense about which an informant had told us, or to a more recent similar offense, or to any more serious offense. (p. 20)

By this criterion, 17 percent were outright "concealers"—slightly more than a sixth of the checked sample. Slightly less than three fourths of the checked sample (72 percent) were "truthtellers." The remainder of the checked sample (a tenth of the cases) could not be classified. These results, of course, may tell us something about the lying rate of the self-reporting respondents (if, of course, the informants were not lying), but they require an assumption or inference to stand as a validation of self-report data as a general enumerator or index of crime patterns. The inference

---

[3] Handy general discussions of reliability and validity in the criminological context can be found in Hirschi and Selvin (1973, pp. 193–215).

[4] As one respondent told Gold (1970) in his self-report study among teen-agers in Flint, Michigan, telling the truth would give the researchers "enough on me to send me up for thirty years" (p. 19).

[5] The memory problem is further discussed in the section titled "Victimization Surveys."

is that if the sample is composed of a large majority of "truthtellers," the self-reporting respondents were not lying about *other* events that they mentioned, their memories were good, and they recognized events as falling within the category asked about. Put another way, this form of validation assumes that an "honest" respondent is also a "correct" respondent.

Validation by Data Provided by the Criminal Justice System. This approach to validation assumes that criminal justice data are themselves valid and reliable measures of deviant behavior, the very thing that self-report studies seek to test (Nettler, 1978, pp. 110–113). Criminal justice records of arrest or conviction are used as a criterion against which to measure concealment by lying, misreporting due to faulty memory, and miscategorization of events.

Erickson and Empey (1963) used juvenile court records to assess the validity of self-report data with samples of youths in Utah. The fact that none of the subjects who had been to court failed to describe that fact, or the offenses for which they were sent to court, convinced the authors of the validity of a finding that the boys averaged 686 self-reported offenses apiece. Farrington (1973) used police data and data from court and diversion records as a test of self-report validity. He concluded that his respondents were generally truthful in self-reporting officially known offenses.

Tittle and Villemez (1977) used crimes known to the police as a test of the validity of data gathered in their self-report study on adults in New Jersey, Iowa, and Oregon. After a weighting and extrapolation procedure, they compared the numbers of self-report assaults and thefts of $50 with the number of FBI index offenses in the categories "aggravated assaults" and "larceny over $50" for the same five-year period covered by the self-report data. They found that:

1. in Oregon approximately twice as many felonious thefts were reported in the survey as were known to the police, and . . . approximately 70 times as many assaults were admitted;
2. in Iowa there were 4 times as many felonious thefts and 200 times as many assaults self-reported as were known officially; and
3. in New Jersey about 13 times as many felonious thefts and about 100 times as many assaults were self-reported as were known to the police. (p. 480)

In view of the general belief in the dark figure of crime, this large difference led the authors to conclude that their self-report data validly estimated the incidence of criminal acts by adults in these states.

External Controls for Lying. Some studies have sought validation of self-report data through external controls for lying by self-report respondents. Clark and Tifft (1966) used a polygraph (lie detector) to assess initial "reporting error." Across a set of thirty-five offenses, 18.5 percent of the original confessions were changed when the polygraph was brought into the picture. The range was from no change (attempted suicide) to over 60 percent change (theft under $2 value). Moreover, the direction of change varied by offense: starting a fist fight was overreported in 17.5 percent of the cases and underreported in 2.5 percent of cases; theft of $2–$50 value was overreported in 2.5 percent of the cases, and underreported in 32.5 percent of the cases. Farrington (1973, pp. 107–108) found that inconsistent reporting (i.e. denying at age sixteen to seventeen offenses admitted at age fourteen to fifteen) was significantly related to the subject's scores on lie scales contained in the New Junior Maudsley Inventory and the Eysenck Personality Inventory administered at age fourteen to fifteen and sixteen to seventeen, respectively. Both of these studies suggest that without external controls, lying is a major problem undercutting the validity of self-report data.

Fair Inference

Fair inference is a shorthand way of saying that when researchers wish to make statements about general patterns in events on the basis of findings from particular research projects, they must pay close attention to a series of design and interpretation problems that may limit or qualify their ability to do so. Problems of fair inference have been particularly important in self-report research. We mention three of them here.

Representativeness. Modern survey technology makes it quite possible to assess patterns within a general population by asking questions of a small sample of that population. This fact, based on probability theory, is well known to social scientists and is exploited very effectively for such commercial purposes as judging the relative popularity of various television shows in order to establish advertising rates or predicting election outcomes for politicians. The efficiency of such activities depends, however, on what population is sampled and how closely the sample population represents the relevant characteristics of the total population from which it is sampled.

Self-report research suffers from unrepresentativeness in at least three known ways.

First, some studies fail to use elementary probability sampling procedures. In such cases, nothing can be said about any group except the respondents themselves.

Second, in those studies that do use proper probability sampling techniques, the population sampled may itself be limited and unrepresentative. Most self-report studies have limited their populations to juveniles. As late as 1977, Tittle and Villemez could list only three self-report studies, including the one they were reporting, that had sampled adults rather than adolescents. Moreover, most of the juvenile self-report studies sample from school populations in only a few places: Short and Nye (1958) sampled high-school students in three small (10,000–25,000 population) cities in the western United States; Dentler and Monroe (1961) sampled junior-high-school students in three small Kansas towns; LeBlanc (1971) sampled fourteen- to sixteen-year-olds in two Montreal neighborhoods; and McDonald (1968) sampled secondary-school boys in metropolitan London. Writing in 1980, Elliott and Ageton could list only three American self-report studies, including their own, that used national probability samples of adolescents.

Third, most self-report studies have been grounded in the sociology of deviance rather than in criminology. The result is that self-report studies have "sampled" from the universe of "deviant" behaviors rather than from the universe of crimes. Some crimes have been included in the lists of behaviors asked about, of course, but they have not necessarily been either a representative probability sample

67

of some criminal code's contents or a set of behaviors that would be generally considered important or serious crimes.

Style of Administration. The method used to put questions to respondents has been thought to pose problems for self-report researchers. The generally accepted techniques involve questionnaires and extensive interviews. There has been considerable suspicion that the format used to ask questions affects the validity and the reliability of the responses. It has been suspected that questionnaires would produce more admissions, and that interviews would produce more reliable responses because ambiguities could be cleared up, missing information could be elicited, and lying could be controlled through probing by the interviewer. Krohn et al. (1974) tested this proposition, finding that questionnaires produced admissions to a larger number of offenses for seven out of the eight behaviors they queried, but that the differences were not statistically significant. Hindelang, Hirschi, and Weis (1981) tested four different modes of SR administration in Seattle: an anonymous questionnaire; an anonymous interview; a nonanonymous questionnaire; and a nonanonymous interview. They concluded that "the results of self-report delinquency research are not dependent on the particular method used in collecting the data" (p. 132). The contemporary consensus seems to be that the interview technique is the better procedure (e.g., Elliott and Ageton, 1980; Tittle and Villemez, 1977; Farrington, 1973; Gold, 1970).

A routine requirement of interview research involves testing for the effect of interviewer bias when multiple interviewers are used because their differential interpretation and recording decisions can introduce nonsubstantive record variation as has already been discussed with respect to police record-keeping variation. In recent research, however, only Farrington (1973, p. 107) has discussed the problem or addressed the issue. In his study, a careful analysis of control data indicated no statistical impact from interviewer bias.

Cut Points and Aggregation Biases. The central statistical data elicited by self-report surveys are statements about the types and frequencies of criminal or deviant acts which respondents have admitted commiting over some fixed time period. The types of acts admitted may range from trivial acts such as theft of a pencil to very serious acts such as murder. Many researchers add different types of acts together (aggregate) to form sets of behaviors. Inappropriate aggregation of different types of behavior can be extremely misleading, suggesting equivalence between types of behavior, such as pencil theft and murder, that are not equivalent.

Self-reported frequencies of criminal or deviant behavior can range from zero to many hundred of acts. Such wide ranges are difficult to comprehend and are usually divided into groupings or sets of frequencies. All of the frequencies within a particular set are then treated as equivalent for analytic purposes. The cut points used to divide a frequency range into sets of frequencies are very important. Well chosen cut points can enhance our ability to understand the patterns in the data. Poorly chosen cut points can obscure or distort the patterns in the data.

Self-report research has been plagued by the inappropriate aggregation of different types of behavior and by the use of inappropriate cut points in dividing frequency ranges. The result has been one of the hottest contemporary disputes in the field of criminology, that is, the dispute about the distribution of offense behaviors across the classes of society. Essentially, the patterns derived from criminal justice data over the past 150 years have suggested a strong inverse relation between social class and crime.[6] That is, higher social classes have lower offense rates. This pattern has been central to causal theories in criminology since the positivist revolution in the late nineteenth century. Yet, many self-report studies claim to find no statistical relation between social class and self-reported offense rates, a finding of critical importance if true (e.g., Short and Nye, 1958; Akers, 1964; Dentler and Monroe, 1961; Tribble, 1972; Tittle and Villemez, 1977; Johnson, 1980).

Recent research, however, suggests that this major apparent difference in patterns is a product of a faulty aggregation procedure. Most self-report studies have used grouped frequency measures. Some have used verbal categorizations rather than counts; that is, the respondents have been asked whether they have committed the offense in question "never," "once or twice," or "three or more times." In some self-report studies, the full range of frequency responses has been collapsed back into truncated clusters of this sort (e.g., Nye and Short, 1957).

Studies using truncated frequency clusters tend to find no relation between social class and frequency of offense behavior (Short and Nye, 1958). This relationship is lacking because the frequency and seriousness distribution for offenses is one in which most respondents report few or no offenses but in which a few respondents report the bulk of all offenses and the bulk of serious offenses. Martin Gold's (1970, pp. 27–32) study in Flint, Michigan, showed that most respondents admitted to very few offenses, but that the most active 17 percent of the respondents accounted for half of all the self-reported delinquent events. The most frequently delinquent 5 percent at the tail of the distribution accounted for 25 percent of the self-reported delinquencies. If differences in offense behavior by social class were important at this extreme end of the distribution, the collapsed data sets would miss them because they are sensitive only to differences at the low-frequency–low-seriousness end of the distribution.

When Elliott and Ageton (1980, p. 104) examined this possibility using the data from the first year of their national five-year panel sample, they found that the high-frequency, high-seriousness tail of the distribution had strong class characteristics. The respondents in this tail were overwhelmingly lower class. This fact would have been missed had they used truncated frequency clusters. Moreover, an examination of studies finding the expected class differential shows that they used a full frequency analysis, whereas those showing no class differential used truncated frequency clusters. The most important finding of the early self-report literature appears to have been reduced to a methodological artifact.

Victimization Surveys

Victimization surveys take the same straightforward approach to the enumeration of crime used in the self-report studies: they ask people to tell us about the crimes

[6] Hindelang, Hirschi, and Weis (1981) argued that, in fact, the criminal justice data show no class-based patterns, so there is no inconsistency to be explained. Most scholars disagree with this position.

that have been committed against them. The responses that people give are totaled (for a relevant jurisdiction and time period) and are cross-analyzed against the fundamental demographic and socioeconomic characteristics of the respondents, such as sex, age, race, marital status, and family income.

Victimization studies are also used to assess the validity of criminal justice statistics in a number of ways: they are used to assess the validity of criminal justice statistics as enumerators of crime; they are used to assess, by considering variations in the rate at which self-recalled victimizations are reported to the police, the validity of criminal justice statistics as an index of crime; and they are used to assess the validity of offender characterizations drawn from arrest or conviction or prison statistics.

Victimization research began in the mid-1960s and it has been conducted almost exclusively by governmental agencies. The mainstream of research has been in North America; only the United States and Canada have made major national commitments to systematic victimization surveys. The Netherlands and Britain have recently begun periodic national victimization research. Occasional studies have been funded elsewhere (e.g., Sparks's study in London, 1976; Hauge and Wolf's study of violence in Denmark, Norway, and Sweden, 1974), and the technique has occasionally been used to measure crime incidence and crime patterns (e.g., Brantingham, Brantingham, and Molumby, 1977).

The President's Commission Studies: 1965–1967

The President's Commission on Law Enforcement and Administration of Justice pioneered the development of the victimization survey as an alternative to police statistics and criminal justice statistics as a measure of the amount and distribution of crime in America. Three studies were undertaken: a pilot study in Washington, D.C.; a second-stage study in three cities; and a national survey.

The Pilot Study

The pilot study was conducted in Washington, D.C., during the spring and summer of 1966. Three police precincts formed the geographic and jurisdictional base for the study. A probability sample of homes was drawn, and a random member of each household was selected for interview. The initial sample size was 707 residences; 511 interviews were eventually successfully completed. Each subject was asked to recall whether she or he had been the victim of any of a fairly lengthy list of crimes since New Year's Day, 1965.

The purpose of the pilot study was twofold: to establish the existence of the dark figure of crime and to develop the best techniques for investigating the dark figure with a minimum of technique-generated bias. The pilot study was successful on both counts: it caught a number of methodological problems that have proved to be very important in the subsequent development of victimization research (Hindelang, 1976a, pp. 24–26), and it demonstrated that victimization surveys could give very different enumerations of crime from those found in the police statistics (Biderman et al., 1967).

The key finding of the pilot survey was that the dark figure of crime is real and that it can be probed through the reports of victims. Depending on the offense, the pilot survey found from three to ten times as many criminal incidents as were recorded in the police files.

The Second-Stage Study

The second-stage, three-city study had two principal purposes: to survey criminal victimizations among businesses and organizations in selected high-crime areas in Boston, Chicago, and Washington, D.C.; and to survey criminal victimizations among residents in Boston and Chicago by means of techniques modified in the light of the pilot study.

This second study demonstrated there was more business crime than was reported by the police, that shoplifting was a major problem, and that victimization was not evenly distributed among businesses: some businesses reported multiple victimizations, whereas others reported few or none. For example, about 20 percent of the surveyed businesses reported being burglarized during the period covered in the study, but because some reported multiple victimizations, the victimization rate was calculated to be 32 per 100 businesses (Hindelang, 1976a, pp. 27–28; Reiss, 1967).

The National Study

The third major victimization study conducted for the President's Commission was a national sample survey by the National Opinion Research Center (NORC) at the University of Chicago. This study used a multistage national probability sample[7] of 10,000 households. One respondent was interviewed per household, and a maximum of two victimizations per household were queried in depth, though larger numbers of victimizations were tallied. Data were collected in such a way as to make reported victimizations comparable with the *Uniform Crime Reports* index offenses.

This study demonstrated, yet again, that more crimes occurred than the police knew about. Roughly twice as many incidents of personal violence and more than twice as many individual-property victimizations were estimated to have occurred on the basis of the respondents' recollections as were recorded in the FBI *Uniform Crime Reports*.[8]

Table 4–2 compares the estimated crime rates for the seven index offenses with the UCR crime rates for 1965. The UCR figures have been adjusted downward to take into account the fact that the NORC did not make estimates for business or organizational victimizations, whereas the UCR reported all index crimes regardless of the type of victim involved. Note that the NORC estimates for homicide and motor vehicle theft are lower than the UCR rates, and that the NORC rates for rape are four times higher and for burglary are three times higher than the UCR rates.

[7] A sampling procedure that uses areal units such as census tracts and city blocks instead of people for all but the last steps in the procedure in such a way that the sample is representative of the target population but is not spatially representative. For further discussion, see Chapter 6.

[8] Note that sample surveys of victims of crimes do not provide an enumeration of victimizations. A correctly drawn representative sample, however, should allow us to estimate, within error limits, what the number of events for the whole population might be.

TABLE 4–2. American Crime Rates, 1965 (Rate Per 100,000 Population)

Crime	UCR Rate	Victimization Survey: Estimated Crime Rate
Murder	5.1	3.0
Forcible rape	11.6	42.5
Aggravated assault	61.4	94.0
Robbery	106.6	218.3
Burglary	299.6	949.1
Theft ($50 and over)	267.4	606.5
Motor vehicle theft	226.0	206.2
Violent crime	184.7	357.8
Property crime	793.0	1,761.8

SOURCE: President's Commission on Law Enforcement and Administration of Justice, *Crime and Its Impact: An Assessment,* Task Force Report. (Washington, D.C.: Government Printing Office, 1967b), p. 17.

Independently collected statistics that measure homicide and auto theft demonstrate that the UCR rates provide *better* enumerations of these crimes than do victimization survey estimates. The reasons include the problem that sample surveys have in identifying rare events (such as homicide) and the concrete reportability of dead bodies and missing cars. In any event, subsequent major victimization surveys have *not* collected information on homicide victimizations.

The NORC survey also explored the reasons why people did not report criminal victimizations to the police when they occurred. Nonreporting ranged from a high of 90 percent of consumer frauds unreported to a low of 11 percent of perceived auto thefts. The majority of nonreporting victims felt that the matter was private, or did not want to harm the offender, or thought that the police could not do anything about the offense anyway. In essence, people appeared to have rational reasons—principally related to judgments about the appropriate role of the police, the possible effectiveness of the police, or the importance of the criminal incident—for *not* reporting their victimizations to the police.

All these initial surveys had severe methodological problems that undercut the continuing utility of their detailed findings. The problems have been cogently analyzed by Hindelang (1976a). The studies did, however, establish the viability of the victim survey in the measurement of crime and gave rise to the creation of an important new source of systematic information about criminal events: the National Crime Survey.

The National Crime Survey

The National Crime Survey began as a collaboration between the U.S. Department of Justice and the U.S. Bureau of the Census. Following the recommendations of the President's Commission on Law Enforcement and Administration of Justice, Congress created the Law Enforcement Assistance Administration (LEAA) within the Department of Justice in 1968. The LEAA, in turn, created a bureau that was to become the National Criminal Justice Informaton and Statistics Service (NCJISS) in 1969, and that has been known as the Bureau of Justice Statistics since 1980. The NCJISS proposed a massive, ongoing, national victimization survey to provide an alternative measure of the national crime problem. Two large-scale series of victimization surveys were begun in mid-1972. The national-crime-panel series provides annual national estimates of criminal victimizations. The city-sample series has, to date, provided surveys of criminal victimizations in each of twenty-six large American cities (Hindelang, 1976a, pp. 45–76).

The National-Crime-Panel Series

Since 1973, the Bureau of Justice Statistics and its predecessors have published an annual national report called *Criminal Victimization in the United States*. Publication has come approximately two years following the calendar year covered in any particular report. Each report is based on the results of an ongoing panel sample of some sixty thousand residences and other dwelling units selected by the Bureau of the Census.

In the panel sampling procedure, the full sample is divided into six rotation groups, each of which is interviewed once every six months. A new rotation group enters the national sample each six months, replacing a group that is phased out after being in the national sample for three years. Interviews involve separate screening and detailed questioning of every member aged twelve years or older in each sampled household.

The reports for 1973–1976 also contain national estimates of commercial and organizational victimization based on a national sample of 39,000 business establishments, which were divided into six monthly interview groups of 6,500 businesses each. Each monthly interview group was interviewed once each six months. The commercial program was suspended in 1977 (Penick and Owens, 1976, pp. 10–12; NCJISS, 1979a, pp. iii, 85–86).

The national-crime-panel series makes estimates of the incidence of six personal crimes, four crimes against households, and, for 1973–1976, two commercial crimes. The personal crimes covered are rape, robbery, aggravated assault, simple assault, personal larceny with contact (i.e., purse snatching and pocket picking), and personal larceny without contact. The household crimes covered are burglary, larceny of less than $50, larceny of $50 and over, and motor vehicle theft. The commercial crimes covered were robbery and burglary.

The construction and size of the sample permit the estimates of the victimization rates for each crime category to be broken down in a number of interesting ways. *Victim* characteristics are analyzed by sex, age, race, marital status, household composition, family income, educational attainment, occupational status, household size and tenure, locality of residence (a metropolitan–nonmetropolitan, central-city–outside-central-city scheme is used), and kind of business. *Offender* characteristics for crimes of personal violence are analyzed by sex, age, race, and stranger–nonstranger status. *Crime* characteristics are analyzed by time of occurrence, place of occurrence, number of offenders, use of weapons, victim self-protection, physical injury to victims, and work-time losses caused by criminal victimizations.

The national surveys also measure crime-reporting behavior in two ways. One measure estimates the percentage of victimizations reported to the police by crime

73

type for various sociodemographic groupings within the victim population. The second measure reports the reasons that people give for *not* reporting offenses to the police.

The City-Sample Series

The city-sample series conducted victimization surveys in twenty-six large central cities between 1971 and 1975. These cities can be grouped by category and survey date. Eight cities (Baltimore; Dallas; Cleveland; St. Louis; Atlanta; Portland, Oregon; Denver; and Newark) comprised the impact-cities group designated to receive special, extensive financial support for a variety of crime prevention and crime control programs from the Law Enforcement Assistant Administration. As an element in the evaluation of the impact-cities program, the eight impact cities were surveyed in 1972 and again in 1975. The nation's five largest cities (New York, Chicago, Philadelphia, Detroit, and Los Angeles) were surveyed twice, in 1973 and again in 1975. Thirteen additional large central cities were surveyed just once, in 1974: Minneapolis, Milwaukee, Cincinnati, Pittsburgh, Oakland, San Francisco, San Diego, Boston, Buffalo, Houston, Miami, New Orleans, and Washington, D.C.

Each city was sampled in an essentially similar fashion. Approximately ten thousand households and between one thousand and five thousand commercial establishments, depending on the city, were sampled by means of a stratified cluster sampling technique. Interviews were conducted in a six-week period by locally hired enumerators. Respondents were asked to recall criminal victimizations over the twelve months prior to the interview rather than the shorter six-month period used in the national panel series.

The questionnaires used in the cities asked about the same crimes and collected the same sociodemographic background information gathered by the national-panel-series surveys. In addition, half of the households were asked a series of attitude questions designed to gather perceptions of crime and the police. The attitude subsamples were asked about national and neighborhood crime trends, about the perceived characteristics of offenders, about their personal chances of victimization, and about the accuracy of the media's portrayal of crime. Fear of crime was explored in terms of feelings of safety, the impact of crime on mobility and activity, and the impact on decisions when the respondents were moving. The respondents were also asked a series of questions about police performance. Thus, the cities sample provides more information than the national panel sample, but in cross-sectional or two-point time series rather than in ongoing time series (Inter-University Consortium for Political and Social Research [ICPSR], 1978; Hindelang, 1976a, pp. 77–103; Penick and Owens, 1976, p. 13; NCJISS, 1979c).

Victimization Surveys in Canada

The Federal Ministry of the Solicitor General in Canada is in the beginning stages of research using the victimization survey as a supplement and alternative to criminal justice statistics. Work in Canada has, to date, concentrated on the development of an improved and less costly method for conducting victimization interviews. The procedures used in the American National Crime Survey are enormously

74

expensive. Current Canadian efforts are centered on the use of telephone surveys that use random-digit dialing to generate a sample of people for interview and that also conducts a telephone interview of the person answering the randomly dialed number. Large-scale pilot studies have been conducted in Edmonton, Alberta; Hamilton, Ontario; and Vancouver, British Columbia. Ministry officials say that the results of the pilot studies are quite comparable to the results produced by parallel studies using the more complex and expensive American survey techniques. A national survey was conducted in early 1982. The results are not yet available.

Problems with Victimization Surveys

Victimization survey data have as many problems as criminal justice data or self-report data when used as measures of crime. Some problems are technical; others are fundamental. The technical problems involve such things as sample construction, question sequencing, and inter-interviewer reliability. Most of these problems can be corrected through experimentation and pilot study. However, a number of fundamental problems remain. These can be classed into four main groups: coverage, comparability, memory effects, and validation problems.

Coverage

Victimization surveys cover only a small portion of the behaviors covered by either criminal justice statistics or self-report studies. The American *Uniform Crime Reports* provide statistics on crimes known to the police for eight offenses and arrest statistics for twenty-one categories of crime; the National Crime Survey collects data on only ten types of crime, some of which represent subdivisions of general legal categories (e.g., larceny from a person with contact, larceny from a person without contact, and household larceny are descriptive subdivisions of the legal and UCR category "larceny–theft"). The Canadian victimization surveys, when brought fully online, will cover only a very limited number of the offenses contained in the Canadian *Uniform Crime Reports*. Sparks's study in London (1976; Sparks, Genn, and Dodd, 1977) explored only assaults, thefts, burglaries, motor vehicle thefts, and vandalism, compared with the sixty-three categories of indictable offenses contained in the English statistics on crimes known the police.

To date, victimization surveys have given only very limited coverage to the range of jurisdictions included in other sources of criminal statistics. The surveys conducted for the President's Commission surveyed selected areas or populations within three cities. The National Crime Survey has conducted surveys in twenty-six central cities. By contrast, the American *Uniform Crime Reports* for 1975 presented statistics for 212 metropolitan areas and for 2,269 cities with ten thousand population or more, as well as for suburban counties, for rural counties, and for other police jurisdictions such as universities. Canadian victimization surveys have been conducted in at least parts of 4 cities, whereas Canadian police statistics covered 719 cities in 1977.

The American national-level surveys can be broken down in such a way as to provide state-level data but cannot be used for county or city estimates of victimization patterns. The NORC survey (Ennis, 1967) used a sample that was too small to permit the responses to be broken down even into regional estimates. Nevertheless, a breakdown was undertaken, producing preposterous results (Hindelang, 1976a, p. 32). Geographic location codes that were contained in the early national samples gathered by the National Crime Survey were deliberately suppressed in order to protect the privacy of the respondents by making regional breakdowns impossible (Penick and Owens, 1976, p. 185). This procedure was later modified to permit state victimization estimates. State estimates for New York, California, and Texas had been published by early 1982. Thus, place coverage was as limited as behavior coverage.

Comparability

Victimization survey data are plagued by many of the comparability problems also found in personal accounts of crimes, criminal justice statistics, and self-report studies. There are problems of definition, problems of comparability across time, and problems of jurisdictional comparability. These problems are significant and mean that victimization estimates of crime occurrence must be used at least as cautiously as the other data sources.

Definitional comparability problems abound in the victimization studies. To the extent that they are designed to assess the validity and reliability of police statistics, these studies are particularly flawed by having adopted different definitions of events, different definitions of crimes, and different counting rules for events.

Victimization surveys count recalled *victimizations,* not recalled crimes. This, of course, is not a problem where a single incident, such as a wallet's being picked from the respondent's pocket, has a single victim; nor is it a problem in the low-volume violent crimes, where most police statistics programs have adopted the "one victim, one crime" counting rule. It is a problem in the large-volume property offenses, because police statistics count transactions, whereas victimization surveys count victims. The tendency would be to inflate the count of property victimizations compared with crimes counted by the police. Assume a burglary in which three roommates suffer a loss of property. Police statistics would count this incident as a single offense, a burglary. A victimization survey might count this incident as three offenses, one for each person who lost property (three thefts), or it might count it as *four* offenses (one household burglary and three personal thefts without contact). (Hindelang, 1976a, pp. 91–97.)

All language is slippery stuff, likely to hold many different shadings and gradations of meaning for different people. As a result, police statistics have comparability problems because different recording officers give different meanings to terms such as *aggravated assault* or *robbery.* The same problem applies, in three ways, to victimization survey data.

First, contextually it is quite likely that people will reinterpret events that they previously considered too trivial or too private to report as crimes and will report them as victimizations when questioned in an interview. We have two reasons for thinking that this is so. First, many victims say that they have not reported crimes because nothing could be done anyway. Table 4–3 shows the reasons for the

76

TABLE 4–3. Reasons for Not Reporting Victimizations to Police, 1977

Reason	Personal Crime (%)	Household Crime (%)
Nothing could be done, lack of proof	30.8	36.1
Not important enough	25.6	30.1
Police would not want to be bothered	6.2	8.9
Too inconvenient or time-consuming	3.1	2.4
Private or personal matter	5.6	5.4
Fear of reprisal	0.8	0.4
Reported to someone else	15.9	3.2
Other, or not given	12.0	13.4

SOURCE: National Criminal Justice Information and Statistics Service. Criminal Victimization in the United States, 1977. (Washington, D.C.: Government Printing Office, 1979a), p. 70.

nonreporting of personal and household offenses given by the respondents in the National Crime Survey panel series for 1977. This information leads us to suspect that people make rational judgments about the seriousness of offenses in deciding whether to report them to the police, and that the seriousness threshold is *different* depending on whether the offense is reported to the police or is reported to a survey agent during an interview.

Second, research by the Urban Institute in Cincinnati has demonstrated that UCR-compatible definitions of crime are extremely vulnerable to varying interpretations by different respondent and interviewer combinations, and that they produced extremely varied and unreliable victimization counts for personal and household crimes in successive city victimization surveys conducted by the Urban Institute, by the Behavioral Sciences Laboratory at the University of Cincinnati, and by the National Crime Survey (Clarren and Schwartz, 1976; Tuchfarber and Klecka, 1976). This finding led the Urban Institute to state a rule about the tendency of victimization surveys to enumerate large numbers of cimes unknown to the police: "given a large representative sample from an American city, *the upper bound for the number of crimes that could be elicited is limited only by the persistence of the interviewer and the patience of the respondent"* (Clarren and Schwartz, 1976, p. 129; italics in original).

A related problem is found in the varying interpretations and recording practices of different interviewers. Though this is a generic problem common to all survey research (including self-report surveys of crime), and though a considerable technology has been developed to reduce inter-interviewer variability in the interpretation, recording, and coding of respondents' answers, Levine (1976) has argued that it is a much greater problem in victimization surveys than is ordinarily supposed, particularly in the city series. In a recent public lecture, Skogan (1980) stated that unpublished studies of interviewer variation for the twenty-six city surveys show that there is considerable consistency among the interviewers used in any particular city survey, but that the variations in interpretation used by groups of interviewers in different cities have been so great that the city surveys are practically worthless for comparative proposes.

Like self-report research, victimization surveys suffer from the problem of temporal incomparability. With the exception of the National Crime Survey panel series, most studies have been conducted in such a way as to collect data for time periods that are different from standard police statistical reporting periods, so that significant adjustments must be made if they are to be compared with police data. The NORC national sample (Ennis, 1967), for instance, used a reference period that asked about crimes occurring between the summer of 1965 and the summer of 1966, covering the last half of one UCR reporting period and the first half of another UCR reporting period. Courtis's (1970) victimization study in Toronto covers roughly fifteen months, from the beginning of 1968 to the end of the first quarter of 1969. The two sets of city surveys that have been conducted in the five largest American central cities also used twelve-month reference periods rolling over fifteen months from January 1972 through March 1973, and from January 1974 through March 1975 because it took several months to interview all the respondents (NCJISS, 1976b). This problem appears to be generic to all but panel-design victimization surveys, so that most victimization data must be subjected to substantial adjustment if they are to be compared with the other information sources.

Victimization surveys use different counting bases from other forms of crime information. Victimization surveys count victimizations, whereas police data count crimes, and self-report studies count delinquent acts. As has already been indicated, these categories involve different definitions of the basic thing being counted, so that cross-comparison is difficult. Victimization surveys and sources of police statistics frequently use different bases in calculating rates; for example, the *Uniform Crime Reports* calculate rates of crimes per hundred thousand population, whereas the National Crime Survey calculates personal crimes as rates per thousand population aged sixteen and over; household crimes as rates per thousand households; and commercial crimes as rates per thousand businesses.

Finally, victimization data and police statistics are frequently geographically noncomparable. Most victimization surveys allocate victim occurrence to the place of residence or the place of business of the respondent, regardless of where the crime occurred. Thus, a Detroit resident who is robbed while on vacation in Miami and subsequently recalls the crime during a city victimization survey will have his victimization recorded in the Detroit victimization statistics. A Miami resident who is robbed while attending a convention in Detroit and who returns to Florida after the Miami city victimization-survey will not have his victimization counted at all. Police statistics, on the other hand, record crimes according to where the criminal event takes place, regardless of where the victim lives. Thus, in the Detroit–Miami example, the Detroit robbery will be recorded in the Detroit police statistics, the Miami robbery will be recorded in the Florida *Uniform Crime Reports*.

The problem of geographic comparability is, of course, important only to the extent that population mobility patterns cause large population flows into and out of particular survey or statistical areas. Though research into this problem has been limited, the research that has been done suggests that a very large population flow has a substantial effect on the comparability of police statistics and victimization survey data. Hindelang's (1976a) analysis of theft and assault victimizations in the eight impact cities (Atlanta, Baltimore, Cleveland, Dallas, Denver, Newark, Portland, and St. Louis) had to be tempered by the fact that net commuter inflows (the number of people living outside the city and working in the city minus the number of people living in the city and working outside the city) increased the city population at risk inside the eight cities each day by 25 percent. Atlanta and St. Louis had net commuter inflows that increased the daily at-risk population by over 30 percent, and only Baltimore had a net commuter inflow as low as 10 percent (pp. 403, 405). Sparks's (1976) victimization survey in London showed similar flow problems. Some 17 percent of all crimes known to the police in Kensington (one of the London areas surveyed) had been committed against nonresidents of the area, and a significant proportion of the victimizations reported by Kensington residents had been committed against them elsewhere (p. 61).

Memory Effects

People have fallible memories. They misremember what happened, they misremember when things happened, and they misremember where things happened. People sometimes also forget altogether that things have happened.

Faulty memory, of course, is a generic problem for all survey research that seeks to recover information about the past. Therefore, it is clearly a problem for self-report studies and for memoirs and other personal accounts of crime and criminal careers, but it has been explored most thoroughly in the context of victimization survey research.

The possibility that memory problems might substantially affect the data gathered in victimization studies was recognized in the earliest studies conducted for the President's Commission on Law Enforcement and Administration of Justice. The Washington, D.C., pilot study (Biderman et al., 1967) pointed to two different problems: forgetting and telescoping.

Forgetting is the process of memory decay over time. It can take two forms important to victimization. First, people can completely forget that an event occurred. Second, they may remember the event but may have trouble placing it in the correct time period. If either or both forms of forgetting take place, we would expect to find that the largest proportion of recalled victimizations is reported for the last part (i.e., the most recent part) of the reference period, and that progressively fewer victimizations are reported as we move backward in time and toward the beginning of the survey reference period.

Telescoping is a product of the decaying memory for temporal detail and the respondent's desire to give the interviewer what he or she wants, that is, some recalled victimizations. In telescoping, the respondent recalls old victimizations that occurred before—sometimes long before—the beginning of the reference period and reports them to the interviewer as having occurred at the beginning of the reference period. The two processes obviously give very different perspectives on when the majority of the victimizations have occurred.

In fact, attempts to test the impact of these two memory problems suggest that *both* processes affect the temporal patterning of victimization recall, but that forgetting is a more important problem than telescoping. The original Washington, D.C., pilot study concluded that temporal patterning would be badly distorted by these two problems unless a series of surveys repeated at fairly short intervals were used (Biderman et al., 1967). The NORC national survey tested quarterly variations in recalled victimizations against quarterly variations in UCR reported crimes as a control and found both forgetting and telescoping effects.

Studies conducted in the pilot phase of the National Crime Survey demonstrated that both forgetting and telescoping affected recall as measured against the offenses that the respondents were known to have reported to the police in Washington, D.C., in Baltimore, in Cleveland, in San Jose, California, and in Akron and Dayton, Ohio. Telescoping was found to add to the reference period up to 20 percent of police-recorded crimes known to have occurred before the start of the reference period. Forgetting slightly reduced the number of victimizations recalled, but more important, forgetting made it difficult for the respondents to place the month of occurrence correctly as time passed (Hindelang, 1976a, pp. 45–71; Penick and Owens, 1976, pp. 32–48).

Sparks's (1976) respondents in London misrecalled the date of 41 percent of the victimizations they had previously reported to the police, and they telescoped into the reference period 19 percent of offenses known to have occurred before the reference period (pp. 48, 52).

Without some procedure for time bounding, that is, for controlling memory problems, we can expect that victimization survey estimates of total victimizations will be inflated by about one fifth by telescoping and will temporally misplace a significant proportion of events.

Validation Problems

Victimization surveys face the same validation problems that plague self-report studies. One problem is lying by respondents. The other problem is finding some independent external source of information against which to assess the reliability and the validity of the data gathered by interviewers.

On the face of it, respondents in victimization surveys have much less reason than respondents in self-report studies to lie to interviewers. Levine (1976), however, has made out a fairly extensive list of reasons for suspecting at least some respondents of lying about past victimizations, such as lies to support false insurance claims or improper income-tax deductions; to dramatize the crime problem; or to help the interviewer. The possibility of lying has not been explored particularly seriously in victimization survey research, certainly not to the extent that it has been explored in the self-report literature.

The University of Michigan commercial victimization survey for the President's Commission (Reiss, 1967, pp. 151–152) asked interviewers to judge the "credibility" of the respondents reporting victimizations. The interviewers questioned the respondent's credibility in only about 2.5 percent of the cases. Otherwise, this problem area remains largely unexplored.

The problem of external validation sources for victimization survey results is much the same as the problem in the self-report studies. No ultimate measure of the "true" incidence of crime is available. Self-report studies have not, to date, been conducted in a way that renders them definitionally, temporally, spatially, or jurisdictionally comparable to victimization surveys, nor have they sampled populations that are even vaguely approximate. They are not therefore available as a validation measure.[9] Therefore, police statistics are the basic source of validation. Temporal variations in the *Uniform Crime Reports* have been used to assess general patterns in the temporal distribution of recalled victimizations (Ennis, 1967), and "reverse record checks" using crimes reported to and recorded by local police forces have served as the principal validation check on the impact of memory problems in both England and America. Victimization surveys are in the same position as the self-report studies in that they must rely on the "inferior" data sources that they were designed to replace to establish their own reliability and validity.

Chapter Summary

Criminologists have developed two alternatives to criminal justice records as principal sources of information about crime and criminals. Both methods involve the use of survey research techniques in order to illuminate the dark figure of criminality. Self-report studies ask people to confess the crimes that they have committed. Victimization surveys ask people to describe the crimes that have been committed against them.

Self-report studies were first conducted in the 1940s, and have been conducted from time to time by different researchers in England, Canada, and the United States ever since. Self-report studies have established a number of important facts. They have shown that most people commit at least one offense at some time in their lives. They have shown that the difference in male and female offense rates apparent in criminal justice records probably reflect differences in behavior. They have shown that a great many offenses never become known to the criminal justice system. They have established that only a few people commit serious criminal offenses, and that fewer still admit to frequent commission of serious offenses. Self-report studies have also generated one major controversy: criminal justice records indicate that the frequency and seriousness of criminal behavior are inversely related to social class. Some self-report studies, in contrast, have suggested that the frequency and seriousness of criminal behavior are unrelated to social class.

Self-report studies are subject to a variety of problems. Few have been conducted in such a way that their findings can be directly compared with those of other self-report research or directly compared with the information derived from criminal justice statistics. Self-report studies also have major unresolved technical problems which limit our faith in their reliability and validity as measures of the dark figure of criminality.

Victimization surveys were first developed for the President's Commission on Law Enforcement and Administration of Justice in the 1960s as a method for probing the dark figure of criminality. The U.S. Department of Justice has conducted an annual national victimization survey since 1973 and conducted victimization surveys in 26 large American cities during the mid-1970s. Canada conducted its first

---

[9] The national-juvenile-panel self-report series conducted by Elliott and associates (e.g., Elliott and Ageton, 1980) may eventually prove suitable for this purpose.

81

national victimization survey in 1982. Unique victimization surveys have been conducted by a variety of individual researchers in Canada, England and the United States.

Victimization surveys have established a number of important facts. They have, like the self-report studies, shown that far more crimes occur than ever become known to the criminal justice system. They have demonstrated that police statistics are excellent enumerators of such crimes as murder and auto theft, excellent indices of commercial crimes such as robbery and burglary, and reasonable indices of such important crimes as robbery and household burglary. They have also demonstrated that police statistics are poor indices of such crimes as rape, assault, and theft.

Many of the patterns found in police statistics seem to be duplicated in victimization survey results. Intercity variations in crime and victimization rates seem to be similar. Police and victimization descriptions of criminal assailants seem to produce similar patterns. Trends for such crimes as robbery and burglary seem to have been similar during the 1970s.

Victimization surveys have a number of problems which make them poor substitutes for criminal justice statistics. Compared with police statistics their coverage in time, in space, and of different types of crime is very limited. They are subject to many of the interpretation and recording problems common to criminal justice records. They are also subject to a variety of problems created by the faulty memories of survey respondents. Finally, victimization surveys are a very expensive way to gather information about crime.

Self-report studies and victimization surveys are valuable techniques for probing the dark figure of criminality. They have established a number of important facts about patterns of crime and criminality. Both methods are afflicted with technical problems which limit their usefulness as substitutes for criminal justice statistics.

5

Using the Sources of Information About Crime

Introduction

People who want to use the various sources of information about crime in order to find and analyze patterns are faced with a set of problems: (1) no single source of information about crime can be taken to be error free; (2) each source has peculiar biases and flaws; (3) some sources are available only once or only sporadically, so that they are difficult or impossible to use for temporal analysis; (4) some sources cover limited areas or limited populations, or they are the memoirs of individuals, and their spatial or social generality is thus limited; (5) some sources are subject to policy variations, and others are subject to all of the infirmities of sample-survey research; (6) various sources define and measure incompatible things, in incompatible areas, and during incompatible times; and (7) no measure yet devised fully plumbs the depths of the dark figure of unknown crime.

Two strategies can be used to retrieve ordered information from the uncertainties of criminological data. The first strategy requires an assessment of the relative strengths and weaknesses of a particular data source with respect to a particular problem when it is the only data source available. A clear example of such a situation is research into historical crime patterns. No consistent self-report data are available prior to the year 1976. No consistent victimization data are available prior to the year 1973. No consistent police data are available in the United States prior to 1933, or in Canada prior to 1920, or in England prior to 1857. Court data measuring indictments and/or convictions, however, can be traced backward in reconcilable form for very long periods of time.

In such a circumstance, the problem becomes this: How much do the conclusions that we draw from one data source distort the conclusions that we would draw if we had *other* sources of information about crime? The answer to this question must be found in the inferences that we draw about the relationship of our data source to other sources of information in circumstances where multiple sources of information exist and can be compared. The conclusions that we draw when using this strategy are necessarily weaker and more tentative than those that we would draw if we had unflawed data or if we could follow the second strategy.

The second strategy dictates that whenever possible, the researcher use multiple sources of information about the issue under study. The appearance of similar patterns in several independent information sources permits us to come to strong conclusions despite the data imperfections that would force us to weak and tentative conclusions if we were restricted to a single source of information.

Assessing Single-Source Information

One critical issue facing contemporary criminologists is the assessment of the relative values of official data, self-report data, and victimization data. There are two reasons. First, the official and the self-report data form very different pictures of the association between criminal behavior and a number of important social patterns and indicators. The conclusions that we draw about the relative truth of these competing pictures have important consequences for the theories that we might construct to explain crime occurrence. Second, self-report and victimization data are available for limited times and places and, compared with official data, are enormously expensive to gather. The manner in which these data sources reflect consistent or inconsistent patterns of crime can place real limits on our ability to draw conclusions about crime patterns at all.

Uniform Crime Reports and
Victimization Surveys

The starting point for a comparative analysis of pattern consistencies between the various sources of information about crime has involved the American *Uniform Crime Reports* (UCR) and the American national victimization surveys. From the beginning, it was apparent that the victimization surveys, because they were sample surveys, would do a poor job of measuring extremely rare crimes such as homicide. The 1967 survey by the National Opinion Research Center (NORC) elicited reports of only two homicides in a national sample of ten thousand households. Viable estimates of homicide incidence could not be made (Ennis, 1967).

Homicide Statistics

As it happens, homicide is one of the few UCR crime categories that may be tested against some other, independently gathered source of information. The national Center for Health Statistics (CHS) vital statistics program gathers data on causes of death that are derived from the death certificates filed by attending physicians or by coroners following postmortem examination. These data are categorized according to a system developed by the United Nations in 1957, and a homicide category is included. Hindelang's (1974) comparison of the two data sources

84

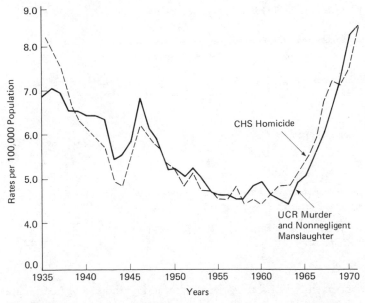

Figure 5–1. Rates of homicide in the United States as reported by the *Uniform Crime Reports* and the Center for Health Statistics, 1935–1971. [Source: M. J. Hindelang, "The Uniform Crime Reports Revisited" *Journal of Criminal Justice* 2/(1974): 1–17. Copyright 1974, Pergamon Press, Ltd. Reprinted with permission.]

(UCR and CHS) showed them to be in substantial agreement over the time period 1935–1971 (see Figure 5–1). Both sources show a decline from high homicide rates in the mid-1930s to low rates from the mid-1950s to the mid-1960s, as well as a very sharp rise to much higher rates again after 1965. In a subsequent analysis of a longer series (1936–1975) using various additional corrections to render the data more comparable, Cantor and Cohen (1979) found a correlation of +0.98 between the UCR and CHS homicide rates.

UCR and vital-statistics homicide data also correlate strongly across jurisdictions. The correlation between UCR homicides and vital-statistics homicides across the sixty-seven counties of Florida in 1972, for instance, was +0.99.

This near-perfect relationship between these two sources of information led victimization researchers to conclude that the *Uniform Crime Reports* provided a very good measure of homicides over time and from place to place, a measure superior to any measure that could be obtained from victimization surveys. Accordingly, the National Crime Survey (NCS) does not gather information on homicide.

Intercity Correlations

Nelson (1979) examined the relationship between UCR crime rates and NCS victimization rates for the twenty-six cities included in the NCS city sample in the mid-1970s. He assessed the city-by-city correlation of the two measures for the crimes of motor vehicle theft, robbery, burglary, assault, and rape (see Table 5–1).

TABLE 5–1. UCR and NCS Crime Rate Correlations
for Twenty-six Cities,

Crime	Zero-Order Correlations (r)
Motor vehicle theft	0.91
Robbery with a weapon	0.81
Burglary	0.69
Robbery without a weapon	0.56
Simple assault	0.05
Rape	0.04
Aggravated assault	−0.36

SOURCE: Reprinted from James F. Nelson, "Implications for the
Ecological Study of Crime: A Research Note," p. 26 in William H.
Parsonage (Ed.), *Perspectives on Victimology,* © 1979 Sage Publications, Inc., with permission.

He subdivided robbery into two categories—with and without a weapon—and subdivided assault into simple assault and aggravated assault categories, consistent with NCS practice.

Clearly, the UCR data index the patterns of motor vehicle theft and robbery with a weapon very well and burglary and robbery without a weapon moderately. By contrast, the UCR and NCS patterns for simple assault, rape, and aggravated assault are only weakly related. Nelson concluded:

> Because UCR rates exist for nearly every city in the United States, whereas only twenty-six cities were included in the NCS city data, it appears that the UCR data should be used to analyze the ecological correlates of theft crimes. In general, the close correspondence of theft rates between NCS and UCR data adds validity to the use of the UCR data as a measure of the relative number of theft crimes. (p. 27)

Ecological Patterns

Spatially grouped estimates of the relationship between police data and victimization data are much harder to find and assess. Mawby (1981, 1979) compared police crime rates and victimization rates for selected areas in Sheffield, England, and found similar patterns for crimes against adults and households, but different results for crimes against juveniles. Hindelang (1974) compared regional and state orderings of UCR crime rates with the regional orderings by victimization rate produced by the NORC national survey and found the two orderings to be similar. The NCS national panel series was not designed for regional analysis. Its geographic indicators have been suppressed, so that no large-scale assessment of relative UCR and NCS geographic patterns can be made. However, there are no data, to date, that suggest that NCS and UCR geographic patterns are grossly dissimilar.

Commercial Crime and Commercial Victimization

The NCS decision to suspend the collection of data on commercial burglary and robbery victimizations in 1977, without explanatory comment (National Criminal Justice Information and Statistics Service (NCJISS), 1979a:iii), leads to a reasonable inference that the action was taken because the continued collection of these data was not cost-effective, given consistently high rates of reporting to the police. Commercial robbery victimizations were reported to the police at rates of 86–90 percent in 1973–1976. Between 73 and 81 percent of all commercial burglary victimizations were also reported to the police during this period. These are very high and very consistent reporting rates.

Information about the incidence of some event gathered from a probability sample of a population is an estimate of the incidence of that event in the entire population. Such an estimate cannot be exact; there is always a margin of error or confidence interval surrounding the estimated value. Small differences between estimates produced by successive surveys, which fall within the range of the confidence interval, cannot be said to be different from one another. They are chance variations attributable to the process of probability sampling.

Variations in the reporting rate fall within the sampling confidence intervals and cannot be said to be real changes. In short, it is reasonable to conclude that UCR statistics do a good job of indexing the pattern changes in commercial robbery and burglary from place to place and from time to time.

Consistency of Reporting Rates

The reporting rates for most of the other offenses surveyed by the NCS national panel series have remained remarkably consistent over the period 1973 through 1979. About 48 percent of all household burglaries and about 70 percent of all forced-entry burglaries have been reported to the police nationally each year. About 68 percent of all attempted motor vehicle thefts and about 88 percent of all completed motor vehicle thefts have been reported to the police. About 53 percent of all personal robberies have been reported to the police. Rape-reporting rates have appeared to fluctuate more widely, but even these variations have not been statistically significant. Larceny rates have shown statistically significant changes, but the fluctuations have been in the vicinity of 25 percent of all personal and household larcenies, and the principal variations have involved the lowest-value offense categories. Assault rates have also been stable: around 45 percent of the offenses have been reported to the police, though reporting rates on aggravated assault dropped significantly from 1976 to 1977 (NCJISS, 1976b, 1976c, 1977b, 1979a, 1979b).

The stability of these various victimization reporting rates reflects importantly on the analytic value of police statistics. Since early in the nineteenth century (Quetelet, 1842; Bonger, 1916), criminologists have been forced to *assume* that criminal justice statistics bear some invariant indexing relationship to the real crime rate over time. This relationship cannot be directly addressed by victimization reporting rates because victimization surveys do not measure all the crimes that occur, but to the extent that they measure a much larger proportion of total crime than police statistics do, we can now assert that the traditional criminological assumption appears to be reasonable, at least with respect to the crimes of burglary, robbery, and motor vehicle theft. On the other hand, we must be suspicious of using police statistics concerning rape, assault, and common theft.

Crime Pattern Comparison

Another approach to the assessment of the relative merits of police and victimization statistics is to compare the detailed crime-information patterns that can be abstracted from the two data sources. Howard (1975) compared descriptive information about personal and commercial robberies derived from an NCS methodology test conducted in San Jose, California, in 1970, and from San Jose's computerized police Crime Analysis, Program Evaluation, and Research System (CAPER) records of known offenses for 1971 and 1972. Personal robberies were compared for seven categories of data collected by both data sources. The patterns were statistically identical for five of the categories: victim's sex, victim's age, number of victims, victim–offender relationship, and number of offenders. The patterns were statistically different for two categories: victim's race (the police data showed more white victims and more Mexican-American victims than did the victimization survey) and time of occurrence (the police data showed a relatively even distribution across three eight-hour periods, and the victimization data showed 53 percent of the offenses happening between 6 A.M. and 6 P.M.). Commercial robberies were compared on four data items: number of offenders apprehended, amount of loss, weapon, and time of occurrence. The patterns were statistically similar for all four items. Howard concluded that a sophisticated police-information system can capture essentially the same information, patterned in the same way, as that gathered by a victimization survey, at half the cost. The CAPER system, of course, is an extremely sophisticated police-information system, and robbery is among the best-reported offenses.

Hindelang (1978) compared the race of arrested robbery, rape, and assault offenders derived from UCR data with descriptive racial information about offenders derived from victims' descriptions of offenders collected in the 1974 NCS panel-series national survey. He found that the percentages of offenders classified as "white," "black," and "other" were identical for robbery. For rape, aggravated assault, and simple assault, black offenders were overrepresented by about ten percentage points in the UCR arrest data compared with the NCS victimization data. These studies seem to show that, at least for the offense of robbery, police statistics can be used in the confident expectation that a large number of the patterns found in them will be the same as the patterns found in victimization data.

Self-report, Victimization, and Police Statistics

The way in which the findings of the three major statistical sources of information about crime and criminals fit together is important because police statistics and many early self-report studies produced distinctly different pictures of the distribution of criminal behavior across the many social classes and ethnic groups that comprise complex contemporary societies. Criminal justice statistics in general and police arrest statistics in particular have generally been taken to demonstrate that lower-class people and some ethnic minority groups (e.g., blacks in the United States and Native Indians in Canada) commit a disproportionately high percentage of known crimes. The criminological result of these patterns in the police data has been the construction of a variety of etiological theories that attempt to account for the causes of this lower-class–ethnic disposition to commit crimes. Self-report studies of delinquent and criminal behavior, by contrast, seem to show that there is no difference in the frequency or seriousness of offending behavior between classes or races. The criminological result of these self-report findings has been the construction of etiological theories that explain differential class and race conviction rates in terms of the bias or the selection mechanisms of the criminal justice system.

Hindelang's (1978) study of the race of offenders identified in UCR arrest data and NCS victimization data showed that the patterns from these two data sources were more consistent with each other than either was with the patterns of offending behavior by race found in the self-report studies. Though the quality of fit differed by offense type, he concluded that "regardless of whether the UCR or the victimization survey data are taken as the indicator, blacks are substantially over-represented in relation to their representation in the general population" (p. 100).

Elliott and Ageton's (1980) analysis of a national panel-series self-report study of delinquent behavior showed strong social-class differentials in both frequency and seriousness of criminal behavior, consistent with the patterns found in police data. Beyond these two studies, the three data sources have not been frequently compared with respect to a single criminological problem.

Police Statistics and Other Criminal Justice Statistics

Since Sellin's classic analyses (1931, 1937, 1951) made the point that discretionary decisions in the processing of criminal cases, such as the decision to arrest, or the decision to indict, or the jury's decision to acquit, have the effect of filtering out large numbers of cases at each successive point in the proceedings, criminologists have generally assumed that only the statistic of "crimes known to police" reasonably indexes general patterns of crime and criminality. Other criminal justice statistics based on records of indictments, convictions, or prison receptions have been assumed to distort trend and offense patterns, and their use has generally been avoided in research. This outcome is unfortunate for three reasons. First, the assumption that it is based on has remained largely untested; it is a basically unscientific assumption based on received wisdom. Second, this assumption hampers comparative research, because despite the frequent repetition of Sellin's (1931) charge that the United States has the *worst* criminal statistics of any advanced country (e.g., Vetter and Silverman, 1978 p. 38; Wolfgang, 1963), many advanced countries do not consistently collect or publish police statistical series. France, for instance, publishes only a *conviction* series, and Australia has no national police statistics. Third, this assumption hampers historical research on crime because no police statistical series exist prior to 1857 and no police, as we now understand that term, existed prior to 1829, and pre-twentieth-century criminological research *must* rely on court statistics. According to the assumption, the findings of such research are invalid or distorted *prima facie*.

It is possible, however, to assess how well *other* criminal justice statistics index police statistics through both cross-sectional and temporal procedures. Archer and Gartner (1980), for instance, examined the temporal correlations between crimes known to the police and prosecutions or convictions for eight nations over various lengths of time for various sets of offenses. For Canada, over the years 1919–1943, they found very high correlations between crimes known and convictions: +0.90 for murder, manslaughter, and assault; +0.93 for robbery and burglary; and +0.94 for theft. Their full analysis was for sixteen nations. The median correlations between sets of criminal justice statistics across all sixteen countries and time series were +0.85 for homicide; +0.86 for rape; +0.92 for assault; and +0.90 for robbery and other property offenses with violence, such as burglary.

Though they argued that the statistics on crimes known to the police are still critical for cross-sectional research, Archer and Gartner concluded that "poor indicators are in most cases a consistent fraction of good indicators. As a result, good and poor indicators are generally interchangeable as measures of a nation's offense rate trend" (p. 440). And again, they said, "In summary, the infatuation of two generations of social scientists with the offenses known indicator may have been overstated and indiscriminate . . . the evidence reported here indicates that longitudinal designs do not require this indicator" (p. 444).

The English data show a longitudinal indexing capacity. The correlation between crimes known to the police and high court convictions during the period 1913–1965 is 0.85. The nineteenth-century data, when the crimes known to the police (CKP) data are known to have been erratically collected (Radzinowicz, 1945; pp. 188–189), show a correlation between CKP and high court convictions of 0.54 for the period 1857–1892. As late as 1907, the introduction to the *Criminal Statistics* maintained that "it is usually immaterial whether the figures of offenses committed (i.e., reported to the police), of persons tried, or of convictions are used— the results as regards increase and decrease of crime substantially coincide in most cases" (Radzinowicz, 1945, p. 189).

As a general guide to research, it is better to use the statistics on crimes known to the police. However, in circumstances where they are not available, it is quite possible to use other criminal justice data to measure patterns in crime.

Using Multiple-Source Information About Crime

In some circumstances, it is possible to use several different sources of information to address a specific criminological research problem. When such a strategy is possible, it should be adopted as the preferred procedure. All sources of information about crime and criminals are flawed. When we find consistent patterns in several different kinds of information sources, however, we are justified in treating such patterns as presumptively (though not conclusively) valid. When patterns found in different sources conflict, the use of additional information sources may resolve the issue.

A classic example of the multiple-source strategy is the work of Clifford Shaw and Henry McKay, whose studies of delinquency patterns in Chicago and other American cities shaped the field of enquiry now known as the *ecological approach* to crime and also formed the core set of empirical findings on which all subsequent American delinquency research has rested. Shaw and McKay (1931) combined criminal justice records of the spatial distribution of the homes of juvenile delinquents with in-depth case studies of individual delinquent careers in an attempt to assess the social causes of criminal behavior. Their case studies included criminal justice records of officially known delinquent acts; the delinquent's personal memoir of his criminal career; extensive interviews with parents, teachers, neighbors, siblings, and friends; an analysis of play-group and friendship activity patterns; and an extensive clinical analysis of physical, mental, and social health. The criminal justice data set was analyzed against the census and other aggregate social data and pointed toward specific *sorts* of neighborhoods as the locus of criminal behavior. The case study data were used to assess the specific social patterns within neighborhoods that correlated with extensive criminal careers. Together, the two data sources pointed to a collapse of neighborhood social institutions in concert with the development of a criminal tradition within the neighborhood as the *cause* of a propensity to commit crimes. This is the theory of the cultural transmission of criminality.

A more recent example of the use of multiple information sources in research is the work of Hagan, Gillis, and Chan (1978) in Mississauga, Ontario, a very large suburb of Toronto. They were interested in testing the impact of police perceptions and expectations of crime frequency in different neighborhoods of the city on the official delinquency rates of those neighborhoods in order to assess the relative strength of three different theoretical explanations of the persistent correlation between delinquency and social class. They actually used six different sources of information about the distribution of delinquent behavior within the city: the police records of known delinquent offenders; the police records of citizen complaints about delinquency; self-reported delinquency and victimization rates gathered in a survey of high-school students; police assessments of the relative delinquency problem in each neighborhood within the city; and police assessments of *why* particular neighborhoods had more or less delinquency than expected.

The first five data sources were combined with several important social and environmental measures for each area of the city in a statistical modeling procedure called *path analysis*. The results showed that the official delinquency rates of an area were determined by a complex of complaint rates, police perceptions, victimization rates, residential mobility rates, housing density, and socioeconomic status. The official delinquency rates of an area were unrelated to either family dissolution rates or self-reported delinquency rates.

From this analysis, it was concluded that police conceptions of the spatial distribution of delinquency are determined by the socioeconomic status and residential density of an area, over and above the citizen complaint rate. This conclusion was tested with the sixth data source (the police interviews) and was qualitatively confirmed through the descriptive phrases used to describe the low-rate areas ("better class of people," "good residential areas," "better class of buildings," "higher income level that doesn't bother the police much") and the high-rate areas ("townhouses and apartments geared to income," "a recent mix of immigrants").

Chapter Summary

The best approach to criminological research is to use multiple data sources. In this respect the work of criminal ecologists such as Shaw and McKay (1929, 1931, 1969) is exemplary. They combined patterns of crime derived from the records of several different criminal justice agencies with the rich detail of criminal events and careers elicited through comprehensive personal accounts provided by offenders in order to develop both a comprehensive description of and a theoretical explanation for juvenile delinquency in American cities.

It is not always possible to use multiple data sources. Historical research into crime patterns, for instance, may be hampered by the fact that self-report data were not collected prior to the 1940s and victimization data were not collected prior to the 1960s. The only crime statistics available for the period prior to 1805 are those found in the records of individual courts. This makes it important to assess the relative quality of criminal justice statistics.

Comparison of the patterns in the American Uniform Crime Reports (UCR) and the American National Crime Survey (NCS) suggests that the UCR data provide a reasonable index of both the spatial and temporal patterns of crime found in the NCS. The rates at which people reported different types of offenses to the police appear to have remained quite stable over the period 1973–1979. The descriptions of criminal events derived from police records and NCS data appear remarkably congruent. Comparison of the patterns found in the UCR, the NCS, and various self-report studies indicate that the three sets of data produce basically congruent pictures. This suggests that in circumstances in which self-report or victimization data are not available, police statistics can be used without fear of massive distortion.

Criminologists have long argued that criminal justice statistics distort the patterns in crime as they increase in procedural distance from the criminal event. Police data are therefore less distorted than and superior to court data; court data are less distorted than and superior to correctional data. This argument appears to have been based on intuition and the logic of discretion in criminal justice, rather than on comparative analysis of various criminal justice statistics. Recent quantitative analyses demonstrate that court data provide good temporal and spatial indices of police data and that prison data provide good temporal and spatial indices of both court and police data. Used with reasonable attention to their limitations, criminal justice statistics provide a reasonable index to the patterns of crime and criminality.

6
Temporal Analysis of Crime

Introduction

Because the available data contain reporting and recording errors, one major problem in crime analysis is understanding the temporal changes in crime and the activity patterns of the criminal justice system. This chapter explores temporal pattern analysis: both visual analysis of graphs and statistical analysis of time series data. A broad range of analytic techniques are discussed. All the techniques discussed in this chapter are used to recognize and understand regularities in temporal patterns, an essential part of temporal crime analysis.

Pattern Analysis

The purpose of studying crime patterns over time is to discover regularities that aid one in understanding the phenomenon of crime. The social, legal, political, economic, and demographic structures of societies change over time. Societal structures are dynamic, not static: laws change; birthrates change; income distributions change; occupational patterns change; economies grow and contract; and migration streams increase and decrease. If crime is related to social, economic, political, and legal conditions, then crime patterns should change over time as society changes. Relating temporal changes in crime to temporal changes in other aspects of society is a potentially powerful way to study and explain crime.

Overall Visual Inspection

The analysis of temporal patterns begins with simple visual inspection. Sometimes it is possible to look at a series of numbers representing criminal justice statistics and immediately see regularities. For example, Figure 6–1 shows the pattern of arrests for major crimes in Boston between 1849 and 1951. A strong down-

93

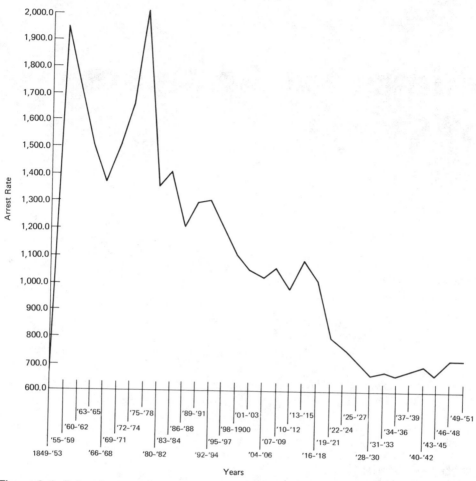

Patterns in Crime

Figure 6–1. Rate of arrests for major crimes in Boston per 100,000 population, 1849–1951. [Source: T. N. Ferdinand, "The Criminal Patterns of Boston Since 1849," *American Journal of Sociology* 73(1967): p. 87. © 1967 University of Chicago Press.]

ward trend is apparent. The pattern is not absolute: there is a dip in the arrest rate from 1866 to 1868, followed by a sudden rise, but from 1875 onward there is an almost steady decline. Such a strong pattern brings many questions to mind. Could the pattern be explained by changes in the criminal justice system? Did the criminal law change, reducing the number of offenses for which arrests could be made? Did police attitudes or behaviors change? Did police detection efficiency enter a sustained decline? Alternatively, does the pattern reflect changes in the incidence of criminal behavior? If so, how does the pattern relate to other social patterns? Did the social structure change? Did economic conditions change?

In analyzing these criminal statistics from Boston, Ferdinand (1967) argued that changes in both socioeconomic structure and police behavior brought about the gradual, but steady, decline in major crime. He argued that the gradually rising standard of living experienced during the entire period worked toward reducing crimes associated with economic distress and social disorganization. He observed that a decline in the wave of immigration from Europe to Boston corresponded with the decline in criminal arrests, and he attributed this correspondence to the social assimilation of the immigrants. He also argued that the police began to ignore common assault, thereby greatly reducing known crimes recorded through arrest.

Ferdinand's analysis of the temporal crime data for Boston was totally visual. He looked at the data, searched for regularities, and tried to think of other social data that exhibited similar patterns. Such a visual analysis is a reasonable way to begin a temporal analysis of crime patterns. A strong pattern, such as the one found in Boston's arrests, triggers a search for other similar patterns that can be used to explain the first pattern.

Unfortunately, strong visual patterns are not always present in time-series data about crime. When no dominant pattern or patterns can be seen through simple inspection, the analysis of temporal statistics requires greater methodological sophistication. Care must be taken to uncover possible distortions of graphic presentation and to break down overall patterns into subpatterns that can be understood.

Time-Scale Analysis

In a systematic analysis of temporal patterns, the first thing that has to be considered is the time scale being used, that is, the *temporal cone of resolution*. Studies of temporal crime patterns may look at, for example, the last five, ten, or fifty years. Temporal analysis can also involve studying yearly, monthly, weekly, or even daily patterns. If the time interval changes, the level of resolution changes. Time is a continuous concept. Temporal studies range from those exploring changes during short time periods to those exploring broad historic variations. Broad historic studies can be thought of as studies at the broad end of a cone of resolution. Short time period studies fall at the narrow end of the cone.

Although time is continuous, the analysis of temporal patterns requires the fixing of a time period. The time interval that is selected sets the level of resolution for the analysis and limits the questions that can be asked. Conversely, if specific questions are being asked, the range of possible time intervals that can be used in the analysis is constrained. For example, temporal analysis can involve examining the rate of crimes known to the police for an extended period, say, for the last hundred years. At this low level of resolution, the analysis will look for large-scale patterns, trends, or regularities over extended time periods. The analysis will usually explore ten-, twenty-, and fifty-year trends and, if any are found, try to relate the trends to comparable trends in social, political, economic, or demographic structures. Large short-term shifts in temporal patterns are interesting if they can be related to sudden transformations in aspects of social life such as legislative reforms, wars, or economic depressions. Year-to-year variations are interesting insofar as they form a part of an overall trend. Except for the trend component, the yearly variations often represent *noise* or *error* when data are analyzed at this low level of temporal resolution. The *noise* is usually ignored.

Temporal analysis need not be multiyear. The cone of resolution can shift to a finer level, away from multiyear patterns, and other questions may be explored. For example, monthly crime data may be studied, and questions about seasonality may be explored. Does crime go up and down depending on the time of the year? Does crime respond to short-term economic changes, or short-term population changes, such as increases in the tourist population? With a finer level of resolution, the overall trends become less important, and the month-to-month variability becomes more important. In this type of analysis, the data are usually *detrended;* that is, trends in the data are mathematically removed, and the short-term variation around the trend is analyzed.

Finally, the *temporal cone of resolution* can be shifted even further, to a very high level of resolution, and weekly or daily patterns may be investigated. Once again, the questions change: When do burglaries occur? On what day of the week? At what time of day? At this level of analysis, the questions and answers usually relate to temporal changes in the opportunities to commit crimes or in the social circumstances surrounding the commission of a crime. When are homes empty? When is it safest to break into a store? When are people likely to be drinking or in situations that often lead to interpersonal violence?

Within the temporal cone of resolution, many levels of analysis are possible. The questions asked change with the level of resolution, but valid and interesting questions are possible at all levels. Temporal crime patterns are made up of hourly, daily, weekly, monthly, and yearly patterns that combine and interact. Any particular study may focus on one level of resolution, obscuring other levels. Across many studies, the focus will—and should—shift in order to describe the dynamics of the temporal changes in crime. There is no single "valid" level of resolution.

Graphical Analysis

Inspection of a graph is usually the first—and sometimes the only—step in temporal crime analysis. Graphs can convey information much more powerfully than a table of numbers. The inspection of a graph begins the search for patterns. Certain specific types of graphs seem to trigger interest. Graphs that rise or fall rapidly (have large positive or negative slopes), that have sharp breaks (points of discontinuity), or that contain noticeable peaks and valleys—all raise questions.

Within the social sciences, temporal sequences (or time series) usually show point-to-point variation. For example, the year-to-year crime rates in any large city in North America or England are not constant; the numbers vary. The numbers may vary because actual crime occurrence rates are changing in a systematic fashion, or because reporting and recording practices are changing, or because there is some natural, random component in all crime rates.

Crime analysis tries to identify the systematic changes and separate them from the random changes. Visually and statistically, one of the techniques that analysts use to separate the random component of temporal change is to try to fit a line to the underlying data, a line that represents the overall pattern of change (Figure 6-2). Many techniques exist for statistically fitting the "best" line, and some of these techniques are described later in the chapter, but at this point in the discussion, it is the visual line that is initially imposed on graphic data that is of interest.

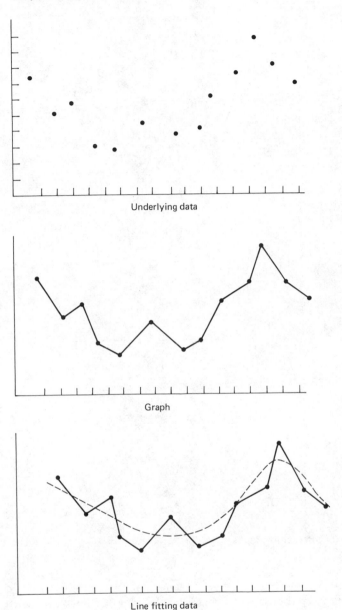

Figure 6–2. Fitting a line to data.

Trends

Although temporal changes always appear to be somewhat erratic, there may be trends within the data. Trends are changes in the recorded data that extend downward or upward. Trends are best seen when one considers the underlying visual or statistical line that can be superimposed on the data. The trends need not be linear; they can be curvilinear, as in Figure 6–3a. Superimposing a trend line is

97

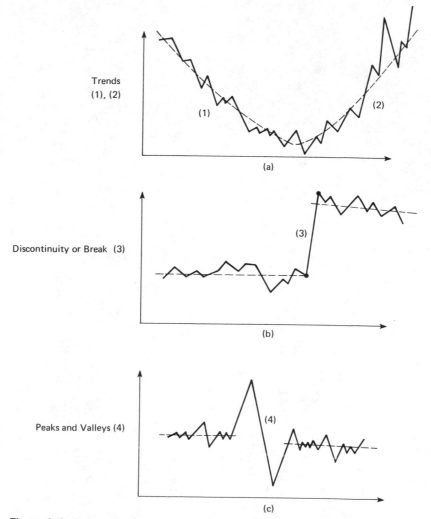

Trends
(1), (2)

(1)   (2)

(a)

Discontinuity or Break (3)

(3)

(b)

Peaks and Valleys (4)

(4)

(c)

Figure 6–3. Points of interest in graphs.

a technique used to simplify the data. Mathematically complex lines can be fitted to data. In fact, data can be fitted perfectly if a sufficiently complicated line (equation) is used. But the goal of fitting a line to a data pattern is to find a "simple" representation that adequately describes the changes. We want to know whether crime is increasing, decreasing, or remaining the same.

The trends that are of most interest in crime analysis are extended downward or upward changes such as those shown in Figures 6–2 and 6–3a. Such trends trigger a search for some force or forces that could have produced the pattern. In historical studies, the focus is usually on the social-structural, demographic, and economic trends that could be considered driving forces behind the crime trends.

Discontinuities

Sometimes a deviation—an upward or downward point-to-point movement of the data—is sharp and out of proportion to the surrounding values (Figure 6–3b). Such a deviation or discontinuity is often the result of a major change in the operation of the criminal justice system, such as a new law, a change in police procedure, or a change in the courts. For example, Figure 6–4 shows the historic variation in the reported burglary and robbery rates in New York City and Chicago between 1935 and 1966. Several sharp breaks are noticeable, the sharpest being a variation in the burglary rate in New York before and after 1950. These sharp breaks reflect changes in police recording practices. In visual temporal analysis, inspection of the data for underlying discontinuities is extremely important. Discontinuities usually represent changes in law or in operation of the criminal justice system rather than behavioral changes.

Peaks and Valleys

Peaks and valleys in graphs (a sharp upward movement followed by a sharp downward movement or vice versa) also trigger interest (Figure 6–3c), especially if there are few large deviations in the data. Peaks and valleys are often the result of short-term social changes such as wars, economic recessions, or short-term migra-

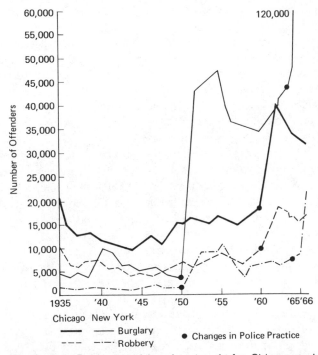

Figure 6–4. Robbery and burglary trends for Chicago and New York, 1935–1966. [Source: Roger Hood and Richard Sparks, *Key Issues in Criminology.* London: Weidenfeld & Nicolson, Ltd., 1970, p. 40.]

99

tion waves. The existence of many peaks and valleys is usually a sign of unstable reporting practices or an unstable underlying phenomenon.

An unstable underlying phenomenon is often a matter of perspective and the numbers used in analysis. When the crime counts being analyzed are small, representing relatively rare events, there is often great variation from one recorded count, or observation, to the next. The best example is the highly variable pattern seen when the number of murders in a limited geographic area are graphed over time. For example, there may be twenty murders one year, thirty-five the next, then only twelve in the following year. The change from twenty to thirty to twelve, when graphed, will look quite jagged. Given this type of variability, no important significance should be given to a single peak.

Graphical Manipulation

The patterns just described—trends, discontinuities, and peaks—are traces of changes over time. Recognizing these patterns through the visual inspection of a graph depends on the manner in which the graph is drawn. The techniques used in preparing graphs can make patterns stand out or can obscure basic relationships.

Adjusting the scale used on the horizontal and vertical axes of a graph is the primary method used to adjust the appearance of a graph. By this means, graphs can be made to appear to flatten out or to rise sharply, that is, to have many peaks and valleys or few major deviations. Adjusting the scale can even make breaks or discontinuities stand out.

The data on convictions for drug offenses in England and Wales between 1954 and 1972 (Table 6–1) is a good example. There was a major rise in convictions, particularly cannabis convictions. Graphically, we can make the rise seem astronomical or merely large by changing the scales on the horizontal and vertical axes. For example, marijuana convictions were relatively stable or slowly rising in England and Wales from 1954 until 1964. In 1964, the English, in response to a perceived problem in the use of "soft" drugs and polyaddiction, enacted the Drugs (Prevention and Misuse) Act. This act (which increased the numbers of drug offenses), combined with a movement toward middle-class use of soft drugs, greatly increased the number of people who were "violating" drug laws. At the same time, the police changed their enforcement patterns and began rigorous action against soft-drug users (Brantingham, 1975a). These factors worked together to produce a major increase in drug convictions.

Figure 6–5, graphed in a relatively straightforward manner, shows this increase. The years form the units on the horizontal axis; the number of convictions, in increments of 500, form the vertical axis. In this graph, the increase appears to have been rapid and quite large.

If we change the scale used on the horizontal and vertical axes, the increase can be made to look less dramatic. In Figure 6–6, the scale for the years has been collapsed into three-year averages; the conviction scale has been collapsed into increments of 1,000 instead of 500. These changes in scale make the increase in convictions look smoother and less sharp, but by no means flat. Figure 6–7 shows a transformation that radically changes the visual impact of the graph. In this figure, the vertical axis has been changed to a logarithmic scale, so that increases

100

TABLE 6–1. Convictions for Drug Offenses, England and Wales, 1954–1972

Year	Opium	Manufactured Drugs *	Cannabis	Subtotal	Synthetics †	Total (all drugs)
1954	28	47	144	219	—	219
1955	17	37	115	169	—	159
1956	12	37	103	152	—	152
1957	9	30	51	90	—	90
1958	8	41	99	148	—	148
1959	18	26	185	229	—	229
1960	15	28	235	278	—	278
1961	15	61	288	364	—	364
1962	16	71	588	675	—	675
1963	20	63	663	746	—	746
1964	14	101	544	659	—	659
1965	13	128	626	767	958‡	1,725
1966	36	242	1,119	1,397	1,216	2,613
1967	58	573	2,393	3,024	2,486	5,510
1968	73	1,099	3,071	4,316	2,957	7,273
1969	53	1,359	4,683	6,095	3,762	9,857
1970	66	1,214	7,520	8,800	3,388	12,181
1971	48	1,485	8,695	10,288	5,149	15,377
1972	95	1,949	11,941	13,985	5,028	19,013

*Heroin, morphine, cocaine, Pethidine, Methadone, etc.
†Amphetamines and LSD, first controlled by Drugs (Prevention of Misuse) Act 1964.
‡ 1965 figures include the last two months of 1964 in Synthetics.
SOURCE: Reprinted by the permission of the publisher, from; "The Medico-Penal Model of Drug Abuse Control: The English Experience," by Paul J. Brantingham, in *Drug Abuse Control: Administration and Politics* edited by Richard Rachin and Eugene Czajkoski. (Lexington, Mass.: Lexington Books, D. C. Heath and Company), Copyright 1974, D. C. Heath and Company.

by powers of 10 are represented by increases of one unit on the scale. The impact of such a logarithmic transformation is to take a rapidly rising, curvilinear trend and convert it to an almost linear visual trend.

Changes in scale change graphs in predictable ways. The variability in a graph can be visually reduced by an alteration in the time dimension (compare Figures 6–5 and 6–6). If yearly data instead of monthly data or multiyear averages instead of single-year values are used, the graph will be smoother. Conversely, graphing at finer levels of temporal resolution will give the appearance of increasing—and actually will increase, in most cases—the variation in the data. Apparent variability can also be decreased by an increase in the scale on the vertical axis.

Finally, variability can be changed through logarithmic (log) transformations. As described above, rapid, geometric increases are made more linear. On a log scale, changes of large values are represented by small changes in log values on the graph. Conversely, changes of small values are represented by proportionally larger changes in the log values on the graph. When one is using logs, the change from 10 to 100 is the same as the change between 100 and 1,000, or 1,000 and 10,000. Log transformations accentuate differences in small numbers and reduce differences in large numbers.

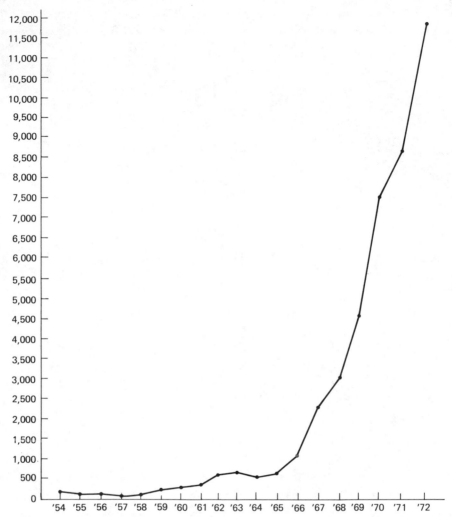

Figure 6–5. Cannabis convictions, England and Wales, 1954–1972. [Source: Based on data in Table 6–1.]

Graphs can be used to convey much information, but the representation of information is not independent of the mode of presentation. Graphs can accentuate or minimize patterns. Although visual analysis is usually the first step in time series analysis, it must be done carefully and with an awareness of possible distortions. Whenever feasible, the visual analysis of graphs should be done in conjunction with a numerical analysis.

Numerical Analysis

Numerical analysis primarily involves the search for a mathematical model that can be used to describe a temporal pattern. A time series is made up of a series of

102

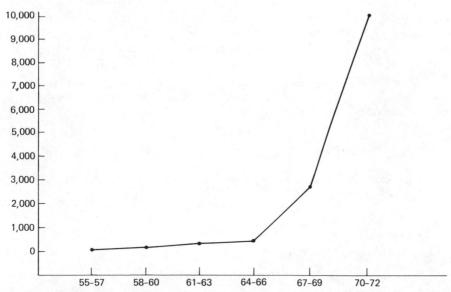

Figure 6–6. Average cannabis convictions for three-year periods in England and Wales, 1955–1972. [Source: Based on data in Table 6–1.]

numbers or values arranged in a temporal order, so that each number represents an observation for a fixed point in time. The numbers are arranged in the order of their temporal occurrence. The numbers, or data values, in the time series usually vary. Either the underlying values of the phenomenon being recorded actually vary, or there is measurement error, or both.

The purpose of time series analysis is to find an underlying process that can

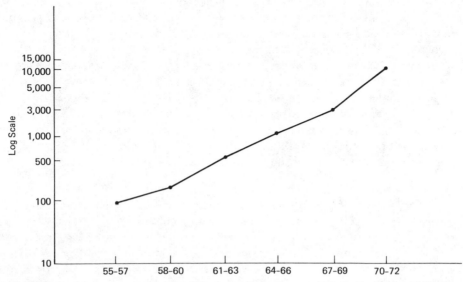

Figure 6–7. Average cannabis convictions for three-year periods in England and Wales, 1955–1972 (log scale). [Source: Based on data in Table 6–1.]

103

reasonably be expected to have produced the values found in the time series. The underlying process is the model for the time series. The model can then be used either to help understand—what social scientists call *explain*—the time series or to predict future values in the series. The first use of the model, the explanatory use, helps to advance knowledge about crime and crime causation and helps to build the empirical base for theory. The second use of the model, the predictive use, helps policymakers to react to and plan for changes in crime patterns.

Basic Time Series Model

The basic model used to describe a time series is one that breaks the time series down into three components:

1. Trend.
2. Seasonality.
3. Random fluctuations.

If we look at the model the other way round, any particular value in a time series is made up of a trend component, a seasonal component, and some random or irregular component. The process of breaking down a time series into its trend, seasonal and random components is called the *decomposition* of a time series.

Trends

The basic approach of decomposing time series data into trend, seasonality, and random fluctuations has been used extensively in time series analysis. But even with its long history, the elements of the model do not have uniformly fixed, precise definitions. The definitions are intertwined with the cone of resolution used in the analysis. The first component (the trend) refers to an overall, general change in the values in the series. A trend is a general increase or decrease in the time-series data values over an extended period of time. Individual point-to-point variations may be positive or negative. The trend is the overall multipoint pattern rather than the minor point-to-point changes.

The appearance of a trend is dependent on the cone of resolution. For example, in monthly crime patterns, what appears to be a trend—that is, a relatively smooth change over an extended (monthly) period—may only appear to be a peak or a minor variation in an investigation of multiyear patterns. What is recognized as a trend depends on the level of resolution. There can be weekly trends, monthly trends, or yearly trends. At each higher level of analysis, what appeared to be a trend at a lower level may disappear or become a peak.

Seasonality

The second component of a time series (seasonality) is also somewhat difficult to define. Seasonality is sometimes referred to as the *cyclic component* in a time series, and it is generally used to describe a recurrent upward or downward movement in the data. In monthly data, the presence of seasonality means a pattern over many years, where the same months appear over and over again as high-crime months and other months repeatedly appear as low-crime months. Cyclic patterns may also occur in daily data, where crime peaks are seen in the late evening hours. Seasonality is tied to the level of resolution: hourly patterns are not seen in weekly data; weekly patterns are not seen in monthly data; and monthly patterns are not seen in yearly data.

Recognizing seasonality in time series data is easiest if the cyclic pattern is highly regular. If, say, in monthly data, the peak occurs in the same month year after year, then the seasonal pattern is apparent. This type of seasonality is evident in the increase in burglaries around Christmastime each year. The date of Christmas is fixed, so the peak is relatively fixed. But suppose there is an annual increase in burglary around Easter, a time when many people take vacations and are away from home. Noticing this peak in the data would be somewhat more difficult than noticing the Christmas peak. The date for Easter varies from year to year, and any associated peak in burglary would also vary. Analysis of seasonality, as all analysis, must temper numbers with knowledge.

Random Fluctuations

Within any given time series, the trend and seasonality components may account for much of the variation in the data values. After trend variation and seasonal variation are accounted for, there will be some variation left. This remaining variation is called the *random* or *irregular component* in the time series.

Given the problems of definition and the commingling of definitions with the level of resolution in the analysis, it is still possible to decompose any particular time series down into its trends, seasonality, and random components (Figure 6–8).

Mathematical Formulation

The basic model for a time series can be written mathematically. For example, the crime rates for a period of five years can be written in the following time-series notation:

(4321.7; 4522.6; 5011.2; 4968.1; 5215.8)

where each number represents the crime rate per 100,000 population for a year and the numbers are listed in the order of the years.

In general mathematical notation, a five-year time series would be denoted as:

$(Y_1, Y_2, Y_3, Y_4, Y_5)$

where Y_1 stands for the crime rate in the first year of the series; Y_2 stands for the crime rate in the second year of the series, and so forth.

In general, the notation Y_i stands for the crime rate for a fixed, but unspecified, year in the series. With the use of this notation, the basic time-series model may be written as follows:

$$Y_i = T_i + S_i + Z_i \qquad (1)$$

where:

T_i is the trend component;
S_i is the seasonal component; and
Z_i is the random or irregular component.

105

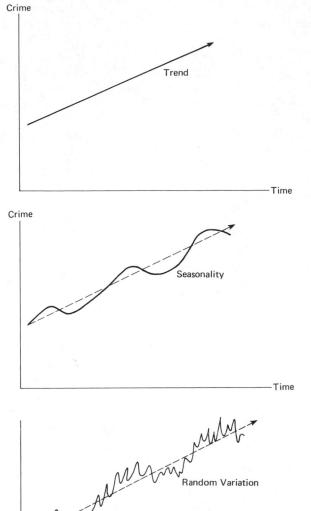

Crime

Trend

Time

Crime

Seasonality

Time

Random Variation

Figure 6–8. Components of Variation in a Time Series.

Equation (1) represents the basic model for a time series. It may be applied to any time series. However, not all of the components need be present in any particular time series. It is possible to have a time series that has no trend component; that is, over the length of the time series, there is no discernible trend. Such a series is called a *stationary time series*.

Series that have trends are called *nonstationary time series*. The analysis of a nonstationary series usually involves (1) determining what transformations of the data are necessary to transform the nonstationary series into a stationary series; (2)

106

transforming the data; and (3) analyzing the transformed series. Both stationary and nonstationary series may have a seasonal component.

Basic Statistical Techniques

Correlational Analysis

In searching for patterns in data, criminologists have traditionally relied on statistical techniques, often correlational analysis. In correlational analysis, two variables, or characteristics of interest, are studied, and their joint variation or covariation is examined. Put simply, one examines the values of two variables over repeated observations to see if the values follow similar patterns. For example, over time, the crime rate and the unemployment rate in a city may be recorded. If when the unemployment rate is high the crime rate is also high, and when the unemployment rate is low the crime is also low, the two variables are positively correlated. The variables are negatively correlated if they move in opposite directions. If when one variable increases the other variable decreases, the correlation is said to be negative. Correlations may be positive or negative. They are positive when variables move in the same direction and negative when they move in opposite directions.

Correlations are normalized coefficients; that is, they are constructed in such a way that the range of possible values is fixed. Correlational coefficients range from -1 to $+1$. The strength of the correlation is not dependent on the scale values used to measure a variable. Correlations do not change when crime rates are measured per 1,000 population or per 100,000 population. Because correlations have fixed upper and lower limits it is possible to compare the strength of the relationship between diverse pairs of variables.

When the value of the correlational coefficient is $+1$ the relationship between the two variables is perfect; increases or decreases in one variable are perfectly matched by increases or decreases in the other variable. When the value of the correlation coefficient is -1, increases in one variable are matched perfectly by decreases in the other. The relationship is perfect, but one variable increases while the other decreases. Such perfect relationships are theoretically possible, but in practice, they are never found in social science research. Having such a perfect relationship is equivalent to finding no error or random fluctuation in the data. When two variables are totally unrelated, their correlational coefficient is zero.

In criminological research, correlations greater than ± 0.6 are usually considered strong and interesting. Depending on the context, smaller correlations may also be considered interesting.

Coefficient of Determination. The correlational coefficient calculated from the data is denoted by the letter r. The square of the correlational coefficient, r^2, is called the *coefficient of determination.* It represents the proportion of variance in one variable that is statistically "explained" by variance in the other variable.

Variance is a measure of the dispersion of the data. It measures how closely the data are to the mean or average, that is, how clustered the data values are around the average value. Variance is an accepted measure of variation used in statistics. If two variables are perfectly related, so that changes in one variable can

107

TABLE 6–2. Relationship Between r and r^2

r	r^2	Meaning of r^2
±1.0	+1.0	100% of variance explained
±0.8	+0.64	64% of variance explained
±0.6	+0.36	36% of variance explained
±0.3	+0.09	9% of variance explained
±0.1	+0.01	1% of variance explained
0	0	No variance explained

be used to predict changes in the other variable perfectly, then 100 percent of the variance in the first variable is said to be "explained" by the variance in the second variable. In such a situation, the correlational coefficient would be +1 and, consequently, the coefficient of determination, r^2, would also be 1 because 100 percent of the variance would be explained. Because r^2 represents a percentage or proportion, it is easily understood and is often used to describe the strength of a relationship.

The coefficient of determination also ranges from −1 to +1, just as the correlational coefficient does, but because it is the square of the correlational coefficient, it follows a slightly different pattern (see Table 6–2).

As can be seen from the table, with a moderate correlation of +0.6 only 36 percent of the variance is statistically explained. A small correlation of +0.3 represents only 9 percent of the variance explained.

Regression Analysis

Regression analysis is another common statistical technique used in criminological research. Regression analysis, which is related to correlational analysis, is a statistical technique used to estimate the value of one variable based on the value of another variable.

Regression analysis is probably most easily described by means of an example. Consider the relationship between the crime rate and poverty. Criminologists often assume that the crime rate is positively correlated with poverty; that is, when the proportion of the population who are poor is high, it is expected that the crime rate will also be high. This hypothesized relationship can be tested by a look at crime rates and the percentage of the population living below the poverty level. Table 6–3 contains the correlation coefficients for the U.S. Standard Metropolitan Statistical Areas (SMSAs)[1] over 250,000 population obtained by correlating each SMSA's UCR index offense rates for 1970 with the percentage of its population living below the poverty level in 1970. As can be seen in the table, except for the murder rate, none of the pairwise correlations is even moderate. With murder, only 28 percent of the variance is explained ($r^2 = 0.28$).

---

[1] SMSAs are part of the U.S. Census Bureau classification scheme for cities. Although the definition of SMSAs is rather complex, they can generally be considered equivalent to urban clusters of counties with a population of fifty thousand or more.

TABLE 6–3. Correlations Between Crime Rates
and Percentages of Poor in SMSA's over 250,000
Population, 1970

Crime Rate	Correlation	r^2
Murder rate	+0.53	0.28
Rape rate	+0.21	0.04
Robbery rate	−0.06	0.004
Assault rate	+0.27	0.07
Burglary rate	+0.19	0.04
Larceny rate	+0.04	0.002
Auto theft rate	−0.11	0.01

The murder rate, or any other crime rate, can also be related to the percentage of people living in poverty through regression analysis. In the terminology of regression analysis, the murder rate is the *dependent variable*, and the percentage of poor is the *independent variable*. Through regression analysis, murder rates can be statistically predicted, within limits, by another variable—in this example, the percentage of the population living below the poverty income level.

Relating the two variables through regression analysis is done by fitting the following equation to the data:

$$Y_i = b_0 + b_1 X_i + e_i \tag{2}$$

where:

Y_i is the predicted murder rate for a given SMSA;

X_i is the percentage of poor in the same SMSA;

b_1 is the parameter representing the slope;

b_0 is the intercept of the equation; and

e_i is an error-of-deviation term.

In essence, a straight line is fitted through the data. If the percentage of poor is used as the scale along the horizontal axis and the murder rate is used on the vertical axis, then the crime rates for the SMSAs can be graphed as in Figure 6–9. The values spread across the graph but around the regression line.

Regression analysis is a technique used to find a line that can "best" represent the pattern formed by the data. The technique used to find this best fitting line is called the *ordinary-least-squares method*. This method finds the line that minimizes the square of the vertical deviations of the data from the line. The vertical deviation for any particular data point is the distance from the point to the line, the distance being measured vertically (see Figure 6–10). The deviations are squared so that positive and negative deviations are weighted equally and will not cancel out. The squared deviations are then summed to give a total measure of how far the points are away from the line. The ordinary-least-squares method finds the line that minimizes these squared deviations. The vertical deviations are the error terms in equation (2). The calculated error terms or deviations are called *residuals*.

When a line is fitted to the data, there are two parameters that are worth

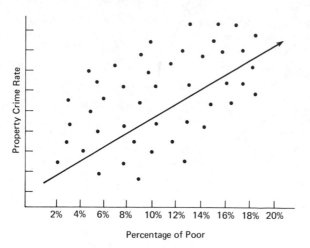

Figure 6–9. Regression line.

noting. A line has a slope and an intercept. In equation (2), the intercept, where the line crosses the vertical axis, is b_0. The slope or angle away from the horizontal axis is b_1.

The fitted equation does not have to be a straight line. More complex functional forms can be fitted to the data. Equations such as:

$$Y_i = b_0 + b_1 X^2 + e_i \qquad (3)$$
$$Y_i = b_0 + b_1 \log x_i + e_i \qquad (4)$$

can be used. In equation (3), the independent variable is squared, and the squared value is related to the dependent value. In equation (4), the log of the independent variable is calculated, and the log values are related to the dependent variables.

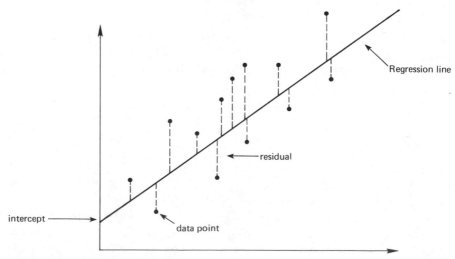

Figure 6–10. Regression line.

Multiple-Regression Analysis

In most criminological research, bivariate relationships, that is, relationships between two variables, tend to be weak. Multiple-regression analysis, which is the logical extension of the simple regression analysis described in the previous section, is the technique often used to explore complex, multivariable relationships. In multiple regression, several independent variables are used to explain or predict the dependent variable. Through multiple regression, it is possible to see if several variables, taken together, can explain or statistically describe the variance of the dependent variable. More complex relationships can be modeled by means of multiple-regression analysis.

The basic model used in multiple-regression analysis is just an extension of the two-variable regression analysis:

$$Y = b_0 + b_1 X_1 + b_2 X_2 + \ldots + b_n X_n + e \qquad (5)$$

where:

the dependent variable Y is modelled or explained by $X_1, X_2, \ldots, X_n$ independent variables;
the b_i's are the parameters of the model;
and e is the error term.

The model is linear; the parameters are joined in an additive fashion. The parameters have meanings similar to the parameters in simple linear regression: b_0 is the intercept; the b_i's are partial slopes. The equation is a line in a higher-dimension space or hyperspace. Although it is not possible to conceptualize such a line, it is the logical extension of adding variables to equation (2).

In correlational analysis and simple linear regression, r^2, the coefficient of determination, is a measure of association. It indicates what proportion of the variance in one variable can be explained by the variance in the other variable. In multiple-regression analysis, the comparable coefficient is R^2. This coefficient gives the proportion of the variance in the dependent variable that is explained by all the independent variables taken together. R^2 is a measure of how well the regression model fits the data.

Using the murder rates in all SMSAs in the United States as an example, it is possible to see the power of multiple-regression analysis. As can be seen in Table 6–4, several socioeconomic and demographic variables can be shown to be associated with the murder rates in SMSAs. None of the variables, however, individually explains more than 49 percent of the variance in the murder rate. The largest individual correlation is -0.70. When this value is squared, the resultant r^2 is only 0.49. But when the variables are taken together, they jointly explain 72 percent of the variance: 72 percent of the variance in murder rates in large SMSAs can be statistically explained by the variation in values of six variables, primarily variables measuring poverty and the presence of minorities.

Regression Assumptions. Regression analysis is a potentially powerful tool in criminology. It provides a technique for looking at the joint impact of many variables. Regression makes it possible to build more complex and realistic models.

111

TABLE 6–4. Regression Model for Rates in SMSAs; Correlations with Murder Rate

	r	b	R^2
Percentage in poverty	+0.53	0.51	0.72
Percentage of females in the work force	+0.13	0.30	
Percentage of blacks × percentage in poverty	+0.64	−0.21	
Log of the population	+0.18	4.60	
Percentage of household workers	+0.69	3.37	
Percentage nonblacks × mean school years completed for blacks	−0.70	−0.20	
(intercept)	—	0.51	

But regression analysis, as any statistical technique, is dependent on mathematical and statistical theory. When regression techniques are to be used, certain assumptions about the data have to be made. Violating these assumptions—that is, using the technique on data that do not meet the assumptions—may have serious consequences and may invalidate the result of the analysis.

Assumptions are primarily made about the behavior of the error term in the model. The errors are the deviations between the value for the dependent variable predicted by the regression equation and the actual values of the dependent variable. Three assumptions are made:

1. *Zero mean.* The error terms must have a mean or average value of zero.
2. *Common variance.* The variance that is a measure of spread or dispersion of the error term must be the same for all points on the regression line. The error term values or the spread of data around the regression line cannot be small at one place on the regression line and large somewhere else.
3. *Independence of Errors.* The error terms must be independent. There can be no correlation between errors.

If these assumptions are met by the data, then it can be shown, mathematically, that the ordinary-least-squares method described earlier produces the best linear unbiased estimators. In essence, the technique works well if the assumptions are met. Unfortunately, meeting these assumptions proves particularly difficult in time series regression. The difficulty in meeting these assumptions and some ways to circumvent the problems that arise are discussed in the following sections. Regression is a popular technique, but it cannot be used blindly with time series data.

Regression Analysis of Time Series

General Regression Model

Criminologists who explore historical patterns of crime and criminal justice usually want to use familiar tools. As a result, analytic studies often use the correlation and regression techniques. For example, the crime rates for a series of years might be correlated with the unemployment rates for the same years; or crime might be correlated with other economic indicators, such as the cost of a major food staple. Similarly, regression equations can be created where the crime rates for a series of years are regressed on social, economic, or demographic characteristics for those years. A model such as the following can be created:

$$Y_T = b_0 + b_1 X_T + e_T \tag{6}$$

where:

Y_T is the predicted crime rate for a given year;

X_T is the independent or explanatory variable, such as the unemployment rate: and

e_T is the error term.

Autocorrelation. Equation (6) may appear simple and straightforward, but several problems can arise. A common problem is that the error terms—what are usually called the *residuals*—are correlated. This correlation is called an *autocorrelation*, or *serial correlation*. Values of the residuals may be correlated with residual values for different or lagged time periods. For example, residual values may be correlated with residual values from a previous time period, and every residual value may be related to a preceding value. Residuals may be compared with any previous residual value.

Autocorrelations occur between adjacent residual values or residuals separated by many time periods. The existence of autocorrelations should be easy to accept. Consider a variable such as the percentage of people living below the poverty line. Year to year, this percentage will vary, but it is reasonable to expect that the percentage of people in poverty in one year is related to the percentage in poverty in the previous year.

When the residuals are correlated, ordinary-least-square regression techniques do not work well. The variance, or spread of the data, is underestimated. This means that estimates of how well the model fits are incorrect. The usual estimate of how well the model fits, R^2, *will tend to be inflated, or larger than it should be, when the residuals are correlated.* A model may appear to fit very well but, in fact, may be incorrect and may only appear to fit well because there is an autocorrelation. This is a serious problem in criminological research. Multiple regression is a popular technique, even with time series data. If the data are autocorrelated, the values for R^2 will be too high. Variables may be thought to be highly related to crime when, in fact, the relationship is only the result of misapplying a statistical technique.

Tests for Autocorrelation. Because autocorrelations can produce serious consequences statistically, it is important to check the residuals and to make adjustments when serial correlations are found. Patterns in residuals can be explored several ways. As with original time series, residuals may be inspected visually. Residuals can be graphed, and patterns, or deviations from randomness, can be checked.

Numeric techniques for checking residuals also exist. The best-known statistic is the Durbin-Watson statistic. It is specifically designed to test the autocorrelation for residuals lagged or separated by one time period.

Details of the Durbin-Watson statistic can be found in any introductory time-series text or econometric text. Good descriptions are found in Maddala (1977) and Fuller (1976).

Adjustments for Autocorrelations. If there are no significant autocorrelations in the data, then models using ordinary-least-squares regression are appropriate. If the residuals are correlated, then the data must be adjusted before ordinary-least-squares regression techniques can be used. A commonly used adjustment technique is to transform the data by means of first differences and then to use the first differences in the regression analysis. Transforming the data by means of first differences means taking each value for a particular variable and subtracting from it the value of the variable from the previous time period. By this method, yearly crime rates would be transformed from a time series of crime rates into a time series of increases or decreases in crime rates.

In mathematical notation, a time series model would be transformed as follows by means of first differences:

$$Y_T = b_0 + b_1 X_T + e_T \tag{7}$$
$$Y_T - Y_{T-1} = b_1 (X_T - X_{T-1}) + (e_T - e_{T-1}) \tag{8}$$

Equation (7) is the original time-series model. Equation (8) is the model equation when the data are transformed by first differences. Each value for the independent variable is replaced by the first difference value. These transformed values can then be used in regression analysis. Care must be taken in using first differences. If the original data were not autocorrelated, transformation by means of first differences may introduce autocorrelations into the data.

Lagged Models

When one is building a regression model to describe temporal crime patterns, it is sometimes theoretically necessary to consider a lagged model. In a lagged model, the current value of the dependent variable is related to previous values of the independent or explanatory variables. The use of lagged models can be seen in the relationship between crime and economic conditions. It may be hypothesized that any year's crime rate depends on economic conditions, not only in the current year but also in the previous years. Given this hypothesized relationship, the correct model would be:

$$Y_T = b_0 + b_1 X_T + b_2 X_{T-1} + . . . + b_{n+1} X_{T-n} + e_T \tag{9}$$

where:

Y_T is the predicted crime rate for a given year, T;
X_T is an independent variable measuring economic conditions;
$X_{T-1}, . . . , X_{T-n}$ are lagged values for the independent variable; and
$b_0, b_1, . . . , b_{n+1}$ are the intercept and slopes.

Equation (9) can be easily converted into:

$$Y_T = b_1 X_T + Y_{T-1} \tag{10}$$

where the lagged values of the independent variable are replaced by the lagged value of the dependent variable.

Equation (10) can be fitted by regression methods.

Trend Models

Methods for working with trend components in time series are complicated. A brief description will be given here. More detailed descriptions for the statistically sophisticated reader can be found in Fuller (1976), Maddala (1977), or Granger and Newbold (1977).

Trends may be estimated in time series data by means of a regression model where the dependent variable, usually a crime measure, is related to time. The functional form of this relationship can vary from simple to complex, but often it is some type of polynomial, such as:

$$Y = b_0 + b_1 T + b_2 T^2 + e_i \qquad (11)$$

where the time parameter T enters directly into the equation. If time is used as the independent variable, polynomials can be used to fit a trend line to the data.

Sometimes no simple polynomial can be found to fit the trend. In such situations, several polynomials may be grafted together to describe complicated trends (Figure 6–11).

An example of the fitting together of polynomials is found in a study of auto theft by Mansfield et al. (1974). The auto theft rates in Norway and the United States were analyzed by means of a socioeconomic model of crime occurrence that predicted that the rates would vary with the availability of cars to be stolen and the relative mix of professional and amateur thieves. The authors fitted together three regression lines to model the complex curvilinear pattern of auto thefts (Figure 6–12).

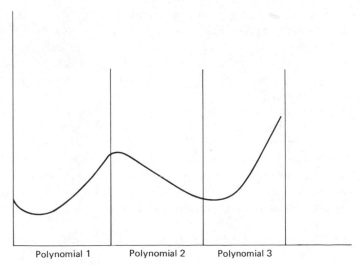

Polynomial 1   Polynomial 2   Polynomial 3

Figure 6–11. Grafted polynomials.

115

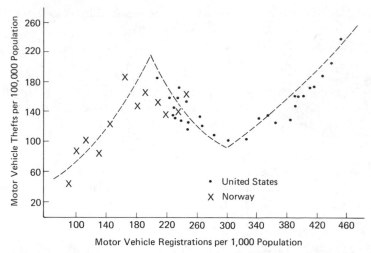

Figure 6–12. Actual and expected motor vehicle registrations and thefts, United States and Norway. [Source: Reprinted from *Social Forces* (Vol. 52, June, 1974). "A Socioeconomic Model for the Prediction of Societal Rates of Property Theft," by Roger Mansfield, Leroy C. Gould, and J. Zvi Namenwirth. Copyright © The University of North Carolina Press.]

Seasonal Models

Seasonal patterns may be explored in many ways. Several methods will be explained in this section: moving averages; seasonal adjustments through dummy variables; and spectral analysis. The methods vary in difficulty from moving averages, the simplest, to spectral analysis, the most difficult.

Moving Averages. The moving-averages method is a method of seasonal adjustment used by criminologists. Each temporal observation is replaced by the average of that observation and the surrounding observations. To create a three-month moving average from monthly data, one would replace each monthly value with the average value of that month and the preceding and succeeding months. For a five-month moving average, the central month's value would be averaged with two preceding and two succeeding months.

Replacing observations by moving averages smooths the data; that is, extreme values are reduced because they are replaced with averages that include surrounding, less extreme values. The more values included in the average, the smoother the resulting values. Moving averages can be used to reduce the effects of peaks and valleys in the data and to reduce seasonal effects. Moving averages may also be weighted to give more importance to the central point in the average. (For a fuller, yet straightforward description of moving averages and their uses, see Firth, 1977.)

Seasonal Adjustments. Seasonal patterns may be handled directly in regression analysis through the use of dummy variables. Dummy variables are categorical variables, variables that represent categories such as sex or race, not continuous variables, such as income or age. Dummy variables may be used directly in regression analysis to adjust the slope or intercept of the regression line for different seasons, in essence to create submodels within the overall model that describe seasonal patterns. Through their use, single estimations may be made for different seasons. Different regression lines can be generated for each season from one general equation. A complete description of the use of dummy variables can be found in any introductory regression text.

Spectral Analysis. Spectral analysis is a general type of statistical analysis used for analyzing time series data. Spectral analysis requires a fair degree of statistical sophistication, but the basic ideas can be presented here. Spectral analysis is used to break down a stationary time series, a time series without a trend, into uncorrelated cycles. Stated another way, spectral analysis involves two steps: first, a series has its trend removed; then, the detrended series is decomposed into a set of cyclic series, each series uncorrelated with the others. Each series has a different period of length. By looking at the presence or absence of cycles of different lengths, it is possible to tell what type of seasonal patterns exist in the data. The length of the cycles reflects the periodicity or seasonality in the data. A time series with a 12-month cycle would have one high period or time of the year. If a time series representing burglary rates were found to have one 12-month cycle with the high period in the summer, we would see seasonality in the data: increased burglary rates in the summer. If no cyclic components were found, then there would be no seasonal variation in the crime rates.

The use of spectral analysis is well illustrated by a study done by McPheters and Stronge (1974b). They examined the reported crimes in a city in Florida for a total of 144 months. They found seasonal cycles for robbery, burglary, and auto theft, but no seasonal cycle for assault. In particular, they found a strong six-month cycle for burglary, that is, two peak periods each year (one in the summer and one in the winter), perhaps reflecting the vulnerability of winter tourists in Florida as well as the usual summer vulnerability of residents. Spectral analysis proved to be an efficient and powerful technique for exploring temporal harmonics in this case, and probably it will eventually become a more general technique used by criminologists.

Chapter Summary

Criminologists work with temporal crime data in order to explore the forces that influence crime patterns. Often analysis consists only of looking at a graph representing the time series and trying to identify patterns visually. Sometimes the visual patterns are clear; sometimes they are obscure.

The analysis of temporal patterns involves looking for trends, discontinuities, peaks and valleys, and seasonality or cycles. These are trigger patterns that begin the search for explanation. When there are not too many gaps in the data, statistical techniques may be used to help uncover patterns. The most popular techniques are correlational analysis and regression analysis.

When statistical techniques are used with time series data, care must be taken.

117

The data must be examined for autocorrelations and transformed if the residuals are correlated. Making adjustments for autocorrelations is particularly important because the presence of autocorrelations will make regression models appear to fit the data well when, in fact, they do not.

But even with the difficulties of doing good time-series analysis, the intellectual rewards can be great. Time series data offer the criminologist an opportunity to explore the impact on crime of changes in the social structure, demographics, and political structures.

7
Modern Temporal Patterns in Crime

Introduction

The crime trends of the past quarter century are extremely disquieting. America, Canada, and England have all experienced massive increases in the known levels of crimes of all sorts. Some components of the total increase, of course, involve rising levels of minor offenses, which nearly everyone agrees are generated as by-products of rising levels of some normal legal behavior such as driving. By volume, traffic offenses represent the most serious set of known offenses in both Canada and England (Hagan, 1977; Home Office, 1979, p. 71; McDonald, 1979, p. 224). Yet the levels of very serious crimes, such as murder, robbery, and burglary, have also increased enormously. The recent trends in serious crime deserve examination and explanation.

Criminologists debate whether the magnitudes of the increases in crime recorded over the past twenty-five years are more apparent than real, that is, whether they may be the product of improved police record-keeping and a greater willingness on the part of citizens to report criminal events. Our survey of the source data about crime suggests that the general trends found in the recorded crime rates in recent years are reasonably accurate indexes of the trends in the incidence of serious crimes.[1] In any case, policymakers in all three countries have reacted to the increase in reported crime as real and threatening. America has seen a succession of presidential commissions on crime and violence; massive growth in both academic criminology and applied criminal justice; and a massive flow of governmental resources into the criminal justice sector at the expense of other areas of social expenditure. Canada and England have experienced much the same: royal commissions on various aspects of crime and criminal justice; substantial efforts at criminal justice reform; a growing criminological establishment; and an increasing flow of pub-

---

[1] See Chapters 2–5 generally. Chapter 5 in particular deals with the fit among the three major sources of quantitative data about crime and criminals: official statistics, victimization statistics, and self-report statistics.

lic funds into crime control. Because policymakers have taken recent crime trends so seriously, it is important to examine those trends.

Both policymakers and academic criminologists tend to react to crime patterns as historically unique and temporally isolated, and to search for solutions without temporal perspective. The crime patterns of any given moment are part of some recent temporal pattern, and that recent pattern is part of a much longer one. The long-term patterns of crime will be considered in Chapter 8. This chapter outlines the trends in serious crime in America, Canada, and England since 1960; and presents some tentative explanations for the trends.

Trends Since 1960 in the United States, Canada, and England

The United States

The trend in reported crime in the United States since World War II has been upward (Figure 7–1). The rates for both violent and property offenses have been rising rapidly. In 1960 there were approximately 161 violent crimes per 100,000 people. In 1980 the violent crime rate was 581 crimes per 100,000 people—a massive increase. Property crimes have increased at a similarly large rate. In 1960 the property crime rate was 1,726 property crimes per 100,000 people. By 1980 the rate had risen to 5,319 property crimes per 100,000 population. Reported crime is rising.

The violent offenses include murder, forcible rape, aggravated assault, and robbery. The property offenses include burglary, larceny–theft, and motor vehicle theft. From 1970 to 1980, violent offenses increased 60 percent, and property offenses increased 42 percent. For a slightly different but longer time period, 1960–1980, which gives a better perspective on the increase, the rate for violent offenses increased 260 percent, and the rate for property offenses increased 198 percent (Federal Bureau of Investigation (FBI), 1972, 1975, 1980). (These rates have been adjusted for the increase in population during the same period; they do not merely reflect population growth.)

Violent Crimes

As already stated, reported violent crime has been increasing in the United States since World War II. Each individual violent offense has a different pattern, and subclassifications within each offense have unique patterns worth exploring. Generally, all reported violent crimes have been increasing.

Murder[2] and Aggravated Assault. Murder and aggravated assault fit together conceptually. They are separated, both legally and factually, by the ultimate quality of the harm done to the victim. Whether a serious assault turns out to be murder

---

[2] We are using *murder* here as a convenient shorthand for the more cumbersome, but more precise, "murder and nonnegligent manslaughter" in the *Uniform Crime Reports* (UCR).

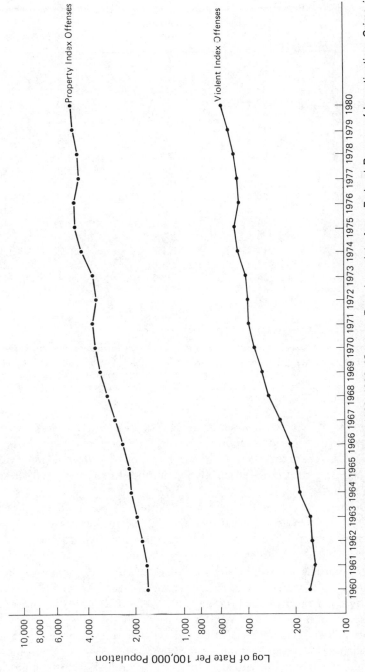

Figure 7–1. Trends in American crime rates, 1960–1980. [Source: Based on data from Federal Bureau of Investigation, *Crime in the United States*. Washington, D.C.: U.S. Government Printing Office, 1972, 1975, 1979, 1980.]

121

TABLE 7–1. Violent Crimes Known to American Police, 1960–1980 (Rate per 100,000 Population)

Year	Murder	Aggravated Assault	"Murderous Attack"	Rape	Robbery
1960	5.1	86.1	91.2	9.6	60.1
1961	4.8	85.7	90.5	9.4	58.3
1962	4.6	88.6	93.2	9.4	59.7
1963	4.6	92.4	97.0	9.4	61.8
1964	4.9	106.2	111.1	11.2	68.2
1965	5.1	111.3	116.4	12.1	71.7
1966	5.6	120.3	125.9	13.2	80.8
1967	6.2	130.2	136.4	14.0	102.8
1968	6.9	143.8	150.7	15.9	131.8
1969	7.3	154.5	161.8	18.5	148.4
1970	7.9	164.8	172.7	18.7	172.1
1971	8.6	178.8	187.4	20.5	188.0
1972	9.2	188.8	198.0	22.5	180.7
1973	9.4	200.5	209.9	24.5	183.1
1974	9.8	215.8	225.6	26.2	209.3
1975	9.6	227.4	237.0	26.3	218.2
1976	8.8	228.7	237.5	26.4	195.8
1977	8.8	241.5	250.3	29.1	187.1
1978	9.0	255.9	264.9	30.8	191.3
1979	9.7	279.1	288.8	34.5	212.1
1980	10.2	290.6	300.8	36.4	243.5

SOURCE: Federal Bureau of Investigation (Annual). *Crime in the United States* (Washington, D.C.: Government Printing Office [Uniform Crime Reports] 1980), N. Parisi, M. R. Gottfredson, M. J. Hindelang, and T. J. Flanagan (Annual), *Sourcebook of Criminal Justice Statistics* (Washington, D.C.: Department of Justice, 1978).

or aggravated assault is often a function of the quality and the speed of medical care, or of random chance in inflicting a wound. In fact, it can easily be argued that the most reasonable crime rate to investigate from a criminological viewpoint is a rate composed of the combination of the number of murders and the number of aggravated assaults.

In 1980, there were 23,040 murders reported to the police in the United States (FBI, 1980). Of these murders, 72 percent were cleared by arrests. In the same year, there were 654,960 aggravated assaults reported to the police (FBI, 1980), a ratio of 28 to 1. Murder, fortunately, is a relatively infrequent offense.

Although murder and aggravated assault can be combined into one crime category, there are differences between the crimes. One difference can be seen in the choice of weapon used in the attack (Table 7–2). Guns are the overwhelming choice of weapon in murders and handguns lead other types of guns. Guns are easily the most lethal weapon. It could be argued that the use of different weapons is the major distinction between murder and aggravated assault. (It would also be possible to argue that those individuals with the more lethal intent choose the more lethal weapon.)

The choice of weapons may be changing. Wolfgang (1966) studied all criminal homicides reported to the police in Philadelphia between the beginning of 1948

TABLE 7–2. Choice of Weapons in the United States, 1980
(in Percentages)

Weapon	Murder	Aggravated Assault
Handgun	50 ⎫	
Rifle	5 ⎬ 62%	24
Shotgun	7 ⎭	
Cutting or stabbing	19	22
Other weapons	13	27
Hands, fists, feet, etc.	6	27

SOURCE: Adapted from Federal Bureau of Investigation (Annual), *Crime in the United States* (Washington, D.C.: Government Printing Office [Uniform Crime Reports], 1980).

and the end of 1952. He explored the basic setting and circumstances of the crime, the relationship between the offender and the victim, and the aftermath of the crime, that is, whether it was solved. In looking at choice of weapon, Wolfgang found that stabbing was the most frequent means of death (p. 84).

Studies, of later time periods, in Houston by Pokorny (1965) and in Chicago by Voss and Hepburn (1968) revealed a different pattern: more shooting deaths than stabbing deaths (Table 7–3). Pokorny's and Voss and Hepburn's studies were for different cities, in different regions of the country, and for different time periods. It is impossible to sort out the effect of temporal change from regional variation. However, the data at least point to the possibility of a change in choice of weapons.[3]

The murder rate per 100,000 population in the United States has doubled since 1960. The aggravated-assault rate during the same period has tripled, with

TABLE 7–3. Changing Choice of Weapons in the United States (in Percentages)

	Philadelphia 1948– 1951	Houston 1958– 1961	Chicago 1965	Northeast 1975	North Central 1975	South 1975	West 1975
Stabbing	38.8	25.4	27.9	26.7	14.2	14.9	19.0
Shooting	33.0	65.4	49.5	51.3	70.7	72.7	59.0
Beating	21.8	5.0	14.7	—	—	—	—
Other	6.4	4.1	7.9	22.0	15.1	12.4	22.0

SOURCE: Data adapted from M. E. Wolfgang, *Patterns in Criminal Homicide* (New York: John Wiley, 1966); A. D. Pokorny,"A Comparison of Homicide in Two Cities" *Journal of Criminal Law, Criminology and Police Science*, 56(1965):479–487; H. L. Voss and J. Hepburn, "Patterns in Criminal Homicide," *Journal of Criminal Law, Criminology and Police Science*, 59(1968):449–508; Federal Bureau of Investigation (Annual), *Crime in the United States* (Washington, D.C.: Government Printing Office [Uniform Crime Report], 1975).

[3] An earlier study of homicide in the United States done by Brearly, *Homicide in the United States* (1932), showed a high use of guns in murders. It is possible that Wolfgang's study is an anomaly.

123

the aggravated-assault rate leading the murder rate in the speed of the increase (Table 7–1; Figure 7–2).

Although the official rates for murder are probably quite close to the actual murder rates, the official rates for aggravated assault probably understate the actual rates. Victimization survey data suggest that police statistics reflect about half of the aggravated assaults that occur. Over the course of the national victimization surveys sponsored by the U.S. Justice Department, (1973–1980), the reporting rate for aggravated assault, including attempts, averaged around 50–54 percent and remained statistically stable from year to year (Bureau of Justice Statistics, 1981, 1982). About 60 percent of aggravated assaults with injury were reported to the police, but only about 50 percent of the attempts were reported. (Bureau of Justice Statistics, 1981). Reporting rates for simple assaults and assaults without serious injury or threat of serious injury were substantially lower, only about 36 percent of offenses reported in the victimization surveys were reported to the police.

Rape. There has been a dramatic increase in reported rape since 1960. The Uniform Crime Report (UCR) rape rate increased from 9.6 per 100,000 population in 1960 to 36.4 per 100,000 population in 1980. National victimization-survey data suggest even higher levels of rape, ranging from a low of 80 admitted rape victimizations per 100,000 population aged twelve or older in 1976, to a high rate of 110 in 1979. Both data sets suggest that the growth in known rape rates leveled, or perhaps declined, in the mid-1970s but have continued to rise since 1977.

Although statistical measures of all crime are, to some extent, unreliable, rape statistics may well be the least reliable. Police statistics clearly underestimate the number of rapes. Many women are reluctant to report rapes to the police. Some victims are afraid of reprisal, some are humiliated and embarrassed by the experience, and some do not wish to experience the humiliation and harassment that the criminal justice system frequently imposes on a rape complainant.

Even the victimization surveys probably underestimate the number of rapes. Victims may be as reluctant to mention a sexual victimization to a survey interviewer as they are to call the police. Further, rape is a relatively rare offense. Because of its rarity, few rapes are actually reported by survey respondents. Estimates gained through a sampling procedure have broad confidence intervals; that is, the sample estimates fall somewhere within a very wide range of possible correct estimates. It is not possible to tell whether the best estimates of the real situation are substantially higher or substantially lower than the estimates given.

Estimates of the proportion of rape victimizations reported to the police during the 1970s range from a high of 58.4 percent in 1977 to a low of 41.5 percent in 1980. These estimates were calculated from a sample survey and, because rape rates are relatively small compared to the sample size, it is not possible to say that any apparent variations in the reporting rate from year to year have been due to actual changes in reporting behavior rather than to sampling.

Robbery. Robbery is the last of the index offenses classified as a violent offense by the U.S. Federal Bureau of Investigation (FBI). Robbery rates have increased from 60 per 100,000 population in 1960 to 243 per 100,000 population in 1980,

124

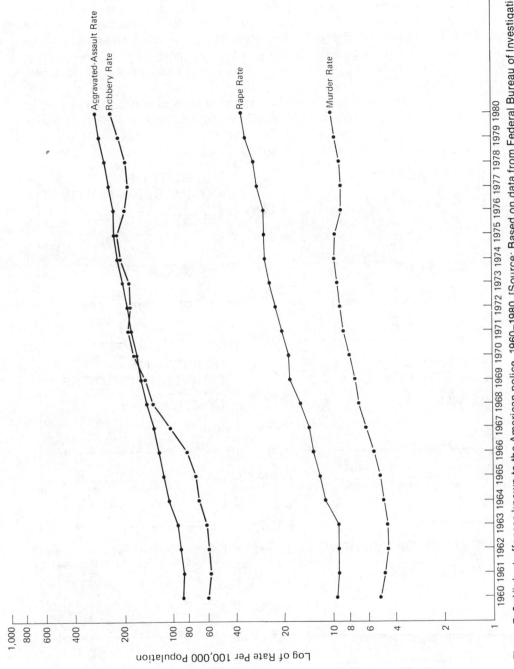

Figure 7–2. Violent offenses known to the American police, 1960–1980. [Source: Based on data from Federal Bureau of Investigation, *Crime in the United States.* Washington, D.C.: U. S. Government Printing Office, 1972, 1975, 1979, 1980.]

125

an increase of around 300 percent (see Table 7–1). It is a particularly interesting offense to study. Robbery is a complex crime category. For example, where people are robbed varies greatly: people may be robbed in the street, as in a strong-arm robbery (purse snatching, which seems much like robbery, is classified as theft by the FBI); people may be robbed in their residences (a burglar who encounters the owner of a home and takes goods from him or her has committed a robbery); people may be robbed in places of business, and the characteristics of places of businesses are highly varied.

As can be seen in Figure 7–3, the pattern of change in robbery rates varies over the possible class of targets, with rates for convenience stores (such as Seven-

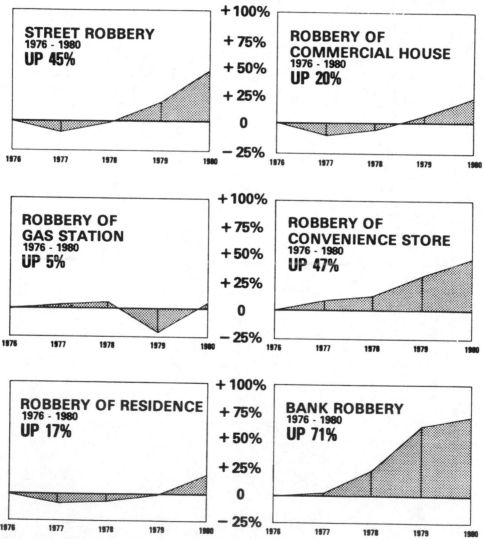

Figure 7–3. Robbery rates in the United States, 1976–1980. [Source: Federal Bureau of Investigation, *Crime in the United States—1980.* Washington, D.C.: U. S. Government Printing Office, 1981.]

126

Eleven stores, Mac's or other corner grocery stores) and banks increasing the most. Although robbery is classified as a crime of violence, and obviously the threat of violence or actual violence exists in the crime, many of the characteristics of robbery are similar to those of property offenses: a person is robbed for money or property; the object of the crime is financial gain, and the means are potentially violent. The rapid rise after 1970 in convenience store and bank robberies makes more sense if the crime is viewed as a property offense. The number of convenience stores, often open late at night or on days when other stores are closed, and branch banks has increased at a rate that far exceeded population growth in the period. Although the robbery rates for these types of businesses have increased dramatically when the rates are calculated on a population base (say, rates per 100,000 population), the rates appear to be increasing less dramatically, if at all, when the rates are calculated on the basis of the number of convenience stores or banks (rates per 1,000 banks or per 1,000 convenience stores, for example).

Support for the idea that robbery is basically a property offense can be found in diverse types of research. Capone and Nichols (1976), working with the locations of the homes of robbers and the target locations, found that the spatial distribution of robberies of chain stores in Miami, Florida, followed a pattern similar to that of shopping behavior. Conklin (1972) also lent support to the idea that robbery is basically a property offense in his research developing typologies of robbers. Building on the work of McClintock and Gibson (1961), he developed a typology that includes (1) the professional robber, who commits offenses in an organized, systematic fashion; (2) the opportunistic robber, who commits offenses in an impulsive manner when the opportunity arises; and (3) the addict robber, who commits the offense when other forms of property offense are not possible. Letkemann (1973) also presented the picture of robbery as a property offense.

Reported robberies have increased rapidly over the past two decades, with two temporary leveling points. In the case of business victimizations, the official statistics accord well with the victimization surveys: about 90 percent of all business robberies reported in the victimization surveys are reported to the police (Parisi, et al, 1978). Commercial robberies can be studied through official statistics with great confidence because the reporting rates are high.

Property Crimes

The property crime category includes burglary, larceny—theft, and motor vehicle theft. Reported property offenses have been increasing rapidly in the last fifteen to twenty years (see Figure 7—4 and Table 7—4).

In 1978 arson was added to the list of Index offenses. In 1980 law enforcement agencies servicing 85 percent of the population were reporting arson offenses. The act of reporting arson cannot yet be considered a sufficiently reliable source to include arson statistics in overall property crime patterns; nevertheless, this topic will be discussed briefly with other property offenses.

Burglary. Reported burglaries increased 228 percent between 1960 and 1980. Robbery was the only offense that, according to official statistics, increased at a greater rate. There were over three million reported burglaries in the United States

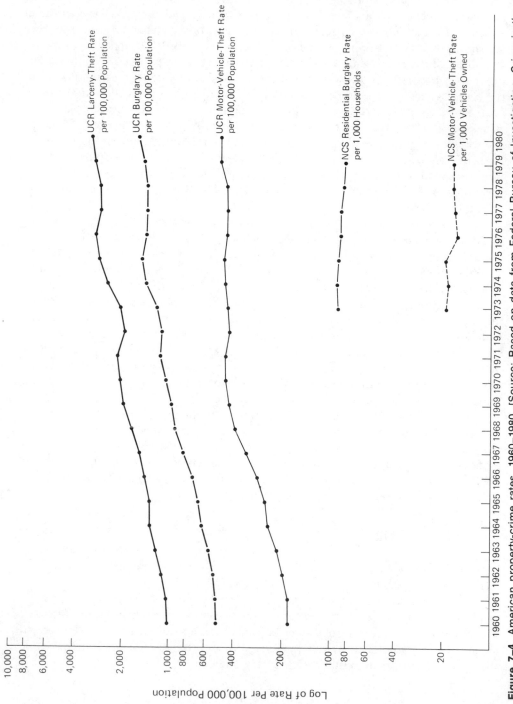

Figure 7–4. American property-crime rates, 1960–1980. [Source: Based on data from Federal Bureau of Investigation, *Crime in the United States.* Washington, D.C.: U. S. Government Printing Office, 1972, 1975, 1979, 1980.]

TABLE 7–4. Property Crimes Known to American Police, 1960–1980
(Rate per 100,000 Population)

Year	Burglary	Larceny–Theft	Motor Vehicle Theft
1960	508.6	1034.7	183.0
1961	518.9	1045.4	183.6
1962	535.2	1124.8	197.4
1963	576.4	1219.1	216.6
1964	634.7	1315.5	247.4
1965	662.7	1329.3	256.8
1966	721.0	1442.9	286.9
1967	826.6	1575.8	334.1
1968	932.3	1746.6	393.0
1969	984.1	1930.9	436.2
1970	1084.9	2079.3	456.8
1971	1163.5	2145.5	459.8
1972	1140.8	1993.6	426.1
1973	1222.5	2071.9	442.6
1974	1437.7	2489.5	462.2
1975	1525.9	2804.8	469.4
1976	1439.4	2921.3	446.1
1977	1410.9	2729.9	447.6
1978	1423.7	2743.9	454.7
1979	1499.1	2988.4	498.5
1980	1668.2	3156.3	494.6

SOURCE: 1980 data calculated from Federal Bureau of Investigation (Annual), *Crime in the United States* (Washington, D.C.: Government Printing Office [Uniform Crime Reports], 1980); Data for other years from Federal Bureau of Investigation (Annual), *Crime in the United States* (Washington, D.C.: Government Printing Office [Uniform Crime Reports], 1979); N. Parisi, M. R. Gottfredson, M. J. Hindelang and T. J. Flanagan (Annual), *Sourcebook of Criminal Justice Statistics* (Washington, D.C.: Department of Justice, 1978).

in 1975. Between 1975 and 1977, the number of reported burglaries dropped slightly, but since 1977, reported burglaries have again increased substantially.

Burglary is a very common offense, even more common than the police statistics show. Victimization survey results indicate that in 1980 over 6.8 million households were burglarized. In 1976, the last year businesses were surveyed, about 1.5 million businesses were burglarized. About half of commercial and residential victimizations were not reported to the police. The pattern of reporting, however, is interesting. Reporting drops off for attempts and entry without force and is greatest for forced entry and commercial crimes. Crimes with the greatest loss and the greatest apparent threat are reported more often.

Victimization data on residential burglary suggest that victimizations per 1,000 households have declined steadily since 1974. Victimization rates are calculated on the number of households. This base is not comparable to the population base used for UCR calculations; moreover, UCR burglary rates contain data for commercial burglaries. The National Crime Survey (NCS) victimization surveys have not reported commercial burglary victimizations since 1976. Although the rate per 1,000 households is probably a more appropriate base rate for considering residential burglary than a rate per 100,000 population, the number of households increased far faster than the population in the 1970s. The two available data bases show very different trends: the UCR shows a plateau in the mid-1970s, followed by rapidly rising burglary rates; NCS victimizations showed declining residential burglary rates through 1979.

Burglary is a crime that affects all income groups and all races. It is a ubiquitous crime. There does not appear to be any strong racial bias in reporting patterns. If anything, there is a tendency toward lower reporting rates by whites. There is, however, an income bias, with lower-income households reporting a smaller proportion of burglaries to the police. The income bias may reflect differential patterns of insurance coverage.

Larceny–Theft. Another ubiquitous crime is larceny or theft. According to official statistics, larceny is the most common index offense, with a rate of 3,156 per 100,000 people in 1980. Larceny has increased rapidly since 1960; 1980 rates were three times those of twenty years earlier. The pattern of increase for larceny is similar to the pattern for burglary. Rates increased rapidly from 1960 until 1972, when they dipped slightly. Rates continued to climb from 1973 until 1976, when they dipped a second time. They have started rising again.

Larceny is a broad crime category and includes such diverse events as shoplifting, bicycle theft, and theft from buildings. The major characteristic of the crimes included in this category is that they involve no force, violence, or fraud. (Purse snatching is a borderline event and perhaps more logically belongs in the robbery category.)

The crimes included in this category are generally less serious and, based on victimization survey results, are poorly reported. Of the personal victimizations for larceny, about 70 percent are not reported to the police. The reporting rate is greater for larceny over $50 than for larceny under $50. In fact, 84 percent of the unreported larcenies in 1973 were for thefts of less than $50 (Skogan, 1977b). The major reasons given for not reporting, in victimization surveys, were "It wasn't worth the effort," "It was unimportant," or "It was inconvenient."

Motor Vehicle Theft. Motor vehicle theft is the last index-crime category for which data are available over an extended period. It includes all thefts of motor vehicles—for joyriding as well as for resale. Completed motor-vehicle thefts are reported to the police at a very high rate. Based on victimization survey results, around 85–90 percent of all completed thefts are reported to the police. This is to be expected: most motor vehicles are insured, and a police report is a necessary component of an insurance claim under the terms of most policies. Official statistics on motor vehicle theft may be used as a relatively accurate measure of the volume of that crime as well as an index of temporal trends.

The trend in officially reported motor-vehicle theft has been upward. In 1980, there were over one million cars reported stolen, with a theft rate of around 500 crimes per 100,000 people. The rate increased 170 percent between 1960 and 1980. As for burglary and larceny, there was a slight decrease in the rate in 1972 and again in 1976–1977. Since 1970, the rate of motor vehicle thefts appears to have stabilized around a fixed mean; that is, the year-to-year figures vary, but the upward trend is no longer there.

Arson. Arson is defined by the Uniform Crime Reporting program as "Any willful or malicious burning or attempt to burn, with or without intent to defraud, a dwelling house, public building, motor vehicle or aircraft, personal property of another, etc." (UCR, 1980). It was added to the list of index offenses in 1978. In 1980 police jurisdictions servicing about 85 percent of the population in the United States were reporting arson to the Uniform Crime Reports. Over 115,000 arson offenses were reported in 1980. Of these offenses, 31 percent were against residential buildings and 22 percent against motor vehicles. About 6 percent of arson attacks were against public buildings and 1 percent against industrial sites. The average damage was $7,745, but the range of damage varied greatly by target. The average reported damage ranged from a high of about $73,000 for industrial sites to $2,500 for motor vehicles (UCR, 1980).

As with other index offenses, arrest data suggest that arson is primarily a male offense. However, of all offenses it has the lowest proportion of black offenders (20 percent) and the highest proportion of persons under 15 years of age arrested. It appears to be a white, juvenile offense primarily directed at residential property.

Summary of U.S. Trends Since 1960

Official statistics show a massive increase in crime since 1960. The increase in crime far outstrips the increase in population. The increases have occurred for all the index offenses, for both property and violent crimes. Of the index offenses, the increase has been most rapid for robbery.

Canada

The Canadian trends in officially reported crime are similar to the trends in the United States. Since 1962, the beginning of the current system of crime reporting, the major violent and property offenses have increased over 100 percent.

The criminal code in Canada, obviously, is different from the codes in the various States, but all are English derivative and consequently are similar to each other. The major violent-crime categories used by Statistics Canada are criminal homicide, attempted murder, manslaughter, wounding, assaults, and robbery. The major property offenses are breaking and entering, theft of a motor vehicle, theft over $200, and theft under $200.

Crime categories are formed by a grouping together of offenses within the criminal code. The categories are similar to categories used in the United States, except for attempted murder, which is reported separately in Canada, whereas it is included in the aggravated-assault totals in the United States, and theft, which is divded into crimes under and over $200 in Canada.[4] There is no division of theft sttistics by value lost in the United States.

---

[4] The breakpoint used to be $50, but it was changed as the effective purchasing power of $50 decreased.

131

In Canada, official statistics are the only major data source available for studying crime patterns. To date, the use of victim surveys has been limited. Canada conducted its first national victimization survey during 1981–1982. It will be some time, however, before Canadian victimization data provide a viable alternative measure of crime.

Violent Crimes

Based on official statistics, Violent crime increased in Canada from the early part of the 1960s until the mid-1970s. From 1962 to 1975, the criminal homicide rate increased 121 percent; the attempted murder rate increased 460 percent; and the wounding and assault rate went up 185 percent. The rape rate increased in number by 161 percent, and the robbery rate increased 252 percent. The rates for all of these crimes leveled, and even declined slightly, in the mid-1970s. But the rates for rape, robbery, and wounding and assault began to rise again at the end of the 1970's. The 1980 rates for these crimes were the highest ever recorded (see Figure 7–5 and Table 7–5).

Although the "official" rates have been increasing, there are no victimization

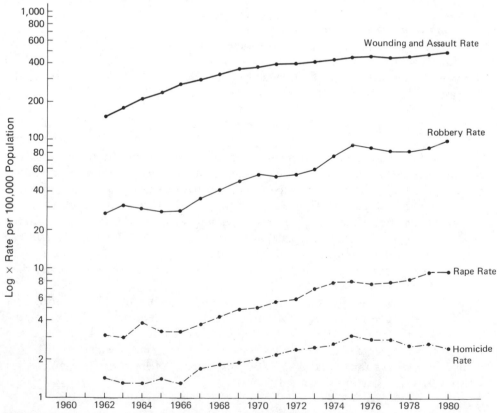

Figure 7–5. Canadian violent-offense trends, 1962–1980. [Source: Based on annual data from Statistics Canada, *Crime and Traffic Enforcement Statistics*. Ottawa: Queen's Printer, (Catalogue 85–205), 1962–1980.]

TABLE 7–5. Violent Crimes Known to Canadian Police, 1962–1980 (Rate per 100,000 Population)

Year	Homicide	Rape	Wounding and Assault	Robbery
1962	1.4	3.1	156.5	26.6
1963	1.3	2.9	179.7	31.1
1964	1.3	3.9	214.1	29.4
1965	1.4	3.3	231.0	28.4
1966	1.3	3.3	272.3	28.5
1967	1.7	3.8	295.3	35.4
1968	1.8	4.3	328.4	40.5
1969	1.9	4.9	351.3	47.8
1970	2.0	5.1	370.9	54.6
1971	2.2	5.7	393.5	52.1
1972	2.4	5.9	398.0	54.2
1973	2.5	7.2	414.5	59.6
1974	2.6	8.1	431.5	75.5
1975	3.1	8.1	446.9	93.4
1976	2.9	7.9	454.0	86.8
1977	2.9	8.0	446.1	83.6
1978	2.6	8.5	452.7	83.7
1979	2.7	9.7	477.0	88.3
1980	2.5	9.7	489.7	102.3

SOURCE: 1962–1975, data prepared by Ezzat Fattah, Department of Criminology, Simon Fraser University; 1976–1980, *Crime and Traffic Enforcement Statistics*, 1980.

surveys to help sort out the reliability of the data. In a situation such as this, it is probably safest to look at the changing patterns of criminal homicide. All logical and empirical evidence points to homicide as being a well-reported offense.

Homicide. Homicide is a rare event in Canada. For example, 707 homicides were recorded by the police in 1977. The homicide rate was 2.9 per 100,000 population, about one third the rate in the United States. Homicide rates peaked at 3.1 per 100,000 population in 1975 and remained high through 1977. Between 1975 and 1980, Canadian homicide rates dropped 19 percent, to 2.5 per 100,000.

Canadians and Americans have different weapon preferences when they kill. In the United States, guns of one type or another are the overwhelming choice of weapon (over 60 percent in 1980). Beating (death by hands, fists, feet, and so on) is relatively rare (6 percent of deaths in 1980). In Canada, guns are still the major weapon used, but beating is a far more frequent cause of death than in the United States. In analyzing all recorded homicides in Canada between 1961 and 1970, Jayewardene (1975) found, among other things, that the methods used for killing were shooting, beating, and then stabbing, in order preference (see Table 7–6).

In another study, done by Tardiff (1967) in Montreal, the choice of weapon more closely corresponded to the pattern in the United States (see Table 7–7). Of the deaths, 56 percent were caused by shooting; 16 percent involved knifing; and

TABLE 7–6. Methods Used for Killing, Canada, 1961–1970 (Percentages)

Shooting	45.1
Beating	23.0
Stabbing	17.1
Strangling	5.7
Suffocating	1.3
Drowning	1.2
Arson	2.6
Other	3.8
Not known	0.2

SOURCE: Adapted from C. H. S. Jaywardene, "The Nature of Homicide: Canada 1961–1970" in R. A. Silverman and J. J. Teevan (Eds.), *Crime in Canadian Society* (Toronto: Butterworth, 1975), p. 298.

2 percent were the result of physical attacks. However, the number of murders studied was small.

More interestingly, Tardiff also looked at the choice of weapon in assaults.[5] The choice of weapon differed for assaults as it did in the United States. Murder or homicide involved firearms more frequently than assaults. Assaults can be distinguished from homicide in part by the type of weapon used in the attack.

Property Crimes

Officially reported property crimes have also been increasing since the early 1960s (Figure 7–6; Table 7–8). The breaking-and-entry rate tripled between 1962 and 1980. The combined rate of thefts over and under $200 increased 195 percent

TABLE 7–7. Choice of Weapon, Montreal, 1964 (Percentages)

	Homicide	Assault
Firearms	56	11
Knife	19	37
Physical	2	23
Other	21	29
None	2	0

SOURCE: G. Tardif, "Les délits de violence à Montreal;" paper read at the 5th Research Conference on Delinquency and Criminality, Société de Criminologie du Québec, Montreal, 1967.

[5] Although Tardiff did not state it explicitly, his category of assaults must include woundings as well as simple assault.

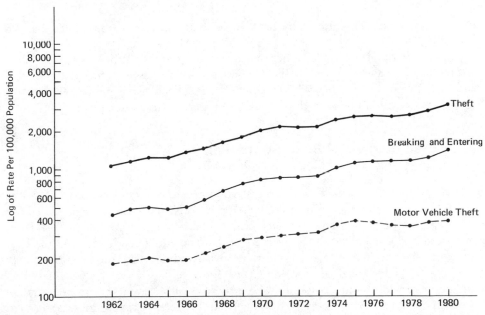

Figure 7–6. Canadian property offense trends, 1962–1980. [Source: Based on annual data from Statistics Canada, *Crime and Traffic Enforcement Statistics*. Ottawa: Queen's Printer, (Catalogue 85–205), 1962–1980.]

TABLE 7–8. Property Crimes Known to Canadian Police, 1962–1980 (Rate per 100,000 Population)

Year	Breaking and Entering	Theft	Motor Vehicle Theft
1962	441.8	1082.9	180.1
1963	497.9	1162.3	196.2
1964	504.0	1231.8	206.8
1965	491.4	1211.1	193.8
1966	510.3	1330.6	198.1
1967	585.9	1441.9	220.3
1968	699.9	1604.3	250.6
1969	769.9	1742.6	284.4
1970	834.4	2013.3	295.4
1971	873.8	2162.8	305.5
1972	875.0	2124.4	322.6
1973	896.3	2163.3	324.0
1974	1039.6	2401.0	371.1
1975	1143.2	2576.0	398.2
1976	1161.1	2609.4	379.2
1977	1162.0	2579.5	361.7
1978	1185.9	2671.7	354.0
1979	1252.3	2898.6	386.3
1980	1462.3	3195.1	392.8

SOURCE: 1962–1975 data prepared by Ezzat Fattah, Department of Criminology, Simon Fraser University; 1976–1980, *Crime and Traffic Enforcement Statistics,* 1980.

135

in eighteen years. The rate of motor vehicle thefts almost doubled between 1962 and 1980.

Against this backdrop of a general increase in property crime rates, it is worth noting that the increase has not been linear. Sharp increases occurred in the early and late 1960s and in the early and late 1970s. There were periods in the mid-1960s and in the mid-1970s during which property crime rates plateaued.

Comparison of U.S. and Canadian Crime Patterns

It is possible to make some cautious comparisons between recent American and Canadian crime rates. The Solicitor General of Canada has constructed comparable indexes of violent and property crimes using the categories and data in the American and Canadian uniform crime reports. The American Violent Crime Index is based on the UCR categories murder, manslaughter, aggravated assault, rape, and robbery. The Canadian Violent Crime Index is based on the Canadian UCR categories capital murder, noncapital murder, manslaughter, attempted murder, wounding, rape, and robbery. The American Property Crime Index is based on burglary and motor vehicle theft. The Canadian Property Crime Index is based on the categories breaking and entering, and theft of a motor vehicle[6] (Solicitor General of Canada, *Statistics Handbook,* 1977).

As can be seen from Table 7–9, official rates for these serious crimes are higher in the United States than in Canada. The difference is greater for violent offenses than for property offenses. The American violent-crime rate is four times the Canadian rate. In Canada, violent offenses account for about 6 percent of the total, and in the United States, violent offenses account for 20 percent of the total. In both countries, violent crimes have increased more rapidly than property offenses in recent years, and in both countries, the patterns of increase have been similar.

Based on aggregate official data (that is, crime reports to which the police respond), the United States has a much more serious crime problem than Canada. The United States experiences more crimes per capita, and a larger proportion of this crime is violent. The actual difference between the two countries may be even greater if the differentially higher reporting rates found by Waller and Okihiro (1978) in a burglary victimization survey of Toronto can be generalized to other crimes and to the rest of Canada. The American "dark figure" may be much larger than the Canadian. When the Canadian victimization surveys undertaken by the Solicitor General are reported, better comparisons will be possible.

England and Wales

English crime trends are generally similar to those found in the United States and in Canada. The levels of violent and property crime have been increasing since the early 1960s, and the rate of increase in crime is far greater than the rate of

---

[6] Theft is omitted because definitional changes in the early 1970s made the American and Canadian figures noncomparable.

TABLE 7–9. Comparison of Serious Offenses in the United States and Canada

Crime Index Offenses	United States		Canada	
	Number	Rate*	Number	Rate
1964 *Total*	2,050,220	1,073	144,777	751
Violent	364,220	191	7,623	40
Property	1,686,000	882	137,154	711
1966 *Total*	2,401,480	1,228	149,500	747
Violent	430,180	220	7,713	39
Property	1,971,300	1,008	141,787	708
1968 *Total*	3,237,510	1,624	207,729	1,004
Violent	595,010	298	11,122	54
Property	2,642,500	1,325	196,607	950
1970 *Total*	3,872,220	1,905	255,594	1,200
Violent	738,820	364	15,077	71
Property	3,133,400	1,542	240,517	1,129
1972 *Total*	4,097,600	1,968	277,076	1,270
Violent	834,900	401	15,751	72
Property	3,262,700	1,567	261,325	1,197
1974 *Total*	4,990,920	2,361	338,682	1,509
Violent	974,720	461	22,011	98
Property	4,016,200	1,900	316,671	1,411
Percentage Change (1964–1974):				
Total	+143	+120	+134	+101
Violent	+168	+142	+189	+145
Property	+138	+115	+131	|98

*Rate per 100,000 population

SOURCE: Adapted from Solicitor General Canada. *Statistics Handbook: Canadian Criminal Justice*-1977 (Ottawa: Information Systems and Statistics Division, Research and Systems Development Branch, Solicitor General Canada, 1977), p. 20.

increase in population. Between 1961 and 1979, the rate of violence against the person increased 395 percent; property crime rates increased 163 percent. The rules used to count crime changed in 1980 making temporal comparisons impossible in many crime categories.

Analyzing temporal patterns of crime in England presents problems similar to those found in Canada. Although the English have many years of official crime data, they do not have a reservoir of victimization data to help triangulate an actual crime pattern. England's efforts in victimization survey work have been limited primarily to the pilot research conducted by Sparks, et al (1977) in Greater London and to some questions included in recent census questionnaires. In the early 1980s a national victimization survey was conducted by the Home Office Research Unit, but its findings have not yet been fully digested and published. What is known about temporal crime patterns must be gleaned from official statistics.

Violent Crimes
Violent offenses against the person have increased dramatically since 1961 (Table 7–10). In 1961, about 18,000 offenses were recorded by the police. By

137

TABLE 7–10. Indictable Offenses Known to Police of England and
Wales, 1961–1979*

Year	Violence Against the Person	Sexual Offenses	Property Offenses
Crimes in Thousands			
1961	18	20	750
1971	47	24	1,565
1976	78	22	1,933
1979	95	22	2,096
Crime Rate per 100,000 Population			
1961	39	43	1,623
1971	96	49	3,196
1976	159	45	3,937
1979	193	44	4,262

*The Theft Act 1968 redefined many offenses of dishonest appropriation of property. Detailed breakdowns by offense are possible, but noncomparable, for the periods before and after 1969. The broad categorizations used here are considered comparable by the Home Office. The 1961 figures have been adjusted to fit post-1968 offense definitions and categorizations. Counting rules were changed again in 1980 producing noncomparable figures for that year.

SOURCE: Adapted from Home Office (Annual), *Criminal Statistics: England and Wales.* (London: HMSO [Cmnd 8098], 1979).

1979, the number recorded had risen to 95,000. The increase in violent offenses has been more rapid than the increase in property offenses.

The rate of violence against the person increased from 38.9 per 100,000 population to 193 per 100,000 between 1961 and 1979, around a 400 percent increase. The property offense rate (burglary, larceny, fraud, and robbery) changed from 1,623 to 4,262 per 100,000, a 163 percent increase. Violent crime showed a stronger relative increase in England than in the United States or Canada.

In the English statistical system, there are many offenses that fall into the category of violence against the person. Not all the violent offenses have been increasing at the same rate. Between 1971 and 1979, some crimes of violence against the person actually decreased, though these offenses were primarily rare or low-volume crimes: causing death by dangerous driving decreased by 69 percent; endangering railway passengers decreased by 43 percent; and abandoning a child under two years old decreased by 45 percent. Except for causing death by dangerous driving, the size of the decreases reflects in part the small number of offenses. Most major violent offenses increased: homicide increased by 37 percent; serious wounding increased by 36 percent; and other wounding increased by 113 percent. Assault increased by 12 percent during this eight-year period.

Homicide is a well-reported offense. The English homicide rate is far lower than the homicide rate in the United States or Canada. In 1979, the English rate was 1.16 homicides per 100,000 population, whereas the Canadian rate was 2.7,

TABLE 7–11. Homicides by Apparent Method of Killing in
England and Wales, 1979

Method	Number	Percentage
By sharp instrument	202	35
By blunt instrument	69	12
By hitting, kicking, etc.	91	16
By strangulation–asphyxiation	104	18
By shooting	49	9
By explosion	1	—
Other	54	9
Not known	1	—
	571*	

*This figure is lower than the number of offenses originally recorded by the
police as homicide. It reflects only those offenses that the courts found to be
homicide.

SOURCE: Adapted from Home Office (Annual), *Criminal Statistics: England
and Wales* (London: HMSO [Cmnd 8098], 1979).

more than twice as high, and the American rate was 9.7, more than eight times as
high.

Because Britain has a strong gun-control law, a small proportion of deaths are
caused by shooting (9 percent). Most deaths are caused by sharp instruments, presumably primarily by knives. The relatively lower murder rate in England may be
a product of the decreased availability of guns. For example, in 1979, guns were
used in only 55 of 629 murders reported to the police (Home office, 1980, p. 62.).
Of these only 8 involved pistols. In the United States, about 50 percent of all
murders are committed with handguns (Table 7–11).

Property Crimes

Property offenses make up the bulk of the serious or indictable offenses in
England and Wales. In 1979, violence against the person, sexual offenses, and
robbery, combined, accounted for 5 percent of the indictable offenses. The most
frequent indictable offense was theft (56 percent), followed by burglary (22 percent). Fraud offenses accounted for about 5 percent of all offenses. These relative
crime mixtures were consistent throughout the 1970s. The pattern in 1970 was
almost identical to the pattern in 1979. Since 1970, the number of property offenses reported to the police appears to be increasing gradually.

Explanation of Recent Trends

The upward trend in crime in the United States, Canada, and England since World
War II calls for explanation. Crime has been increasing more rapidly than the

population. Possible reasons for the temporal changes in crime can be found in changes in the major structures that create the fabric of society. Changes in the demographic, economic, social, opportunity, and criminal-justice-system structures can be seen to mirror, at least in part, changes in the crime pattern.

Demographic Factors

Demography is the social science that studies population growth and change. Demographic studies look at the age structure of populations (the number and percentage of the population falling into different age and sex groupings), fertility and mortality patterns and migration and mobility patterns, and the ethnic composition of society. Demography explores how these patterns and structures interrelate and what factors influence these basic building blocks of population growth and change.

Demographic analysis is extremely important in the temporal analysis of crime. Empirical research in criminology has repeatedly demonstrated that different age groups, different ethnic groups, and the two sexes have different rates of criminal behavior. When the pattern of criminal behavior changes, a likely place to look for an explanation is in the demographic structure of society.

Age

Crimes are disproportionately committed by adolescents and young adults. Few crimes are committed by the very young or the very old. Age-specific rates of criminal activity peak in the teenage years. Traces of this age-specific pattern can easily be seen by looking at the volume of persons found guilty or cautioned for serious offenses in England and Wales in 1979. Among males, the conviction–caution rate for all ages combined was about 20 per 1,000 population. Males ten to thirteen had rates of about 29 per 1,000, almost fifty percent above the overall rate. Males aged fourteen to sixteen had rates of 68 per 1,000, three times the overall rate, and males aged seventeen to twenty had rates of about 62 per 1,000. There was then a sharp and progressive drop in conviction and cautioning rates for each progressive age category: age twenty-one to twenty-four, 35 per 1,000; age twenty-five to thirty, 27 per 1,000; age thirty to thirty-nine, 14 per 1,000; age forty to forty-nine, 8 per 1,000; age fifty to sixty, 4 per thousand; and age 60 and over, 2 per 1,000.

A similar pattern is found in the United States. In 1979, about 33 percent of the persons arrested were between fifteen and twenty years old (FBI, 1979, p. 188). There was a steady decline in the numbers arrested as age increased.

Changes in crime rates or the volume of crime may just reflect a changing age structure, that is, an increase in the number of people in the fourteen to twenty age range. If we look at the problem cross-sectionally, two areas may have identical population sizes but different age structures. If one area has a larger proportion of teenagers, demographically it would be expected to have more crime. Demographic studies do not explain why young people commit more crimes; they just describe the relationship.

The empirical link between age structure and crime can be examined temporally. Age structures vary over time. Demographers usually represent the age struc-

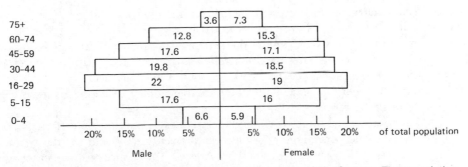

Figure 7–7. Population Pyramid for the United Kingdom, 1980. [Source: The population pyramid was created from mid-year population estimates in Central Statistical Office, *Social Trends 12-1982 Edition.* London: H. M. S. O., 1981.]

ture of an area graphically by using something called a *population pyramid.* In a population pyramid, the proportion of people of various age groupings or cohorts is shown in a chart with the ages on the vertical axis and the population on the horizontal axis. In Figure 7–7, the 1980 population of the United Kingdom is represented by a population pyramid. As can be seen in the graph, the number of people in over age seventy-five was small. This finding should not be surprising. The differentially higher male death rates for people over sixty years of age can also be seen.

The changes in birth rates (live births per 1,000 population) and fertility rates (live births per woman of childbearing age) account for much of the population change in Western societies. Because crime is disproportionately committed by the young, changes in fertility and birth rates can explain part of the increase in crime since 1960. In the years immediately after World War II, the United States, Canada and England experienced what has been dubbed a *baby boom.* Fertility and birth rates soared. What had been a general long-term trend of decreased fertility was temporarily reversed.

Although this baby boom in fertility rates has subsided, the baby boom has had, and will continue to have, profound effects on the three societies.[7] First, new baby industries were created; later, more schools were built. Still later, school enrollments dropped as the children of the baby boom passed school age. In years to come, social welfare systems will have to be developed to handle proportionately larger numbers of retired persons, who will drain pension programs and place extreme pressures on medical systems.[8]

While the children of the baby boom were growing up, their numbers produced a bulge in the population found in specific age groups. During the 1960s, there was a temporary increase in the proportion of the population between ages

[7] The effect in Canada appears to be somewhat less pronounced because in-migration still forms a major component of population growth.

[8] As the children of the baby boom have entered into the family-forming years and had children of their own, there has been a smaller, more dispersed second wave of increased births. This second wave has been caused more by the increase in the number of women of childbearing age than by any increase in fertility.

141

fifteen and twenty, the age most prone to commit offenses. All other things being equal, crime rates would have been expected to rise.

Empirical studies that explore the statistical influence of the age composition of a population on crime rates have generally shown some relationship, though often weak. Both Hasenpusch (1978), working with Canadian data, and Fox (1979), working with American data, found that the percentage of young males is a good predictor of crime rates.

Hasenpusch used three demographic variables in making predictions: (1) total population; (2) the percentage males fifteen to twenty-four; and (3) the percentage of persons living in Census Metropolitan Areas.[9] These variables, together with a time variable used to represent past crime patterns, worked extremely well in predicting crime. Hasenpusch used multiple regression and, because of the obvious correlation between his demographic measures, did not attempt to sort out relative importance.

Fox (1979) conducted a more sophisticated study in the United States in an attempt to predict crime rates. His analysis looked at clearance rates and the size and expenditure of police forces, as well as crime rates. His analysis was based on a set of equations. Because his data were temporal, he checked for autocorrelation and made necessary adjustments. He found that the proportion of the population (nonwhite) between eighteen and twenty-one was significantly related to the violent crime rate, and that the proportion of the population (nonwhite) between fourteen and seventeen was significantly related to the property crime rate (pp. 33–45). Although his variables were not pure age factors (race was included), his results do lend support to the idea that demographic structure does help to explain temporal changes in crime.

A study done by Sagi and Wellford (1968) and a later report by Wellford (1973) showed much weaker support for an age structure variable. The empirical analysis of the importance of age structure in understanding crime patterns is not over. At a conceptual level, age structure should matter, but as is true of all factors influencing crime patterns, age is not the only variable that matters.

Sex

The relative proportion of males to females in the population is also linked to actual crime rates. Criminal behavior, at least serious criminal behavior such as that recorded by the FBI in its index offenses, is primarily a male activity.

Studies of homicide, a well-reported offense where the sex of the offender is usually known, provide strong evidence for the sexual bias in criminal behavior. In one of the earliest studies of homicide in the United States, Brearly (1969) found that in the 1920s about 90 percent of all reported murders with known assailants were committed by males (p. 82). While looking at homicide in Philadelphia in the late 1940s and early 1950s, Wolfgang (1966) found that over 82 percent of the known offenders were male. Similarly, Pokorny (1965) found that 81 percent of the

---

[9] The Census Metropolitan Area (CMA) is the Canadian census designation used to cluster together contiguous municipalities that have fairly large populations, as well as economic ties that are apparent in commuting patterns. It is similar, but not identical, to an SMSA in the U.S. or a conurbation in Great Britain.

offenders in Houston between 1958 and 1961 were male. Voss and Hepburn (1968) found that the percentage was 83 in Chicago in 1965.

Because of the relative statistical rarity of murder, victimization surveys do not include questions about homicides (relatives of victims would respond if questions were included), but official arrest data give evidence of the national trend in the United States in recent years. In 1980, 90 percent of the persons arrested for murder and nonnegligent manslaughter were male (FBI, 1980, p. 10). In 1960, the male percentage was 83 (FBI, 1972, p. 124). This pattern appears to hold true also in Canada and England. The ratio of male suspects to female suspects in Canada between 1961 and 1970 was 8.4 to 1 (Jayewardene, 1975). In England, the rate was around 85 percent male in 1979, but the number of murders was quite small relative to the number in the United States and Canada.

Similar sex differentials occur in other serious offenses. In U.S. arrests in 1980 the male–female differential was large. Males arrested for aggravated assault outnumbered females 7 to 1; for robbery the ratio was 13 to 1. For burglary, 94 percent were male, 6 percent female; and for motor vehicle theft, 91 percent were male, 9 percent female. The highest percentage for females arrested was found in the larceny–theft category, which includes shoplifting. Even for larceny–theft, however, females accounted for only 29 percent of the persons arrested, whereas 71 percent of arrestees were male.

The proportions were remarkably similar in England and Wales in 1979. In the statistics of persons proceeded against for indictable offenses, the male–female ratios are high: 93 percent of the persons proceeded against for crimes of violence were male; 94 percent of persons proceeded against for robbery were male; and 96 percent of persons proceeded against for burglary were male. The female ratio was highest for theft, and even in this category, only 25 percent of the people proceeded against were female, whereas 75 percent were male (Home office, 1979, p. 643).

Whatever the reasons or explanations for the sexual bias shown in official statistics (from the biological maturation processes of males to the sociologically restricted activity patterns of females), the demographic pattern is strong. Males dominate the crime picture. Consequently, areas that have an above-average proportion of males are likely to have above-average crime rates, all other factors being equal. Of course, all other factors are never equal, so the sex ratio becomes, like other factors, a relative predictor of crime patterns.

Race

A population's racial structure is also related to official crime rates. In England and Canada, official statistics are not published by race of victim or offender. The studies that explore the relationship between race and crime rates have primarily been done in the United States and, within that cultral context, overwhelmingly show differential patterns for blacks and whites: it has repeatedly been found that blacks are disproportionately both victims and offenders. Possible explanations for the racial variance include differential economic status, differential law-enforcement patterns, and subcultural patterns within some black communities that tolerate higher levels of crime, particularly higher violence rates. These possible explanations are discussed later in the chapter. The purpose of this section is to present the demographic patterns.

TABLE 7–12. Race of Apprehended Murderers

Study	City	Time Period	Race Black (Percentage)	Nonblack (Percentage)
Wolfgang (1958)	Philadelphia	1948–1952	75.2	24.8
Bullock (1955)	Houston	1945–1949	65.0	35.0
Pittman and Handy (1955)*	St. Louis	1961	82.0	18.0
Voss and Hepburn (1968)	Chicago	1965	77.9†	22.1
Pokorny (1965)	Houston	1958	63.5	36.5
Bensing and Schroeder (1960)	Cuyahoga County‡	1947–1953	76.4	23.6
Block (1977)	Chicago	1975	76.0	24.0
Parisi et al. (1979)	U.S.	1976	53.5	46.5

* Pittman and Handy studied aggravated assault, not homicide, but it is a highly related offense.
† Nonwhite category.
‡ Greater Cleveland.

More research has been done on violent crime than on property crime. The work is primarily cross-sectional; that is, studies exist for specific points in time. An overall temporal pattern can be pieced together from several studies. Such a piecemeal temporal pattern is, of course, weak and is subject to much error. However, general impressions can be formed.

Murder is the offense most often studied. Studies in different urban areas in different time periods have repeatedly shown a relationship between race and murder (Table 7–12). The percentages vary, but murderers turn out to be black in a disproportionate number of cases. It should be noted that the percentages given in the table represent the percentage of the persons arrested who belong to particular racial groups. Percentages such as these create a major problem.

As discussed in Chapter 6, rates or percentages make sense only within a context. If a city were 50 percent black and 50 percent nonblack, then a 50 percent black-offender rate would represent an equal distribution of offenders between races. The percentages in Table 7–12 would make sense, in an absolute way, only if the proportion of blacks within the cities were also known. In a relative sense, none of the cities studied for the time periods covered had black populations over 60 percent, though all the cities had black populations that exceeded the proportion found in the country as a whole (note that the figure for the United States, given in the table, is lower, 53.5 percent, which makes sense when it is noted that the proportion of blacks in the United States as a whole is lower than the proportion in the cities covered by these studies).

Race is a demographic characteristic such as age or sex, but it differs in one way that influences calculations. Within North America, there are few pure Negroes. Most "blacks" have some "white" ancestry. The division into black and nonblack categories is problematic. If 75 percent of a person's ancestors are nonblack, is that person nonblack? The breakpoint in categorization is made not in law (as it is for native North Americans in the United States), but by custom, culture, and subjective impression. It should also be noted that because murder is not gen-

TABLE 7–13. Victimization Rates, United States, 1979*

	Race of Victim	
Type of Victimization	White	Black and Other Races
Rape and attempted rape	73	165
Robbery	552	1,314
Assault: Aggravated	915	1,489
Simple	1,572	1,316
Personal larceny with contact (purse snatching and attempts, pocket picking)	245	601

* Rate per 100,000 whites and nonwhites twelve years of age or older.

SOURCE: Adapted from N. Parisi, M. R. Gottfredson, M. J. Hindelang, and T. J. Flanagan (Annual), *Sourcebook of Criminal Justice Statistics* (Washington, D.C.: Department of Justice, 1979), p. 378.

erally an interracial crime, disproportionate numbers of victims are also "black."

The disproportiontely high number of blacks persists in statistics on other violent crimes. In 1980, the UCR reported that 48 percent of all persons arrested for rape were black; 58 percent arrested for robbery were black; and 36 percent arrested for aggravated assault were black.

The victimization surveys produce a somewhat comparable pattern for victims (Table 7–13). Except for simple assault, blacks and other nonwhites (the racial categories used in victim surveys) are victims at a higher rate than whites. Simple assault is an exception to the general pattern.

The magnitude of the differential risk for different racial groups in an urban area can be seen in a study of homicide rates done in Atlanta by Munford et al. (1976). They found very different rates for blacks and whites, as well as for males, and females (Figure 7–8). In addition, the rates are soaring for blacks in Atlanta, and consequently, the differentials appear to be getting larger.

Blacks also have a higher-than-expected arrest rate for property offenses, though the differential is not as striking as for violent offenses. In 1962, the UCR indicated that 31.5 percent of the persons arrested for property offenses were black, and 68.5 percent were nonblack. In 1980, the arrest figures for index property offenses were 32 percent black and 68 percent nonblack.

The race of the victim of property offenses, once again, follows the arrest pattern. Blacks and other nonwhites have a higher victimization rate for burglary and motor vehicle theft than whites. They have a lower rate for larceny, primarily for amounts under $50 (Parisi et al., 1979, p. 397).

Summary of Demographic Factors

Age, sex, and racial structure are all related to crime occurrences, though not necessarily independently. Work unraveling how demographics affect crime rates is in its infancy. One study by Blumstein and Nagin (1975) points to the potential

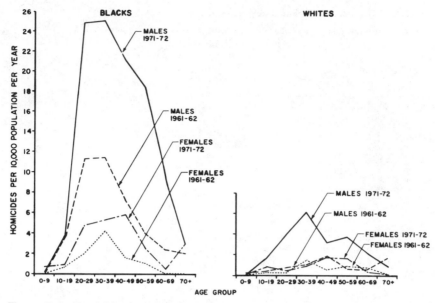

Figure 7–8. Homicide rates by age group, race, and sex, Atlanta, 1961–1962 and 1971–1972. [Source: Reprinted from Robert S. Munford, Ross S. Kazer, Roger A. Feldman, and Robert R. Stivers, "Homicide Trends in Atlanta," *Criminology,* Vol. 14, No. 2 (August 1976), pp. 213–232, © 1976 American Society of Criminology, with permission of Sage Publications, Inc., and the author.]

value of using demographics to predict crime patterns. Using data from Pittsburgh for 1967–1969 and 1971–1972, Blumstein and Nagin explored whether there was an increase in the criminality (proneness to commit offenses) of specific age, sex, and racial groups or whether the criminality of the groups stayed constant and the changes in crime could be attributed to changing demographic mixes. Working with arrests for index offenses, they found that 99 percent of the variance in arrest rates could be explained by the interaction of age, sex, and racial characteristics. Variances in crime rates could be explained by differences in demographic makeup. Although these authors worked with arrests, not reported crime, their work points to the importance of demographic structure. But as the authors stated:

> From these results, one certainly cannot conclude that changes in demographic factors are the major *cause* of the observed variations in arrest rate. Demographic factors are only definitions. If they are well defined, demographic factors will delineate groups of similar people, similar in the sense that they broadly face the same type of economic and social forces. While the nature of those forces are [*sic*] not at all well understood, it seems clear that they are the principal driving force behind the deviant behavior. (p. 226)

Economic Factors

A general thread runs through much temporal analysis of crime: crime should be, at least in part, the result of economic conditions. Many studies of long-term crime patterns try to relate increases in crime to cyclic downturns in business or radical dislocations in the economy, such as wars, depressions, or famines. Studies of crime trends since World War II usually link crime with economic problems. However, empirical studies trying to relate economic factors to crime show mixed results: the relationship between crime and the economy is not evident but is instead complex. To begin to unravel the relationship between crime and the economy, it is necessary to think about how economic changes might influence crime.

Property Crime

At the individual level, it is argued that lack of income creates an inability to maintain an "adequate" standard of living and consequently triggers crime as a means to gain income. Before the massive economic growth of the nineteenth century and the subsequent introduction of major social-welfare programs, crimes of economic necessity were frequent. With the economic growth of the Industrial Revolution and the advent of major social-welfare programs, the danger of people's starving to death decreased, and the argument of economic necessity changed its focus to an argument about perceptions of an "adequate" standard of living. Although governments debate "poverty levels" and social-welfare subsistence levels, it is clear that many people, whether covered by social welfare programs and not, either experience or perceive a need for greater income. The perception or experience of inadequate income may lead to crime as an individual seeks to increase his or her income by illegitimate means. Lack of income is often the result of unemployment. Unemployment also creates excess leisure. This excess leisure is often spent in socializing with others in similar circumstances or in committing crimes when others are working (Figure 7–9a).

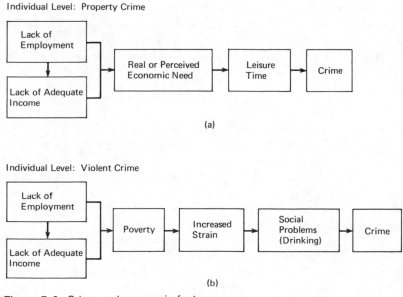

Figure 7–9. Crime and economic factors.

Violent Crime

The arguments linking economic factors and violent crime are slightly different. For violent crimes, lack of employment or lack of income leads to poverty and/or increased economic strain. This strain is thought to produce social problems, which, coupled with excess leisure, often spent drinking or socializing, lead to violent crime (Figure 7–9b).

Mediating Factors

The models shown in Figure 7–9 are simplified, eliminating factors that mediate the linking process.

Individuals do not live in a vacuum. The economic factors that influence crime are really part of a cluster of factors that define a social setting that facilitates or encourages crime. To give a fuller picture, it is worth mentioning some of these factors.

1. *Age.* As discussed before, age appears to have an effect on criminal behavior: the young commit more crimes. Unemployment or lack of adequate income should be viewed in relationship to age. The young suffer from higher levels of unemployment when they enter the labor force than do older people. In addition, many youths are not directly unemployed but have a parent or parents who are unemployed. This unemployment affects the youths indirectly. Age and individual or family unemployment work interactively.

2. *Race.* Race, another demographic factor associated with crime also interacts with economic factors. The unemployment rates for blacks in the United States are higher than for whites and are the highest for black teenagers.

3. *Opportunity.* Crime occurs within a context. The context has both social and opportunity characteristics. In Canada, the United States, and England as well as the rest of Western Europe, there has been an explosion in the ownership of consumer goods. There are many goods easily accessible to anyone who wants to steal. Crime is easier now because there are more accessible targets.

Empirical Studies

Analytic studies exploring the relationship between the economy and crime have produced mixed results. The studies are diverse, working with many levels of aggregation and are usually not directly comparable. Because the data are available, many studies use employment data (and other socioeconomic data) for cities or even countries. The results are then used either to support or challenge general economic models of crime. There is often a large gulf between the concepts behind the models and the type of data used to validate them.

Two well-known studies linking economic conditions and crime were done by Vold (1958) and Fleisher (1966). In examining the relationship between crime and unemployment in the United States during the first part of this century, Vold found no strong, consistent relationship. A study by Fleisher, which covers a more recent period, found a positive correlation between rates of juvenile arrest[10] and unemployment in the United States in three selected cities. Similar results were obtained by Glaser and Rice (1959). Fleisher found additional support for the relationship between unemployment and crime by looking at arrest rates by age and comparing them with the school dropout rate and with the unemployment rate by age for the largest SMSAs in the United States. All three rates peaked at age sixteen.

Many studies using varying definitions and time frames—some time series analysis, some cross-sectional—support Fleisher's findings, at least in a weak way. Distinguishing between whites and nonwhites, Phillips et al. (1972) found a strong relationship between labor-force participation rates and arrest rates for youths age eighteen to nineteen. Within a general economic study in Canada, Avio and Clark (1976) found a significant relationship between mean income and property crime. Krohn (1976), in an international analysis, and Kvalseth (1977), Greenwood and Wadychi (1973), and Ehrlich (1973), within a much broader model-building effort, found support for the idea that economic factors influence crime. The economy and crime are not yet definitively linked for the post–World War II period, but unemployment rates, income levels and labor-force participation rates seem to matter. Geographic studies of crime at the international, regional, and intermetropolitan levels seem to show a strong relationship between crime rates and measures of income inequality (see Chapter 10).

Economic factors are also related to analyses in other parts of the criminal justice system. Economic modeling is used to describe the deterrent effect of conviction and punishment (see for example, Becker, 1968; Ehrlich, 1973; and Greenberg, 1977), as well as the relationship of the economy to the use of sanctions (Greenberg, 1977; and, in general, works of critical criminologists).

Social Factors

Much criminological theory has centered on determining what social factors influence crime. It is beyond the scope of this book to try to repeat all the social arguments about the causes of crime. Generally, studies of social factors and crime have shown that family structures and relationships, peer-group relations, education, and occupational status are related to crime.

Social factors can be broken down into three major categories:

1. Individual rule-learning approaches.
2. Institutional rule-learning approaches.
3. Social systems approaches.

[10] Fleisher found a positive effect for ages 17 and over in the United States. He tested for autocorrelation of residuals in his time series analysis and used first difference formulations when autocorrelations were found. Fleisher's book, *The Economics of Delinquency* is an extremely useful book to read. His time series analysis is straightforward and a good introduction to this mode of analysis for the non-methodologist.

Individual Rule-Learning

Many sociological approaches address the ability or the potential of the individual (or the group, as an agglomeration of individuals) for learning societal rules. Deviant or criminal acts occur when an individual fails to learn appropriate societal rules of behavior. The character or quality of the home learning environment may be deficient: adults at home may not teach children behavior acceptable to the general society. Trasler (1962) presented such an argument.

The character and quality of the "neighbourhood" or peer-group learning environment may also be deficient. An individual may learn rules of behavior that are appropriate in her or his immediate surroundings but inappropriate at a more general social level (Shaw and McKay, 1969; Reiss and Rhodes, 1961; Hirschi, 1969).

The family, neighbourhood, and peer-group learning approaches coexist in the theory of *differential association*. In this theoretical approach, developed by Sutherland (1947), an individual is likely to engage in deviant activities if the contacts that teach attitudes that push in a deviant direction exceed those that teach attitudes that push in a nondeviant direction.[11]

Institutional Rule-Learning

Rules may be learned at institutional as well as group or individual levels. Several sociological approaches address how institutions, primarily schools and prisons, teach an individual to be delinquent or how they fail to teach an individual not to be delinquent. Schools may teach someone that he or she is a failure or an outcast (Cohen, 1955; Hirschi, 1969; Polk and Schafer, 1972). Schools may also fail to teach societal values. Prisons, it is argued, are not only places of containment, but schools for crime (Letkemann, 1973, pp. 122–130). Individuals may learn from institutions as well as from family or friends.

Social Systems

Social systems factors are used in many current explanations of crime. There may be institutional arrangements that facilitate, increase the probability of, or even cause crime. Cloward and Ohlin (1960) argued that societal structures, as they now exist, *block the opportunity* of many individuals to achieve "success." Some individuals, who are identifiable by their socioeconomic characteristics, cannot achieve success by means generally accepted by society: they are blocked from legal success and reach for success by criminal means.

Institutional arrangements may have effects on groups and thus on individuals within groups. For example, Turk (1969), Quinney (1970), Taylor et al. (1973), and others have argued that the political structure of society divides people into competitive groups and that crime is a by-product of this competition. Crime becomes a symptom of a struggle between the people in power and those not in power. Societal structures may also label groups as criminal (Erikson, 1966; Becker, 1963).

Approaches based on social systems use the demographic and economic characteristics of individuals, groups, or even nations to give numerical substance to

[11] If the contacts are weighted by importance, and if *importance* means the strength of the contact's association with deviant activity, it is always possible to show, at an individual level, that the pressures toward deviance exceed those towards nondeviance (or vice versa). Deviant contacts are just weighted more. Thus, at an individual level, the theory cannot be falsified.

150

theoretic ideas. These approaches try to describe the mechanisms that lead to crime.

Social systems have spatial analogues. People live in towns and cities. Much social factors research looks at the social correlates of the geographic arrangements of individuals. This research will be described in the next section.

Urbanization. A strong antiurban bias permeates research and theory building in sociology and criminology. Cities are generally considered bad places, places filled with crime, disease, and strife. It is often implied that crime, disease, and strife are inevitable consequences of cities. Two basic concepts are used in studies of cities: *urbanism* and *urbanization.* Urbanization is the easier concept to understand. Urbanization is the process by which the population of an area, usually a country, shifts from rural surroundings to urban surroundings. Over time, the population leaves rural areas and moves to urban areas.

Several definitions must be given if the concept of urbanization is to make sense. First, *rural* and *urban* must be defined. Although any split into categories is arbitrary, rural areas are obviously lower in population density than urban areas. In the U.S. Census, *urban* is defined as a place with a population over 5,000, though this number is clearly lower than most people would use intuitively for urban concentration. Kingsley Davis (1974) used a more acceptable breakpoint: 100,000 population. Urbanization is the process by which the proportion of the population living in urban areas increases, and consequently, the proportion of the population in rural areas decreases. In 1900, only Great Britain could be considered highly urbanized; now all industrialized nations are also urbanized (Davis, 1974).

Urbanization can be the result of migration from the rural areas to the cities in the same country or from rural or urban areas in one country to cities in another. Either type of movement switches the balance toward urban population if the migration stream to the cities results in a relative increase in city population.

Urbanism is a different, more amorphous concept. Urbanism is the cluster of qualities and characteristics that make a city different from a rural area. Louis Wirth (1938) is probably the best-known scholar who studied urbanism. For Wirth, the characteristics of an urban environment are created by an interaction of the size, the density, and the heterogeneity of an area. Cities are large, densely settled areas with a variety and mixture of people.

According to Wirth, and numerous urban sociologists and criminologists who followed him, urbanism creates problems (Figure 7–10). The *size* of cities increases human interaction, spreading interpersonal dependence until contacts become impersonal. The high *density* in cities leads to the segregation of the city into subareas with, inevitably, some people not belonging anywhere. *Heterogeneity* leads to the segmentation of roles, fluid membership in diversified groups and depersonalization. Wirth's model is a mixture of Emile Durkheim, on the sociological side, and Georg Simmel on the psychological side. From a sociological perspective, size, density, and heterogeneity lead to differentiation, formalization of institutions, and anomie. From a psychological or behavioral perspective, living in an urban environment was thought to lead to overstimulation, nervous-system overload, and possibly social isolation or deviance (Berry, 1973).

Two major analytic approaches have developed from Wirth's theory: (1) structural studies and (2) tension studies (Lodhi and Tilly, 1973). Structural arguments

151

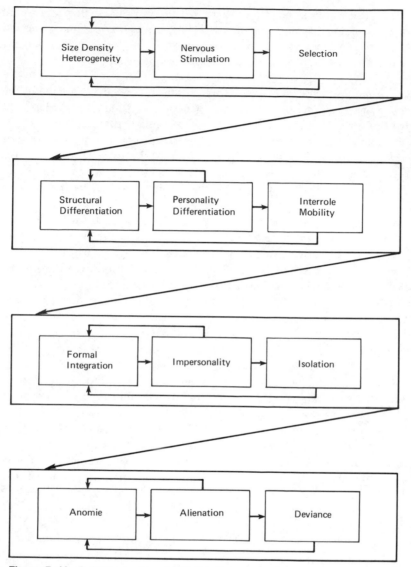

Figure 7–10. A diagram of Louis Wirth's theory of urbanism as a way of life. [Source: B. J. L. Berry, *The Human Consequences of Urbanization.* London and Basingstoke: Macmillan; New York: St. Martin's Press; 1973, p. 16. Reprinted by permission of the publishers.]

emphasize the changes in organization, the arrangements that control interactions between individuals, and the reliance on formal methods of social control. The tension arguments find crime the result of the strains or disorientations associated with urban living. Structural- and tension-oriented studies dominate urban criminology.

Urban–Rural Differences. The change from rural to urban ways of living is associated with changes in the family's structure and economic situation. As city size increases, family size decreases; divorce rates go up; and income goes up. Studies of urban rural differences have produced the traces of interesting patterns. Contrary to an early belief in a rural–urban continuum (that is, a gradual change as societies move from a rural to an urban form), there appear to be complex alterations. Often, there are threshold changes or sharp breaks between rural and urban living.

In the United States, the increase in crime is not linear and does not necessarily peak in the largest cities. Robbery and auto theft are the only offenses that appear to increase consistently as city size increases. The pattern of crime increasing as city size increases is somewhat stronger in Canada, but not totally consistent. The rates of theft and assault or attempted murder are not highest in the largest cities in either the U.S. or Canada. (See Tables 7–14, 7–15.)

In studies of city size and crime, it is often assumed that more is bad. Thus,

TABLE 7–14. U.S. Urban–Rural Patterns, 1979 (Rate per 100,000 Population)

	Murder	Rape	Robbery	Aggravated Assault	Burglary	Larceny–Theft	Motor Vehicle Theft
Total	10.1	35.7	223.3	285.7	1,539.9	3,052.3	513.7
Total cities	11.2	40.7	293.6	332.8	1,725.2	3,601.4	627.4
Group I							
Cities 250K+ *	23.1	71.5	667.8	475.4	2,336.2	3,828.0	1,054.0
Cities 1M++	27.5	66.4‡	832.2	507.6	2,198.8‡	3,055.5‡	1,243.8
(6)							
Cities 500K–1M	21.0	74.1‡	583.1	425.9	2,301.5‡	4,303.7‡	980.0
(19)							
Cities 250K–500K	18.5	76.6‡	507.8	479.6	2,583.0‡	4,496.3‡	843.6
(33)							
Group II							
Cities 100K–250K	11.4	50.3	281.9	357.9	2,114.1	4,355.7	655.4
(110)							
Group III							
Cities 50K–100K	7.2	36.7	193.9	287.7	1,772.9	3,768.9	593.6
(271)							
Group IV							
Cities 25K–50K	5.8	26.6	133.9	253.8	1,476.9	3,607.0	459.3
(605)							
Group V							
Cities 10K–25K	4.5	17.6	77.8	215.6	1,186.5	3,138.6	349.3
(1498)							
Group VI							
Cities under 10K	4.0	15.3	47.2	212.1	1,020.5	2,938.9	265.8
(5,912)							
Suburban areas	5.6	25.4	99.1	225.4	1,302.9	2,793.5	380.9
Rural areas	7.6‡	15.6‡	22.8	148.1	803.0	1,130.0	143.1

* K = thousands.
† M = million.
‡ Rising rate as size class goes down.

SOURCE: Federal Bureau of Investigation, *Crime in the United States-1979* (Washington, D.C.: Government Printing Office [Uniform Crime Reports], 1980), pp. 170–171.

153

TABLE 7–15. Canadian Urban–Rural Patterns, 1977 (Rate per 100,000 Population)

City Size Groups	Homicide	Assault and Attempted Murder	Rape	Robbery	Breaking and Entering	Theft	Motor Vehicle Theft
Groups 1 and 2 Cities 250K+ *	3.5	460.8‡	10.0	156.4	1,330.7	3,088.4‡	461.2
Group 3 Cities 100K–250K	3.2	501.4‡	8.7	104.1	1,314.8	3,160.0‡	472.9
Group 4 Cities 50K–100K	1.6‡	362.4	8.0	63.6	1,258.5	3,198.3‡	399.9
Group 5 Cities 25K–50K	1.9‡	448.1	6.9	56.7	1,173.4	2,972.5	376.2
Group 6 Cities 10K–25K	2.4‡	405.5	4.8	51.3	1,099.1	2,742.7	335.5
Group 7 Cities 5K–10K	1.3	376.1‡	3.9	26.7	831.7	2,195.0	277.5
Group 8 Cities 2.5K–5K	2.2	467.0‡	3.4	16.0	743.4	1,871.1	241.5
Group 9 Cities 750–2,500 pop.	1.7	493.4‡	3.5	12.5	905.3	1,819.4	237.6

* K = thousands.

‡ Rising rate as size class goes down.

SOURCE: Statistics Canada, *Crime and Traffic Enforcement Statistics-1977* (Ottawa: Queen's Printer, 1980), pp. 2-81–2-114.

it is often assumed that density is associated positively with crime and, consequently, that high-density areas experience more crime than low-density areas. Guerry (1833) first explored this problem in the early nineteenth century in France and rejected a relationship between density and crime. In North America, the work of Shaw and McKay (1969) identified the poor areas of cities that had a high density and a high immigrant population as being the areas where crime was highest. The Shaw and McKay thesis has generally been accepted in studies both within and between cities.

Recent American research raises some doubt about the association between crime and high density in cities. Schichor et al. (1979) found that only property crimes with contact (robbery and personal larceny with contact) were positively related to the overall density of a city. Other property crimes had a negative correlation with density. McCarthy et al. (1975) found that various measures of density—such as number of persons per square mile, rooms per dwelling unit, the percentage of the city's population living in dwellings with more than 1.51 persons per room (the U.S. Census definition of crowded living conditions), and population size—were positively related to homicide and assault, but that classic demographic variables such as the percentage of the population that was nonwhite and the percentage of young males in the population were also influential.

A study by Skogan (1977a) directly tested Wirth's ideas, looking at size, density, and heterogeneity and how they related to crime in large American core cities over time. Skogan found that from 1946 to 1951, density was correlated *neg-*

atively with crime. Density became strongly positively correlated with crime in the 1960s. Similarly, city size was negatively correlated with crime until the 1960s and now has only a weak positive association with crime.

City size is related to crime, but not in a simple linear fashion. Density and crime are probably not positively related overall, but only for certain offenses and possibly only within cities with generally decreasing densities. Urbanization itself is related to crime, if at all, in a complicated manner. Urbanization has leveled off in England, whereas the rate of increase in crime has not. In both the United States and Canada, urbanization began later than it did in England and is still continuing. Linking urbanization and crime conceptually is difficult, particularly because rapid urbanization occurred during the latter nineteenth century and early twentieth century, when crime was decreasing in both Britain and the United States.

Opportunity Factors

Crime is not caused by a single factor, but out of the studies of the correlates of crime, one factor emerges that deserves some careful attention. Researchers have traditionally looked for the relationship between socioeconomic or sociodemographic variables and crime. Little attention has been given to the relationship of opportunity to crime. For a crime to occur, there must be both an individual who wants to commit an offense *and* an opportunity to commit that offense. Examining the changing distribution of opportunities to commit offenses can help to explain part of the massive increase in crime since World War II. In a summary of opportunity theory, Mayhew et al. (1976) described "Opportunities that attach to the properties of objects involved in crime" (p. 6) and presented four characteristics that help to show how opportunity and crime are related. Crime is related to:

1. *The abundance of goods.* As more goods enter into circulation, more goods are available to be stolen.

2. *The physical security of goods.* As objects are made more secure, they are more difficult to steal. Conversely, insecure goods may be stolen easily.

3. *The level of surveillance.* Opportunities for crime are mediated by surveillance. High levels of supervision provide some protection.

4. *The occasion and temptation for crime.* For a crime to occur, there must be a moment in time and space when the crime can happen. Insecure cars, even with the keys left in the lock, will not create a crime. A person who wants to steal a car must come across the insecure car. (Mayhew et al., 1976, pp. 6–7)

As these characteristics change, opportunity theorists argue, crime will change.

Opportunity theory is primarily concerned with property offenses. In highly emotional or high-affect crimes, opportunity becomes less crucial. There still must be an opportunity for a violent offense, but emotions usually override factors that might otherwise supply minimal security. One opportunity factor associated with violent crimes should be mentioned. As discussed earlier in the chapter, guns are the most common choice of weapon for murder in North America. In England,

155

which has gun control, only about 10 percent of murderers use guns. The lower murder rate in England may, in part, be the result of the reduced availability of weapons that would make murder easier.

Changing Opportunity Structures

One reason that researchers are becoming interested in opportunity factors is the apparent paradox associated with the study of social and economic factors. Since World War II, economic and social conditions have generally improved for the segments of the population that have higher known criminality rates. In America, during this period, the educational levels of blacks have risen substantially, and median income for black families has risen proportionately with that of whites (though it still lags considerably). At the same time, the number of people living in poverty has dropped (Cohen and Felson, 1979). All this has occurred as official crime rates have soared, even though socioeconomic theories would predict reduced crime. During the same period, the opportunity structure for property offenses has changed in two major ways. First, since the 1940s, there has been a rapid proliferation of durable consumer goods. Constant dollar expenditures increased 105 percent between 1960 and 1970, and household appliance shipments increased from 56.2 million to 119.7 million units (Cohen and Felson, 1979, p. 599). At the same time, the weight of consumer goods has also decreased, so that more targets have become reasonably suitable for theft. The *abundance* of goods has increased, to use Mayhew's terminology.

The second change in the opportunity structure relates to the security of potential targets. Since World War II, there has been a change in individual activity patterns. Routine activity can be divided into three categories: (1) activities at home; (2) activities in jobs away from home; and (3) other activities away from home (Cohen and Felson, 1979). There has been a shift, both at the household and the individual level, away from activities at home and toward activities away from home. This shift increases the probability that an offender will find unguarded targets. In property crimes, this increased probability can be seen in two ways. A higher proportion of houses are empty during the daylight hours; female labor-participation rates are climbing; and the number of single-person households is increasing. The number of households unattended at 8 A.M. as recorded by U.S. Census interviewers, for example, increased about 50 percent between 1960 and 1970. In addition, more people take vacations away from home (Cohen and Felson, 1979, p. 598). Fewer "guardians" are at home to protect property. The move away from home is echoed by a relative increase in residential burglary, particularly daytime residential burglary, compared with other types of burglary. For violent offenses, the shift in activity patterns away from home moves more people into positions of vulnerability on the streets, and in bars and pubs.

In an analysis of postwar crime patterns in the United States, Cohen and Felson (1979) explored the importance of activity patterns in explaining crime trends. Using a household activity ratio,[12] the proportion of persons fifteen to twenty-four

---

[12] The *household activity ratio* is defined as the sum of the number of married, husband-present, female labor-force participants and the number of non–husband–wife households, divided by the total number of households.

in the population, and the unemployment rate for persons over sixteen, they found a consistent, strong, positive relationship between activity and crime. They looked at homicide, rape, aggravated assault, robbery, and burglary (the classic serious offenses) and used straight regression, first-differences, and autoregressive formulations. They found a consistently strong relationship for the household activity ratio, a relationship that was stronger than the one for age grouping and much stronger than the relationship with the unemployment measure. For unemployment, the strength of the relationship was close to zero.

The temporal patterning in recent periods points to the importance of context in understanding crime and the complexity of patterns. The opportunity matrix is changing, society is changing. Crime rates should and do change.

Analyzing detailed opportunity structures in a historical or time-series approach is difficult. One area where it has been possible to perform numerical analysis has been in automobile theft patterns.

Sarah Boggs (1966) first pointed out the importance of counting the number of units "at risk" for any particular crime. In a study in St. Louis, she showed the striking difference in the spatial patterns of auto thefts if the theft rates were calculated on a per-person basis or a per-vehicle-registration basis. From a slightly different perspective, there should be a relationship between motor thefts and the number of motor vehicles on the road. Wilkins (1964) studied this relationship in England between 1938 and 1961 and found a positive link.

Two American studies, by Mansfield, Gould, and Namenwirth (1974) and by Gould (1969), looked at the abundance of motor vehicles and the associated motor-vehicle-theft rate. Both studies found a relationship between motor vehicle theft and the number of motor vehicles, but the relationship was complex. The authors argued that the criminal population is composed of professionals and amatuers. Professionals steal when there is a high return on their investment of time and effort. Amateurs steal when the crime is easy. Therefore, auto theft patterns were expected to vary as the number of registrations increased. When automobiles are relatively rare, the number of thefts should be comparatively high. When registrations are few, the car is a rare, desirable commodity, attractive to professional thieves. As the number of registrations increases, the automobile becomes less attractive to professionals. More is to be gained by looking elsewhere for targets. As registrations become even more numerous, amateurs take over. Cars are abundant, and the owners are less careful about security. Auto theft becomes easy, if not as financially rewarding. Because amateur criminals outnumber professionals, auto thefts rise. Both studies showed such a pattern.

The changing patterns of automobile thefts provide an additional interesting test of opportunity theory. Steering-wheel locks have been installed in all new cars for a number of years. These locks obviously change the security of cars. Mayhew et al. (1976) examined the mix of "newer" and "older" stolen cars and found that the locks, even at an aggregate level appeared to reduce the risk of theft. In 1969, the year that the locks were introduced in England, cars three years old or less ("new cars" before the locks were introduced) represented almost 21 percent of all the cars illegally taken in the London metropolitan police area. In 1973, the "new" cars with steering wheel locks made up only 5.1 percent of all the cars taken (Mayhew et al., 1976, p. 11). However, the risk reduction was relative. The overall

157

auto theft rate increased during this period. In the German Federal Republic, *all* cars were required to have steering-wheel locks installed by a fixed date. When the changeover to locks occurred, all cars were made more secure. Auto thefts decreased 62 percent in the first year (1963), and the decrease has been maintained despite massive increases in registrations (Mayhew, et al., 1976, p. 15).

Seasonality

The importance of opportunity can also be seen in the changing movement patterns of people and commodities. Within a city, there are changes in activity that are associated with crime. Houses and apartments are at the highest risk when the residents are away. Cars are moved around during the day and are often left unobserved during working hours and at night in apartment parking lots. Cars are at the highest risk when they are left unobserved.

At an intercity or regional level, crime is associated with major movements of population. Tourism represents a major movement of people and, as Cohen and Felson argued, creates increased opportunities at the "empty" homes of the tourists. The movement of tourists also may cause problems at the receiving end. In Florida, a high-tourism state, it was found that variations in the number of tourists were related to property crimes, particularly robbery. Crime may be a negative side effect of tourism (McPheters and Stronge, 1974a). Although tourist patterns have not been fully explored, it seems reasonable to expect nonemotional crimes—that is, property crimes—to relate to the changing dynamics of property location: crime moves as property moves.

At a simplistic level, a person who wants to steal a car does not go to a parking lot that is empty. At a less simplistic level, the human ecology concepts of rhythm, tempo, and timing should not be ignored in crime analysis (Cohen and Felson 1979). Cities pulse and change. People move about. Sometimes property is secure, sometimes insecure. The opportunity for crime is variable and is dependent on the movement of people and goods. Opportunities are spatially and temporally bound.

Criminal-Justice-System Factors

Most criminal-justice-system factors influencing crime trends have already been discussed. Several, however, deserve a restatement. It is never reasonable to assume, without examination, that changes in the amount of recorded crime are the direct result of changes in the behavior of individuals. Many institutional factors may influence how much crime is counted. The major criminal-justice-system factors are

1. Changes in options for handling crime.
2. Changes in the institutional application of the existing means for dealing with crime.
3. Changes in society's use of the existing means.
4. Random, unintentional error.

New Options

The history of the criminal justice system has been one of expanding options for dealing with the crime problem. The invention of the police, then prisons, probation, and parole, and, finally, "alternative" means, such as diversion, have created a net-widening effect (Blomberg, 1979). When options are created, they are usually used, as in the transportation planner's adage: "New highways are traffic generators." With a proliferation of the options available to the criminal justice system, behavior that was previously tolerated, ignored, or forgotten may be formally captured by the system.

Varying Applications

It is also argued that the massive increases in crimes known to the police since World War II are the result of changes in applications of the law and changes in police behavior. It has been suggested that much of the rise in reported crime is police-generated. The number of police is increasing faster than the population. This increase in police strength may *drive* or precede the increase in crime. The converse argument is, of course, that the police strength increases in response to increases in crime. It may be impossible to sort out the merits of these two approaches by looking at aggregate crime patterns since World War II. Crime has been increasing; so has police strength. When there are two increasing patterns such as these, it usually cannot be shown that one causes the other.

Differential Societal Use

The increase in officially recorded crime data could also be due in part to an increased willingness of individuals to call the police and report crimes. There is no way to demonstrate definitively whether there has been a systematic shift toward more reporting since World War II. Victimization surveys, where they exist, cover too short a period to give firm answers. However, there has been no appreciable reporting-rate increase over the period covered by the U.S. surveys (1973–present). This lack of increase, even for this relatively short period, lends support to the position that there has been no dramatic change in the rate at which people report crimes to the police, at least no recent shift that can explain massive crime increases. As long as there is no shift, the official data can be used as an index (a fixed fraction) of the actual uncounted victimizations.

In a reporting unit smaller than a country (say, a city) and for specific crimes, there may be reporting changes that do not show up in more aggregate data. Reporting at a local level may be influenced by media exposure (a crime wave) and by police programs.

The variation caused by police programs is worth examining in more detail, because changes in the number of reported crimes may be used to start or to stop specific programs. A current focus in policing is on *preventive policing*. Some police departments are trying to move away from their traditional use of patrol as the means to control crime and toward the use of the community to help control crime. Community relations programs, which were also developed to respond to real conflicts between local communities and the police, have proliferated. These programs—together with programs such as Operation ID, in which articles that might be stolen are marked with a personal, nonremovable identification, and Neighborhood Watch, in which local residents are encouraged to watch for and report unusual behavior—have the potential of increasing the number of crimes reported. In fact, if these programs are working, the amount of reported crime should go up.

159

Community relations programs should improve police relations with the public, making individuals more likely to think that reporting a crime may do some good. Similarly, Operation ID and Neighborhood Watch encourage reporting. When such programs are introduced, the number of reported crimes should go up.

Random Error

All information-gathering systems include error. No figures should be taken as absolutely correct. In record-sampling procedures and surveys such as victimization surveys, the numbers obtained are only estimates, not absolute values. The data gathering systems are also open to administrative error. Two numbers may look different. It may look as if crime is going up or down, but in reality, the changes may not be significant. As more is learned about the reporting systems, the error may be identified as system bias and may thus be reduced. Currently, small differences should generally not be taken too seriously.

Chapter Summary

Since World War II, there has been a massive increase in the number of reported crimes, both violent and property crimes. Although the patterns vary locally there has been an increase in the United States, Canada, and England. Recently, there has been some leveling, but it is too soon to know whether the leveling is temporary.

Arguments about the reasons for the increase abound: Is it real or just apparent? Although these arguments can not be completely resolved through empirical studies, they can be explored through the available data. The reasonable position, as is often the case, seems to be one in the middle. Some crime increase is most likely the result of the operation of the system or the system generating crime. As Pepinsky (1976) stated, a "goal" of much of the criminal justice system is reporting. With this as a goal, it is not surprising that counts have increased. On the other hand, the limited victimization data that exist support the position that official statistics are related to the pattern of victimizations. Reporting rates calculated from victimization data at an aggregate level do not vary significantly from year to year.

The massive increase in officially recorded crime is the result of some system influence, but it also probably reflects changes in society. Social, demographic, economic, and opportunity factors all seem to play a role in temporal crime variation, but in a complicated interplay. The changing mix of social class can affect crime. Changes in the demographic mix of races and ages can be used to predict some crime variation. Economic factors logically should matter, but the empirical support is mixed. Opportunity seems to matter and seems to be a valid analytic concept that should be used more frequently by researchers.

8

Long-term Patterns in Crime

Introduction

The modern crime patterns of England, Canada, and the United States outlined in Chapter 7 are strikingly similar in trend. Crime levels in all three countries have risen sharply and steadily since the end of World War II. By contrast, the levels of specific crime rates and the relative mixtures of crimes in the three countries have differed: England has had the lowest rates and the smallest proportion of violent crimes; the United States has had the highest crime rates and the highest proportion of violent crimes; and Canada has fallen in between on both measures.

Modern crime trends are best understood in historical perspective. Some components of the modern crime trends represent sharp breaks with past patterns, and others are continuations of patterns, cycles, and trends set years or centuries before. Recent advances in historical criminology make it possible to trace the long-term trends in English, American, and Canadian crime over very long periods of time. The English trends can be traced over almost eight hundred years. The American trends can be traced over almost four hundred years. The Canadian trends can be traced for more than a century. When these long-term historical patterns are considered together with the data of historical demographics and economics, as well as institutional, cultural, and political history, it becomes possible to test a wide range of ideas about the structural causes of crime.

Data Sources About Historical Crime Patterns

Most of the sources of information about crime discussed in Chapters 2, 3, and 4 are unavailable to researchers interested in long-term patterns. Victimization surveys date from the mid-1960s and self-report surveys date from the early 1940s. National police statistics date from the 1920s and 1930s in Canada and the United

161

States, and from the 1850s in England. National conviction statistics date from the 1830s in England and the 1870s in Canada. For studies of the crime trends before these dates, historians must rely on the records of local courts and on various personal memoirs.

By assembling information from court records and from memoirs, diaries, publications, folk histories, and the like, criminological historians are able to present relatively complete pictures of crime in different historical periods. Most important, it is possible to say something about crime trends, about the mixtures of crime experienced in different periods, and, occasionally, about the modes of crime or about the characteristics of convicted criminals.

Long-term Crime Patterns in England

Analysis of the long-term patterns of crime in England must be divided into two distinct periods. Recent historical work with the relatively extensive judicial records that have survived from the century and a half before the Black Death devastated Europe in the mid-fourteenth century makes it possible to assemble a picture of the crime patterns in England at the height of medieval civilization. The second analytic period begins with the accession of Elizabeth I to the throne in 1558 and runs, relatively intact, to the present. This modern period can be considered in four separate sequences: the early modern period, 1550–1700; the eighteenth century; the nineteenth century; and the twentieth century. There is a gap of two centuries between the medieval and modern analytic periods that coincides with an era of political and social turmoil touched off by the devastating depopulation caused by the Black Death. The crime patterns of this period are, thus far, known solely from anecdotal sources.

Crime in Medieval England

Homicide in the Thirteenth Century

The patterns of murder in thirteenth-century England are accessible to us through the surviving records of the great itinerant court of justice called the *eyre*. During the thirteenth century, this court, composed of a panel of royal justices, traveled round the country at irregular intervals, visiting each county every few years. The eyre was empowered to try all forms of action that could be heard in a royal court, including criminal accusations. While the eyre was sitting, its authority superseded that of all local courts, and even the royal courts of justice at Westminster would transfer cases back to the county for trial at the eyre.

Homicide cases were a major responsibility of the eyre, which was charged with inquiry into all homicides occurring between sittings. Information about homicide was gained in two ways. A coroner's court inquired into all deaths, sorting cases of death by accident or natural causes from murders. Records of these inquiries were examined and considered by the eyre. The second method involved the indicting jury. Each county was divided into smaller administrative areas called *hundreds* and *boroughs*. When an eyre began, each area was required to produce a jury of

162

twelve men who were questioned by the justices about local crimes, local court convictions and executions, and deaths from violence or suspicious causes. The jury responded with a list of offenses called a *veredicta*. The justices in the eyre proceeded through the veredicta, noting cases in which the offenders were unknown, scrutinizing the cases tried in the local courts since the last eyre, and trying cases in which the jury had named specific people as suspected murderers. Records of these inquiries and trials, called the *eyre rolls,* were handed in at Westminster by the eyre justices at the end of each sitting.

Homicide Trends. James Given (1977) analyzed the eyre homicide records for the counties of Bedford, Kent, Norfolk, Oxford, and Warwick, and the cities of London and Bristol. Using population estimates based on the census recorded in the Domesday Book in the late eleventh century, soon after the Norman Conquest, he was able to estimate homicide rates per 100,000 population for each of these jurisdictions: Bedford, 22; Kent, 23; Norfolk, 9; Oxford, 17; Warwick, 19; London, 12; and Bristol, 4. These levels of homicide are very much higher than modern English homicide rates. Based on crimes known to the police, a statistic likely to inflate the homicide rate relative to court inquiry records, the English rate in 1977 was 0.88 per 100,000 population. The homicide rate of thirteenth-century Bristol was almost five times higher, and the homicide rate of Kent, the county with the highest recorded level, was twenty-six times higher than the modern English homicide rate.

The thirteenth-century homicide rates differ from modern homicide rates in another way: they are highest in the rural counties and generally lower in the cities. A recent general analysis of twentieth-century city–hinterland homicide rates showed the cities to have higher homicide rates in eighteen out of the twenty-four countries surveyed (Archer and Gartner, 1980, p. 450). Contemporary English crime statistics also show higher homicide levels in urban areas than in the countryside.

Homicide rates rose throughout the thirteenth century. In Bedfordshire, for instance, the homicide rate calculated for the eyre of 1202 was 13 per 100,000 population. The rate calculated from the eyre of 1227–1228 was 15. The eyre of 1247 recorded a homicide rate of 23 per 100,000 populatoon, and and the eyre of 1276 recorded homicides at a rate of 28 per 100,000 population. The general upward trend was apparent in most jurisdictions: the average number of homicide victims per month doubled in London between 1244 and 1276, and the rates rose sharply in Norfolk, Kent, and Oxford as well.

Characteristics of Thirteenth-Century Homicide. Homicide was a group activity in the thirteenth century. Only about a third of the cases recorded in the eyre roles accused a single killer; 37 percent of the cases accused groups of two to four killers; 30 percent of the cases named groups of five or more killers and accomplices. Huge groups of twenty-two or more killers were indicted in 5 percent of the homicide cases.

Homicidal groups were often composed of kinship groups or of people with close social ties. A fifth of all group killings involved family members' banding together to attack the victim. Another fifth involved groups of fellow villagers who attacked the victim. Unrelated persons with household ties (masters and servants, or groups of fellow servants) accounted for another 4 percent of group killings. Only about 16 percent of the group killings were definitely attributed to groups of unrelated people hailing from several different places.

Homicide was primarily a male enterprise. Nine tenths of the accused killers were males. Four fifths of the homicide victims were males.

Given (1977) estimated the social class of victims and offenders by using eyre roll data on the net worth of offenders and by looking at the recorded occupations of victims and offenders. Neither data source was complete and both present significant problems.

The criminal process involved the confiscation of the accused person's possessions. Of the persons accused of homicide, 60 percent had no chattel property of any value whatsoever. An additional 24 percent had property worth less than ten shillings. This is a critical cutoff point. Ten shillings was the approximate price of an ox, one half of a plow team, and thus a critical measure of minimum economic security and status in medieval society. Of the accused killers, 84 percent fell below this measure of net worth and must be assumed to have belonged to the lowest socioeconomic stratum in medieval society.[1]

Given (1977) speculated that the majority of accused persons (77 percent) and victims (84 percent) for whom no occupation was recorded in the eyre rolls were peasants. Among the occupations that were listed (official; manufacturer, dealer, trader, or seller; tradesman; agricultural worker; transport worker; and ecclesiastics) only the ecclesiastics stand out. Clergy were demographically overrepresented among accused killers by a factor of 2. The preponderance of the lower classes among the homicide victims and offenders recorded in the eyre rolls might be partially due to the ability of the members of higher social and economic strata to kill and be killed without becoming entangled in the law: they controlled the courts and may not have been prepared to use criminal sanctions against one another.

Robber Bands and Homicide. The robber band formed the most important popular image of the criminal in thirteenth- and fourteenth-century society. On the one hand, the ballad of Robin Hood and his Merry Men celebrated impoverished gentry and yeomen who robbed the rich and gave to the poor in chivalric protest against oppressive rulers; on the other, contemporaries believed it to be deadly dangerous to travel the highways between cities and towns. Neither of the popular images of robber bands appears to have been accurate.

Robbers and bandits played an important role in the patterning of murder: almost 10 percent of all the victims in Given's thirteenth-century homicide data had been killed by robbers or bandits. The victims of robber bands were, primarily, villagers and isolated farmers, not merchants or lords on the highroads. Bandits descended on homes, stripped them of everything of value, and killed the occupants, particularly the women and children. The rise in homicide rates over the course of the century appears to have been caused by the increasing activity of

---

[1] It is not clear how the costs of jailing affected this pattern. In later periods, a jailed accused was required to pay for his own keep, so that by the time of trial, even a moderately wealthy person might have paid over everything he owned to his jailer for bribes or room-and-board fees.

robber bands: the proportion of homicides attributed to bandits increased steadily as the century progressed.

Crime in the Fourteenth Century

The fourteenth century was a period of massive upheaval and social change in Europe. During the first half of the century, the limits of medieval civilization were reached as population growth outstripped increases in agricultural production and manufacturing, creating demand inflation in the prices of everything and throwing a massive marginal class, which had been living at bare subsistence levels, into desperate famine. Institutional order began to crumble.

The Black Death (bubonic plague) entered Europe through the Crimea in 1347. It reached France in January of 1348, and by December, it had reached England. Between January and December of 1349, one third of the population of England died. The plague raged across Europe until 1353. The population of Europe was reduced from around 80 million people to about 60 million people. Population recovery took 150 years, and political and institutional recovery took longer.

The crime patterns of the first half of the fourteenth century have been studied by Barbara Hanawalt (1979). They reveal patterns at once similar to and radically different from the crime patterns of modern England.

By the beginning of the fourteenth century, the eyre was a dying institution, unable to cope with the increasing volume of judicial business in the provinces. The business of trying criminal cases (gaol delivery) was conducted by many different judicial bodies: by the eyre, by the court of King's Bench; by judges holding commissions of trailbaston (so named after criminals who wandered the countryside heavily armed, literally trailing clubs behind them); by judges holding commissions of *oyer and terminer* to try civil lawsuits; and by specially commissioned itinerant judges who were sent out to each county twice a year specifically to try criminal cases. In addition, a series of rival institutions, such as the leet courts (private franchisal courts) and the experimental keepers of the peace, tried and disposed criminal cases. Hanawalt (1979) studied the aggregate crime patterns in the judicial records of all of these institutions, supplemented by homicide and suicide data from the coroners' rolls, for eight counties.

Crime Trends. The levels of crime experienced by fourteenth-century society varied dramatically between 1300 and 1348. Crime levels, moderately high at the turn of the century, declined to their lowest point in the period between 1305 and 1309. There followed a massive rise in crime, which peaked around 1320 at levels four times higher than the prior low. After that, crime levels generally declined for twenty years and then began another, but more gradual, rise that lasted until the onset of the Black Death terminated reasonably reliable judicial record-keeping at mid-century (Figure 8–1).

This temporal pattern is important. Long-cycle variation in crime levels is an important characteristic of many Western societies. Crime levels do not merely rise, they rise and fall and rise again over periods of fifty to one hundred years. Sometimes the reasons for such cycles are easily identified in external conditions, and sometimes they are not. The dramatic rise in English crime between 1310 and 1320 seems to have been related to the burgeoning population and to bad harvests that

165

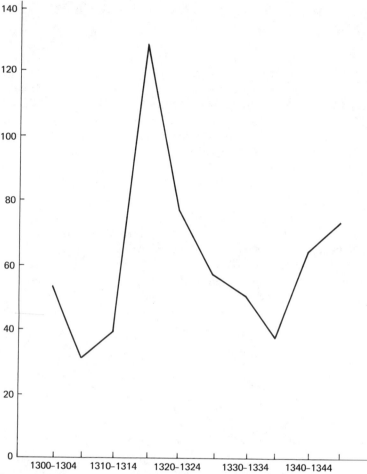

Figure 8–1. English crime trends, 1300–1348 (number of crimes, five-year average). [Source: Adapted from B. A. Hanawalt, *Crime and Conflict in English Communities: 1300–1348.* Cambridge, Mass.: Harvard University Press, 1979, p. 241.]

triggered famines. There was a dramatic shift in the relative proportions of burglary and homicide during the peak crime period, with burglary rising to its highest relative level and homicide dropping to its lowest relative level in this half-century.

Crime Characteristics. The relative levels of different types of crime (the crime mix) of the fourteenth century were distinctively different from the crime mix found in modern England (Table 8–1). Although property crime dominates the records of the crime mix of both periods, violent crime, particularly homicide, was far more prevalent in the fourteenth century than it is today. Theft accounted for 39 percent of all indictments between 1300 and 1348, burglary accounted for 24 percent. Burglary is relatively more important than theft in modern indictment figures. Arson, rape, and treason were minor components of the crime mix in the fourteenth

TABLE 8–1. Crime Mixtures in England, 1300–1348 and 1977

Crime	Percentage of Indictments 1300–1348	Percentage of Indictments 1977
Larceny–Theft	39.3	32.0
Burglary	24.1	42.1
Robbery	10.3	6.9
Homicide	18.6	1.0
Receiving	6.2	15.3
Arson	0.8	1.7
Rape	0.5	1.0
Treason	0.2	0

SOURCE: Calculated from data in B. A. Hanawalt, *Crime and Conflict in English Communities: 1300–1348* (Mass.: Harvard University Press, 1979), p. 272; Home Office (Annual) *Criminal Statistics: England and Wales* (London: HMSO, 1978 [Cmnd 7670]), pp. 272–278.

century, as they are now. Receiving, the crime of handling stolen goods, was somewhat less than half as important in the fourteenth century as it is in the modern crime mix.

The most important difference in the medieval and modern crime mixes is the difference in the relative importance of homicide. In 1977, homicide indictments accounted for about 1 percent of all indictments for this set of serious offenses.[2] In the fourteenth century, homicide accounted for almost a fifth of all criminal indictments. Hanawalt (1979) cautiously estimated that the homicide rate in London during the first half of the fourteenth century varied between 36 and 52 per 100,000 population. She estimated that a person living in London during that period ran a greater risk of death from homicide than from accident (pp. 98–99). The homicide rate in London in 1978 was about 1.6 per 100,000 population, or twenty-two to thirty-two times lower than the homicide rates of the fourteenth century.

Crime was a male problem in the fourteenth century. There were nine male offenders for every female offender. There were nine male victims for every female victim.

Crime was a problem for the lower ranges of the social order, perhaps because the nobility and the gentry refused to permit themselves to be brought to the bar. Hanawalt's examination of the court and social records of the Ramsey Abbey Villages showed that the wealthier villagers (the landholders, merchants, and tradesmen) were more often indicted for crime than the very poorest villagers, but studies of a number of other villages suggest that the villagers of different socioeconomic strata appeared in the court records in proportions roughly equal to their representation in the population.

[2] There are many additional crimes in the modern crime statistics, of course. The comparison in Table 8–1 and the accompanying text is based on a roughly comparable set of serious offenses found in both fourteenth-century and modern crime statistics. Only very large differences ought to be noted.

Criminal Bands in the Fourteenth Century. Criminal bands play as important a role in the imagery of fourteenth-century society as they did in that of the thirteenth century. Scholars have found no more evidence of social bandits who fit the romantic image of Robin Hood in the fourteenth-century data than they have found in the thirteenth-century data. Real fourteenth-century bandits did not rob from the rich and give to the poor: they descended on peasant homes; stole food, clothing, household goods, and livestock; raped the girls and women; and killed all witnesses. They engaged in robbery, extortion, and murder for hire. The robber bands of historical record appear to have been wholly indiscriminate about the social rank of their victims, choosing them on the basis of opportunity, proximity, or ease of attack. Exceptions to this pattern seem to have occurred only when these bands had been hired to harass or kill some specific victim, or when the band leader had a personal quarrel with a specific victim.

The social composition of fourteenth-century criminal gangs was a microcosm of the broader society. These bands seem to have been composed of landless knights and impoverished landholders, professional criminals and rootless vagabonds, Oxford dons and landless laborers. A large proportion of criminal band members seem to have been churchmen, who had the ability to claim benefit of clergy and avoid hanging for their felonies. The largest and longest-lasting of the criminal gangs—such as the Coterel gang, which terrorized Nottinghamshire and the Peak District in the late 1320s and early 1330s—had political connections with local gentry and ecclesiastics. They often worked for, or in concert with, the nominally law-abiding, drawing support and sharing booty. (Hanawalt, 1979; Bellamy, 1964, 1973).

Crime in Early Modern England: 1550–1700

There is a two-hundred-year gap in our information about English crime that stretches from about 1350 to about 1550. Internal and foreign wars, political and religious struggles overshadowed criminal justice and the need for careful judicial record-keeping. Judicial records were lost through poor storage, periodic housecleaning, fire, and deliberate or incidental destruction in the course of battle. The records that remain are scattered, in broken series. Historians of crime have so far remained reluctant to assert much about the character and patterns of crime during this period.

Beginning with the accession of Elizabeth I to the throne in 1558, judicial record-keeping became more systematic, and record preservation has been better. In recent years, historians have begun to trace the patterns of English crime for a number of counties in very thorough fashion. With caution, it is possible to trace the general crime trends from the mid-sixteenth century to the present.

The Early Modern Justice System

The justice system of this period was essentially a system of judicial courts and commissions. Primitive policing agencies existed—the constable, the sheriff, and the day watch—and there was some growth of what we would now think of as correctional agencies. But the arrest of criminals remained mostly a matter of self-help on the part of the victim, and the punishment of criminals remained mostly a matter of capital execution or corporal punishment.

Two principal criminal courts dominated the trial of criminal cases during the early modern period. *Assizes* were traveling judicial commissions composed of judges from the permanent superior courts sitting at Westminster. Their powers were derived from temporary commissions of assize, of goal delivery, or of oyer and terminer. The country was divided into six circuits, each of which was visited by assize judges twice a year. By custom, capital felonies were reserved for trial by assize judges. *Quarter sessions* were quarterly sittings of a quorum of the justices of the peace for a particular county. Justices of the peace were individually empowered to make inquiries, to take informations, to issue warrants, to conduct preliminary examinations of accused persons, and to take recognizances (promises made on pain of automatic fine) to keep the peace. A quorum of two or more justices of the peace was empowered to try and determine crimes committed within the county. General sessions of the peace were held four times a year and had the power to try most indictable offenses, though capital offenses were usually reserved for trial at assizes.

London had no assize visitation. The court of King's Bench exercised complete and plenary power to try all criminal cases. Situated in Westminster, it exercised nominal assize jurisdiction over the principal components of the metropolis: the county of Middlesex, the City of Westminster, and the City of London. In practice, however, it tried so few criminal cases that the general sessions of the peace of the three metropolitan jurisdictions became plenary criminal trial courts, meeting at least eight times annually in order to handle the volume of cases.

Three forms of prosecution were permitted. Private prosecution was called *appeal of felony*. The appellant filed suit by means of a writ, just as he would in a civil case. The appellee pleaded to the charges, and trial was joined. The appellant paid the costs of prosecution himself. If he lost, he risked punishment for having brought false suit or damages for having defamed the acquitted appellee. Prosecution could be commenced by an information filed directly with a court, charging a specific person with crime. Where a justice found, after preliminary examination in court, that there was evidence to support the information, the accused was bound over to face trial at the quarter sessions or the assizes. The most common form of prosecution was by means of grand jury indictment. Accusations were presented to a sitting grand jury in the form of bills of indictment. Bills found to be supported by evidence were followed by the issuance of indictments. An accused was required to plead to the charges in the indictment, then stand trial.

Criminal trials during this period have been characterized by Cockburn (1972) as "nasty, brutish, and essentially short" (p. 109). Felony defendants were not permitted legal counsel (a disadvantage not changed until 1836). Prosecution witnesses gave evidence on oath, but defense witnesses gave their evidence unsworn. The trial judge controlled the proceedings at all stages and, until the 1670s, had the power to punish jurors for bringing in verdicts that he felt inappropriate.

Cockburn (1972) estimated that 88 percent of accusations resulted in bills of indictment and that 75 percent of felony trials resulted in convictions. Only about 10 percent of felony convictions actually resulted in capital executions. An extensive system of mitigations saved most of those convicted from the gallows: jury under-

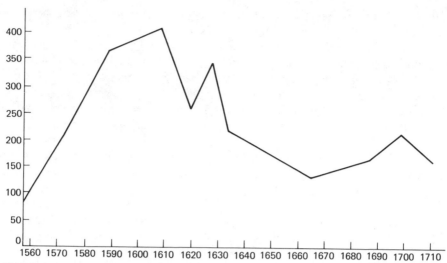

Figure 8–2. Incidents of criminal indictments in England, Home Circuit, 1560–1710. [Source: J. S. Cockburn, *A History of English Assizes: 1558–1714.* Cambridge: Cambridge University Press, 1972, p. 102. Reprinted with permission.]

valuation of stolen goods; benefit of clergy (exercised by an average of 20 percent of all convicts); commitment to service in the galleys; transportation abroad; and pardons (pp. 127–133).[3]

Crime Trends

The period between 1558 and 1700 was marked by three crime waves (Figure 8–2). The first crime wave, a sustained, major rise in crime levels during the reign of Elizabeth I, lasted for half a century, from 1559 to about 1600. The crime patterns of three counties on the perimeter of metropolitan London (Essex, Kent, and Sussex) have been analyzed for this period: all show major crime rises. Crime rates in Essex rose from about 70 felonies per 100,000 population in 1559 to about 360 felonies per 100,000 in the peak year of 1598. Crime levels at the end of Elizabeth's reign were four to eight times higher than those at the beginning of her reign (Cockburn, 1977; Samaha, 1974).

Cockburn (1972) analyzed the annual variations in assize indictments for the Home Circuit from 1560 to 1710. The Home Circuit was one of the six assize circuits into which the country was divided. It comprised five counties on the northern, eastern, and southern perimeters of London: Hertfordshire, Essex, Kent, Surrey, and Sussex. The aggregate pattern for the five counties shows the first major wave and two smaller waves. The second crime wave is composed of a strong decline from the crest of the first wave around 1610 to a trough around 1620, then a sharp rise to a peak in about 1630. The peak of the second wave was followed by a forty-year decline in indictments, reaching a trough in about 1670. The third crime

---

[3] For further reading, see Baker (1977) and Cockburn (1972).

170

wave followed with a thirty-year increase in indictments, peaking in about 1700, and declining again until 1710. ·

Crime Characteristics

The levels of crime in early modern English society appear to be tied to the crime mix. At the beginning of the Elizabethan period, 13 percent of the persons accused of serious crimes in Essex were accused of crimes of violence against the person, 40 percent were accused of robbery or burglary, and 47 percent were accused of theft. In 1598–1602, when crime levels were three times higher, accusations for violent crime dropped to 7 percent of the total, accusations for robbery and burglary dropped to 21 percent of the total, and accusations for theft rose to 72 percent of the total. The comparable figures for Essex in the period 1668–1713, during the third crime wave, show that 18 percent of accused persons were accused of crimes of violence, 24 percent of robbery or burglary, and 58 percent of theft. The first great crime wave was strongly associated with a growth in the problem of theft. The third peak, at the end of the eighteenth century, was associated with a major rise in the relative importance of crimes of violence.

In some ways, the rise in crime at the end of the seventeenth century was more serious than the much larger rise in crime levels at the end of the sixteenth century. The first great crime wave during this period was caused principally by a rise in theft and other crimes against property, whereas the numbers of violent crimes against the person stayed the same or even declined. Overall crime levels rose, but the most dangerous crimes declined. In the crime wave that closed the seventeenth century, the numbers of all kinds of crime rose, making this period more dangerous, even though the overall crime rate was lower.

Homicide rates appear to have declined substantially in the early modern period. Cockburn (1977) calculated the annual average homicide rates per 100,000 population at 7 in Essex, 14 in Sussex, and 16 in Hertfordshire during the Elizabethan period (pp. 55–56). The homicide rate in Sussex dropped to about 3 per 100,000 population at the end of the seventeenth century. The homicide rate in Surrey dropped from around 5.3 in the 1690s to about 2.3 per 100,000 population in the 1720s (Beattie, 1974, p. 61). Homicides were less tied to the commission of other felonies than they were in the late medieval period. Instead, the vast majority of murders "occurred during acts of sudden, unpremeditated aggression and resulted from attacks with a variety of knives and blunt instruments" (Cockburn, 1977, p. 57).

Crime was a male activity in Elizabethan Essex: 90 percent of the persons accused of crime were male. Crime was also a lower-class activity in Elizabethan Essex. The landowning social classes were demographically underrepresented in judicial records: gentlemen comprised about 2.2 percent of the county's population, but only 1.1 percent of the persons charged with felony; yeomen, (wealthy landholders of common birth) constituted about one third of the county population, but only 10 percent of the charged felons; other landholders (peasants or husbandmen) comprised 20 percent of the county population but only 7.5 percent of charged criminals. By contrast, the unpropertied classes contributed the largest share of known criminals: half of the people charged with felony were identified as laborers;

another 25 percent of the known criminals were identified as tradesmen such as butchers, tailors, blacksmiths, and carpenters (Samaha, 1974, pp. 26–27).

Vagrants and Crime

The romantic criminal gang played no important role in the early modern imagery of crime: Robin Hood was replaced by the shabby stranger, the vagabond, and the vagrant. The Elizabethans thought that vagrants—wandering paupers living by means of robbery, theft, and fraud—were the principal source of crime. The draconian antivagrancy statutes adopted during this period specifically blamed vagrants for the rising crime rate (Chambliss, 1964).

Elizabethan and seventeenth-century vagrants were mostly young, single males. They traveled the roads and highways of England in a rhythm set by the agricultural calendar (Laslett, 1971; Beier, 1974; Cockburn, 1977). Vagrants were principally involved in opportunistic thefts. Cockburn (1977) said that the pretrial records of three different counties show "quite clearly the prevalence of vagrants and their association with . . . opportunistic thieving. . . . Vagrants concentrated on isolated or empty dwellings, goods left unattended, solitary or obviously gullible victims" (p. 63). Scholars are not yet in agreement on whether vagrants ought to be viewed as professional criminals or as victims of economic circumstance wandering the countryside and stealing for subsistence, but it appears that much of the Elizabethan crime wave can be attributed to the activities of vagrants.

Crime in the Eighteenth Century

The crime patterns of the eighteenth century form an important bridge between the preindustrial crime patterns of the medieval and early modern periods and the crime patterns of the modern, urban, industrialized world. By the end of the eighteenth century, a number of the important characteristics of modern crime patterns had become fully fixed, whereas medieval and early modern criminal justice institutions had been pushed to their logical conclusions and could no longer be adapted to the control of new forms of crime. The crime patterns of the eighteenth century gave rise to the Classical School reform movement that established the modern institutions of criminal justice in the period between 1764 and 1850.

The Eighteenth-Century Justice System

The criminal justice system of the eighteenth century was inefficient, unfair, savage, and corrupt by modern standards. The criminal law was based on the theory of terror. The agencies of justice were wedded to ideas of self-help and private enterprise, and they stressed the importance of form rather than function.

The growth of cities and towns during the seventeenth century had been matched by a proliferation of quasi-police agencies. Some, like the offices of sheriff or constable, were historic administrative offices charged with law enforcement. Others, the day watches and night watches, were newly created institutions. None was charged with a routine duty to prevent crimes or to arrest and prosecute offenders. Instead, arrest and prosecution were private functions. Private citizens could sometimes seek the aid of law enforcement officers but could not always count on receiving it.

In the absence of preventive police, Parliament sought to encourage law enforcement through a system of rewards paid to persons successfully prosecuting criminals and a system of immunities and pardons given to criminals turning crown evidence against co-offenders. This system helped create a class of professional "thief takers," who solved crimes and prosecuted criminals for the rewards.

Thief taking was a business well suited to corruption. Johnathan Wild, for instance, used his reputation as a thief taker to organize virtually all of London's underworld in the 1730s. Wild commissioned thieves to steal goods. In his role as thief taker, he approached the victim and offered to secure a return of the goods, no questions asked, for a fixed percentage of their value. Thieves who refused to cooperate with this system were captured and prosecuted by Wild and his agents: the renegade was hung, and Wild collected his reward from the courts and enhanced his reputation as a detective. Wild was eventually hung on the evidence of a lieutenant with whom he had a falling out (Howson, 1970). Other thief takers, epitomized by Peachum in *The Beggar's Opera*, entrapped innocents by enlisting them as accomplices in the commission of crimes and then turning crown evidence against them in exchange for immunity from prosecution and a reward.

The majority of victims were left to self-help. Victims seeking legal authority for their efforts at self-help, or commencing prosecutions for all but the most serious of crimes, went to a justice of the peace for a warrant. Most of the immediate problems of criminal justice in the eighteenth century—problems of investigation and accusation, of the punishment for petty offenses, and of the commencement of prosecutions for serious crimes—were handled with informality by lay justices of the peace sitting at home or in local gathering places.

The notebooks of Justice William Emmett of Bromley in Kent reveal the range of local, lay justice. He dealt with public profanity and stolen goods, cricket played on Sundays and assaults on public officers, illegal hunting and fights in public houses. In 1711, Emmett gave search warrants to William Wicker "to search for goods stolen from him on Thursday night being the 6th of March," and to John Drury "to search for stoalen wood and hedg stealers [*sic*]." In 1712, Emmett gave arrest warrants to Edmund Say, bricklayer, against John Jones, schoolmaster, for "abuseing, strickeing, and wounding the said Edmund Say in the execution of his office" as a parish officer, and to Thomas Phillips, laborer, against James Grim, who "had beaten, brused, and wounded" Phillips. Each warrant gave the victim the authority to undertake law enforcement functions commonly exercised by modern police (Melling, 1969, pp. 146–149).

Serious crimes were tried at the assizes or the quarter sessions, which were not much changed from the early modern period. The substantive criminal law, however, became more savage through the theory of deterrence by terror. The range of capital felony expanded enormously during the eighteenth century. In 1680, there were perhaps fifty capital offenses. By 1810, English criminal law defined about nine hundred behaviors, scattered through 200 different statutes, for which an offender could be hung (Radzinowicz, 1948).

The law was never as severe in operation as it appeared on paper. Juries defied the law by refusing to convict, or by bringing in partial verdicts that reduced capital felonies to noncapital misdemeanors. A significant proportion of criminal business was shifted from the assizes to the quarter sessions. The proportion of capitally convicted offenders actually hung declined throughout the century. An extensive system of pardons and reprieves, operating through political and social patronage systems, developed in concert with new forms of punishment, particularly the practice of transporting convicted felons to penal colonies in America and Australia (Radzinowicz, 1948; Hay, 1975; Beattie, 1977). The principal forms of punishment were hanging, transportation, whipping, and fines. Imprisonment did not become a major form of punishment until the nineteenth century.

Crime Trends

Crime rates cycled through two major peaks in the eighteenth century (Figure 8–3). The upward trend that began in the 1680s continued to a peak in the 1720s. This peak was associated with waves of robbery in London, and with a major outbreak of violent crime and political unrest (called *blacking* because the offenders wore blackface as a disguise) in the countryside west and south of London. The Waltham Black Act (9 Geo. 1, c.22) enacted at the peak of this crime wave is one of the most savage in common-law history: it created more than fifty capital offenses, ranging from extortion to poaching to the malicious destruction of trees; it applied retroactively to activities that had been legal when they were done; and it permitted trial and condemnation in absentia.

The second peak occurred in the 1750s and was followed by a long decline, with an upturn at the end of the century. Criminal-justice reform efforts begun during the mid-century crime wave developed into the great Classical School transformations of English criminal justice in the early nineteenth century (Radzinowicz, 1948; Thompson, 1975; Beattie, 1974, 1977).

The trends in London look somewhat different, depending on the crime, the location, and the measure employed. Radzinowicz (1948) traced the patterns of capital convictions in London and Middlesex assizes from 1750 to 1800. Convictions declined from a peak in 1750 to a half-century low in 1760, then climbed to a peak in the early 1780s and declined thereafter. Beattie (1977) traced the assault and property crime rates in urban Surrey, which had really become the southern half of metropolitan London, over the period from 1660 to 1800. Assault rates rose from 1660 to peaks in the 1720s and 1730s, declined to a low in 1760, jumped to a minor peak in the late 1760s, and declined again until the end of the century, when they began a general rise. Property crime rates peaked around 1715 and around 1750 and were climbing again in 1802.

Crime trends in rural Surrey and Sussex were different from the London pattern. Property crimes declined from 1660 to about 1770, then showed a strong increase from 1770 into the nineteenth century. The assault rate increased slightly in rural Surrey throughout the eighteenth century, but it declined steadily from 1660 to 1802 in Sussex.

The Crime Mix

Property crime came increasingly to dominate the crime mix of the eighteenth century. The homicide rate in Surrey dropped from 5.3 per 100,000 population in the 1690s, to about 2.3 in the 1720s, to less than 1.0 between 1795 and 1802; in Sussex, it dropped from around 3.0 in 1700 to about 1.0 in 1800. During the crime wave of the 1750s, robbery accounted for 11 percent of property crime in-

174

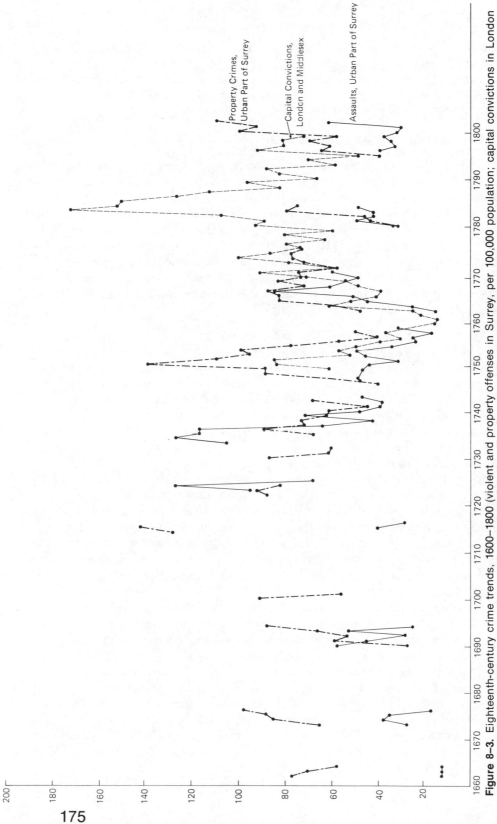

Figure 8–3. Eighteenth-century crime trends, 1600–1800 (violent and property offenses in Surrey, per 100,000 population; capital convictions in London and Middlesex, number per annum). [Source: Surrey: J. M. Beattie, "The Pattern of Crime in England, 1660–1800," *Past and Present* 62(1974):47–95; London and Middlesex, L. Radzinowicz, *A History of English Criminal Law from 1750: vol. 1. The Movement for Reform.* London: Stevens, 1948.]

175

dictments in urban Surrey; other capital property crimes such as burglary accounted for about 9 percent, animal theft for 3 percent, grand larceny for 32 percent, and petty larceny for 45 percent. Assault rates exceeded property crime rates in urban Surrey during the 1720s and 1730s but were otherwise generally lower.

Crime in the Nineteenth Century

The historical record of crime in England in the nineteenth century is remarkably different from that of earlier centuries in three ways. First, the modern institutions of criminal justice were developed during the nineteenth century. Crime trends can be examined through police and correctional records as well as judicial records. Second, comprehensive central collection of criminal statistics developed during the nineteenth century. It is possible to examine national crime trends and mixtures directly, rather than by inference. Third, criminologists examined the limitations of nineteenth-century crime statistics in detail. Conclusions drawn from nineteenth-century data can be much firmer than those drawn from earlier records.

The Nineteenth-Century Justice System

The English criminal justice system was in a state of collapse at the beginning of the nineteenth century. The twin doctrines of encouraging private law enforcement through rewards and deterring offenses through terror were generally believed to have failed. Policing was both haphazard and corrupt. The criminal law was a shambles—a vast, unsystematized amalgam of statutes, cases, bylaws, and customs that was both unknown and unknowable. The courts used unfair procedures against uncounseled defendants, and juries routinely ignored both plain facts and law in order to avoid felony convictions. Capital sentences were only rarely executed. Transportation to the American colonies was no longer possible, and transportation to the Australian penal colonies was a slow and expensive business. Convicts were increasingly placed at hard labor on the prison ships (the "hulks") floating in the Thames. Crime rates were rising. The streets of the cities were dangerous for all.

Nineteenth-century criminal-justice reform created the core institutions of the modern criminal justice system. Patrol police, charged with a duty to prevent crimes and to arrest and prosecute criminals, were invented in nineteenth-century England. The London Metropolitan Police were created in 1829. The success of the new police was so spectacular that by 1856, all local governments were required to institute new model police forces. Criminal procedure was reformed, the laws of evidence were solidified, and legal defense counsel were permitted in court on a routine basis. The criminal law was simplified, consolidated, and reduced in savagery, though it was never codified. The summary jurisidction of magistrates' courts was expanded substantially, and the felony jurisdiction of the quarter sessions and the assizes was reduced. Imprisonment slowly replaced capital and corporal punishment as the principal form of punishment. By the 1850s, the squalid local jails and the floating prison hulks had been replaced by a system of local and national prisons (Radzinowicz, 1948; Silver, 1967; Thompson, 1968, pp. 532–533; Gatrell and Hadden, 1972; McConville, 1981).

176

Crime Trends

Crime trends in nineteenth-century England (Figure 8–4) can be traced through many different sources. National judicial statistics were collected episodically from 1805 and annually from 1834. National police statistics date from 1857. Regional time series are available for London and for Lancashire. All of the criminal statistics show similar patterns: a vast tidal wave of crime that began in the late eighteenth century and rose to a peak in the late 1840s, then declined for the remainder of the century.

Historians and criminologists think that the statistical trends in the English data reflect the real patterns of crime occurrence in the nineteenth-century. Gatrell and Hadden (1972) argued that the apparent decline in crime after 1850 must be real because it occurred during a period in which the modern police developed into efficient engines for discovering and recording crime. The magnitude of the declining trend after 1850 occurred when the police, as a social institution, should have caused a major inflation in the known crime rates. Tobias's (1972b) general survey of nonstatistical sources of information about crime levels—parliamentary papers; newspaper, magazine, and pamphlet accounts; and the personal diaries of individuals—reinforces the reality of the trends in the statistics. These sources show a general rise in public and private concern about crime from the beginning of the century until about 1850. After mid-century, concern about crime declined for fifty years.

London and Lancashire had crime trends that followed the national pattern. The indictable crime rates in London rose in the early part of the century and reached a peak in the late 1840s. After 1850, crime rates generally declined for the remainder of the century (Gurr et al., 1977, pp. 65, 111). Murder, assault, and theft rates followed the general trend. Robbery rates had two peaks, in the 1820s and in the 1870s, whereas the burglary rates went against the general trend, rising throughout the nineteenth century. The crime rates in Lancashire peaked around 1840 and declined for the remainder of the nineteenth century (Gatrell and Hadden, 1972:375).

The Crime Mix

The English crime mix shifted away from simple property crime toward violent property crime such as burglary and robbery over the second half of the nineteenth century. In 1860, simple property crime without violence accounted for 89 percent of the crimes known to the police; property crimes with violence accounted for 6 percent; and violent crimes against the person accounted for about 3 percent. In 1910, property crime without violence accounted for 79 percent of the crimes known to the police; property crimes with violence accounted for 13 percent; and violent crimes against the person accounted for 4 percent. By any imaginable standards, nineteenth-century crime was preeminently property crime.

Crime in Twentieth-Century England

The structure of the English criminal justice system has remained relatively stable since the early twentieth century. The principal institutional innovations

177

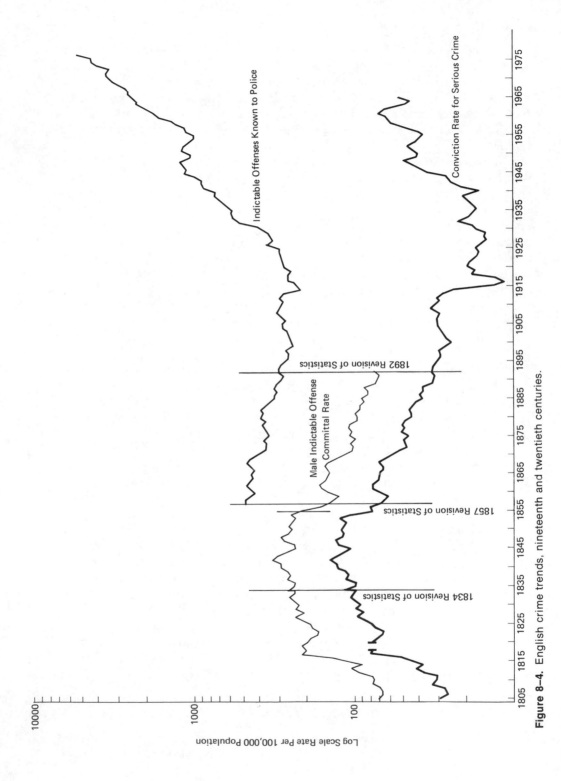

Figure 8–4. English crime trends, nineteenth and twentieth centuries.

178

include the consolidation of small police forces into large operating organizations covering large jurisdictions; the introduction of juvenile courts and a system of offender probation around 1908; the consolidation and expansion of the prison system; and the introduction of parole in 1968. The most startling structural change involved the abolition of the assizes and the quarter sessions, and their replacement with a new system of crown courts for the trial of indictable crimes in the early 1970s. Criminal justice statistics have been collected in essentially similar form since 1893.

Crime Trends

The general decline in crime that began in the second half of the nineteenth century lasted until 1914. After that date, English crime rates have generally increased, except for a period immediately after World War II, when, for a decade, crime rates leveled and then actually fell. The massive and rapid rise in the rates of known crimes over the past quarter century that was outlined in Chapter 7 is unprecedented in English history. The crime rates of the late 1970s were twenty-five times higher than the crime rates of 1914, and ten times higher than the indictable crime rates recorded in the 1850s, during the nineteenth-century crime peak.

The Crime Mix

The twentieth-century English crime mix continues trends that developed in the latter half of the nineteenth century. Although property crime still dominates the mix, there has been an ominous shift away from simple property crimes such as theft and toward violent property crimes, such as burglaries and robberies. In 1900, simple property crime accounted for 81 percent of crimes known to the police; property crimes with violence accounted for 10 percent; and violent crimes against the person accounted for about 5 percent. By 1930, simple property crimes made up 75 percent of the mix; property crimes with violence had increased to 18 percent; and violent personal crimes continued to account for about 5 percent. In 1960, simple property crime had further declined to 72 percent of the mix; property crime with violence had increased to 21 percent of the mix; crimes of personal violence continued to account for about 5 percent.

Compared with reported-offense levels in 1900, the reported-offense levels in the early 1960s make the shifting composition of the crime mix quite clear. Reported break-in attempts were about forty-two times higher in 1963 than in 1900, shop break-ins were twenty-six times higher, and house break-ins were fourteen times higher. By contrast, simple and minor larcenies were up by only a factor of 10, and frauds and false pretenses by a factor of 12. Larceny from the person—pocket picking—had increased a miniscule 1.5 times over the sixty-year period. Murder rates actually declined slightly from their 1900 levels. The overall rates for the full set of reported indictable offenses increased by a factor of 11 over the period 1900–1963. Property crimes with violence clearly increased much more rapidly than simple property crimes or crimes of violence (McClintock and Avison, 1968, p. 30).

179

Long-Term Crime Patterns in America

Permanent English settlement of North America dates from the early seventeenth century. Settlement began on the eastern seaboard and moved west only slowly at first. Records of crime in some eastern cities span a period of three hundred years, but the periods covered become much shorter as we move progressively west. California, for instance, has no common-law crime pattern for analysis prior to the mid-nineteenth century. The early settlements were radically different societies: Massachusetts, Pennsylvania, and Maryland were theocracies, but of very different persuasion; New York was a secular trading colony; Virginia and the Carolinas were manorial cultures based on chattel slavery; and Georgia was a penal colony. Nothing like common use of the criminal law emerged until after the Civil War (1861–1865) and nothing like national crime statistics was collected until the 1930s. Still, by examining the extant records of crime in different places at specific times, it is possible to assemble a long-term picture of American crime patterns.

Crime in the Seventeenth Century

Our picture of seventeenth-century American crime—for the present, at least—is largely based on the crime patterns of Essex County in Massachusetts (Table 8–2). Salem, with its infamous witch trials and executions of 1692, forms the geographic and historical core of the county. This fact, combined with the survival of detailed judicial, governmental, and social records, has made seventeenth-century Essex a major subject of scrutiny by social and legal historians, psychologists, and criminologists. Studies of crime in other colonies tend to be anecdotal, such as Semmes's (1938) study of crime in Maryland, or excessively technical, such as Goebel and Naughton's (1970) study of criminal procedure in colonial New York. This is true, in part, because of the limited number of records made in the first place,

TABLE 8–2. Convictions in Essex, Massachusetts, 1651–1680 (Rates per 1,000 Population)

	1651–1655	1656–1660	1661–1665	1666–1670	1671–1675	1676–1680
Church related	3.6	18.5	31.5	18.6	6.7	3.2
Contempt of Authority	8.0	9.2	8.9	11.9	12.5	7.6
Fornication	7.8	6.2	4.4	5.1	8.5	10.2
Disturbing the peace	1.3	2.5	3.0	4.4	2.8	2.7
Crimes against Persons and Property	8.7	7.7	10.2	8.9	7.5	9.2
Other	12.9	8.8	6.7	4.9	5.8	8.4
Total	42.3	52.9	64.7	53.8	43.8	41.3

SOURCE: Adapted from K. T. Erikson *Wayward Puritans* (New York: Wiley, 1966), p. 175.

in part because many records have not survived, and in part because the existing records present difficult problems of legal interpretation. Thus, the crime patterns of this period of American history can be understood in only the most tentative fashion.

Crime Trends

The conviction rates of Essex County, Massachusetts, show striking variations over the thirty-year period 1651–1680. The total conviction rate varied by 50 percent over the period, climbing from a low of about 42 convictions per 1,000 population in 1651–1655 to a peak of almost 65 per 1,000 in 1666–1670, then descending to about 41 per 1,000 in 1676–1680. The crime patterns in the 1680s and 1690s are much less clear, as they are compounded by struggles between the king's colonial administrators and the colonial legislature over political control of the agencies of government, by social unrest occasioned by the French threat from Canada, and by the infamous witchcraft trials of Salem. To the extent that they have been sorted out, conviction rates appear to have risen during the late 1680s and early 1690s (Erikson, 1966; Konig, 1979).

The Crime Mix

The crime mix varied substantially over the thirty years for which conviction data have been analyzed in detail. In the period 1651–1655, traditional serious crimes against persons and property accounted for 21 percent of the criminal convictions in Essex county; fornication accounted for 18 percent; contempt of authority for 19 percent; and crimes against the church for about 8 percent. During the peak that occurred a decade later, the crime mix was substantially different: although their rate had risen, crimes against persons and property accounted for only 16 percent of the criminal convictions; fornication dropped to 7 percent; contempt of authority dropped to 14 percent; and crimes against the church rose to 47 percent of all convictions! The crime mix of 1676–1680 returned to something like the earlier pattern.

This variation in the crime mix, in concert with the crime trend for the period, illustrates a common pattern in American crime data. As Lawrence Friedman (1973) has observed, the criminal law is something more than a statement of current morality, it is "a vehicle for economic and social planning, and an index to the community's division of power" (p. 64). Americans seem always to have seen the criminal law in this way, and to have used it as a convenient device for dealing with problems of social order quite different from the dangerous and expensive problems prohibited by the laws of felony and misdemeanor. Rapid and sharp rises in the overall crime rate have frequently reflected periods of change in the incidence of nuisance behavior or disputes about the structure of the social order rather than changes in the incidence of common crime. Changes in the crime mix indicate these periods.

The crime rise in seventeenth-century Essex County was general, but the magnitude of the peak reflects an intense social dispute between the Puritan religious order of Massachusetts and the evangelical Quakers, who insisted on preaching deviant religious doctrine. Crimes against the church jumped from about 8 percent of the mix during more normal times, to almost half during the height of the

181

Quaker problem. Prosections for fornication, always important in colonial America, dropped from 18 percent of the crime mix to only about 7 percent during the crime peak. Common-law crimes dropped from 21 percent of the crime mix to about 16 percent at the peak.

Crime in the Eighteenth Century

The crime patterns of eighteenth-century America are available through studies of a number of cities, particularly the colonial metropolises of Boston, New York, Philadelphia, and Charleston. All four cities had relatively low crime rates in the period 1700–1750, and sharply rising crime rates during the second half of the century. Crime rates rose to very high levels after 1780, and the trend continued into the early part of the nineteenth century. Figure 8–5 presents estimated crime curves for the four cities based on a limited number of data points measuring prosecutions per 100,000 population and a number of nonstatistical accounts of crime trends.

Boston

Boston began the eighteenth century with a relatively small crime problem. During the first third of the century, the prosecution rate for all crimes averaged about 537 per 100,000 population. More than half of the prosecutions were for essentially minor offenses against morality or for drunkenness. Crimes against property were prosecuted at a rate of 123 per 100,000, and crimes of violence were prosecuted at a rate of about 37 per 100,000 population (Ferdinand, 1980). As late as 1760, Boston had low rates of crime compared with other American cities. Thereafter, the pressures of urban growth, of political agitation and war, and of social change combined to increase Boston's crime rate. By the late 1760s, "the inability of the Boston watch to preserve the famed nocturnal security of former times frightened many substantial citizens" (Bridenbaugh, 1955, p. 298).

Boston's crime rate appears to have continued to soar until at least the mid-1820s. Ferdinand (1980, p. 198) showed that the total prosecution rate in 1824 was 4,436 per 100,000 population—an eightfold increase in this measure of crime in eighty years. Moreover, the relative crime mix had changed dramatically for the worse. Common-law crimes, dangerous to persons and property, were far more numerous. Violent crimes against the person accounted for 32 percent of all prosecutions in 1824, compared to only 7 percent eighty years earlier. Property crimes accounted for only 19 percent of prosecutions. Drunkenness and morality prosecutions accounted for about a third of offenses in 1824, compared with half of all prosecutions in the early eighteenth century.

New York City

New York City appears to have experienced a U-curve in crime trends. It had a period of relatively high crime rates in the early part of the century, followed by a period of relatively lower crime rates in the 1720s. Crime rates began to rise again in the 1730s, and the rise accelerated rapidly and continuously after 1760. Greenberg (1976) found a prosecution rate for serious crimes of 300 per 100,000 population in New York State in 1703, and the much lower rate of 150 per 100,000

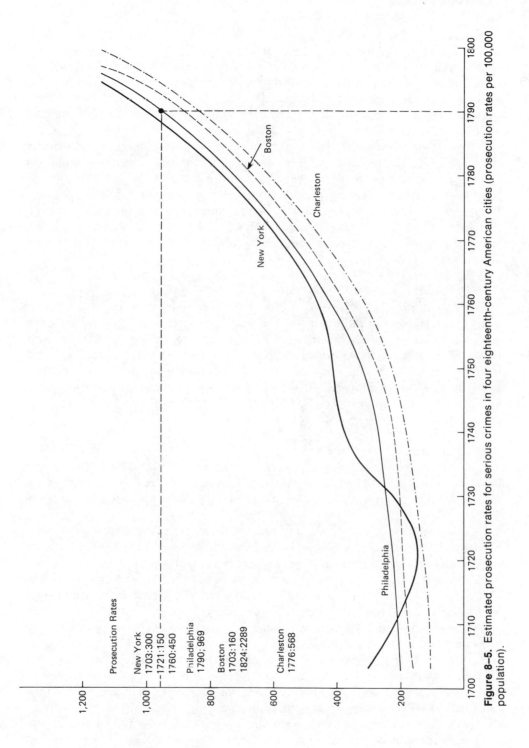

Figure 8–5. Estimated prosecution rates for serious crimes in four eighteenth-century American cities (prosecution rates per 100,000 population).

183

population in 1723. New York City itself had a prosecution rate of 450 per 100,000 population in the period after 1750. Bridenbaugh (1955) also noted that crime became a significant problem in New York City after 1750. By the 1770s, New York had a reputation as the most dangerous of the American cities and as a base for criminals operating on an intercolonial scale. Vice areas became firmly established in waterfront locations during the latter part of the century, as well (Inciardi, 1978, p. 32).

New York's crime mix also changed over the course of the eighteenth century. Comparing the two periods 1691–1749 and 1750–1776, Greenberg found that theft had risen from 17 to 24 percent of prosecutions; that public order crimes had risen from 6 to 9 percent of prosecutions; and that crimes of violence had risen from 13 to 28 percent of prosecutions. Many contemporary commentators thought that most of the rise in crime in the latter part of the eighteenth century could be attributed to increased levels of homicide, robbery, and burglary (Bridenbaugh, 1955).

Philadelphia

Philadelphia, America's largest city in the eighteenth century, had America's worst crime problem through much of the era. Crime rates were high and the courts dealt with frequent cases of theft, robbery, rape, assault, and murder in the period before 1750. Reform of the nightwatch in 1750 appears to have reduced the crime levels for almost a decade, but the crime rates rose again in the 1760s and thereafter. By 1790, when Philadelphia served as the national capital, its conviction rate for serious crimes was 969 per 100,000 population (Bridenbaugh, 1955, pp. 113, 302; Hobbs, 1943).

Charleston

Charleston had relatively low crime rates prior to the 1760s. Crime rates began to rise sharply in the latter third of the eighteenth century. Charleston had annual prosecution rates on the order of 622 per 100,000 population in the period 1769–1776.

Charleston's crime mix was very different from the crime mixes found in the northern colonial cities during the late eighteenth century. Violent crimes against the person accounted for about 10 percent of all prosecutions in Middlesex County, Massachusetts, circa 1776, but accounted for 54 percent of all prosecutions in Charleston. Crimes against property accounted for 13 percent of prosecutions in Middlesex County, but 38 percent of prosecutions in Charleston. Crimes against order and morals—such offenses as bastardy, fornication, riot, and vagrancy—were a major problem for the criminal justice system in Middlesex County, Massachusetts, accounting for 58 percent of prosecutions! In Charleston, by contrast, these offenses constituted a mere 3 percent of prosecutions. The special differences between Massachusetts society and South Carolinian society is reflected in two other categories of crime: crimes against the church and authority constituted 18 percent of prosecutions in Massachusetts but do not appear at all in South Carolina data for the late eighteenth century. Slave-related crimes constituted 3 percent of Charleston prosecutions circa 1776 but do not appear in Massachusetts data for the period (Hindus, 1980, p. 64).

Charleston's social patterns were, at base, radically different from those of the other major colonial cities. In some senses, Charleston was much closer in spirit to Georgian London than any of the other colonial cities, serving as an urban gathering spot for a landed society founded on plantation agriculture and chattel slavery. In many ways, then, it is not surprising to find Charleston's crime problem to have been different from that in theocratic Boston. What is perhaps most startling is the difference in violence. This difference has persisted throughout American history.

Crime in the Nineteenth Century

The general trend of crime in nineteenth-century America is remarkably consistent with contemporary patterns in England. The rising crime rates observed in American cities in the late eighteenth century continued to increase through the first half of the nineteenth century, reaching a peak in the 1850s. Crime rates generally declined from the late 1850s until about 1930.

The general trend is visible in both state and city data. Massachusetts data have been charted for the period 1836–1873. (Figure 8-6). They show the 1850s peak for total crimes; for crimes against morality, order, and chastity (such as fornication or drunkenness); for crimes against property; and for crimes against the person. All of these crime categories show secondary peaks in the years immediately after the Civil War. South Carolina crime data for the period 1801–1860 show a very high peak in the period 1811–1820, then rise to a half-century peak in the 1850s (Hindus, 1980, pp. 72, 77).

Arrest data for individual cities show similar patterns (Figure 8–7). New York City data for the period 1845–1870 show a clear peak in the 1850s (Miller, 1977, p. 101). Buffalo data show a crime peak in the early 1870s, followed by a period of generally delining crime rates lasting 80 years (Powell, 1966, 1970). Boston arrest data show peaks in the 1850s and 1870s, followed by generally declining arrest rates until after World War II (Ferdinand, 1967). Chicago arrest trends declined from 1870 to 1920 (Gurr et al 1977, p. 647). Oakland felony arrest trends showed declining rates from 1875 to 1910 (Friedman and Percival 1981). The general trend for 23 large cities has been charted by Monkkonen (1981) and is shown in Figure 8–7.

The Crime Mix

The character of crime changed over the course of the nineteenth century. Data on crime mixes are most clearly available for Boston and other northeastern industrial cities. The general pattern is a shift from a crime mix dominated by crimes of violence against the person and crimes against order in the first half of the century to a crime mix dominated by property crime in the second half of the century. This shift in crime mix has been documented for Boston and Salem, Massachusetts, and for New Haven, Connecticut. By contrast, newer industrial cities seem to have had crime mixes dominated by property crime through much of their existence. Rockford, Illinois, for instance, had a crime mix dominated by property offenses from its beginnings in 1840 and never experienced any major change in its ratio of property to violent crime (Ferdinand, 1978, 1980).

New York City showed the modern property- and order-dominated crime

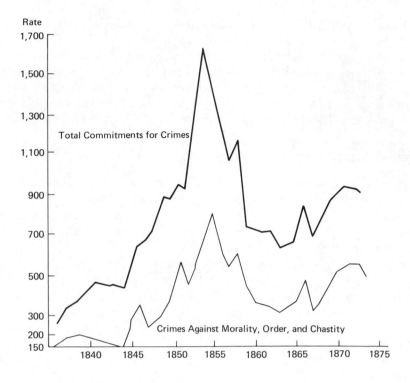

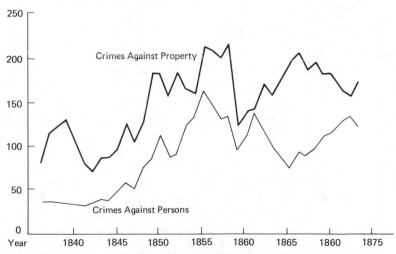

Figure 8–6. Crime in Massachusetts, 1836–1873: Trends in jail and prison commitment rates (per 100,000 population). [Source: Reprinted with permission from *Prison and Plantation: Crime, Justice, and Authority in Massachusetts and South Carolina, 1767–1878,* by Michael Stephen Hindus, p. 72. Copyright 1980, The University of North Carolina Press. Studies in Legal History Series.]

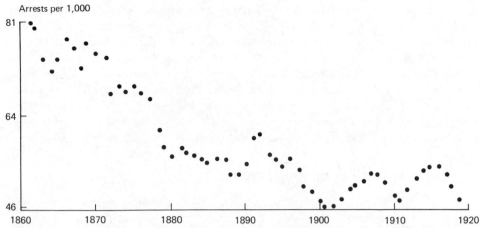

Figure 8–7. Arrest trends in Urban America between 1860–1920. [Source: Eric H. Monkkonen, *Police in Urban America: 1860–1920*. New York, N.Y.: Cambridge University Press, 1981, p. 73. Reprinted with permission.]

pattern in the period 1845–1850. New York police made 144,364 arrests during the period. Nearly all of these arrests were for violations against public order or for petty thefts or minor assaults. One fourth of all the arrests were for drunkenness, another one fifth for drunk and disorderly behavior, and another one seventh for disorderly conduct. Together, these categories totaled 59 percent of all arrests. Petty theft accounted for 10 percent of arrests, and minor assaults accounted for another 10 percent. Vagrancy accounted for 8 percent of the arrest totals. Among serious crimes, parallels of the modern FBI index-offenses together accounted for about 3 percent of all arrests. Even arrests for index offenses were dominated by property crime: murder arrests amounted to 1 percent of index arrests; rape to 3 percent; aggravated assault to 10 percent; robbery to 4 percent; burglary to 19 percent; and serious theft to 63 percent of index arrests (Inciardi, 1978, pp. 58–59).

Temperance movements—and, consequently, drunkenness—played an important role in the politics and law enforcement of the late 19th and early twentieth centuries (Gusfield, 1963). Campaigns against drunkenness by means of criminal law enforcement had the same sort of impact on the overall arrest rates of nineteenth-century cities that campaigns against improper sexuality and improper religious dogma had in the late seventeenth and early eighteenth centuries. This fact is clearly visible in the burden that drunkenness arrests and prosecutions placed on the criminal justice system of many cities during this period. Ferdinand (1980) has shown that drunkenness prosecutions accounted for only 13 percent of the rate of known crimes in Boston in 1824, but for 59 percent of all arrests in 1884–1885. By 1967, drunkenness had dropped back to 41 percent of all arrests. Drunkenness accounted for 25 percent of all arrests in New York circa 1850 (Inciardi, 1978, p. 58) and 20 percent of all arrests in Philadelphia in 1858 (Johnson, 1979, p. 127). Drunk-and-disorderly arrests in Chicago in the 1870s and 1880s fluctuated from a low of 46 percent of all arrests in 1878 and 1879 to a high of 62 percent of all arrests in both 1872 and 1885 (Johnson, 1979, p. 128).

The impact of drunkenness arrests on the apparent overall crime level gives a clear example of the interplay between policy and criminal records. Drunkenness, of course, is a troublesome and obnoxious behavior, but it cannot be classed with the traditional crimes against persons and property in either the danger it presents or the inconvenience it causes. Still, the fluctuation of this offense's importance in the total crime mixes of Boston and Chicago should be cautionary. Crime waves can be artificially induced by the adoption or enforcement of unpopular laws or laws that focus on behaviors at the margin of acceptable conduct. The creation of an artificial crime wave by the use of the criminal sanction against drunkenness was predicted by Jeremy Bentham, in disdainful tones, two centuries ago (1776).

Crime in the Twentieth Century

The United States began collecting national criminal statistics in the twentieth century. Homicide rates can be calculated from vital statistics data on causes of death recorded on death certificates beginning in 1900, though complete participation by all states did not occur until the 1930s. State-prison population statistics giving an annual national index of serious offenses have been collected since 1926. The uniform crime reporting system has collected national data on crimes known to the police since 1933.

Crime Trends

Arrest data for many cities show essentially similar crime trends during the first half of the twentieth century: the decline per capita in arrests for serious offenses that began in the nineteenth century continued until about 1930; then, the rate began to rise. This general pattern appears to hold for Boston, for Buffalo, for Oakland, and for New York City. Chicago arrest data show a massive arrest peak during the 1920s, during the celebrated era of gang warfare, but otherwise, they conform to the general pattern.

The national crime trends drawn from the *Uniform Crime Reports* exhibit general patterns consistent with those found in the arrest data for individual cities. The decline in crime rates that began in the nineteenth century apparently bottomed out in the 1930s. The rates for the seven original index offenses have apparently risen since that time.

Uniform Crime Reports data must be used with caution. The time series is short: the Federal Bureau of Investigation did not begin collecting data until 1933. Participation in the program was originally voluntary and remains so for many jurisdictions today. The early national estimates provided by the UCR contain wide margins of error: the number of reporting jurisdictions varied substantially from year to year before World War II, and the rules for offense classification and reporting developed almost by trial and error. Still, for purposes of trend analysis, the data are useful (Figure 8–8).

The overall rate of violent crimes against the person known to the American police declined until about 1940, then began to rise. The trends for both robbery and aggravated assault were consistent with the overall trend. Rape rates have generally increased since the establishment of the UCR. Murder rates generally declined from 1933 until the mid-1960s.

The overall rate of property crimes known to the American police declined

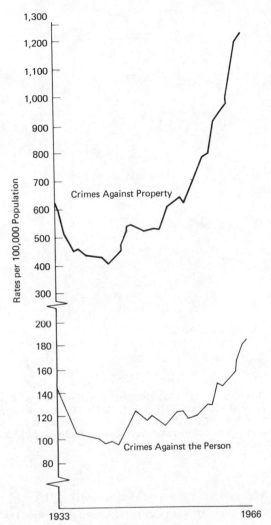

Figure 8–8. UCR crime-rate trends, 1933–1966. [Source: President's Commission on Law Enforcement and Administration of Justice. *Task Force Report: Crime and Its Impact: An Assessment.* Washington, D.C.: Government Printing Office, 1967a, pp. 19–20.]

sharply from 1933 until the early 1940s, then began the sharp postwar rises detailed in Chapter 7. Both burglary and motor vehicle theft followed the general trend. Rates for larceny $50 and over, by contrast, have generally risen since the UCR first began collecting data.

The UCR national arrest estimates show a general upward trend from 1933 onward. Arrests per 100,000 population numbered 255 in 1933, 308 in 1935, and 461 in 1940. Arrest rates declined during World War II but began to rise again in the postwar era. Arrests numbered 460 per 100,000 population in 1946, 525 in 1950, 1,133 in 1955, and 1,944 in 1960.

Homicide Trends

Because of the special character of criminal homicide, much longer American times series exist for it than for any other offense. Figure 8–9 fits three extant homicide time-series convering the period 1881–1977 together onto a single graph.

189

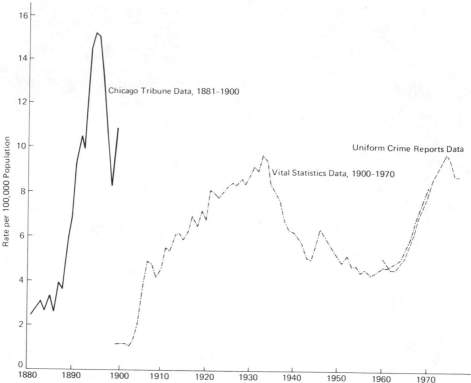

Figure 8–9. U.S. homicide rates, 1881–1977. [Sources: 1881–1900 data in J. A. Inciardi, *Reflections on Crime*. New York: Holt, Rinehart and Winston, 1978, p. 51. 1900–1977 data from B. J. Wattenberg (ed.), *The Statistical History of the United States from Colonial Times to the Present*. New York: Basic Books, 1976; Federal Bureau of Investigation, *Crime in the United States: 1977*. Washington, D.C.: U.S. Government Printing Office, 1978.]

The *Chicago Tribune* series covers the period 1881–1900 (Inciardi, 1978, p. 51). The *Vital Statistics* series, compiled initially by the Census Bureau and now by the National Center for Health Statistics, covers the period 1900–1970. The program began in 1900 with ten states reporting causes of death based on physicians' death certificates. In 1920, 80 percent coverage of the U.S. population was achieved. In 1933, 100 percent coverage was achieved. The *Uniform Crime Reports* series began in 1933 but is graphed only from 1960.

The *Chicago Tribune* series indicates that homicide rates rose substantially in the late 1880s, peaking at very high levels in the mid-1890s. Homicide rates then dropped substantially. This series should be used with extreme caution for any purpose except trend assessment. Direct comparisons should not be made with the homicide rates shown in the *Vital Statistics* and UCR data.

The *Vital Statistics* series shows long cycle variation in American homicide rates, with periods of approximately forty years between peaks. The very sharp rise in homicide rates between 1900 and 1930 is exaggerated by the fact that the earliest reporting states were in New England, a region that all other data sources indicate has very low homicide rates. Areas subsequently joining the reporting system had higher homicide rates. Sutherland (1947, p. 33) long ago showed that the cyclic trend in the data occurred even when study was limited to the original 1900 reporting areas. Homicide rates peaked in 1933 (when 100 percent coverage of the United States had been achieved) at 9.7 per 100,000 population. The cyclic decline that followed the 1933 peak eventually reached a low rate of about 4.5 homicides per 100,000 population in the mid-1950s. The massive rise in homicide rates that has occurred in recent decades returns the United States to the levels of homicide of the early 1930s and perhaps the 1890s.

The *Uniform Crime Reports* criminal homicide series shows the same pattern found in the *Vital Statistics* series. The two time series are, in fact, highly correlated. Because they are collected by substantially different data-recording systems, the fact that they both show the long cycle in homicide rates since 1933 suggests that the cyclical pattern is real. The homicide cycle, by itself, suggests that the 1980s should show a leveling and then a decline in homicide rates. The magnitude of the current crime wave, as discussed in Chapter 7, is such that other forces may override the cyclic trend.

Long-Term Crime Patterns in Canada

Canada is the youngest of the three nations considered in this chapter. The current federal state was formed in 1867 as a confederation of various British colonies and possessions in North America. The nation grew in stages, adding the Pacific crown colony of British Columbia in 1871; defining the prairie provinces of Alberta and Saskatchewan in 1905; and adding the North Atlantic colony of Newfoundland in 1949.

The historical trends in Canadian crime can be traced for only about a century. Though Canadian history dates from the seventeenth century, little research has, as yet, been conducted into preconfederation records of crime. No published work yet explores the detailed character and fluctuations of crime at the local or provincial level in the way that historians have explored crime patterns in the villages, towns, and counties of England or colonial Massachusetts. Consideration of Canadian crime trends must be based on centrally gathered statistical data about criminal convictions.

The Canadian criminal justice system is structured differently from both the English and American systems. Canada has a single national criminal code enacted by the federal government. Criminal procedure and the generic organization of criminal courts are both defined by federal law. The provincial governments have full responsibility for law enforcement. Local, provincial, and federal governments all have police. Courts are operated by provincial governments, though senior-level judges are appointed and paid by the federal government. Both the federal government and the provincial governments operate correctional systems. Though less integrated than the English criminal justice system, the Canadian system is far more integrated than the American system. (See, generally, Griffiths, Klein, and Verdun-Jones, 1980.)

One result of the structure of the Canadian government and the integration of the Canadian criminal justice system has been the collection and publication of crime statistics on a national basis since 1876. National judicial statistics exist for the period 1876–1973. National statistics on crimes known to the police have been collected since 1920. These data can be used to assess the trend in crime levels over a period of slightly more than a century.

Crime Trends

Canada's crime pattern, over time (Figure 8–10), seems to be quite different from the English and American crime pattern. The English and American trends both describe a vast, cyclic curve. From the mid-nineteenth century until sometime in the first third of the twentieth century, both England and the United States had continually declining crime rates. Crime rates in both countries have risen since the 1930s. This general pattern in trends is also apparent in the historical crime data for Sweden, Australia, and Norway (Gurr et al., 1977; Mukherjee, 1981).

Canada never experienced the late-nineteenth-century decline in crime rates that characterized the crime trends of so many other countries. Instead, the Canadian trend has been similar to the general trend in criminal convictions in France, which showed a steady increase in known levels of crime from 1825 to the mid-1970s (Zehr, 1976; Davidovitch, 1961).

The Canadian crime trend rose steadily from 1880 to 1970. Charges for all indictable criminal-code offenses rose from around 120 per 100,000 population in 1880 to around 520 per 100,000 population in 1970, more than a fourfold increase. Convictions for serious offenses rose from around 80 per 100,000 population in 1880 to about 450 per 100,000 in 1970, more than a fivefold increase.

The Province of British Columbia has consistently had the highest of reported conviction rates since entering confederation (Figure 8–11). The conviction rate rose from about 200 convictions per 100,000 population in 1890 to about 600 convictions per 100,000 population in the early 1970s. The linear trend in the British Columbia conviction time-series has a positive slope of 4.3, which means that the level of the base-year conviction rate doubles about every fifty years.

The second striking feature of the Canadian crime trend is the abrupt and massive crime wave that occurred around 1914. The crime wave is present in the conviction data of every province, though it crested in 1913 in some provinces, and in 1914, 1915, or 1916 in still others. The 1914 crime wave appears to have been uniquely Canadian: nothing like it appears in the English, American, or French crime data for that period.

Evidence of the impact of the temperance movement on the arrest data for American cities, and the way in which a temperance drive could induce an artificial crime wave, might suggest that the 1914 Canadian crime wave could be attributed to the introduction of some new law, some new agency of law enforcement, or some new policy on prosecution. Research to date is tentative, but none of these possibilities seems to explain the 1914 crime wave: no major modifications of the criminal code occurred during this period, Canadian prohibition was still some years away, and no major modification seems to have occurred in the structure and organization of criminal law. Moreover, the 1914 crime wave seems to have been generally present across all categories of crime: the rise, the crest, and the decline

192

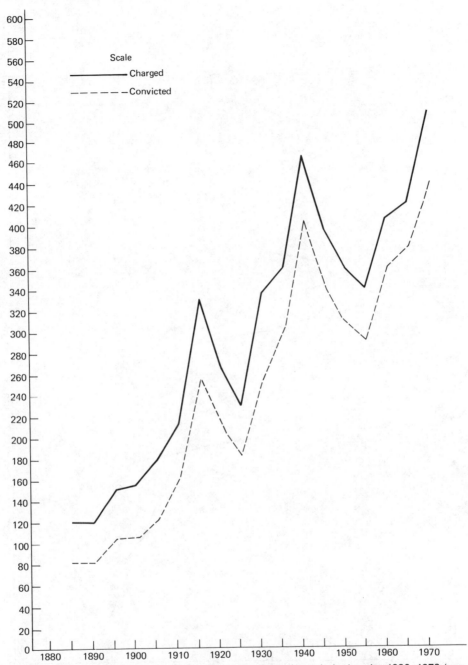

Figure 8–10. Rate of persons indictable under Canadian criminal code, 1880–1970 (per 100,000 population). [Source: J. Blanchard and R. G. Cassidy, *Crime and Criminal Process in Canada: 1880–1970 and Beyond.* Ottawa: Statistics Division, Solicitor General of Canada, 1975 (CANJUS Project Report No. 21; Statistics Division Report No. 2/75, p. 19.]

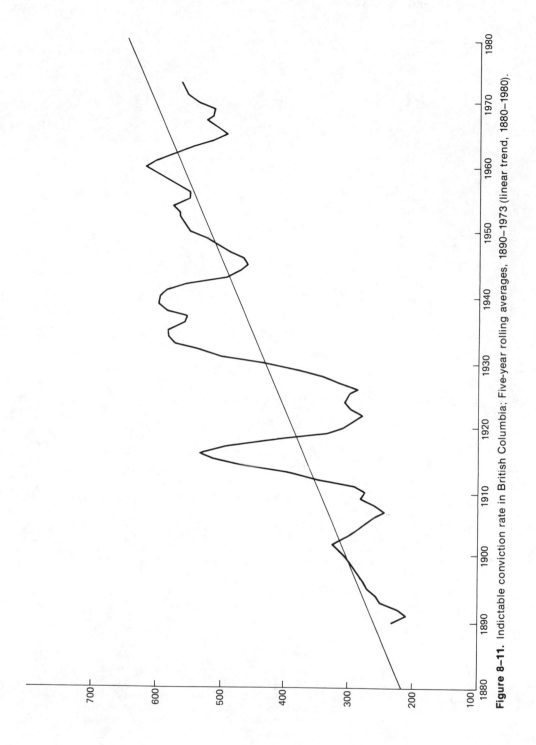

Figure 8-11. Indictable conviction rate in British Columbia; Five-year rolling averages, 1890–1973 (linear trend, 1880–1980).

194

are there in the homicide data, in the theft data, and in the data on convictions for summary offenses such as vagrancy and public drunkenness. The Canadian crime wave of 1914 appears not to have been artificially induced by policy changes. Why it occurred remains a matter for future research.

The Crime Mix: 1880–1970

Canada's relative crime mix changed substantially between the late nineteenth century and the mid-twentieth century. The change in the relative proportions of violent crimes against the person, violent crimes against property, and simple property offenses followed trends familiar from the changing crime mixes in England and the United States during this period. Although simple property crimes continued to dominate the crime mix, the relative proportion of violent crimes against the person declined substantially, and the relative proportion of violent crimes against property increased.

Canada followed the English classification system for grouping crimes during most of the past century. Under this system, crimes against the person include murder, manslaughter, all other forms of homicide except suicide, kidnapping, all forms of assault and battery, and all forms of sexual offenses. Crimes against property with violence include the breaking-and-entering offenses, robbery, and extortion. Simple crimes against property without violence include theft, receiving stolen goods, fraud, embezzlement, and obtaining property through false pretenses. There is a residual "other" category as well. It includes arson and vandalism, forgery, suicide, a number of vice-related offenses, and, beginning in 1923, narcotics offenses. (Urquhart and Buckley, 1965, p. 636).

The change in the quality of crime experienced by Canadians is apparent in a comparison of the indictable crime mix of 1886 with that of 1960, as shown in Table 8–3. It is clear that violent personal crimes declined, whereas burglary and robbery became major problems.

There was also a major transformation in the mix of minor, high-volume offenses. Minor crimes such as public drunkenness and traffic violations are so frequent that they account for the major share of all penal convictions. In 1881, for instance, drunkenness convictions alone amounted to 34 percent of all criminal

TABLE 8–3. Canadian Crime Mix (Percentages)

	1886	1960
Violent Crimes Against the Person	21	9
Violent Crimes Against Property	8	23
Crimes against Property Without Violence	59	54
Other Indictable Offenses	12	12

SOURCE: Calculated from M. C. Urquhart and K. A. H. Buckley *Historical Statistics of Canada* (Toronto: Macmillan, 1965).

court convictions, when indictable and minor crimes were combined. Taken together, liquor and drunkenness offenses accounted for 40 percent of all Canadian convictions in 1881. But there was a drastic change. By 1955, drunkenness and liquor offenses accounted for only 6 percent of all Canadian criminal convictions. The change in British Columbia was even more dramatic. Drunkenness and liquor offenses accounted for 59 percent of all convictions in 1881, but only 9 percent of all convictions in 1955 (Popham and Schmidt, 1958, pp. 37–38, 52–53). This change is accounted for by the advent of a new form of offense, the motoring offense. Since 1901, minor traffic offenses have come to dominate both the summary convictions and total criminal convictions. Quantitatively, traffic violations have become Canada's most important single crime problem (Hagan, 1977, p. 55).

Long-term Crime Trends: Approaches to Explanation

The very long-term trends in crime experienced by England, the United States, and Canada raise several important criminological questions: (1) Why have the English homicide rates declined so steadily and permanently over the past eight hundred years? (2) Why have English and American crime rates oscillated in similar long cycles over the past four hundred years? (3) Why is the Canadian pattern so different from the pattern found in other common-law countries? The present state of criminological knowledge permits no generally agreed-on explanation for any of these questions. It is possible, however, to outline sets of elements that most criminologists would agree will probably play an important part in the explanations that are finally developed. These elements include demographics, economics, urbanization, the criminal justice system, opportunity patterns, and a pair of very fuzzy but important concepts, modernization and civilization.

The Decline in English Homicide Rates

One of the most remarkable long-term patterns documented in this chapter is the decline in English homicide rates over the past eight hundred years. At their peak in the late thirteenth and early fourteenth centuries, homicide rates approached 30 per 100,000 population and constituted almost a fifth of all known offenses. By the late Elizabethan and early Stuart periods at the close of the sixteenth and the beginning of the seventeenth centuries, homicide rates had dropped to around 14 per 100,000 population. Between the 1690s and the early nineteenth century, English homicide rates dropped to about 2 per 100,000 population. They have remained very low ever since.

The principal sources of explanation for this dramatic decline in the level of lethal violence over time must be sought in the process of modernization and the advance of civilization. Neither concept is particularly satisfactory, yet each represents a reasonable bundle of ideas that help understanding.

By *modernization,* we mean a process of social change that includes the development of a more complicated productive technology and a consequently growing economic interdependence of people, together with the development of an increasingly neutral and rule-bound system of government. Modernization also seems to include a shift of population toward urban residence and work, and an increase in transportation and the flow of information.

Our grounds for asserting that the modernization process may be responsible, in part, for the decline in England's homicide rate over the centuries are thin, but plausible. When we seek to understand temporal processes under circumstances that do not permit a replication of observations over time, one alternative is to look, cross-sectionally, at the contemporary world and to examine the crime rates in places that exhibit characteristics of social, economic, and cultural complexity similar to those we think obtained in England at different times in the past. This procedure is, of course, a poor substitute for the observation of another temporal sequence, but it is a common process in science, used by astronomers, geologists, anthropologists, and sociologists alike.

The cross-sectional data suggest that modernization ought to be considered a major candidate to explain declining homicide rates. Contemporary nations having very high homicide rates exhibit many features in common with medieval England: agrarian economics bound in a quasi-feudal structure of large, manorial landholders and subsistence-level peasant farmers; extreme inequality of wealth; a very small political elite; a primate city; high mortality rates in general; and low literacy. Such countries today exhibit enormously high levels of homicide and violent crime in general, as well as relatively low levels of property crime.

The United Nations' (1977) world survey on crime in the 1970s showed that the relative crime mix for "developing" countries was 43 percent crimes against the person, compared with a generalized world pattern of only 20 percent violent crimes against the person, and a rate for "developed" countries of only 10 percent violent crimes against the person. Arrayed along a developmental scale from medieval to contemporary English social organization patterns, the countries of the world show a progressive decline in homicide rates and a progressive shift in their crime mixtures away from violent crimes against the person and toward property crime (Wolf, 1971). (See Table 8–4.)

The second element in an explanation of the long-term decline in English homicide rates is the advance of civilization. By that, we mean a change in cultural and ethical values toward a greater appreciation of the value of human life, together with the development of social mechanisms that make the taking of human life dangerous, socially, for the killer and at the same time provide alternative methods of dispute settlement. One index of advancing civilization is the development of a reasonably efficient and reasonably neutral system of legal rules for crime control and dispute resolution. The large decline in English homicide rates in the seventeenth and eighteenth centuries corresponds to the development of an available and independent judiciary (Harding, 1966).

Any such set of explanations, of course, must be viewed with some caution. Both Canada and the United States are historical heirs to the decline in English homicide rates and are subject to the forces of modernization and civilization that are responsible for the decline. Canada has a very low homicide rate (2.5 per 100,000 population in 1979). But the United States has much higher murder rates than might be expected from this source of explanation alone (9.7 per 100,000 popula-

TABLE 8–4. Distribution of 37 Interpol Nations According to High/Low Murder/Larceny Rates per 100,000 Population and a Number of Conventional Criteria of Developmental Status. 1962

Member countries of Interpol for which statistical information was available for the years 1961–1962 from the sources mentioned at base of table put down in rank order from left to right (1 = highest rank i.e. lowest MR:LR ratio)

Criteria of Development (MR = Murder rate per 100,000 population of crimes known to the police; LR = Larceny rate per 100,000 population of crimes known to the police)	Sweden	Norway*	New Zealand	Denmark			Federal Germany		Israel		Japan	Finland	Holland			Eire	Italy		Malaya	Tunisia	Nigeria	Tanganyika	Ceylon	Sudan	India	Uganda	Malagasy	Ghana	Libya	Peru	Pakistan		Syria	Ethiopia	Thailand	Cambodia	Philippines
	1	2	3	4	5	6	7	8	9	10	11	12	13	14	15	16	17	18	19	20	21	22	23	24	25	26	27	28	29	30	31	32	33	34	35	36	37
MR < 6 and LR > 600	X	X	X	X	X	X	X	X	X	X	X	X	X	X	X																						
Low infant mortality	X	X	X	X	X	X	X	X	X	X	X	X	X	X	X	X																					
Low proportion of pop. in rural occup.	X	X	X	X	X	X	X	X	X	X			X	X	X		X																				
High degree of urbanization	X	X	X	X	X	X	X	X	X	X	X	X	X	X	X	X	X													X			X				
> 5 telephones per 100 population	X	X	X	X	X	X	X	X	X	X	X	X	X	X	X	X	X																				
High economic development	X	X	X	X	X	X	X	X	X	X	X	X	X	X	X	X	X																				
< 20% illiterates	X	X	X	X	X	X	X	X	X	X	X	X	X	X	X	X	X																				
> 100 newspapers per 1,000 pop.	X	X	X	X	X	X	X	X	X	X	X	X	X	X	X	X	X																				
Westernized, not colonial	X	X	X	X	X	X	X	X	X	X	X	X	X	X	X	X	X																				
High MR or Low MR and low LR																X	X	X	X	X	X	X	X	X	X	X	X	X	X	X	X	X	X	X	X	X	X
High infant mortality																	X	X	X	X	X	X	X	X	X	X	X	X	X	X	X	X	X	X	X	X	X
High or medium proportion in rural occup.											X	X				X		X	X	X	X	X	X	X	X	X	X	X	X	X	X	X	X	X	X	X	X
Low degree of urbanization																		X	X	X	X	X	X	X	X	X	X	X	X		X	X		X	X	X	X
< 5 telephones per 100 population																		X	X	X	X	X	X	X	X	X	X	X	X	X	X	X	X	X	X	X	X
Economic underdevelopment																		X	X	X	X	X	X	X	X	X	X	X	X	X	X	X	X	X	X	X	X
> 20% illiterates																		X	X	X	X	X	X	X	X	X	X	X	X	X	X	X	X	X	X	X	X
< 100 newspapers per 1,000 population																		X	X	X	X	X	X	X	X	X	X	X	X	X	X	X	X	X	X	X	X
Not westernized or colonial status																		X	X	X	X	X	X	X	X	X	X	X	X	X	X	X	X	X	X	X	X

* Based on figures from 1961. ** Larceny concerning property valued at less than 50 dollars not included.

SOURCE: P. Wolf "Crime and Development: An International Comparison of Crime Rates" *Scandinavian Studies in Criminology* 3(1971):114. Oslo: Universitetsforlaget. Reprinted with permission.

tion in 1979). Any general rules drawn from the long-term experience of England must be tempered by other sources of explanation when one is looking at the homicide rates of other countries.

The Long Cycles in Crime

Both England and the United States have exhibited similar long-term crime trends over a period of between three hundred and four hundred years. These trends have taken the form of a repeating cycle with peaks around 1600, around 1720, around 1850, and possibly at present. Major troughs have fallen in the mid-eighteenth century and the early twentieth century. Gurr (1979) has called these great cycles "tidal waves" of crime. He argued that they represent real events and cannot be dismissed as artifacts of criminal-justice-system data recording.

Any complete explanation of these long cycles lies sometime in the future, when a great deal more research has been done. A number of likely candidates for inclusion as elements in the eventual explanation can currently be identified. All represent long-term structural changes in the social systems and environments in which crimes occur.

Demographic Changes Over Time

Chapter 7 examined some of the short-term influences of demographic changes on the post–World War II crime rates of England, Canada, and the United States. In particular, the impact of the postwar "baby boom" on crime rates in the 1960s and 1970s and the further consequences expected for the crime rates of the 1980s and 1990s were discussed. Such changes in population pyramids—in the proportion of males in the crime-prone ages in particular—in the past might have produced some impact on the crime trends. Still, baby booms or short-term depopulations of the sort caused by epidemic disease—for example, the outbreak of plague in London in the 1660s killed somewhere between 15 and 25 percent of the city's total population (Wrigley, 1969)—merely represent brief dislocations in much longer-trend patterns. Long-term patterns seem to be related to much more fundamental demographic changes caused by changes in fertility and mortality and by large and permanent migration streams.

The long-term demographic patterns in England and Wales are shown in Figure 8–12. There was a major rise in population from the Norman Conquest until the mid-fourteenth century, with the peak just before the onset of the Black Death. A major decline in population during the last half of the fourteenth century was followed by recovery and an accelerating rate of population increase, which rose to another peak in the early seventeenth century. There was a period of population stability from the mid-seventeenth to the mid-eighteenth centuries. A third major period of population growth, associated with the Industrial Revolution, began in the late eighteenth century.

A comparison of this pattern with the long-term crime pattern is suggestive. Major crime waves crested in the mid-fourteenth, and early seventeenth, and the mid-eighteenth centuries. The long-term English crime pattern is strongly connected with the demographic pattern over two and one half cycles. Increasing pop-

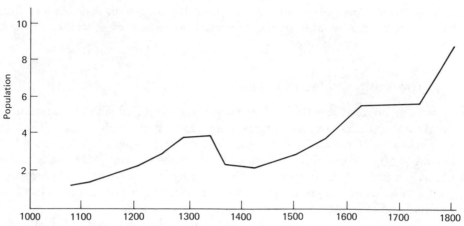

Figure 8–12. Long-term population trends in England and Wales, 1000–1800 (in millions). [Source: E. A. Wrigley, *Population and History*. New York: McGraw-Hill, 1969, p. 78.]

ulations are associated with increasing crime rates from time immemorial until the mid-nineteenth century.

There was a strong association between rapid population growth and rapidly rising crime rates at the beginning of the nineteenth century as well. After 1850, however, the aparent close association between long-term demographic patterns and crime waves appears to have changed. The population growth continued unabated throughout the nineteenth and well into the twentieth centuries. The crime wave, however, peaked about 1850 and entered a long decline that lasted until after World War I.

The mechanisms of association between population growth and crime waves in the preindustrial era appear to be Malthusian. The Malthusian model of demography and society assumes fixed resources for the production of the necessities of life and also assumes that human population grows until it reaches the limits of production, so that per capita, people live at bare subsistence. But because goods are not equitably distributed, a few people will be rich, others will be comfortable, and most will live at or below the subsistence level. The pressures on people to commit crimes in order to survive will be enormous. Thus, population growth creates the structural conditions for crime waves, whereas declining population removes these structural conditions and crime rates should decrease (Samaha, 1974, pp. 33–34).

At the microlevel, a Malthusian model of crime would predict two patterns: (1) property crimes centered on the theft of foodstuffs, fuel, and clothing; and (2) short-term fluctuations in crime keyed to the economy of foodstuffs. Both of these patterns obtained throughout the preindustrial period in England. Food, clothing, and fuel were the objects of theft and house break-ins during the crime wave that crested in the early fourteenth century (Hanawalt, 1979); and they were the central objects of theft in the seventeenth and eighteenth centuries as well (Beattie, 1974; Cockburn, 1977b; Thompson, 1975). Crime rates, particularly theft rates, fluctuated with the price of food, particularly during periods of population growth.

Strong associations between the theft pattern and variations in the cost of grain were especially apparent during the rising population and crime waves in the fourteenth, the early seventeenth, and the late eighteenth centuries (Hanawalt, 1974, 1979; Samaha, 1974; Cockburn, 1977b; Beattie, 1974).

Population growth also has impact on criminal opportunities. Increasing population implies an increasing number of households and householders, multiplying the possibilities for housebreak-ins (Laslett, 1971). Increasing population implies increasing population density, either in the villages or, after migration, in the cities. In either location, increasing population density implied in the preindustrial world, just as it does now, an increase in the number of human social interactions. Personal crime appears to be some power function of the number of human social interactions, so that increasing population implies a massive increase in such personal crimes as murder, assault, robbery, and pocket picking.

At the same time, population growth implies a major increase in the number of targets for property crime. More people need more hardware and cloth, more furniture and more services. The proliferation of consumer goods is a proliferation of criminal opportunities. As Beattie (1974) put it in the context of crime in eighteenth-century London:

> [there was] a rapid increase in river traffic, in number of warehouses and docks and in the amount of goods being transported in and out of the capital by road and water. Shops became more numerous and began to display their goods in a way that made them more attractive and accessible to thieves as well as customers. (pp. 92–93)

The Malthusian model of demographic change and crime does not fit the American crime pattern at all well. Although American crime rates exhibit the same cyclic pattern seen in the English crime data, American population growth has not shown any cyclic patten of rise and decline. Since European settlement began in the early seventeenth century, the American population has grown at a startling rate, averaging 35 percent per decade between 1650 and 1800, 31 percent per decade in the nineteenth century, and 16 percent per decade in the twentieth century.

The reason that population growth does not appear to have had such a powerful impact on American crime rates is the absence of critical restraints on land and food production. Through most of North American history, population pressures could be, and apparently were, absorbed by the opening of the continent to agriculture and by the exploitation of the abundant forests and other natural resources.

The divergence between English crime patterns and English population growth patterns in the nineteenth century reflects the general impact of the Industrial Revolution on a wide variety of human patterns. The productive advances in agriculture and in industrial goods, as well as the development of new transport and communication technologies, removed the immediate threat of Malthusian starvation from huge segments of English, European, and North American society, reducing the pressure to commit crimes in order to survive. Advances in public health changed the character of the population as well: people lived longer, and families became smaller, with fewer children. The proportion of the growing populations of England and America falling into the high-crime-prone age brackets of adolescense declined.

The structural connection between population and crime attentuated. Other things became more important determinants of the long-term crime trend (Wrigley, 1969; Lane, 1974).

Changes in the Criminal Justice System

Changes in the criminal justice system constitute another element in any plausible explanation of the long-term trends in English and American crime rates. Such changes may involve the definition of new crimes or the abolition of old ones, the creation of new institutions of justice or the abolition of old ones, or major changes in the policies followed by the agencies of the law. Any of these changes may constitute a structural change in the conditions and consequences of historical trends in crime. Conversely, it may be the case that specific institutions of criminal justice have only a limited effective life because the social conditions for which they were created change and they cannot adapt far enough and fast enough to new conditions to continue as effective controls on crime. The combination of these two processes— loss of institutional vitality and the creation of new institutions especially designed for specific crime problems—may explain the cyclic long trends in English and American crime rates. The evidence for this explanation takes the form of institutional collapse and creation at crime wave crests and troughs.

During the great crime wave in the early fourteenth century, the last forms of Anglo-Saxon and Norman criminal-justice institutions collapsed. The system of criminal trials by justices in Eyre was largely abandoned. In place of Saxon laws and Norman courts, new systems of laws and new courts were created. Justices of the Peace (local magistrates charged with criminal jurisdiction) were created. The felonies were defined more precisely and made capital offenses. The royal commissions of goal delivery, oyer and terminer, and trail baston were devised to allow the speedy and flexible dispatch of royal justice courts to specific trouble spots. The problems of urban crime, particularly robbery in market towns and on the highroads that connected them, were addressed in the Statute of Winchester of 1285, described in its preamble as "a statute to abate felons." Townspeople were made responsible for solving robberies occurring within the town or paying fines. Landholders abutting highroads were required to clear the verges of the roads so that robbers could not lurk there. Towns were also required to create night watches to patrol against crime. Finally, the Statute of Treason of 1352 defined high crimes against the state and the administration of justice (Harding, 1966, pp. 59–87; Radin, 1936, pp. 219–244; Plucknett, 1960, pp. 89–90.) We do not, of course, know what impact these system reforms had on the subsequent crime trend because the Black Death introduced what Harding has characterized as two centuries of anarchy.

The great crime wave that built in the late Elizabethan period and crested in the early seventeenth century was accompanied by a number of major criminal-justice innovations. The criminal law was expanded in two ways: there was a substantial expansion of the number of nonclergiable felonies (the creation of new crimes for which people could be hung), and the law of vagrancy was fully converted to a device for the control of wandering bands of itinerant criminals (Harding, 1966; Samaha, 1974; Chambliss, 1964). The role of central administration became more important to the courts. Assize jurisdiction expanded and was regularized into the power to try and punish major crimes, at the expense of justices of the peace on the one hand, and of the old gaol-delivery commissions on the other (Cockburn, 1972). The judicial functions of the justices of the peace were crystallized and bureaucratized: petty sessions met four times a year to try serious misdemeanours and minor felonies. The police function, such as it was, was supplemented by a system of rewards paid to informers for the prosecution of criminal offenders. A system of professional informers working in concert with the justices' clerk quickly developed in many counties, some, according to Harding (1966, p. 77), operating detective agencies. The first recognizable correctional institutions, the Bridewells— houses of correction where vagrants were to be punished and youthful offenders trained in job skills—were created during this crime wave (Harding, 1966, p. 85; Rusche and Kirchheimer, 1968).

Old institutions and laws were replaced or buttressed by new laws and new institutions during the seventeenth-century crime wave. These innovations were followed by a long decline in crime that lasted until the late eighteenth century.

During the long period of lower crime rates, one important minor crime wave occurred in the 1720s. It was accompanied by one of the most ferocious innovations in the history of criminal law: the Black Act. Concern about poaching and extortion—perhaps merely criminal, but perhaps politically motivated—produced a single act creating something like thirty-five new capital offenses, ranging from extortion to the malicious destruction of trees. Radzinowicz (1948, p. 76) calculated that with accomplice liability taken into account, the Black Act actually defined somewhere between 200 and 350 different behaviors for which the death sentence could be imposed. The act was made retroactive to apply to behaviors occurring during the year prior to its passage. Conviction could occur in absentia and was automatic if a charged offender failed to appear for trial at a fixed date.

The Black Act remained in effect for a century and appears to have been used as a mini-criminal code by prosecutors (Thompson, 1975; Radzinowicz, 1948). Moreover, the Black Act exhibits the method by which eighteenth-century legislators attempted to cope with perceived short-term crises during the era of relatively low crime rates: the passage of specific capital criminal laws. This method led to an enormous expansion of the criminal law but had little effect on crime. It became part of the system discarded in the innovations designed to meet the crime wave of the nineteenth century.

The nineteenth-century crime wave began in the latter part of the eighteenth century and crested about 1850 in both England and America. The systemic changes made in response to this crime wave created the main forms of the criminal justice systems we have today: the police, prisons, juvenile institutions, and a codified criminal law.

The police were an outgrowth of discontent with the traditional watch system created during the medieval crime wave and the reward–informer system created during the seventeenth-century crime wave. The old institutions were seen as inefficient and corrupt. They produced neither effective street patrol nor the systematic solution of crime nor the consistent prosecution of offenders. A combination of Enlightenment thinking, utilitarian theorizing, and pragmatic experimentation with patrol police at the Bow Street magistrate's office and on the Thames River provided a scheme for a new preventive police. The London Metropolitan Police were created in 1829 and proved a major success. The force was copied, more or less, in other cities throughout England and North America. The wide-scale adoption of preventive police forces corresponded with the crest of the crime wave in both countries (Critchley, 1978; Miller, 1975; Lane, 1971).

Prisons, as systematic substitutes for traditional corporal and capital punishments, were developed over the course of the nineteenth-century crime wave. Their development was dictated by Enlightenment thought and what we now call the Classical School of criminology. Prison architecture and the prison regime seem to have been designed in America, with competing systems from Pennsylvania and New York shaping specific developments throughout North America and Europe (Mannheim, 1972).

Juvenile reformatory schools of an essentially similar nature evolved in America, in England, and in Europe at the same time, under the pressures of the crime wave. Juvenile offenders played a major role in the English and American crime waves. They were a major problem in the period before the 1850s in England and the 1870s in America. Some time after mid-century, juvenile offenders ceased to be the central focus of the crime problem, in part because of the impact of the new reformatory schools (Tobias, 1972b; Lane, 1974).

The criminal law was reformed by simplification, by systematization, and by a change in the character of the sanctions during this period. Formal codification proceeded in America, in Canada, and in Europe. It has never occurred in England. Capital offenses were cut from lengthy lists of fifty to two hundred to small lists of very serious crimes, such as treason, murder, rape, and robbery.

Criminal procedure was also reformed. The American Constitution provided for notice of charges, for legal counsel, for the privilege against self-incrimination, for freedom from unwarranted searches, for bail, and for due process of law. English courts permitted defense counsel in court as a matter of right after 1835.

The full panoply of systematic changes—keyed to a utilitarian theory of fair warning, of swift and certain apprehension, and of measured punishment—was intended to change the structure of the social environment so that criminals would be deterred from crime. The new system became fully developed at mid-century, and crime rates declined for eighty years.

The twentieth-century crime wave began in the 1930s, or perhaps in the late 1950s. The effects of World War II make it difficult to say for certain. There have been no major systemic changes in the institutions of criminal justice since the 1870s or 1880s. The current crime wave may, in part, be a function of criminal institutions whose specific methods and techniques have become outmoded through social change or criminal adaptation or both. If so, we cannot expect to see a major deflection in the current crime trend until the structured conditions of crime control have been altered by the creation of new, more responsive agencies of justice.

Structural Economic Change

Long-term structural change in economic organization and productivity ought to be reflected in major changes in the level and quality of crime, in the ways in which short-term changes in the crime rate relate to different economic indicators, and in the forms of punishment. This argument is principally made by criminologists following various versions of Marxist socioeconomic analysis (e.g., Rusche and

Kirchheimer, 1968; McDonald, 1976; Bonger, 1916). The assertion of fundamental relations between economic organization and other forms of social organization need not be solely Marxist in its conclusions (e.g., Beard, 1935), not even in criminology (e.g., Thompson, 1975; Zehr, 1976; Samaha, 1974).

Although often alluded to in criminological debate, very little actual research has focused on the relation between changing crime patterns and major changes in the structure of economic organizagion. Speculations are possible, however, and suggest that this might prove a very fruitful field for social scientists. Speculations in this field suggest one way of explaining the long-term decline in English homicide rates and the general tidal waves of crime.

Periods of Major Economic Change. Two major periods of economic change are easy to identify: the mercantile revolution that followed the discovery of the Americas by Europeans at the beginning of the sixteenth century, and the Industrial Revolution, which radically changed the productive capacity of human industry in the period between 1750 and 1800.[4]

The Mercantile Revolution. The mercantile revolution transformed the economy of Europe from a collection of unrelated local systems into a highly productive trading system featuring world-spanning economic activity and an increasing division of labor for both individuals and nations. It coincided with the development of national states, with major religious wars, and with colonial settlement and exploitation. Wallerstein (1976) has argued that this period marked the formation of capitalism as a dominant mode of economic activity and the triumph of the cities and the bourgeoisie over manorial agriculture.

The last part of the sixteenth and early part of the seventeenth centuries were the critical period. They marked the collapse of the Hapsburg–Hispanic empire and the rise of the Protestant trading states: the Dutch and the English. It was a period of massive economic expansion, but also of rising prices. It was a period of search for public order and for labor.

The great early-modern crime wave coincided with the growth of English mercantile preeminence. As the economic transformation stabilized in the mid-seventeenth century and the expansion moved into decline, the crime wave also entered a long decline.

The Industrial Revolution. The Industrial Revolution—the application of powered machine technology to the production of goods—transformed England and then the rest of the world during the late eighteenth and early nineteenth centuries. Industrial production, personal income, and population all exploded. The population of England increased from about 6 million in 1750 to over 9 million in 1800. It then doubled to 18 million in the next half century and almost doubled again to 33 million in 1900. This population increase was made possible by an industrial system that harnessed the power of water and steam, that converted cottage industry to the large, specialized factory, and that demanded a large and disciplined work force. The growing population was converted into the needed work force and was clothed, housed, and fed in unprecedented numbers.

---

[4] The precise dating of the start of either of these periods is a matter of much scholarly dispute. For a general economic history of the Industrial Revolution, see Cipolla (1973).

The period of major economic growth was also a period of major growth in crime rates. The crime wave was apparently fed by two different elements in the economic transformation. First, it was fed by the need to tame the urban crowd, to convert it from a mob of casually employed hedonists who pursued current impulse without regard to longer-term consequences into a work force committed to regular employment, to predictable behavior, and to the pursuit of long-term economic gain. The process may be considered an ongoing one, yet most of its effect was probably complete by the middle of the nineteenth century. The rise of crime accompanied what E. P. Thompson (1968) has called the "making of the English working class" and in part must be seen as a change in expectations of behavior. In Roger Lane's (1974) words:

> there began a marked change in the normal standards of behavior among, eventually, all classes of the population. The new standards were essentially those of the increasingly dominant middle class. And by the middle of the Victorian Era, the violently cavalier behavior of the aristocracy, the desperate criminality and callous brutality of the working classes had largely surrendered to the forces of society. (p. 287)

The development of this ideological hegemony must surely have driven crime rates up, as previously tolerated behavior was brought to heel by means of the criminal law.

Second, the Industrial Revolution produced massive sets of new opportunities for crime, particularly theft, robbery, and burglary, as goods multiplied in an unprecedented manner and as dwellings and businesses crowded together in increasing numbers. Crime rates soared until criminal justice reform began to modify the growth of opportunity. As E. P. Thompson (1968) suggested:

> the standard-of-living of the average criminal . . . rose over the period up to the establishment of an effective police force (in the late 1830's), since opportunities for pilfering from warehouses, markets, canal barges, the docks, and railways were multiplying. Probably a good many casual workers supplemented their earnings in this way (pp. 292–293)

This interpretation of the impact of the Industrial Revolution also suggests a way to understand the break in the crime wave at mid-century and the long "era of good feeling" and declining crime rates that followed. The police, a national presence after 1856, had some deterrent effect and may also have contributed to the reinforcement of the nineteenth-century behavioral ideology (Gorer, 1955). A major behavioral change had taken place by mid-century. Fewer crimes were committed. Finally, the continual expansion of real per capita income produced by the Industrial Revolution produced sufficient well-being for the masses so that crimes ceased to be events of economic desperation. Gatrell and Hadden's (1972) careful and detailed analysis of nineteenth-century data show a major break at mid-century: up to that point, the crime rate was strongly, inversely correlated with the business cycle, dropping in expansions and rising sharply in recessions; after about 1860, the relationship changed, and crime and business cycles become positively, but weakly, correlated.

The Postindustrial Era. The great twentieth-century crime wave, through which we are now living, might be seen as the result of yet another vast structural change in economic organization. Over the course of the twentieth century, and increasingly since 1969, England, Canada, the United States—and the rest of the world— have been caught in a high-technology revolution in which the demand for highly skilled and professional labor has increased, but the demand for unskilled industrial labor has declined, as factory jobs are taken over by automated machinery. The demand is for computer technicians, for electronics experts, and for biological engineers to fill jobs that require talent and years of expensive education.

In Roger Lane's (1974) analysis, this new economic organization of society is responsible for the rising crime rates of the current wave, particularly the enormously high crime rates of urban minority groups:

> in this "Post-Industrial Age" of technological unemployment, unskilled migrants to the city have not experienced the kind of industrial discipline experienced by earlier generations of immigrants. The restraints imposed by school, police, sumptuary legislation are thus no longer related naturally to the underlying business of making a living, and may be rightly regarded as irrelevant by much of the population in the inner city. (p. 303)

The Anomalous Canadian Crime Pattern

The Canadian crime pattern has differed from the English and American pattern in two significant ways. It exhibited a continual rise in rates during a period when the American and English rates both declined (1880–1930), and it showed a major and explosive crime peak in 1914, a period when both England and America had relatively low crime rates.

The explanation for these differences appears to lie in a different demographic and industrial history. Canada was largely a cluster of wilderness colonies of the British Empire until the 1870s. As such, its economic base was principally agricultural and extractive and its population small and rural, until confederation consolidated the various British North American possessions into a single state. Industrialization, large-scale immigration, and, therefore, population growth and urbanization all occurred after 1871.

Economic Structure

The pressures of industrialization, which everywhere push toward high crime rates, were experienced in Canada during a period when the major transformation had already been completed in both England and the United States. Structurally, Canada experienced the conditions of the 19th century crime wave at the end of the 19th and the beginning of the 20th centuries.

Canada's major period of industrialization was both later and more gradual than that of England and the United States and more closely resembled the pace and timing of industrialization in France. Canada's historical crime trend also resembled that of France, which experienced a steady upward growth over the period 1825–1950 (Davidovitch, 1961; Zehr, 1976). Since World War II, major segments of the Canadian economy have become increasingly linked to the American economy. Recent Canadian crime trends tend to mirror recent American crime trends, though at much lower levels.

Demographic Structure

Since 1850, Canada has had very stable population growth, rising from about 3.6 million population in 1871 to about 24 million in 1981. This population growth has been fueled, historically, by natural increase rather than by immigration. Net immigration to Canada was negative (that is, more people left Canada than moved to Canada) from 1861 to 1901 and from 1931 to 1941. Net immigration was positive from 1901 to 1921 and has been positive since World War II.

The only period in which the national demographic structure was massively altered by immigration was between 1901 and 1915. New immigration actually accounted for more of the population growth between 1901 and 1911 than did natural increase. The tide of immigration rose from 55,000 in 1901 to 212,000 in 1906, to 331,000 in 1911. It peaked at 400,000 immigrant arrivals in 1913. Of Canada's total population in 1913, 5 percent arrived as immigrants in that year alone. One-fifth of Canada's total population in 1913 had arrived as immigrants within the prior four years.

Just as the major demographic change represented by the Post–World War II baby boom corresponded to a major rise in the crime rates of England, Canada, and the United States in the 1960s, the large structural change in Canada's demographic picture caused by this wave of immigration was reflected in the major crime peak of 1914. That crime wave rose with the immigration wave and receded with it. The correlation between immigration and convictions over the period 1886–1960 is trivial ($r = -0.1$), but for the period 1886–1913, the correlation is positive and very strong indeed ($r = +0.86$).

The strong connection between immigration and criminal conviction rates might reasonably be given a number of different theoretical interpretations by criminologists. Most interpretations are likely to be related to the idea of social conflict. Lorne Tepperman (1977), for instance, explained the strong positive correlation between crime and immigration in the early twentieth century as a function of the Canadian acceptance of structural social inequality: "a fear and hatred of immigrants contained within a need for their talents and energy" (p. 236). In his version of social conflict, a repressive elite used the criminal law and the machinery of justice to cow and control the tendencies toward social and economic change—and, presumably, equilization through social and economic leveling—implicit in large-scale immigration. Crime rates rose with high levels of immigration because powerful elites needed more criminal convictions in order to maintain their position as the power elite.

Sellin (1938) might have explained rising crime rates during periods of high immigration as a function of cultural conflict, in which the legalized conduct norms of the receiving society and the immigrants differ. The crime rate rises as immigrants engage in behavior that was legal in the old country but is illegal under the laws of the new country. Social disorganization theory (e.g., Shaw and McKay, 1969) might explain this association in terms of social-control breakdown in immigrant neighborhoods, where people find themselves caught between the old conduct norms, which no longer control them, and the new conduct norms, which they do not yet understand.

Another approach, opportunity theory, might argue that massive immigration causes social and physical change in a number of ways that expand the opportunities for crime. Any expansion of opportunity is likely to be accompanied by an expansion of the number of criminal events. Opportunity expands because of the growth of service and consumer economies, the increased number of people, and the increased number of households at risk. Opportunity also expands because immigration disrupts established neighboring patterns and otherwise effects the daily activity patterns of many people. Such changes are now known to create more criminal opportunities and seem always to be more associated with rises in the crime rate.

Urbanization Pattern

The process of urbanization (the structural transformation of residence patterns from rural to urban, in which the majority of a nation's people come to live in large cities rather than being scattered on farms and in small villages) seems to be associated with rising crime rates. The Canadian urbanization pattern has differed from both the English and American patterns. Both England and America experienced different periods of maximal and minimal urban growth. The Canadian pattern, by contrast, has been one of constant urban concentration. In 1871, only 20 percent of Canada's population lived in urban areas. By 1901, 37 percent lived in cities. By 1956, more than 65 percent of Canada's population lived in urban areas.

This steady process of urbanization is mirrored in the steady growth of the crime rate. Urbanization might explain crime rates in two ways. First, the concentration of more people expands the opportunities for crime, both in terms of social interactions and in terms of concentrations of property. Second, the movement of rural emigrants into cities creates some form of cultural conflict or social disorganization that sends crime rates soaring. Zehr (1976), using French data, has demonstrated that high crime rates are associated with both urban density and the rate of urban growth. Thus, one reasonable explanation for the long-term trend in Canadian crime is the urbanization pattern over time.

Structural Changes and Crime

No single explanation for the long-term trends in English, American, and Canadian crime should be sought. Important changes in the social, demographic, and economic structures of a society are usually closely associated with one another as well as with rising crime rates. The massive population growth of England in the late eighteenth century was closely associated with the Industrial Revolution, and both were associated with urbanization and with a major transformation in political ideology known as the Enlightenment. The causal orderings of these changes and the way in which they related to the nineteenth-century crime wave as a set remain very much a matter of dispute among historians and social scientists. What can be said about structural changes in society is that any major structural change seems to be associated with rising crime rates. Thus, structural change indicators can be used as predictors of major changes in the long-term crime trend.

Chapter Summary

English crime rates have varied in major cycles over a period of eight hundred years. Major peaks have occurred in the early fourteenth century, the early seventeenth century, the early eighteenth century, and the mid-eighteenth century. American crime rates have exhibited similar cyclic patterns since the mid-seventeenth century, with a major peak in the mid-nineteenth century. Canadian crime rates exhibit a different trend, generally rising since 1880. Major upswings in the crime trends of all three countries can be associated with major changes in economic organization, in demographic structure, and in the organization of criminal justice.

The nature of crime has changed over time. It is much less violent and much more connected with property now than it was in times past. English homicide rates have declined steadily, by a factor of 18, from the fourteenth century to the present time. The crime mix in all three countries has changed radically over the past century and a half: the relative importance of crimes of violence against the person has declined substantially; the relative importance of crimes of violence against property, such as robbery and burglary, has increased substantially. The nature of offenders has also changed substantially over time. Offenders are now, in the aggregate, much younger than they used to be.

We now appear to be caught in a major upward trend in crime rates that began in the late 1920s or early 1930s. This upswing has resulted in levels of crime unprecedented during past ages. It may be the product of major structural changes in society produced by the communications and automation revolution.

9
Spatial Analysis of Crime

Introduction

This text explores both the spatial and the temporal characteristics of crime. The previous chapters described the temporal patterns. The remaining chapters describe the spatial patterns. The spatial patterning of crime is the hidden dimension of crime. Criminology frequently uses spatially based data to explore nonspatial theories of crime. Data for countries, cities, or subareas in cities are related to crime rates and the strength of the relationships used to support or refute social theories. Areal units, such as cities or neighbourhoods in a city, are often used as a counting base for enumerating crime. Crimes are counted within the units; socioeconomic characteristics are also tabulated for these units and then related to crime. For example, the percentage of poor people or the percentage of unemployed people or the percentage of black people is calculated and statistically related to property, violent, or specific crime rates.

Data are collected and relationships explored from a social or economic perspective. The same data could be explored from a spatial perspective, and new or complementary relationships might be uncovered. Much criminological research is social, but it could be augmented with spatial research. Harvey (1973) provides an excellent exposition of the differences between the sociological and geographic imaginations. According to Harvey, describing the general approach of C. Wright Mills, the sociological imagination

> enables the possessor to understand the larger historical scene in terms of its meaning for the inner life and the external career of a variety of individuals. . . . the first fruit of this imagination . . . is the idea that the individual can understand his own experience and gauge his own fate only by locating himself within his period, that he can know his own chances in life only by becoming aware of those of all individuals in his circumstances. (Harvey, 1973, p. 23)

The geographic imagination

enables the individual to recognize the role of space and place in his own biography, to relate to spaces he sees around him, and to recognize how transactions between individuals and between organizations are affected by the space that separates them. It allows him to recognize the relationship which exists between him and his neighbourhood [and] his territory. (Harvey, 1973, p. 24).

Ultimately *social* scientists must accept space and geography in their theories, and geographically oriented researchers must accept social relations. Sociology and geography are complementary. It is the interaction of the geographic and the sociological perspectives that produces the understanding necessary to form analytic frameworks in criminology and criminal justice. This text explores the spatial and social dimensions of crime.

This chapter presents basic analytic techniques that can be used to study the spatial dimension of crime. These techniques include those used to study point patterns, such as locations where crimes occur; those used to study flow patterns, such as the movement patterns of criminals when they are picking targets; and those used to analyze spatial aggregations of crime data.

Analysis of Absolute Locations

As with temporal analysis, special techniques have been developed for spatial data. Spatial information is information that has locational coordinates attached to it, that is, information that can be interrelated based on position. A simple example is crime occurrence data, which include the address of the location of the crime as well as specifics about the criminal act. Addresses can be translated into positions on a map, and because of the reference system on a map (often longitude and latitude), the points can be interrelated.

A more complex example of spatial data is information about stops on a public transit system, say, a subway or a metro. The information might include only an ordered list of the stops on various service lines, but with the ordered list, as well as knowledge about the junction points connecting two lines, it would be possible to reconstruct how someone moved through the subway system. Distance is not measured, but movement is. As a criminological example, it would be possible, by the use of relational locational data, to see if vandalism in subways clustered on one line or at adjacent stops. Vandalism could be high on one line but low on another line that is nearby. The spatial interrelationship can be seen only if the relative location of the stops is considered.

A final type of spatial analysis involves ecological analysis. Human ecology, which is a derivative of plant and animal ecology, considers people as groups occupying a territory. The study of the interaction of these groups, with associated territorial changes, forms the core of human ecology. Analytical ecological studies often lose touch with their conceptual base and become exercises in correlating the characteristics of areal units. Criminology has a long ecological tradition, both in its pure conceptual form, which looks at space, and in its statistical form, which uses ecological units as a base of statistical analysis.

Point Data

Point information is information with a locational component. Any discussion of point information immediately raises issues of levels of resolution and mapping techniques. Both point data and temporal data can be analyzed at many levels of resolution. As described in Chapter 6, temporal crime data can be collected at hourly, weekly, monthly, or yearly intervals (or can be aggregated to hourly, weekly, monthly, or yearly totals). The research questions change with the level of aggregation or the length of the time interval.

Similarly, spatial crime data can be collected by specific address (down to apartment unit or even room), by police patrolling area, by predefined administrative units (such as census tracts), by city, by region, or by country or cluster of countries. The occurrence of, say, a burglary at a specific store has many levels of locational information attached to it: the absolute street address of the store; the placement of the store in the city; the placement of the city in the region; and the placement of the region in the country. Analysis done on the highest-resolution point data (the building location for burglary) often looks at opportunity structures. High-resolution spatial data coupled with high-resolution temporal data provide a dynamic trace of the movement of offenders and victims in time and space, particularly the dynamic changes that relate to the movement of criminal targets and changes in surveillance patterns. Analysis at a city, region, or country level involves exploring grosser level characteristics with a spatial component. For example, crime can be correlated with migration patterns, locational flows of capital as economies grow and decline, the spatial patterning of law enforcement, or court behavior. People do not move about randomly within a city, region, or country; people's patterns of movement are spatial biased. Similarly, the movement of money and goods is spatially biased and can be related to other spatial patterns, such as crime patterns.

Mapping

The analysis of spatial data begins with visual inspection. The data are represented on a map, and the map is inspected for patterns. Crime mapping can be done several ways.

1. Data can be represented as points or dots on a map. Most police departments keep "pin" maps of current crimes.
2. Data can be represented for areas by shadings or colors. In a map using shading, dark usually means *more* and light means *less*. The number of shading levels or colors used is arbitrary and depends on the choices made by the person constructing the map.
3. Data can be represented as contours. In contour mapping, points of equal value are connected by lines. The lines form contours. Areas between con-

tour lines are considered of equal value. Most weather maps showing temperature are contour maps.

Figure 9–1 demonstrates the results of the various types of mapping. Changing the type of mapping can radically alter the visual interpretation of the data.

Dot Maps

Data presented in the form of a dot map are usually fairly unambiguous. If the spatial distribution of one crime is being mapped, then dots of any form or

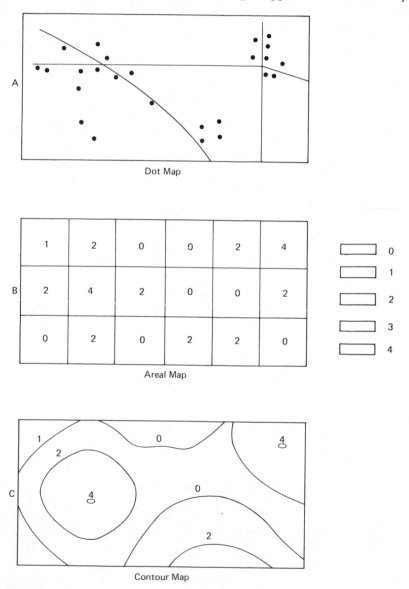

Figure 9–1. Identical crime data mapped three ways.

214

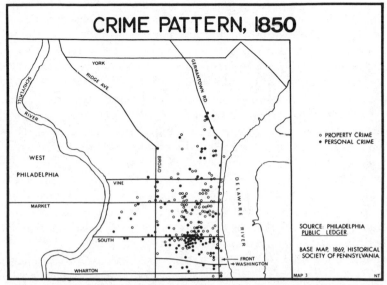

Figure 9–2. Dot map showing locations at which crimes were known to have occurred in Philadelphia, 1850. [Source: D. R. Johnson, *Policing the Urban Underworld: The Impact of Crime on the Development of the American Police, 1800–1837.* Philadelphia: Temple University Press, 1979, p. 74. Reprinted with permission.]

color can be used. Dot maps can be exciting visually, and they easily reveal patterns. The use of dot maps has a long history in criminology (see Figure 9–2, the map of violent and property crime locations in Philadelphia in 1850). Dot maps clearly show clusters and linear elements.

Areal Maps

Representing data in areal units also has a long history (see, for example, the maps prepared by Guerry [1831] showing crime in France in 1825). Producing areal maps of crimes is, however, not as straightforward as producing dot maps. Crimes can be spatially located in very fine detail by dots. The streets, the buildings, and even the rooms where crimes occur, can be mapped. Areal mapping requires the aggregation of highly specific spatial data into broader areas.

Two basic types of areal units are used with crime data: (1) administrative units and (2) arbitrary coding units. The category *administrative unit* covers the range of spatial units designed primarily by government to organize the delivery of services, to provide common areal units for diverse reporting functions, and to provide an areal basis for government allocation and representation. Countries, states, provinces, counties, and cities are major administrative units. These units have clear political as well as administrative purposes. Other administrative units exist that are less well known but that are used extensively in criminological work. The most frequently used units are those developed by the agencies that gather census data. In the United States, the Census Bureau takes the census; in Canada the responsible agency is Statistics Canada; and in England [1] the Office of Population Census and Surveys carries out the census. The United States performs a census every ten years. Both England and Canada perform a five-year minicensus as well as the full ten-year census. The census has become a major data source for criminologists because the census not only counts people but also gathers socioeconomic information. This information is frequently related to crime data.

The names of the census units used to report counts vary from country to country, but basically similar divisions exist. England, the United States, and Canada divide the country into a series of nested units; that is, the country is first completely divided up into large areas, and then these large areas are further subdivided. The subdivision process is repeated several times until finally the whole country is divided up into small units, units that may be as small as one city block. At different stages in the subdivision, areal units are created that match governmental units. For example, in Canada a province is both a governmental unit and a census counting unit. Similarly, the three countries have census areal units that match municipalites or incorporated cities.

The primary units used in crime-related research are cities or municipalities and sub-city divisions called *census tracts*. Cities or municipalities are legal units, with fixed boundaries. People in these units elect local government bodies, and the local governing bodies, in turn, provide many services.

Within cities, there is much variety: land uses change; housing types change; density changes; and the characteristics of the residents change. Therefore, there is a need to gather sub-city-level data that capture these changes yet provide meaningful areal units. The major census sub-city area is a census tract. Census tracts are nonlegal (they have no legal purpose) subdivisions of a city; they are designed by the census to have boundaries that remain fixed for fairly long intervals. In the United States, they are usually designed with an initial population of around four thousand people and have initial boundaries that surround relatively homogeneous population groupings. The boundaries are often drawn on major roads.

Division into relatively long-standing areal subdivisions, such as those used by the census, has advantages. Information from one census can be compared with that of other censuses. Other agencies can be convinced to collect data in these predefined subdivisions because they can be certain that other data will exist at the same level of aggregation. Relatively fixed subdivisions do, however, create problems for spatial studies. Units such as census tracts are created at a fixed point in time. Cities grow and change. The population of a census tract changes over time. The original homogeneity of the tract may disappear, so that tract data (which are often an average for a tract) become meaningless or difficult to analyze statistically.

Finally, census tract boundaries are usually drawn on major roads. Crime frequently clusters along major roads; consequently, what appears to be a visual cluster of events on a dot map is often diffused in the average figures for several tracts. In Figure 9–3, there are six census tracts with associated crime totals that vary from two to five. From the map, only one tract appears to show many crimes (Tract 2),

---

[1] A census is carried out in all of Great Britain. The discussion and comparisons in this text are restricted to England and Wales and consequently the discussion of the census is restricted and general reference is made only to England.

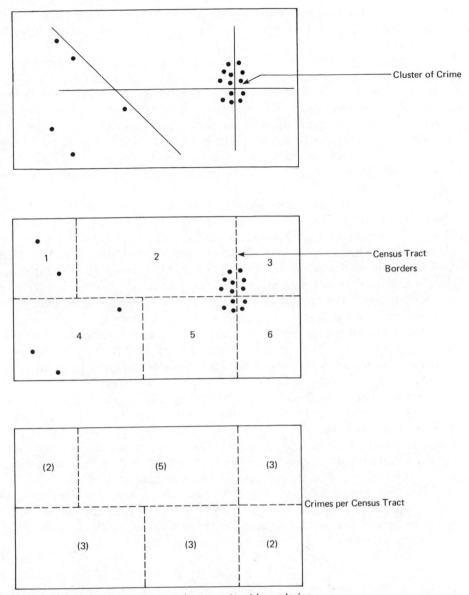

Figure 9–3. Census locations and census tract boundaries.

and the rest of the tracts seem to be about equal in crime. However, visual inspection of the dot map clearly reveals a cluster of fourteen crimes at the intersection of two roads and few crimes elsewhere. Tract-level information cannot show this cluster because the cluster occurs at tract boundaries.

Somewhat analogous problems exist for cities. A city may grow beyond its legal boundary. In this case, crime that is actually associated with one urban area will be divided into two or more administrative counting units. In addition, because cities are legal units, they vary greatly in size and reasons for existing. Some

217

cities have a dense core area and a lightly developed fringe. Other cities are more uniform in density. Comparing the crime rates for cities of such diverse urban forms must be done with care.

The census bureaus are not oblivious to the problems of using administrative units such as cities for research. In the United States, Canada, and England, systems for dividing up the country into units have been devised that make more sense for social science research. Those of primary importance to criminologists are the systems used to identify urban areas. As mentioned before, the legally defined limits of cities often do not correspond with the actual urban form. Urban areas may grow into each other; an urbanized area may spill over the city limits, legally defined cities might not be completely urbanized and may contain rural areas as well as urban areas.

To handle the first two problems, urban areas growing together, or growing past legal boundaries, the various census bureaus have created a tabulation category in which information from contiguous urban areas is clustered together. In the United States, this category is the Standard Metropolitan Statistical Area. A Standard Metropolitan Statistical Area (SMSA) consists of a grouping of counties having more than fifty thousand population and having an urban core and integrated commuting patterns.[2] The purpose of the SMSA is to cluster together counties that are tied economically and spatially. The FBI reports crime data for SMSAs.

Canada has a similar census designation, a Census Metropolitan Area (CMA). A CMA consists of a cluster of municipalities that have the following two characteristics: a labor market area with a population of 100,000 and an urban core with an urban fringe linked by work and commutation patterns.

Spatial analysis in Canada is more difficult. The Centre for Justice Statistics of Statistics Canada, the crime reporting agency in that country, tabulates crime data not for CMAs, but for something they call a Metropolitan Area. These Metropolitan Areas do not match the census metroplitan categories. The crime data for individual municipalities must be retabulated and totaled for the census categories so that crime data can be compared with census metropolitan data.

England groups urban areas into conurbations. Conurbations are an aggregation of local authority areas with an economic center of high commercial and business activity and low residential activity. As in Canada, police data are not tabulated for conurbations and must be hand-calculated.

The census bureaus have also developed techniques for separating the rural from the urban parts of census administrative units, such as legally defined cities. Such a split would be ideal for criminological research, but easily available police data are publically tabulated only for whole cities (or counties). Separating the rural from the urban areas would require analyzing original address-level police data and classifying the addresses into rural-fringe and urban-core categories.

Areal maps can also be created without the use of census areas or legally designated areal units. The areal units used in crime maps are just categories for tabulation. Crimes are summed within a census tract, and the rates are calculated. Crimes are then totaled for a city, county, state, or province. The advantage of

---

[2] The largest urban clusterings in the United States—New York and Los Angeles—are called Standard Consolidated Areas and are made up of clusters of SMSAs.

using existing administrative units rests in the capability of comparing characteristics across units. If the purpose of mapping is just to describe a spatial distribution, then using other areal units may be preferable. One can subdivide the area to be mapped—say, a city—by laying a grid over the area. A grid or lattice can be of any shape or size, but common lattice patterns are squares, hexagons, or diamonds. Crimes are counted within the grid cells.

The advantages of areal mapping by means of grid cells are numerous. The size of the cells can be made regular, so that one area does not dominate the map. The lattice can be placed so that clusters of crimes have a better chance of appearing as high counts in one or a few cells, instead of being distorted as they are in many census-tract counting schemes. The lattice can be arranged, when one is working with city data, to avoid having a border line of a cell fall on a main road, thereby reducing the probability of splitting a natural crime cluster in an unnatural way. But as noted before, data gathered under lattice structures cannot be directly cross-related to administrative units.[3]

Contour Maps

Dot maps and areal maps are commonly found in criminological studies. Contour maps are less common but are found frequently enough so that they should also be discussed.

In contour mapping, it is assumed that the process or activity being mapped is continuous, that is, that a value for the activity can be found for every point on the map. Rain fall, temperature, and altitudes are three continuous data sets that are mapped naturally by a contour map. The easiest way to picture a contour map is to think of a topographical map of the world. High-altitude locations are represented by physically or visually high points or by colors. Rain, temperature, and altitude are continuous properties.[4]

Crimes occur at specific points but can be considered continuous and mapped as contours. The crime rates perceived by residents of Summit County, Ohio, for 1972 are mapped in Figure 9–4. High points on the contour surface represent areas perceived to have high crime rates (Pyle, 1976). For a contour map of crime data, information is collected for areal units (lattice cells or administrative units). The totals collected for each areal unit are viewed as being the value at a control point at the center of the units. The values of each control point are compared with those of the surrounding control points. It is assumed that the values increase or decrease in a direct linear fashion from one control point to the next. For example, if one control point has an associated crime rate of 500 and the nearest control point has a value of 200, it is assumed, for the purpose of constructing the contour map, that all of the points between the two control points take on values between 500 and 200 and that the values decrease as the points move away from the higher control point, finally decreasing to 200 at the other control point. Contour mapping can

---

[3] When lattices are used, they are sometimes related to administrative units by the use of cells smaller than the administrative unit. Lattice cell totals are then aggregated and proportionally allocated to the administrative unit. The aggregation process can reintroduce the tabulation problems associated with administrative units.

[4] To map continuous processes such as these, sample values must be drawn. At that point, a continuous process becomes a point representation.

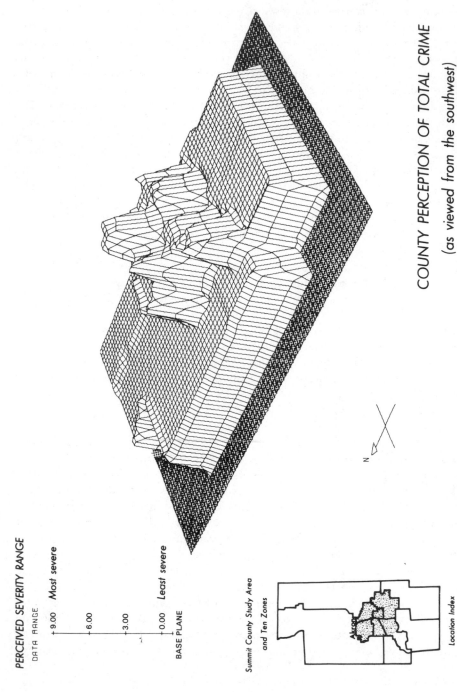

PERCEIVED SEVERITY RANGE

DATA RANGE.

9.00 Most severe

6.00

3.00

0.00 Least severe

BASE PLANE

COUNTY PERCEPTION OF TOTAL CRIME

(as viewed from the southwest)

N

Summit County Study Area
and Ten Zones

Location Index

Figure 9–4. Contour map of crime perceptions in Summit County, Ohio. [Source: G. F. Pyle, "Systematic Sociospatial Variation in Perceptions of Crime Location and Severity," in D. Georges–Abeyie and K. D. Harries (eds.), *Crime: A Spatial Perspective.* New York: Columbia University Press, 1980, p. 226.]

produce pretty visual images but, because of the assumption of continuous change, may be deceiving.[5]

Numerous variations on the basic contour algorithm are possible. The change from point to point can be considered nonlinear instead of linear. Imaginary boundary lines can be drawn midway between control points, effectively dividing the map into contour areas; data values may be considered equal from a control point to the boundary line, and then may be changed to another control value when the boundary is crossed. Finally, control points of equal value can be connected, forming contour lines. The distance between contour lines then shows the rise or fall of a contour surface.

All mapping techniques are basically unidimensional. Only one variable can easily be mapped at one time. Several techniques have been tried for producing composite maps of two or more variables, none very successfully. Dot maps can be executed in several colors or shapes. Areal maps may be produced with overlays, each overlay representing one variable. Maps may also be produced for a composite index. The variables to be mapped (say, crime rates for several crimes) can be combined into one index value (say, a composite crime rate) and the index value mapped. These techniques either become visually complex or lose substantial information.

Analysis of Relative Locations

Spatial analysis usually proceeds beyond the visual inspection of a map. Numerical descriptions of the distribution of data are needed. Two standard descriptions are presented here: (1) the center of mass and (2) nearest-neighbour analysis.

Center of Mass

When one has a series of numbers, an obvious first statistic to generate is a mean. Given the crime rates for the various states, it is reasonable to calculate the average crime rate. In spatial data, the equivalent mean value is the center of mass. Given a distribution of crimes across a city, where is the central location of crime? What point on the map represents the spatial center of the distribution of the crime data? Centers of mass exist for all spatial distributions, just as mean values do for any series of numbers. To understand what a center of a spatial distribution is, it is easiest to consider the example of retail store locations. During the last thirty years, the population of cities has generally been increasing. As cities have grown, there has been a relative shift of retail stores from a central location to peripheral locations, usually spatially biased in certain directions. Strip commerical development on highways has increased in the United States and Canada. Shopping malls have also been built at peripheral locations, but not uniformly on the periphery. If the retail store locations of most cities were mapped thirty years ago, there would

---

[5] A fuller discussion of contour mapping can be found in almost any geographical text. A good discussion can be found in Haggett (1965).

221

have been a clear clustering toward the centers of urban areas. Conceptually, the stores would cluster around some central mean point. Now, if the retail stores in the same cities were mapped, there would be many more locations away from the center. If a mean location were picked, it would be placed away from the downtown concentration and toward the peripheral locations.

One finds the central mean location for a spatial distribution by taking the map, superimposing a coordinate system on it (often longitude and latitude), and measuring the relative location of the point data using the imposed coordinate system. The data now have locational coordinates. The locational coordinates for the horizontal and vertical axes are then averaged.[6] These average values are the coordinates of the center of mass.

By the use of calculated centers of mass, it is possible to tell whether the locus of criminal activity is shifting in a city. It is also possible to tell where patrol cars should be placed to minimize the response time in answering calls about crimes. Finally, the center of mass can be used to help unravel some of the visual complexities of multicomponent maps. As discussed before, visual inspection of spatial distributions becomes difficult if several distributions are being compared. Overlay maps are confusing. If several crime distributions are being compared, the centers of mass for each distribution can be calculated and the central points compared. If the centers are widely dispersed, then the distributions are dissimilar. If the centers are clustered, then the distributions may be similar.[7]

Nearest-Neighbor Analysis

The center of mass is a measure of central tendency. Point data are much richer than just mean values. Patterns can be seen and clusters or regularities noticed. Nearest-neighbor analysis is a numeric technique used to classify point distributions as clustered, regular, or random (or more clustered than random, more regular than random, and so on). Figure 9–5 shows idealized crime patterns in a city. The locations are purposely simplified to show clustered, regular, and random patterns.

City-level crime data are often clustered (Figure 9–2). Usually, several prominent clusters can be seen, with a scattering of points away from the clusters. When crime locations are clustered, some clustering of targets or clustering of criminals should be suspected. Commercial crimes obviously cluster because retail stores, through zoning, are forced to cluster. Residential crimes sometimes give a more diffuse picture, possibly a random pattern. Regular crime patterns are highly unusual.

Nearest-neighbor analysis developed from plant ecology and involves deter-

---

[6] If longitude and latitude are used for the coordinate system, care must be taken in finding averages. Longitude and latitude are measured in minutes and seconds. Because these have a base of 60, not 100, the measurements must be converted to decimal equivalents before being averaged.

[7] Quite different distributions can produce the same center of mass, just as different distributions of nonspatial data can have the same mean. A variance equivalent is available for spatial data. This calculation can be used to identify the dispersion around the center of mass. See R. Hammond and P. S. McCullagh (1974) for a description of spatial dispersion measures.

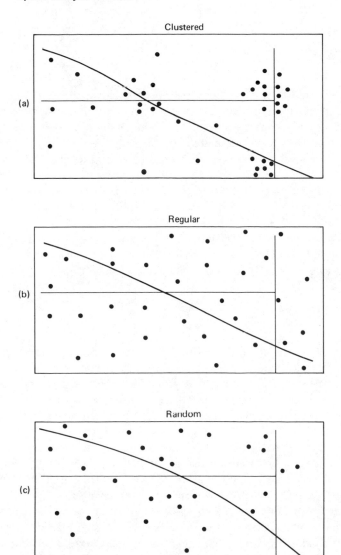

Figure 9–5. Point distributions of crime in a city.

mining how the spacing of dot locations differs from what would be expected in a random pattern. The actual average spacing between points is compared with the expected spacing if the distribution were random. The difference between the actual and the expected spacing describes whether the spacing is clustered, random, or regular.[8]

---

[8] See David M. Smith (1975) for a description of nearest-neighbor analysis and an example of its use. See R. Hammond and P. S. McCullagh (1974) for a description of the limitations of nearest-neighbor analysis.

Statistical Analysis

When crime data are collected by area (either governmental administrative units or a specific researcher's analytic frameworks), the data can be statistically analyzed by means of the techniques described in Chapter 6 (as well as many others that are not described in the chapter but are described in standard statistical texts). Spatial data, however, have their own special problems. The results of spatial analysis are inexorably tied to the areal units used. There are strong aggregation biases in spatial statistics: statistical relationships change as areal units get larger or smaller. Improper inferences can be made if one gathers data for a unit of one size and uses them to draw conclusions about units of other sizes. Inferences made about small areal units from data gathered on larger units fall into the category of *ecological fallacies*. The ecological fallacy and problems associated with the size of the geographic unit being analyzed will be described in the following sections.

Problems with Spatial Units

Relative Size

In areal collection of spatial data, individual data are aggregated into values for areas, and then the areal data are analyzed. In most criminological research, the data are already aggregated before the research begins. Most areal studies are done on crimes within cities and between cities. For intracity analysis (analysis within a city), data are often supplied by a police department for patrol areas or other administrative service areas.[9]

In intercity analysis, crime totals and census totals for the cities form the most common data base. The areal units used are usually legally defined municipalities or cities, and because of the multipurpose reasons for creation of the areal units, they have inherent flaws, which were discussed earlier in the chapter.

The statistical relationships uncovered in spatial analysis depend directly on the relative size and shape of the areal units used. Specifically, correlations based on areal data may change radically as the areal collection units change. Consider the following example, in which a region is arbitrarily divided up into three different configurations (Figure 9–6). The first (Figure 9–6a) configuration has six cells of equal size; the second (Figure 9–6b) collapses two cells together; and the third (Figure 9–6c) collapses four of the original cells together. The number of crimes per square mile and the population per square mile are known in each of the original cells. The correlation between crime and population is $r = +0.715$ for the first configuration (Figure 9–6a). For the second configuration, the correlation rises to $r = +0.875$ (Figure 9–6b). For the third configuration (Figure 9–6c), the correlation drops to $r = +0.500$. *The underlying data have not changed, but the correlations have.*

The amount of distortion in correlational analysis when one is using irregu-

---

[9] Individual crime data are sometimes the base for studies. These data, usually address level data, are often immediately totaled to patrol areas or census tracts by researchers.

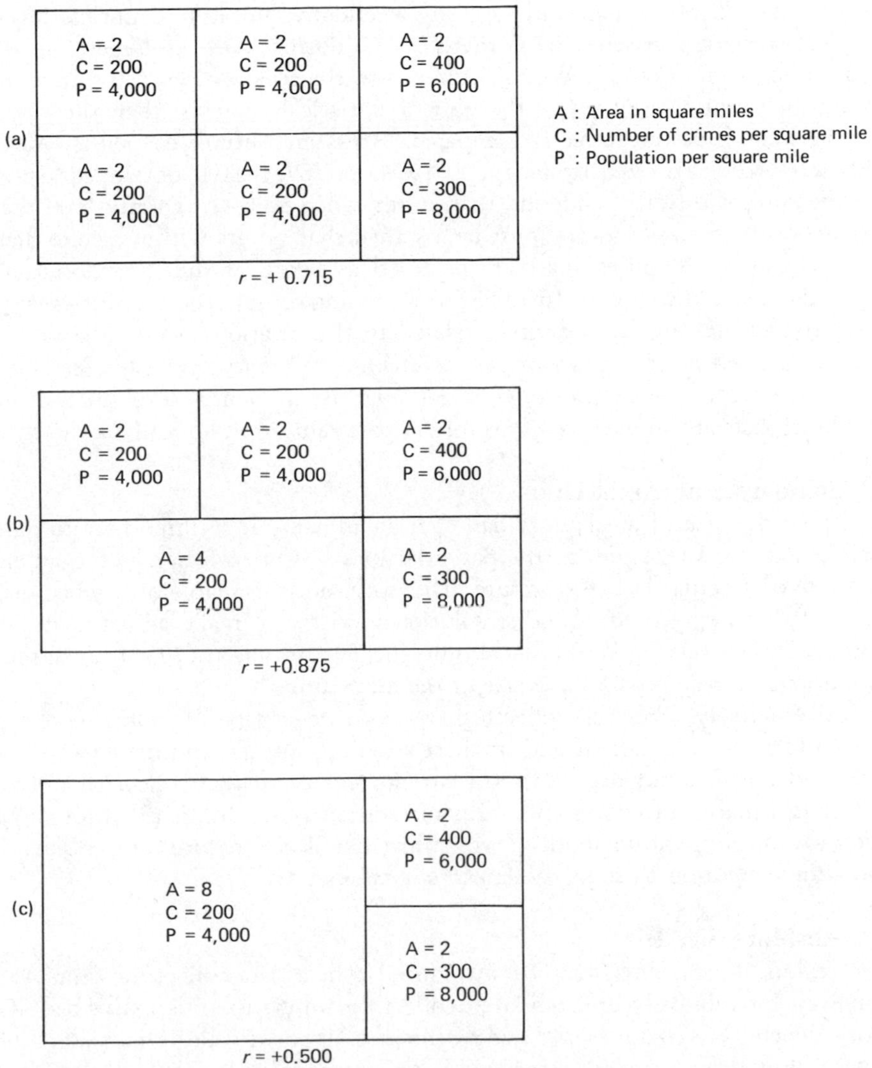

A = 2 C = 200 P = 4,000	A = 2 C = 200 P = 4,000	A = 2 C = 400 P = 6,000
A = 2 C = 200 P = 4,000	A = 2 C = 200 P = 4,000	A = 2 C = 300 P = 8,000

(a)

A : Area in square miles
C : Number of crimes per square mile
P : Population per square mile

$r = + 0.715$

A = 2 C = 200 P = 4,000	A = 2 C = 200 P = 4,000	A = 2 C = 400 P = 6,000
	A = 4 C = 200 P = 4,000	A = 2 C = 300 P = 8,000

(b)

$r = +0.875$

(c)

	A = 2 C = 400 P = 6,000
A = 8 C = 200 P = 4,000	A = 2 C = 300 P = 8,000

$r = +0.500$

Figure 9–6. Effect of size on correlational coefficients. [Source: Adapted from A. H. Robinson, "The Necessity of Weighting Values in Correlation of Areal Data," *Annals of the Association of American Geographers* 46/1956: 234, as reported by P. Haggett, *Locational Analysis in Human Geography.* London: Edward Arnold, 1965, p. 202.]

larly sized collecting units depends directly on the variability in the sizes (Haggett, 1974, p. 203). Care must be taken in analyzing irregularly sized areal units (such as states or provinces, counties, cities, and subareas within cities, such as census tracts) where the data for each collecting unit, because of the nature of the statistical techniques, are viewed as being centered at one point.

MacCarty (as cited in Haggett, 1974, pp. 203–204), in an analysis of industrial location, provided strong documentation of the effect of variably sized reporting units. In the continental United States, the size of the states ranges from 267,339 square miles for Texas to 1,214 square miles for Rhode Island, with a clustering of states around 60,000 square miles. Using a random sample of counties, MacCarty found less variation in size (San Bernardino, California, was the largest, at 20,160 square miles; Ohio County, West Virginia, was the smallest, at 109 square miles). If states or counties are used as the unit of statistical analysis, then the values for large or small areas are directly compared. Areas are shrunk to points. McCarty, Hook, and Knos (as cited by Haggett, 1974, pp. 203–204) developed a preliminary measure of the size reduction that occurs when state- or county-level data are used. If one uses state data, it must be assumed that points within a state that are, on an average, 120 miles apart are regarded as being at the same location. For county data, the distance is 16 miles. For criminological studies, this means that if property crimes are, for example, related to the locations of retail stores in the states, *then crime locations that are, on an average 120 miles from retail store locations must be regarded as being located at the same point.* At a county- level analysis, stores and crimes that are an average of 16 miles apart cannot be logically separated.

Standardizing Areal Units

Since the size of areal units has such an impact, it is important to consider possible statistical remedies to the potential biases. One solution is to gather data using a fixed, regular lattice structure. This solution is available only when original point data are being used. Another solution is to try to make adjustments in calculations for the varying sizes of areal units. A. H. Robinson (1956) suggested that observations be weighted for the size of the areal unit.[10]

Alternatively, irregular collecting areas can be grouped to form more regular shapes and sizes. The largest and smallest areas can also be eliminated—or may be considered outliers and dropped. Any attempt to regularize collection units after the fact is a matter of compromise. Regularization is accomplished through aggregation and/or elimination, both of which lose detail and reduce sample size. There is no simple solution to this problem in spatial analysis.[11]

Absolute Size Bias

Technical problems may be introduced when data-collecting units vary in size. Even for relatively uniform-sized collecting units, there is a size bias. Correlations generally increase as the size of the areal reporting units increase. Correlations computed for variables associated with single points are called *individual correlations*. Correlations computed for areal units are called *ecological correlations*.

One can compute an individual correlation between income and education by drawing a sample of individuals, determining their income and education, and then computing the correlation coefficient using the standard formulas. One can compute an ecological correlation between income and education by taking a sample of census tracts (or counties, or cities, or states), determining the average income and

---

[10] Robinson suggested that the standard deviation formula be adjusted as follows:

$$\Delta_A = \sqrt{((\Sigma AX^2 / \Sigma A) - (\Sigma AX / \Sigma A)^2)}$$

where A is the size of the collecting unit.

[11] See, generally, P. Haggett, *Locational Analysis in Human Geography* (1974), for an excellent description of qualitative problems in spatial analysis and possible solutions.

average educational level of the people in the tracts (counties, cities, or states), and computing the correlation coefficient in the standard way using the tract (county, city, or state) values as the data. An individual correlation relates properties of people or single points. Ecological correlations relate properties of groups or areas.

In the terminology of the previous section, the correlations are calculated between areas with the areas regarded as single points. The areas become data points. Statistically, in ecological correlations, no information is known about what goes on within the area. The variation within the areal units is lost.

Research that uses large areal units as the data reporting base generally reports higher correlations than studies on smaller areas. In a study by W. S. Robinson (1950), the correlation between the percentage of black people and illiteracy in 1930 for the nine multistate U.S. Census Bureaus divisions was +0.946, an extremely strong relationship. When the correlation was recomputed for states instead of divisions, the value dropped to +0.773. For individuals, the correlation dropped to +0.203, a major reduction from the +0.946 value. The underlying data did not change; only the size of the reporting unit changed. The reason for the increase is fairly clear. As the size of the reporting units increase, the variability between the data points being used in the analysis decreases. When any areal unit is used instead of individuals, the measures used represent some composite picture of individual variability. If mean values are used (say, average income), one value for average income replaces a range of incomes. The relative importance of individual high and low incomes disappears, and their values are subsumed within the average. As the size of areas increases, the importance of any individual value that goes into the areal measure decreases, and the areal measures become more stable.

As a simple example, there is more variability in the height of children in any given Grade 4 class than there is in the average height of students in each of several Grade 4 classes. Similarly, there is less difference between the average heights of Grade 4 students for several schools than between the average heights of the individual classes. Obviously, from a logical point of view, numerical examples could be constructed that do not show this general pattern. In the natural environment, odd counterexamples rarely occur. From a predictive point of view, it would be more difficult to predict the height of one Grade 4 student than to predict the average height for a school.

From a criminological perspective, the smoothing of data can be seen from a residential burglary example. On any particular street, it would be difficult to predict which homes will be broken into. Burglary is a rare enough event so that it would be difficult to identify individual prospective victims. If the number of burglaries were counted for several clusters of blocks, it would be possible to see which clusters of blocks had many burglaries and which had few. Although it would be difficult to identify prospective individual targets, it would be easier to identify clusters of blocks where burglaries would be more likely to occur. If the clusters were clustered—particularly if high first-level clusters were joined with other high ones, and low first-level clusters with other low clusters—then it would be even easier to identify the superclusters with a high probability of future burglaries. It would still be difficult to identify individual buildings that might be victimized. Correlations for the larger units should be higher, the predictive and descriptive tasks are easier. Correlations for smaller units are generally smaller. As described in

Chapter 6, prediction and correlation are tied together. Predictions can be made with confidence when correlations are high.

Although correlations generally increase with the size of the unit of analysis, the size of the increase may be minimal and, logically may not even occur. However, whenever large correlations are found for large areal units, questions should be raised about whether the high correlation is an aggregation effect and whether correlations for smaller units should be calculated.

Ecological Fallacy

Correlations vary with the size and the shape of areal units; the numbers vary, and the technical analyses vary. Researchers and writers on crime have more difficulty adjusting their analytic framework as the analyses move up and down through the spatial cone of resolution than they do adjusting their units of analysis. The generic term *ecological fallacy* is applied to research arguments that inappropriately apply conclusions reached from the data from one spatial level of analysis to another level. Most often inappropriate conclusions are drawn when areal data are used to infer the characteristics of individuals. The ecological fallacy problem is obviously logically tied to aggregation bias and the identification of areas as points, but it is of sufficient interest so that it deserves separate discussion.

Criminological theories attempt to explain crime by looking at the factors that influence behavior at an individual or group level. *Differential association, blocked opportunity theories, and strain theories* all flow from *sociological imagination* and look at people alone or as they fit into groups. Crime and socioeconomic data are usually available in areal totals. The temptation exists to use areal relationships to test individual or group theories. If crime is related to unemployment at a census-tract level, it is very tempting to conclude that individual unemployment is related to individual commission of crimes. It is tempting to conclude that unemployed people commit more offenses than employed people. This shift to an individual level can not be made, of course, only from knowledge about the relationship between crime and unemployment at a tract level. Areal relations do not define associations for individuals. Knowing the ecological correlation does set limits on the range for the individual correlations; but the range may even be great enough to move a correlation from a positive to a negative value.

The range of variability is large. For example, if an area were divided into two subareas—say, census tracts (Figure 9–7)—and measurements were taken on two variables, and if the measurements were identical for the two variables in the two tracts, it would be quite easy to draw the conclusion that there was a relationship at a smaller level of spatial aggregation. However, if the two census tracts were subdivided into smaller areas (the next level of U.S. census subdivision is a block group), there might be no association. Figure 9–7 shows what can happen to apparent relationships as areas get smaller. Uniform tract averages of 20 on Variable A and −5 on Variable B are decomposed into block-group totals that appear unrelated. To borrow terminology from contingency table analysis, the tract analysis works with the *marginal totals* of the block-group data. Variation within the tracts is not known when the analysis is performed at tract level.

Ecological analysis should involve asking the right questions of the data. If

228

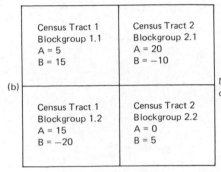

Figure 9–7. Ecological fallacy.

one follows a single crime through a spatial cone of resolution, the varying patterns and appropriate research questions can be seen. Figure 9–8 is a contour map of the burglary rates in the United States in 1971. Generally, the Southwest had the highest rates. At this level of analysis, reasonable research should be directed toward exploring regional demography and regional flows of goods or people.

Even in high-crime regions, crime is not uniformly high. On a map of Florida alone (Figure 9–9), a pattern of high and low areas emerges within a state that has a generally high burglary rate. Although Florida had generally high rates, there were many areas within the state with low rates:

This level of analysis [intrastate] can lead to finer resolution of questions raised at the national level. It permits first crude cuts into rural/urban and socioeconomic analysis of crime regions and also begins to provide meaningful operations research and re-

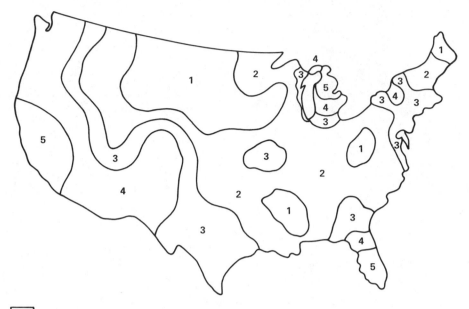

5	1619.9 – 1939.8
4	1299.9 – 1619.8
3	979.9 – 1299.8
2	659.9 – 979.8
1	339.8 – 659.8

Figure 9–8. Burglary rate pattern in the United States in 1971. Burglary rates were calculated per 100,000 population for each state. Five levels of burglary rates were mapped. Level 1 = 339.8–659.8; Level 2 = 659.9–979.8; Level 3 = 979.9–1299.8; Level 4 = 1299.9–1619.8; Level 5 = 1619.9–1939.8. [Source: P. J. Brantingham, D. A. Dyreson, and P. L. Brantingham, "Crime Seen Through a Cone of Resolution," *American Behavioral Scientist* 20/1976:263.]

source allocation information for criminal justice professionals (Brantingham, Dyreson and Brantingham, 1976, p. 286)

If we take one city within Florida, Tallahassee, the pattern once again becomes complex (Figure 9–10). There are two peaks (bimodal) and a generally declining burglary problem away from the two peaks. Individual analysis is not yet possible at this level, but distinctive patterns at this level should draw attention to land uses, traffic and people movements, and location of public institutions.

The city pattern can be broken down even further. A high-crime census tract in Figure 9–10 devolves into high and low areas when mapped at a block-group or cluster-of-blocks level (Figure 9–11). Neighbourhood crime analysis can begin at this level. Finally, a crime rate within a block group can be mapped at a block level (Figure 9–12). In this case, perceived uniform crime rates at a block-group level once again reveal modulations. Block-level data can be used to pinpoint prob-

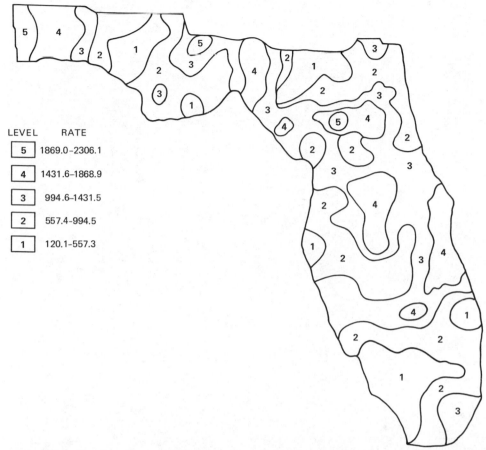

Figure 9–9. Burglary rate pattern in Florida in 1971. Burglary rates were calculated per 100,000 population for each county. Five levels of burglary rates were mapped: Level 1 = 120.1–557.3; Level 2 = 557.4–994.5; Level 3 = 994.6–1431.5; Level 5 = 1431.6–1868.9; Level 5 = 1869.0–2306.1. [Source: P. J. Brantingham, D. A. Dyreson, and P. L. Brantingham, "Crime Seen Through a Cone of Resolution," *American Behavioral Scientist* 20/1976:266.]

lem areas for police operations and to identify areas to explore at the individual level of analysis (Brantingham, Dyreson and Brantingham, 1976, p. 272).

Aggregation errors will not be made if minimal care is taken to pose questions that can be answered by the data. The biggest source of potential error is the temptation to use areal data to infer individual relationships.

Analysis of Flow Data

Up to this stage the description of spatial techniques has involved only the analysis of point patterns or aggregations of point data. Human spatial behaviour, however,

231

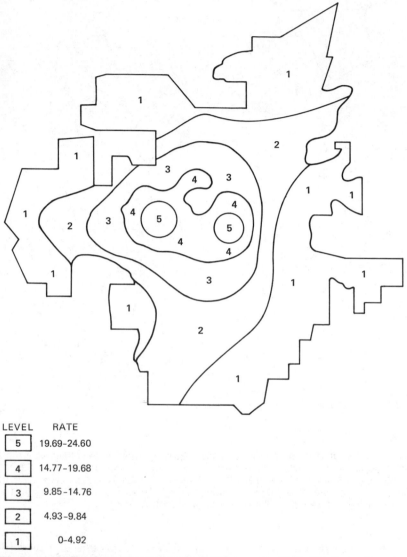

LEVEL	RATE
5	19.69–24.60
4	14.77–19.68
3	9.85–14.76
2	4.93–9.84
1	0–4.92

Figure 9–10. Burglary rate patterns in Tallahassee in 1970. Burglary rates were calculated per 1,000 population for each census tract. Five levels of burglary rates were mapped: Level 1 = 0–4.92; Level 2 = 4.93–9.84; Level 3 = 9.85–14.76; Level 4 = 14.77–19.68; Level 5 = 19.69–24.60. [Source: P. J. Brantingham, D. A. Dyreson, and P. L. Brantingham, "Crime Seen Through a Cone of Resolution," *American Behavioral Scientist* 20/1976:267.]

is primarily movement to and from fixed points. Movement and point patterns are linked. This link is particularly evident in crime analysis. Crimes usually occur at a fixed point in space.[12]

The criminal and often the victim are movable. For a crime to occur, a person

---

[12] To simplify the discussion, crimes such as hijacking an airplane and robbery in a moving car will be ignored.

232

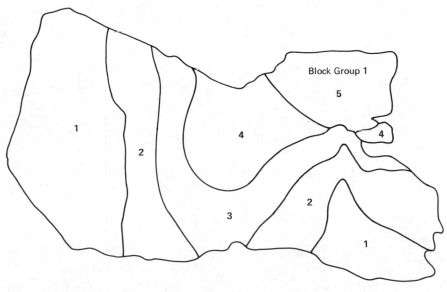

Burglary Rate per 1,000 population

5	15.55–18.27
4	12.82–15.54
3	10.10–12.81
2	7.37–10.09
1	4.63–7.36

Figure 9–11. Burglary rate patterns in Census Tract 20 in 1970. Burglary rates were calculated per 1,000 population for each block group. Five levels of burglary rates were mapped: Level 1 = 4.63–7.36; Level 2 = 7.37–10.09; Level 3 = 10.10–12.81; Level 4 = 12.82–15.54; Level 5 = 15.55–18.27. [Source: P. J. Brantingham, D. A. Dyreson, and P. L. Brantingham, "Crime Seen Through a Cone of Resolution," *American Behavioral Scientist* 20/1976:270.]

who is motivated to commit an offense and an attractive target must intersect in time and space. At a broader geographic level, patterns of crime in cities, regions, or countries may relate to spatial flows of people, goods, or employment. A flow perspective adds temporal and spatial dynamics to the study of crime.

Analysis of Nodes and Routes

The movement of people in an urban area is not uniform. Anyone who has traveled through a city is well aware of differences in mobility patterns. There are certain places that attract large numbers of people and others that do not. The movement of people in a city over the course of a day is an intricate process of agglomeration and dispersion. In the morning, adults from diverse residential areas funnel toward work locations, and children move toward schools. Work locations are obviously fewer than residential locations, and schools are still fewer than work

233

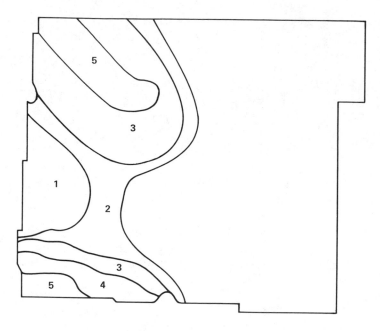

Rate per 100 population

5	5.37–6.7
4	4.03–5.36
3	2.69–4.02
2	1.35–2.68
1	0–1.34

Figure 9–12. Burglary rate patterns in Block Group 1, Tract 20 in 1970. Burglary rates were calculated per 100 population of each census block. Five levels of burglary rates were mapped: Level 1 = 0–1.34; Level 2 = 1.35–2.68; Level 3 = 2.69–4.02; Level 4 = 4.03–5.36; Level 5 = 5.37–6.7. [Source: P. J. Brantingham, D. A. Dyreson, and P. L. Brantingham, "Crime Seen Through a Cone of Resolution," *American Behavioral Scientist* 20/1976:271.]

locations. Work locations, in turn, cluster. There are commercial areas of town, financial areas, and industrial parts. To get to these restricted work areas, people travel along major arteries. Children filter through residential and commercial areas to get to school. The flow patterns change with the time of day and the day of the week. Similarly, flows between cities and countries are not uniform. Migration streams develop and die off; capital flows differentially; communications flow differentially. Certain cities are centers, focuses of activity. The centers of activity at individual, city, regional, or national levels are *nodes* or *nodal points*. The paths leading to the nodes are often called *routes*. The analysis of nodes and routes is the analysis of the spatial dynamics of crime.

For criminology, the interesting spatial questions include: What are the detailed spatial dynamics of crime? What influences the spatial dynamics of crime? How can these spatial patterns be analyzed? This chapter addresses the third question and provides the basic tools for the spatial analyses of crime described in subsequent chapters.

Spatial dynamics are time-dependent, representing movement over time. The movements over time can, in essence, be summed, and nodes or places of high activity can be identified. For example, for people, the patterns of movement in an urban area can be looked at over an extended period of time, and the locations that are the destination of many *trips* can be identified. More fully, the *origins* and *destinations* of trips can be identified. O-D (origin–destination) surveys reveal much of the spatial dynamics of movements and interactions in a city.

Striking movement patterns can be seen through an analysis of crimes. In fact there is a subarea of crime analysis, *crime-trip analyses,* that studies the travel patterns associated with different types of crimes. Capone and Nichols (1976) provided a classic example of crime-trip analysis. They extensively studied criminal mobility in Miami, Florida, uncovering differential trip patterns for various types of robbery. The importance of trip analysis can be seen in Figure 9–13. Capone and Nichols found that robbery trips—the distance a robber will travel to commit an offense— vary with the distribution of targets, the location of the residences of robbers, the relative attractiveness of the targets, and the relative risks associated with crimes.

To understand spatial analysis, one must understand several definitions. A *node* is simply the origin or the destination of a trip. As with all spatial analysis, questions of level of resolution immediately arise. If one looks at the movement patterns of a person, within a home, the nodes are all the locations where a person stops moving. During the course of a day, a person moves from bed to other specific points in the house, such as the kitchen sink, the dining table, or a favourite chair.[13]

The beginning and end points of *inside trips* are nodes. High-activity points are those locations that are nodes for repeated movements or trips and/or are nodes for many people. The refrigerator, the kitchen sink, the bathroom, and points in front of the television are high-activity points in most houses.

At a less fine level of resolution, an urban level, the nodes are the end points of individual trips outside the house. High-activity nodes are nodes for many people at many different times. At an even lower level of resolution, cities as a whole can be considered nodes if they are the origin or the destination of intercity trips. High-activity cities are the origin and destination of many trips.

The trips between nodes are routes. As with nodes, questions of level of resolution arise. People follow fairly fixed routes within homes or work places. Major routes within homes can be seen easily by inspecting worn areas of carpets or floors.

Outside the home, routes are the paths between higher order nodes such as school, home, and work. If specific information is available, routes can be mapped in great detail: the actual roads followed can be identified or the intersections crossed. Routes followed by many become major traffic arteries or major pedestrian paths.

Often, detailed information about routes is not available. Route or trip infor-

---

[13] There is no logical end to fine tuning the cone of resolution. Movements within a chair could even be considered movements from one nodal position to another.

Figure 9–13. Miami robbery trips, 1971. [Source: D. Capone and W. J. Nichols, "Urban Structure and Criminal Mobility," *American Behavioral Scientist* 20/1976:205.]

mation may be limited to directional information (identification of general direction traveled), time information (identification of length of time a trip took), or distance information (identification of distance traveled).

Route or trip information is the basis of much spatial analysis and modeling. Movement patterns are dynamic and the analysis of criminal- and victim-movement patterns are an important part of the spatial analysis of crime. The following sections present several major techniques for modeling movement.

Distance-Decay Modeling

Movement is patterned. There are high-activity nodes; origin—destination maps show this strongly. There are many ways to analyze movement. Several are discussed here, but they all depend on a conceptual model of movement. The simplest conceptualization is as follows: People generally move about in a purposeful manner; that is, movement is a search process. If a specific good is being searched for, and there are two available products, all things being equal, the closer product or occurrence of the good will be chosen. From a criminological perspective, if a person is searching for a target to rob and several potential targets exist, all things being equal, the closest target will be chosen. All things are never equal, but it is argued that on the whole, there is a strong spatial bias that results in more short trips than long trips within any particular category of crime. More burglaries occur close to the home of the offender than far away. More robberies also occur close to the home of the offenders, but *short* robbery trips may be longer than *short* burglary trips because the distribution of "targets" is different. Within a crime classification, occurrences should decline with distance. In comparisons of several types of crime, the rate of decline with distance varies. The well-documented phenomenon of the decline of the number of trips with distance is called *distance decay*.

In their studies, Capone and Nicholas (1976) performed classic distance-decay modeling. They found that for all robberies in Miami, 33 percent of the trips were less than one mile, and over 50 were within two miles. For open-space robberies (robberies occurring out-of-doors, in parks and on the street), 36 percent occurred within one mile of the home location of the offender and around 60 percent within two miles. For robberies in fixed premises, 23 percent were within one mile, and 41 percent were within two miles of the homes of the offenders.

Capone and Nichols next fit the data to a functional form. In Chapter 6, simple linear regression and multiple regression were described. In these techniques, the straight line is found that *best* describes or fits the scatter of data points. There may be no good straight line that can be made to fit the data, as is the case with much distance data. Functional forms other than a straight line must be used to describe most distance data. The three standard functions commonly used are

1. The Pareto function.
2. The exponential function.
3. The Pareto-exponential function.

The *Pareto* function has the form:

$$Y = a\ D^{-b} \tag{1}$$

237

where:

Y is the calculated number of interactions for nodal points at distance D.

In a burglary example, for a given distance, D, Y is the estimated number of burglaries.[14]

A Pareto function is appropriate when there is a disproportionately large number of nodes or interactions close to the origin point.

The second function is the *exponential* function, which has the form:

$$Y = a \, e^{-bD} \tag{2}$$

where:

the distance measure is now the exponent of the natural logarithm called e.[15]

The exponential function works differently from the Pareto function and, if fit to data, estimates fewer short trips or nearby interactions. It is a function that often fits shopping trips for major purchases.

The final equation combines the exponential and the Pareto. It has the form:

$$Y = a \, D^{-b} \, e^{-cD} \tag{3}$$

and can be used to model complex patterns with many interactions either close by or far away.[16]

Capone and Nichols fitted Miami robbery data to these three functions and found that the Pareto-exponential, with its inherent flexibility, worked with all types of robbery. The Pareto and exponential, however, fit different types of crimes. Given the functions that work, several of their results conform well with what is known about urban structure. For open-space robberies, the function that projects many occurrences close to home works best. Open space is ubiquitous. It is reasonable to expect that more crimes will occur close to home because, all things being equal, interactions are more likely close to home. For fixed-premise robberies, however, some travel is obviously necessary if no targets are close to the home base. The function that underestimates close events, the exponential, fits best. It must be remembered that the exponential underestimates close events *within the general context of declining frequency*. All the functional forms describe a distance-decay process. In studying spatial patterning, care should be taken to understand the various forces or factors that influence criminal mobility, such as the location of targets, the security of targets, and the general movement patterns of criminals.

Gravity-Potential Modeling

Statistical evidence exists for a distance-decay phenomenon. Generally, people interact close-by if possible. However, at the same time, there is strong visual evi-

---

[14] The number of burglaries must be normalized on some areal unit such as square kilometers to adjust for the increasing potential area as distances increase.

[15] Logarithms can be calculated to any base, but the standard bases are 10 and e. Any introductory college algebra book contains descriptions and examples of both natural and base 10 logs.

[16] There are other functions, most notably *gamma,* used with distance data.

dence that movement patterns are directional and purposeful. Gravity-potential modeling is a type of modeling that merges distance decay with concentrated nodal patterns.

Gravity-potential modeling has its history in social physics, a historical attempt to translate laws of physics into social science laws. In physics, the gravitational pull of bodies of equal size decreases with distance, or stated another way, large bodies of high mass have a higher gravitational pull than smaller bodies at the same distance. The interaction of size (mass) and distance can be used to calculate gravitational pull. These ideas have been translated almost directly into sociogeographical terms: the interaction of any two bodies (locations) in geographic space—say, the interaction of cities or census tracts within a city—is a function of their relative masses (usually measured in population terms) and the distance between them. Large population centers, close together, have more interactions than equal-sized population centers further apart, and if there are two population centers of unequal population, the larger one generates more interactions. In social physics, interactions may be telephone calls, trips, letters, moves, or any number of social or economic exchanges.

The simplest form of the gravity model is:

$$I = \frac{k\, P_i P_j}{D_{ij}{}^2} \tag{4}$$

where:

I is the number of interactions between
two locations, i and j;
P_i is the population in place i;
P_j is the population in place j;
k is a constant of proportionality; and
D_{ij} is the distance between place i and place j.

The formulation of the model is crude. The constant of proportionality changes with each study; other variables may be substituted for population; the distance measure, which is the denominator that shows declining interactions as distance increases, may be other than squared (D^2). Generally, gravity modeling, particularly at an aggregate flow level, works fairly well (see Lowe and Moryadas, 1975, Chapter 9, for an excellent description of the strengths and weaknesses of gravity modeling and its various forms).

The attraction between any two locations can be modeled with equation (4). By means of the sums of interactions, a gravity potential surface can be created. Any particular place has potential interactions with many locations. Pairwise potential interactions may be modeled with equation (4). For a specific place, the sum of all its potential pairwise interactions is a measure of its attractiveness and is its gravity potential. The attractiveness or pulling power of any particular place is a function of its own size (usually its population) and the size of the surrounding areas.

Gravity modeling, first used by Stewart (1948) and Zipf (1946) in North America, and reformulated by Stouffer (1959) as an *intervening-opportunities model*, has primarily been used in demography and planning. However, it has great potential in research on crime patterns. At an intraurban level, criminological research has primarily been carried out by the use of census-tract data in an aspatial manner. But crimes cluster, often along tract borders, and looking at the crime in an individual tract misrepresents obvious visual patterns (see Figure 9–3). Ideas from gravity modeling can be used to construct tract measures that represent the patterns in surrounding tracts as well as the initial tract. Interaction variables are probably more representative spatial patterns than single, isolated variables. Although gravity modeling is almost uniformly ignored in criminology, there is one exception. Smith (1976) used various formulations of gravity models to analyze crime-trip data in Rochester, New York. He found that the simple model—equation (4)—using just population and distance, explained 37 percent of the variance in crime trips. A modified gravity model using aggregate arrests and crime with distance explained 65 percent of the variance in crime trips.[17]

Graph Theory

Nodes of high criminal activity can be identified. Crime-trip analysis and gravity modeling give some substance to spatial movements. Actual spatial behavior can be modeled through *graph theory*. Graph theory is an area of mathematics that explores *connectedness*. A graph represents a number of points or locations as vertices and indicates whether any two points are connected by a path. A street map of a city is a graph. The intersections are vertices, and the roads are the connections between vertices. An airline map of routes is also a graph. The cities serviced are the vertices; the routes are the paths. A map of a country is also a graph. The cities are the vertices; the roads between the cities are the paths connecting the vertices. A graph in the form of a route or road map makes it easy to see connections. Is it possible to get to City A from City B by plane without a stop (crossing another vertex)? Is there a direct route in a city between two places, or does the trip involve many intersections and indirect turns? The maps tell us something visually about connectedness or accessibility.

It is possible to take maps and convert them into a mathematical matrix form to compute values for connectedness and accessibility and to identify high-accessibility points and low-accessibility points.

Gravity-potential modeling assumes easy accessibility in all directions. In fact, all sociological and criminological studies that are based on area units such as census tracts implicitly assume either that distance is not a constraint or that movement in all directions is equally easy. However, the accessibility of the various subareas within a city may have a lot to do with the amount of crime in different areas. An area inaccessible to the general public is also inaccessible to the average young offender. For migratory criminals, accessibility between cities may influence moves and, consequently, crime patterns.

A map may be transformed to a table or matrix by the identification of locations or points of interest. These locations are the vertices and become the row and

---

[17] The gravity formulation was necessary. The arrest–crime measure was a poor predictor when used alone.

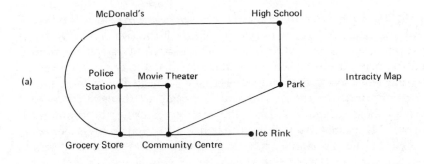

(a)

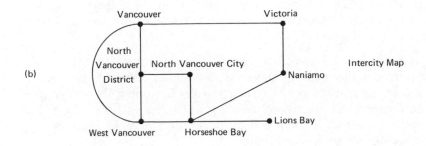

(b)

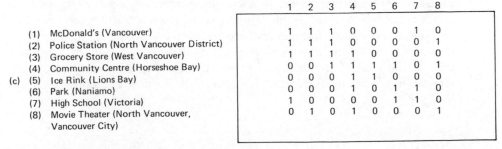

(c)

		1	2	3	4	5	6	7	8
(1)	McDonald's (Vancouver)	1	1	1	0	0	0	1	0
(2)	Police Station (North Vancouver District)	1	1	1	0	0	0	0	1
(3)	Grocery Store (West Vancouver)	1	1	1	1	0	0	0	0
(4)	Community Centre (Horseshoe Bay)	0	0	1	1	1	1	0	1
(5)	Ice Rink (Lions Bay)	0	0	0	1	1	0	0	0
(6)	Park (Naniamo)	0	0	0	1	0	1	1	0
(7)	High School (Victoria)	1	0	0	0	0	1	1	0
(8)	Movie Theater (North Vancouver, Vancouver City)	0	1	0	1	0	0	0	1

Figure 9–14. Connectivity matrix and original maps.

column headers for a matrix. In Figure 9–14, two maps are transformed into identical matrices. The first map, an intracity map, identifies high-activity nodes and indicates how they are connected by roads. For example, in Figure 9–14a, to travel from the McDonalds to the grocery store, you could go directly or pass the police station or take a longer route past the high school, the park, and the community center. If you are really interested in a long ride, you could add on a trip from the community center to the movie theater, to the police station, and finally to the grocery store before getting to McDonalds. The second map shows connections between cities in and around Vancouver, Canada. The lines now represent connections between the cities and stand for many varying roads.[18]

---

[18] Some liberties were taken with the actual connections between the cities, in order to produce an example that has interesting numerical results.

Figure 9–14 shows the connectivity matrix—or *incidence matrix,* as it is called—associated with these maps. A *1* is entered in the matrix if the two points (vertices) are connected directly; a *0* is entered otherwise. The pattern of 0s and 1s mimics the patterns on the map. It can be seen from the map that the community center (Figure 9–14a) and Horseshoe Bay (Figure 9–14b) are connected with more places than any other point. Similarly, the ice rink and Lions Bay are the least connected. In the connectivity matrix (Figure 9–14c), the row representing the community center (alternatively, Horseshoe Bay), Row 4, has five 1's or four connections with other places. (One of the 1's represents a connection of the community center (Horseshoe Bay) with itself. The ice rink (Lions Bay) has only two 1's and consequently only one external connection.

The value of converting maps to graphs comes from the ability to perform arithmetic on the connectivity matrix. Several simple measures that can be derived from the matrix will be discussed.[19]

1. *Associated Number.* The associated number for any particular vertex is the maximum distance that must be traversed to all other vertices. The distance is measured by the number of intervening vertices (including the termination vertex). In Figure 9–14, the movie theater is a distance of 1 from the police station, and the ice rink is a maximum distance of 4 from McDonalds. The associated number for the ice rink is 4.

2. *Accessibility Index.* The accessibility index is a global measure of connectedness of any particular vertex. It is the sum of the distances from a particular vertex to all others in the graph. The distance between North Vancouver City and the other vertices and the distance between Lions Bay and all other vertices can be found in Table 9–1. The accessibility index for North Vancouver City is the sum of the distances to the other vertices, or 13. Lions Bay's accessibility index is 16. North Vancouver City is more accessible than Lions Bay.

TABLE 9–1.

Node	Distance from North Vancouver City to Other Nodes	Distance from Lions Bay to Other Nodes
Vancouver	2	3
North Vancouver District	1	3
Horseshoe Bay	1	1
Lions Bay	2	0
Nanaimo	2	2
West Vancouver	2	2
Victoria	3	3
North Vancouver City	0	2
Totals	13	16

[19] A fuller explanation of graph theory and networks can be found in Kansky (1963).

3. *Beta Index.* The beta index is another connectivity measure, but one that relates to the whole graph. It is the ratio of paths (usually called *edges*) to vertices or to nodes.

$$\beta = \frac{e}{v} \qquad (5)$$

where:

e is the number of edges; and
v is the number of vertices.

A low value for the beta index indicates few paths; a high value, many paths. The graphs in Figure 9–14 have eight vertices and ten edges, giving a beta index of 1.25, which is low. The minimum index value is 0.5.

4. *Gamma Index.* The gamma index is a bounded measure of connectedness, ranging from 0 to 1.0. It is the ratio computed from the actual number of paths to the maximum number of paths:

$$\gamma = \frac{2\,e}{v(v-2)} \qquad (6)$$

For the graphs being used here the gamma index is 0.41.

Graph measures have not been fully exploited in spatial criminology. In regional science, graph measures are used in studies of economic development, where dense, highly connected route networks are usually associated with technological development. Sociology uses simple graph theory to explore social-interaction networks. In crime analysis, graph-theory measures have the potential value of distinguishing the spatial structure of several cities or subareas of a city. In an imaginative study by Bevis and Nutter (1977), which is discussed in more detail in Chapter 12, beta indexes were calculated for subareas in Minneapolis and correlated with burglary rates. Although accessibility was not associated with burglary in a global sense, within generally high-burglary areas the least accessible subareas had lower crime rates. Auto thefts have also been found to be strongly associated with the location of cars in areas accessible to main arteries (Muir, 1978).

Graph-theoretic measures, although underutilized in current criminology, may provide an areal link between the sociological and the geographic imagination. Are city areas that, by socioeconomic criteria, are considered high in crime linked spatially? Are some of these areas isolated? How are these areas connected spatially to high-criminal-opportunity areas? Does the varying accessibility to potential targets influence areal crime rates? The questions are almost endless, and the field of research is almost virgin.

Diffusion Modeling

Distance affects interactions in a negative exponential manner; that is, interactions decrease with distance at a faster-than-linear rate. Connectedness and accessibility affect interaction. Distance and connectedness can be merged conceptually in diffusion modeling. For example, how are ideas transmitted from one person to another? By personal contact? Through the media? Ideas gain importance for certain groups and are transmitted to other groups. Innovations in police management filter through the police community, but how? Outbreaks of violence occur in a city and spread to other cities, but how? Drug usage patterns change. How do these changes occur spatially? Diffusion researchers attempt to build models that describe how ideas travel through space and through social groups. The spatial aspects of diffusion research are described here, but briefly, because criminology has been slow to answer diffusion questions.

Diffusion is thought to occur in two major ways: (1) through a model hierarchy and (2) through contagion processes. Diffusion is time-dependent, can be interrupted by boundaries or barriers, and may even occur through a combination of hierarchical and contagion mechanisms.

Hierarchical Diffusion

Hierarchical diffusion occurs in a descending manner through nodal systems. If cities are considered nodes in a system of cities, ideas can be thought to work their way through the cities from the largest toward the smallest. New ideas are usually developed or first appear in large cities, then are transmitted to or adopted by the next largest cities, and then by smaller cities. As ideas move down through the hierarchy, there comes a point where ideas spread outward from the cities into contiguous areas, but the diffusion generally spreads from large to medium-large to small cities. (Hagerstrand, 1952; Berry, 1971).

The introduction of nonlegislated innovations in the criminal justice system probably follows a hierarchical diffusion process.

Contagion Diffusion

The diffusion of information about criminal techniques and good target locations probably follows a contagion model. As might be expected by the name, contagion is a type of diffusion modeling based on the transmission of ideas through personal contact. The spread of a flu virus is a good example of contagion diffusion. The flu is transmitted after personal contact, but not all people contacted get the flu. In contagion modeling, ideas spread outward through contact networks from a base point. Because contacts tend to be greatest close to a home-base point, contagion diffusion can visually appear to spread out through contiguous space. The diffusion need not be smooth, and some areas may be jumped. The spread of crime technique through people in prison is a classic example. Information is spread by personal contact, but when people get out of prison, they disperse, taking new knowledge with them to be spread to contacts at other locations.

Contagion modeling, with its spatial aspects, is another link between sociological and geographic approaches. Social network analysis and the study of the transmission of ideas through social networks, an area of research in sociology, has an obvious geometric analogue.

Spatial Theories

Criminology and criminal justice research are generally based on social theories. The spatial articulation of these theories or spatial theories that describe social behavior are generally ignored or understudied. This last section of the chapter contains short summaries of some of the major spatial approaches in human geography. Spatial theories can be divided into three categories: (1) macro; (2) meso; and (3) micro approaches. Macrotheories look at the spatial differentiation of large areas (countries or multicountry regions). Mesotheories explore spatial differentiation at an intracountry or regional level. Microtheories explore patterns within urban areas or cities or small regions.

Macroanalysis

Countries grow and change. Two basic approaches, not necessarily contradictory, are taken in describing the growth and change of countries or multicountry regions. Countries are seen as passing through stages of growth and development. These growth stages are associated with social, economic, and spatial configurations. Countries were all initially agrarian. If a country develops into a modern industrialized country, it passes through stages in which first, raw materials are exported and finished products imported; then, a national industrial base begins to grow and goods are produced within the country, and raw materials may even be imported for domestic industry. Finally, the economy of the country begins to be dominated by national industry (possibly later by service functions) and international links become strong (Friedman, 1966). With the growth or decline of nations comes a host of demographic and economic changes, which are often associated with crime. Crime may well be the by-product of national maturity.

The growth and change of countries can also be viewed without reference to stages of development. Countries grow and change as the result of flows of people and capital. Macrotheories are really migration theories about what attracts people (or capital) and what drives people (or capital) away. The push and pull of relative attractiveness within general multicountry economic patterns sets the stage for varying crime patterns.

Mesoanalysis

Within a country, subareas grow or decline. Cities increase or decrease in size. Regional economies prosper. The spatial dynamics of crime are not independent of urban and regional spatial dynamics. Generally urban and regional science theories and concepts have not been used to analyze intercity crime patterns. Intermetropolitan crime patterns have, instead, been analyzed within a social context. Several theories are mentioned here in the hope that they may trigger increased and more diversified interest in mesolevel analysis.

Growth Poles

Perroux (1950), the "inventor" of the concept of growth poles, thought that within an economy, there are clusters or centers of activity that are so strong that they can trigger or influence activity in other clusters. He also thought that these high-activity centers attract other activities. Growth poles are growth centers that cause development. Perroux conceived of growth poles in a purely economic sense, the pole being an industrial grouping such as electronics firms that cause growth in other areas and attract growth themselves. Perroux's ideas were quickly given a geographic component. Growth poles became cities that were thriving, attracting more people and money, and that were influencing the surrounding areas in a positive manner, stimulating more growth. Growth pole theory and later ideas of growth centers have been used to guide public investments. In regional economic development, growth centers are identified and encouraged to grow through infrastructure development, or centers that have the potential to be growth centers are force-fed government money in an attempt to trigger self-continuing growth. For criminologists, the question has never been asked: How does crime relate to growth centers? Does crime flourish as other industrial and commercial concerns flourish? Is crime unrelated to the dynamically growing cities, cities that have wide influence within a region? Growth pole theory points to an awareness of the spatial and temporal variability of economies, an awareness that far transcends simple measures of the percentage of unemployed or average income.

Hierarchy of Cities

Tied somewhat to concerns about centers of economic growth are concepts of the hierarchy of cities. Cities, like nations, do not exist in a vacuum. People move and communicate between cities; products are shipped; money flows. Cities are linked into systems of cities. Any particular city does not interact equally with all other cities. Interactions are stronger with, or biased toward, selected other cities. The pattern of unequal interaction can clearly be seen around large cities such as New York, London, or Los Angeles. Cities around these giants have more contact with the core city than with each other. Commuting patterns, newspaper circulation patterns, phone calls, and money all flow more to the core city.

In any region or nation, a network of city interactions can be mapped. Interactions between cities can be measured along many dimensions (e.g., trips, business communication, and product flow), but generally, a dominant city appears, surrounded by that city's sphere of influence. Several levels of domination may exist. A particular city may deal primarily with the core city but, in turn, may be the core for several other cities or towns. Hierarchies of dominance exist.

Hierarchies are often measured by population size. When the population of the cities in a large, industrialized area or a country are listed, there usually are many small cities, fewer middle-sized cities, and, finally, a small number of large cities. In agrarian economies, there is often a sharp break in the number of small towns and large cities, with few cities of an intermediate size.

Within any system of cities, there are many connections. From a spatial, criminological point of view, many questions can be raised: Do city systems have similar crime patterns? Do dominant cities within a system, usually the commercial centers, have a disproportionate amount of acquisitive crime? What are the mobility and demographic characteristics—and consequently, the crime characteristics—of the cities within a system? Do these characteristics relate to a city's place in the urban hierarchy? Once again, the concept of a system of cities provides a mechanism for considering the spatial location of crime. Considering the crime in each city totally independently of the crime in surrounding cities loses a potential analytic dimension. The predictive and explanatory power of social theories can be increased by the addition of a spatial dimension.

Microanalysis

Spatial analysis at the macro- or mesolevel is deficient and is underexplored in criminology. More spatial analysis has been done at the microlevel or intracity level. However, many of the studies have not shown a sophisticated knowledge of urban spatial form. Three general urban form models are presented here:

1. The concentric zone model.
2. The sector model.
3. The multiple-nuclei model.

These models provide the conceptual framework for interpreting the spatial distribution of crime within a city and for interpreting the studies discussed in chapters 11 and 12.

Concentric Zone Model

In 1925, E. W. Burgess published a paper describing the spatial organization of cities (Burgess, 1925a). His thesis, subsequently called the *concentric zone theory,* has had a more profound impact on urban sociology and urban criminology than any other single piece of research. Simply, Burgess argued that urban land uses tend to form concentric use zones around a central-core business area, called today the *central business district.* Although Burgess's ideas have been attacked in recent years, they did and still do dominate urban criminology.

E. W. Burgess lived and wrote in Chicago and, after observing that city and other North American cities, postulated that, given a level plane with no natural barriers or pre-existing cities and equal accessibility in all directions, a city would grow outward from its central business core, forming concentric zones of similar land uses. His ideas were well grounded in ecological concepts. People *compete* for land. In order to expand in population, a social group (species?) must gain more space by *invading* surrounding areas, *contesting* for the areas, and finally dominating or taking them over. Burgess wrote in a time of high immigration and rapid growth of cities. Chicago changed rapidly and continually; neighborhoods did grow and change. His model emphasized change.

The concentric zone model consists of five zones. Each zone surrounds the previous zones:

1. The central business district. This is the area of major commercial activity.
2. The zone in transition. This is an area of mixed industrial and residential use. Industry competes for space in this zone with low-price housing.
3. The zone of working-class homes. This is the next zone out and contains more expensive housing than in Zone 2, but it is not considered expensive. This zone, however, is not delapidated or rundown like Zone 2.
4. The residential zone. This zone contains high-priced residential housing, both in apartments and in exclusive districts.
5. The commuters' zone. The commuters' zone is an unbounded zone containing satellite cities and the suburbs.

Burgess did not assert that this model would fit all cities or even any cities perfectly. It is an idealized model that he felt bore a resemblance to several U.S.

247

cities. The model has, however, been picked up and applied more literally by criminologists (Shaw and McKay, 1931), who have studied the distribution of the residences of delinquents in Chicago. Shaw and McKay (1931, 1969) borrowed Burgess's model in its literal form and calculated delinquency rates for (somewhat arbitrarily defined) zones. Their work began a whole school of research labeled *criminal ecology*. Criminal ecology includes many subareas: studies of natural areas associated with crime, studies of distance-decay gradients of crime from core business areas, and statistical studies of underlying spatial clusterings. The general school of criminal ecology is covered in depth in Chapter 11.

Although the concentric zone theory of E. W. Burgess triggered much criminological research, the model itself has many problems. It is idealized and far removed from real cities. The concentric zone hypothesis requires a uniform plane; rivers, mountains, and other natural barriers cannot be handled in the model. The model depends conceptually on a large core shopping area and a surrounding industrial zone—in essence, an industrial city. Finally, the model presupposes equal accessibility in all directions and no government policies that shape land use. Concentric zone theory is an idealized model, not a real-world model.

Sector Model

Homer Hoyt (1939), working for the U.S. Federal Housing Administration in the 1930s, proposed another theory of urban form, *sector theory*. Using housing data for blocks, Hoyt constructed maps based on housing cost for several American cities. He found a tendency for housing of similar cost to align itself within a sector beginning at the core instead of an circular zones. He found that expensive housing was located on prime land with good accessibility to the central business district. Hoyt's model introduced the concept of differential accessibility. Major transportation arteries influenced the location of residences: high-income people bought attractive land and high accessibility. High-income people could buy housing close to the central business district if they wished.

Hoyt's model has conceptual problems, too. He did not consider nonresidential locations, except peripherally; he, as Burgess, assumed a central commercial core or a *one-center* city.

Multiple-Nuclei Model

Harris and Ullman (1945) provided yet another modification to concentric zone theory, a modification that, in essence, creates a flexible model of a city, a model that is not tied to a single central core. They argued (1) that cities grow not from single centers, but from many points; and (2) that the specialization of areas within a city depends on differential factors, factors that influence spatial patterning. Several specialization factors are worth mentioning:

1. Retail districts require good accessibility.
2. Certain activities repel each other; that is, they are rarely located close together. The classic example, used even by Hoyt, is industry and expensive housing.
3. Like activities often group together if there is increased profit associated

248

with closeness. Financial, commercial, and entertainment areas tend to appear over time in a city.

4. Some activities cannot compete for high rents and end up locating in undesirable sites. (Harris and Ullman, 1957, p. 244–245)

A city's form depends on initial accidents of location and several driving forces that govern growth. Multiple-nuclei theory, however, is so flexible that almost any urban form is possible. The predictive power of the concept is low.

Beginning with a diverse growth model such as multiple nuclei, many complex mathematical models and several interesting conceptual models have been developed. Two conceptual approaches are worth noting. Timms (1971) described a city as an *urban mosaic,* where urban form really devolves into the joining of clusters of relatively homogeneous areas. No form is ultimately constrained. Pahl (1970) and Rex and Moore (1967) drew legitimate attention to government policies and how they influence the spatial location of people. Particularly in England, there appears to be a *housing class* created by government housing policy. The location of people who depend on the government for housing is the result not of individual decisions or even of decisions based on market forces, but of decisions based on governmental policy.

In spatial criminological studies, it is necessary to understand the underlying urban form and to see crime in relation to what exists in the city. As is discussed much more fully in Chapter 11, crime patterns may be incorrectly interpreted if the patterns are being analyzed against an inaccurate urban backcloth.

Chapter Summary

The spatial analysis of crime requires the merger of the geographic and sociological imagination. Spatial patterning of crime occurrences is related to the spatial patterning of the functions that are thought to influence crime. Spatial analysis requires, as does temporal analysis, careful attention to methodology.

Locational data can be analyzed individually as point data or as areal data. Point data maintain high levels of locational specificity and can reveal much just by visual inspection. Statistically, point data patterns can be studied to identify the center of mass and to compare the patterns with general random and clustered distributions.

In criminology, point data are usually collected into areal units. With these aggregations come specific conceptual and statistical problems. Aggregation produces size bias, often inflating correlations. Researchers often incorrectly use aggregate data to explain lower-level or individual relationships. The appropriate research questions are tied to the level of analysis.

Locational data can also be regarded as flow data. Crime trips can be studied and modeled. The spatial mobility of criminals in a city is a special case of general mobility. Patterns of mobility are often studied by means of distance-decay models, where increased interactions close to home are explored, and through gravity-potential modeling, where the attractiveness of areas is specifically modeled.

249

Graph theory and diffusion modeling are areas of geographical research that are rarely used in criminology, but that have potential conceptual and technical relevance. Graph theory transforms movement and the linkages in a city into a pattern of connectedness. Mobility is viewed within a framework of potential mobility. Diffusion research explores the spatial traces of the transmission of ideas. Future work in the geography of crime is likely to make use of both graph theory and diffusion concepts.

Spatial analysis of crime is often performed in an atheoretic manner or within a sociological framework, which does not use spatial concepts. Spatial frameworks are necessary to an understanding of what is happening. Briefly, the intermetropolitan analysis of crime should probably be viewed within the context of a system of cities. Cities do not function independently; they form links with other cities. These links influence regional economies, cultures, and demographies, three areas that relate to crime. Patterns of crime will make more sense when placed in geographical context. Intrametropolitan analyses of crime require a knowledge of urban form, both social and geographic.

Currently, criminological research appears either to have adopted simplistic models of urban form (such as the concentric zone, where cities are conceived of in idealized fashion with a single center and uniform accessibility) or to have rejected urban form as relevant because simplistic models such as the concentric zone model do not fit well. The spatial backcloth of urban crime occurrences must be more fully developed and used to help describe spatial variability.

10

Macrospatial and Mesospatial Patterns in Crime

Introduction

The spatial patterning of crime can be analyzed through a cone of resolution at many different levels. This chapter explores the lowest level of spatial resolution: world, national, and intercity crime patterns. Chapter 11 examines crime at a higher level in the cone of resolution: intracity crime patterns. Chapter 12 examines patterns at the highest level in the cone of resolution: the geometry of criminal events.

The World Crime Pattern in Recent Years

The distribution of some kinds of crime among the countries of the world can be assessed and mapped from two data sources. The United Nations conducted a world survey of crime rates and crime problems among its member states in the mid-1970s. The International Criminal Police Organization (Interpol) has collected data on crimes known to the police and on criminal convictions since 1950. Each of these data sets is subject to all of the generic problems of official crime data discussed in Chapters 2 and 3. These problems are compounded because the reporting is a strictly voluntary process not subject to verification; because many countries have elected not to report; because, for many countries, crime is a politically sensitive issue so that crime data may be suppressed as a state secret or may be falsely reported; because of the varied definitions of crime in different national penal codes; and because of language difficulties.

The United Nations survey of world crime rates for the period 1970–1975, based on responses from sixty-four nations, provides world crime rates for ten different categories of crime: intentional homicide; assault; sex crimes; kidnapping;

251

robbery; theft; fraud; illegal drug traffic; drug abuse; and alcohol abuse. The total world rate for all ten offense categories was 1,311.2 offenses per 100,000 population. Table 10–1 shows the world rates for each of the specific offense categories. (Also see Figures 10–1 and 10–2.)

The UN Study also established regional crime rates for six different geopolitical areas of the world: (1) North Africa and the Middle East; (2) Asia; (3) Eastern Europe; (4) Latin America; (5) the Caribbean; and (6) the culturally and economically interdependent regions Western Europe, North America, Australia, and New Zealand. Regional comparisons show that Latin America had very high levels of homicide, whereas the Caribbean reported extraordinary levels of assault. Asia, Latin America, and the Caribbean reported very high levels of robbery. The Western Eruope–North America—Oceania region had high levels of theft and fraud. Eastern Europe reported relatively low levels for all categories of crime. (The Eastern European region was composed of only two reporting countries, Poland and Yugoslavia. Whether the data from these two countries was accurately reported is unclear.) The Caribbean region reported the highest overall crime rate.

A comparison of the crime mixes (the relative proportion of total crime accounted for by each of the various crime categories) reveals striking regional differences (Table 10–2). Theft dominated the crime pattern of Western Europe–North America–Oceania, constituting 76 percent of the reported crime rate. Theft accounted for 59 percent of the reported crime rate in Eastern Europe, but assaults accounted rather ominously for almost a third of the total crime in that region. Assaults accounted for, respectively, 36 percent and 35 percent of the reported crimes in the Middle East–North Africa and the Caribbean regions. Robbery ac-

TABLE 10–1. World and Regional Crime Rates, 1970–1975

Crime Category	Crime Rates per 100,000 Population						
	World Rates	North Africa and Middle East	Asia	Eastern Europe	Latin America	Caribbean	Western Europe, North America, Oceania
Intentional Homicide	3.9	4.7	2.3	0.7	8.2	6.7	2.1
Assault	184.1	163.6	38.4	65.9	36.6	852.2	126.1
Sex Crimes	24.2	22.2	22.6	5.6	12.3	33.9	29.2
Kidnapping	0.7	0.8	0.5	0	3.1	0	0.1
Robbery	46.1	13.0	100.2	7.3	89.4	82.8	26.9
Theft	862.4	153.1	137.5	121.5	95.6	1,302.8	1,580.3
Fraud	83.3	13.7	22.2	5.1	8.2	96.7	159.2
Illegal Drug Traffic	9.8	19.2	4.1	0	2.1	22.9	5.8
Drug Abuse	28.9	6.0	18.4	0	0.3	54.9	45.1
Alcohol Abuse	67.8	61.0	1.9	0.7	91.8	3.3	101.8
TOTAL	1,311.2	457.3	348.1	206.8	347.6	2,456.2	2,076.6

SOURCE: United Nations, *Crime Prevention & Control: Report to the Secretary General* (New York: United Nations [A132/150], 1977), pp. 9, 26.

253

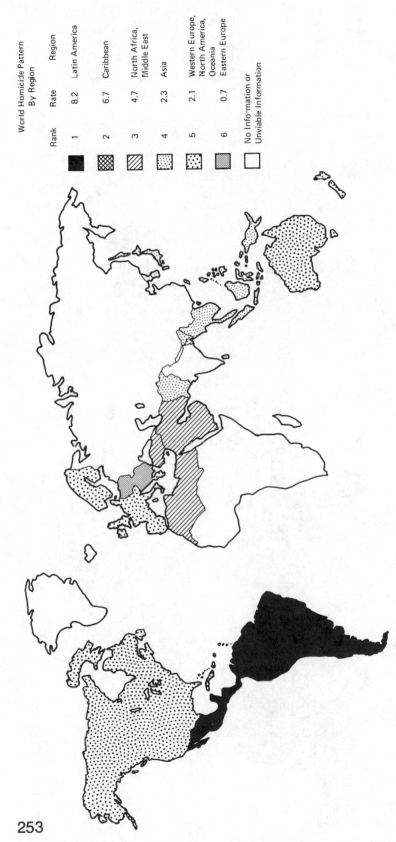

World Homicide Pattern By Region

Rank	Rate	Region
1	8.2	Latin America
2	6.7	Caribbean
3	4.7	North Africa, Middle East
4	2.3	Asia
5	2.1	Western Europe, North America, Oceania
6	0.7	Eastern Europe
		No Information or Unviable Information

Figure 10–1. Homicide regions, 1970.

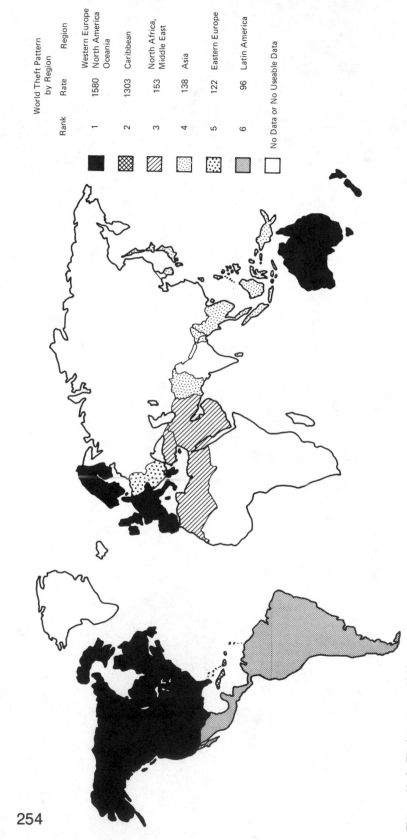

Figure 10–2. Theft regions, 1970s.

World Theft Pattern by Region		
Rank	Rate	Region
1	1580	Western Europe, North America, Oceania
2	1303	Caribbean
3	153	North Africa, Middle East
4	138	Asia
5	122	Eastern Europe
6	96	Latin America
		No Data or No Useable Data

254

TABLE 10–2. World and Regional Crime Mixes (in Percentages) 1970–1975

	World Rates	North Africa and the Middle East	Asia	Eastern Europe	Latin America	Caribbean	West Europe North America and Oceania
Intentional Homicide	0.3	1.0	0.6	0.3	2.0	0.3	0.1
Assault	14.0	36.0	11.0	32.0	11.0	35.0	6.0
Sex Crimes	2.0	5.0	6.0	3.0	4.0	1.0	1.0
Kidnapping	0.05	0.2	0.1	0	0.9	0	0.004
Robbery	3.5	3.0	29.0	4.0	26.0	3.0	1.0
Theft	66.0	33.0	40.0	59.0	28.0	53.0	76.0
Fraud	6.0	3.0	6.0	2.0	2.0	4.0	8.0
Illegal Drug Traffic	0.7	4.0	1.0	0	0.6	0.9	0.2
Drug Abuse	2.2	1.3	5.0	0	0.09	2.0	2.1
Alcohol Abuse	5.0	14.0	0.5	0.3	26.0	0.1	5.0

SOURCE: Calculated from data in Table 10–1.

counted for 29 percent of all crimes reported in Asia and 26 percent of the reported crimes in Latin America. Alcohol abuse accounted for 26 percent of the total crime rate in Latin America.

The UN survey also noted a major difference in the relative crime mixes of nations at different stages of economic development (Figure 10–3). The world crime mix was 72 percent crimes against property; 20 percent crimes against the person; and 8 percent drug-related crimes. The relative crime mix in developing countries (i.e., countries without an extensive industrial economic base) was 49 percent crimes against property; 43 percent crimes against the person; and 8 percent drug-related crimes. The crime pattern in industrially developed countries was starkly different. Crimes against property accounted for 82 percent of the reported crime, whereas crimes against the person accounted for only 10 percent of the reported crime. Drug offenses accounted for 8 percent of the known crimes in developed countries. The historical association between economic development and changing crime patterns identified in Chapter 5 appears in this cross-sectional survey of crime in the contemporary world. Violence seems to make up a very large proportion of all crimes in preindustrial societies, and to recede, being replaced by crimes against property, in industrialized societies.

The UN survey received little useful response from African nations south of the Sahara Desert. The annual criminal statistics collected by the International Criminal Police Organization, Interpol, do include statistical returns from African countries. Their principal disadvantage is that Communist countries such as Poland, Yugoslavia, the Soviet Union, and the People's Republic of China do not participate in the Interpol program at all. The 1976 Interpol statistics mirror the UN survey findings on the differential crime patterns of developed and undeveloped countries, and they place African nations in the world crime pattern. This is par-

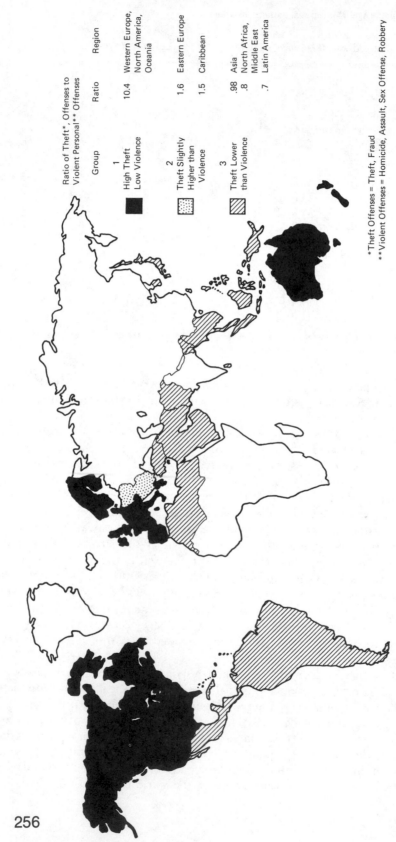

Group		Ratio	Region
1	High Theft Low Violence	10.4	Western Europe, North America, Oceania
2	Theft Slightly Higher than Violence	1.6	Eastern Europe
		1.5	Caribbean
3	Theft Lower than Violence	.98	Asia
		.8	North Africa, Middle East
		.7	Latin America

Ratio of Theft*. Offenses to Violent Personal** Offenses

*Theft Offenses = Theft, Fraud
**Violent Offenses = Homicide, Assault, Sex Offense, Robbery

Figure 10–3. Groups of regions having similar theft-to-violence ratios: Patterns of relative crime mix.

TABLE 10–3. Highest Ranked Countries by Crime Rates Reported to Interpol, 1976

Murder and Attempted Murder			Serious Theft (Robbery, Burglary)		
Country	Rank	Rate per 100,000 Population	Country	Rank	Rate per 100,000 Population
Lesotho	1	137	Bahamas	1	2,126
Nigeria	2	81	Sweden	2	1,847
Peru	3	36	West Germany	3	1,748
Turkey	4	27	U.S.A.	4	1,635
Guyana	5	20	Denmark	5	1,350
Phillipines	6	14	Canada	6	1,266
Kuwait	7	14	New Zealand	7	1,213
Bahamas	8	11	England & Wales	8	1,072
Tanzania	9	10	Netherlands	9	961
Kenya	10	10	Australia	10	937

SOURCE: International Criminal Police Organization (INTERPOL) *International Crime Statistics: 1975–76*. (France: INTERPOL, 1980); Statistics Canada *Crime and Traffice Enforcement Statistics* (Ottawa: Queen's Printer [Catalogue 85–201 annual]), 1977; N. Parisi, M. R. Gottfredson, M. J. Hindeland, and T. J. Flanagan (Annual) *Sourcebook of Criminal Justice Statistics* (Washington, D.C.: Department of Justice, 1978).

ticularly clear in Table 10–3, which shows the ten nations with the highest reported murder rates and the ten nations with the highest reported major theft (i.e., robbery and burglary) rates for 1976. For reported murder, four of the top ten are from Africa south of the Sahara, two are from Latin America, two are from the Middle East, one is from Asia, and one is from the Caribbean. All are countries that can be characterized as economically undeveloped. In contrast, the top ten countries reporting major theft rates are, with the exception of the Bahamas, highly developed industrial nations: Sweden, West Germany, the United States, Denmark, Canada, New Zealand, England and Wales, the Netherlands, and Australia.

State socialist countries are extremely difficult to position in a world mapping of crime. No state socialist country participates in the Interpol crime-reporting program. Poland and Yugoslavia were the only socialist states that responded to the UN survey with usable data (United Nations, 1977, p. 26). The Soviet Union maintains its crime statistics as state secrets, available only to the personnel of the criminal justice system and to selected criminologists with special security clearance (Connor, 1972; Shelley, 1981, p. 109). Data pieced together by a number of different scholars, however, suggest that the crime problem in these countries falls midway between the level and mix of the developed Western nations and the level and mix of the economically undeveloped countries.

The Soviet Union had a total criminal conviction rate of 1,064 per 100,000 population in 1967 (Shelley, 1981, p. 109), compared with a conviction rate of about 1,521 per 100,000 population in the countries of Western Europe, Oceania, and North America in the period 1970–1975 according to the UN survey (1977, p. 26). The Soviet crime mix for 1967 is shown in Table 10–4. It falls between

TABLE 10–4. Soviet Crime Mix, Circa 1967
(in Percentages)

Property Crime	
Theft of State and Public Property	17.0
Crimes Against Citizens' Personal Property	16.0
Hooliganism	24.0
Property Crime Subtotal	57.0
Crimes Against the Person	17.0
Economic Crimes	5.0
Official Crimes	4.0
Vehicular Crimes	5.0
Crimes Against the System of Justice	1.5
Crimes Against the System of Administration	4.0
Other Crimes	6.5

SOURCE: Adapted from W. D. Connor, *Deviance in Soviet Society: Crime, Delinquency and Alcoholism* (New York: Columbia University Press, 1972), p. 150.

the two general patterns found in the United Nations and Interpol data sets: 17 percent of all known crimes were crimes against the person; 33 percent of all known crimes were crimes against state, public, or personal property; and a further 24 percent of all crimes were "hooliganism," a form of disorderly conduct with an antigovernmental flavor (Connor, 1972, p. 150). Shelley (1981) asserted that the Soviet crime mix remained stable for the succeeding decade, and that it was essentially the same in the late 1970s as it had been in 1967. The Soviets used prison far more than the developed Western countries during the 1970s. Juviler's (1976) estimates for the mid-1970s show the following prisoner rates: Sweden, 45 prisoners per 100,000 population; United States 180 prisoners per 100,000 population; and the Soviet Union, 400–600 prisoners per 100,000 population (p. 106).

Explanations for the World Crime Pattern

Explanations for the world crime pattern are tentative and are based on limited empirical evidence. Nineteenth-century explanations tended toward unverified assertions about the criminal propensities of different nationalities and races or toward statements about the impact of climate on crime rates. Quetelet (1842), for instance, formulated the "thermic law" of criminality, according to which national crime mixtures varied with mean annual temperature: cold climates had high property-crime rates and low violent-crime rates; warm climates had high violent-crime rates and low property-crime rates. Modern explanations of the world crime pattern focus on the socioeconomic structure of different societies.

The fundamental modern study was conducted by Preben Wolf (1971), who used the Interpol crime data for twenty-five nations for the year 1972. He examined the socioeconomic development status of nations with high property crime but low violent crime in comparison with nations having low property crime but high violent crime (together with the few nations that reported high rates for both categories of crime or low rates for both categories of crime). Wolf's measures of development were low infant mortality; a low percentage of the population engaged in rural occupations; high urbanization; more than 5 telephones per 100 population; less than 20 percent illiteracy; more than 100 newspapers per 1,000 population; high economic development status; and westernized, noncolonial status. Underdeveloped countries had the reverse pattern. He found that fourteen highly developed countries had high property-crime rates, high total-crime rates, and low violent-crime rates. Underdeveloped countries had high murder rates, low property-crime rates, and low total-crime rates.

A number of studies have looked at specific dimensions of nations as explanatory predictors of the world crime pattern. Wellford (1974) analyzed the Interpol data for seventy-five nations reporting in 1967 and 1968 against population size, gross national product per capita (GNP), and political orientation. GNP correlated positively, and relatively highly, with a number of Interpol crime categories: sex offenses, 0.57; major larceny, 0.40; minor larceny, 0.48; fraud, 0.48; counterfeiting, 0.24; and total crime, 0.28. Neither political orientation nor population correlated strongly with any crime category.

Krohn (1976) extended Wellford's analysis by examining the predictive power of unemployment and income-inequality data for national crime rates reported to Interpol. He found that unemployment was not a powerful predictor of crime rates, but that intersectoral income inequality correlated strongly with homicide, +0.60; with property crime rates, −0.62; and with the total crime rate, −0.41. When he used the partial correlation technique to control the effect of GNP and energy consumption per capita, Krohn still found strong relationships between reported crime rates and income inequality for twenty-four nations. The negative relationship between income inequality and property crime was striking: property crime rates rose as income inequality was reduced! Homicide rates, on the other hand, rose as income inequality increased and fell as income inequality was reduced. Stepwise regression analysis demonstrated that income inequality and GNP could, together, explain significant amounts of variance in the homicide, property crime, and total crime rates of twenty-four nations, whereas energy consumption and unemployment were not powerful predictors.

McDonald (1976) explored the Interpol offender rates for some forty countries during the early 1960s using a large number of social, economic, and governmental variables in an attempt to test the validity of various forms of conflict and consensus based criminological theories. She found that the "societies with the highest rates of official crime were those which were highly urbanized, rich, had many schools, a modern and efficient central bureaucracy and police force, and extensive reliance on impersonal mass media for communication." (p. 155). Murder rates were best explained by a set of social problem indicators: low GNP; inequality; population increase; linguistic heterogeneity; and governmental instability.

Two studies have looked at the world homicide pattern. Quinney (1965) compared homicide rates, levels of urbanization, and levels of industrialization for forty-eight countries for the period 1953–1960. He found strong inverse patterns between both urbanization and industrialization levels and homicide rates: as the proportion of a nation's people living in cities of more than 100,000+ population

259

increased, homicide rates went down; as the proportion of a nation's male work force in nonagricultural jobs increased, homicide rates went down. He concluded that homicide varies inversely with urban and industrial development. Braithwaite and Braithwaite (1980) correlated homicide rates and several measures of income and wealth inequality for twenty-one nations. They found intersectoral income inequality a good predictor of homicide rates.

An explanation of the different crime patterns exhibited by different regions of the world cannot be found in different cultural definitions of criminal or deviant behavior. Newman (1976) surveyed opinions about crime and deviance in rural and urban settings in six very different countries: India, Indonesia, Iran, Italy, the United States, and Yugoslavia. He found a stable core of agreement about the reprehensibility of and the appropriate punishment levels for common crimes (e.g., robbery) in all areas of all six nations. Newman concluded that the common crimes define a set of absolute conduct standards shared by most countries (p. 286). He found a great deal less agreement about the reprehensibility and appropriate treatment mode for victimless crimes, such as homosexual activities or drug taking. The crimes considered in constructing the world crime maps in this chapter, however, seem to be considered seriously criminal everywhere. Differences in penal code contents or in public opinion cannot account for the differences in regional crime patterns.

The pattern of explanation that seems to emerge from the data of these studies involves the impact of modernization on a nation's crime. Modernization is a process that changes a society in many ways. The economy is transformed from subsistence agriculture and resource exploitation to industrial production and service. Income inequality is reduced. The modernizing nation becomes urbanized as larger and larger proportions of its population migrate to large cities. Improved communication and transport systems move people, goods, and information with accelerating speed and density. Government is marked by increasing political stability, by greater efficiency, and by neutrality in many interpersonal disputes. Personal freedom increases.

Modernization creates conditions that change the crime mix and level. Violent crimes are reduced because the conditions of human interaction are changed. Transactions become brief, neutral encounters among strangers, so that irritations do not have time to develop into violent rages. Access to alternative dispute-solving mechanisms in the form of courts, arbitration panels, or the like removes the need for violent forms of self-help. The presence of people in urban settings makes many forms of violence less easy and less safe for the offender. Improved policing systems sweep the uncontrolled violent offenders into prisons, incapacitating them. The urban migration process breaks up traditional subcultures of violence. Property crimes increase enormously because the raw number of opportunities for theft, for breaking and entering, and for vandalism increase in dense communities with ever-increasing quantities of property. Property crimes may also increase in expanding, modernizing economies because relative deprivation, rather than absolute want, becomes an important motivating factor: reduced income inequality may make relative poverty more difficult to bear.

Crime Patterns Within Three Common-Law Countries

England, Canada, and the United States have similar and interesting crime patterns at the world level of resolution: high property-crime rates and relatively low violent-personal-crime rates. Geographic patterns at the world level of aggregation, however, mask underlying differences within nations. Analysis of the spatial distribution of crime within particular nations, using administrative subunits such as the departments in France or the counties in England, was the first scientific research undertaken by criminologists. The national patterns found by early nineteenth-century researchers laid the groundwork for the development of most contemporary criminological theory. The crime patterns of England, Canada, and the United States resolve into regions with very different crime problems when examined at the county, province, or state level. Some regions have very high crime rates, and other regions have low crime rates. Crime mix also varies by region: some areas have problems with violent personal crime but not with property crime; some regions have property crime problems, but not violent crime problems; some regions have problems with robbery but not burglary; some regions have problems with auto theft but not simple theft. Regional patterns sometimes prove interesting and even useful guides to the construction and testing of theories that attempt to explain criminal events or criminality.

Regional Studies in the Nineteenth Century

The Classical School criminological reforms of the early nineteenth century led to the creation of systematic criminal-justice record-keeping systems in much of the European legal world. England developed a crime statistics system between 1805 and 1835. France developed a judicial statistics system, the Compte Generale, in 1825; it is still operational. An effort was even made by the governor of New York State to appropriate funds for the collection and publication of criminal justice statistics for the United States during this period (Guerry, 1831, p. 6). Such statistics were collected and arranged on the basis of the governmental units of each country: in England, for the counties; in France, for the departments. Statistical and cartographic analysis of the crime problem in the different parts of the same country became possible.

The first systematic analyses of crime statistics used data collected by the French system. A. M. Guerry (1831) examined the distribution of criminal charges across eighty-six departments of France for 1825 through 1830 (Table 10–5). He divided the country into five regions of seventeen departments each: the North, which contained Paris; the South; the East; the West; and the Center. When Guerry examined the distribution of crimes against the person and crimes against property, he found striking differences among the regions. The populous, urbanized North had low levels of crimes against the person, but high levels of crimes against prop-

261

TABLE 10–5. Regional Distribution of Crime, France, 1825–1830

Region	Percentage of French Population	Percentage of Crimes Against the Person	Rate per 100,000 Population for Crimes Against the Person	Percentage of Crimes Against Property	Rate per 100,000 Population for Crimes Against Property
North	28	25	5	42	26
South	15	24	9	12	13
East	18	19	6	16	14
West	22	18	5	18	13
Center	17	14	5	12	12

SOURCE: Calculated from data in A. M. Guerry, *Essai Sur la Statistique Morale de la France* (Paris: Chez Crochard, 1831), pp. 9, 10, 38, 42.

erty: with 28 percent of France's total population, it had only 24 percent of the charges for crimes against the person, but 42 percent for crimes against property. By contrast, the rural South, with 15 percent of France's population, had 24 percent of crimes against the person but only 12 percent of crimes against property. The East had crime levels consistent with its proportion of the national population, and the West and the Center had levels below their share of the population. In terms of rates per hundred thousand population, the South had rates of crimes against the person almost double the rates in the other four regions; the North had property crime rates double those of the other four regions. These patterns were displayed on multicolor maps that clustered the departments with similar crime levels together.

Guerry sought to explain the differential distribution of property and personal crimes in terms of variations in wealth, in literacy, and in population density across the departments. He found that the wealthiest departments had the highest rates of property crime, whereas many of the poorest departments had the lowest property-crime rates. Further analysis led him to conclude that the wealthy departments had high levels of manufacturing and commerce, whereas the poorer departments did not. Property crime was, in part, a function of opportunity. Second, he reasoned that the relative deprivation of the poor in wealthy, urban departments would seem much greater to them than the absolute poverty experienced by the residents of the poorer departments. The greater gap between the incomes of rich and poor in the rich departments would serve as a strong motive for property crimes. Guerry found that the departments with the highest literacy levels had the highest property-crime rates, whereas those with the lowest literacy levels had the highest rates of crimes against the person. A comparison of population density with crime led him to conclude that population density was unrelated to crime.

Quetelet (1842) analyzed the same data, finding the same regional patterns. His analysis pressed beyond that of Guerry's, concluding that neither education nor poverty had any substantial impact on the distribution of crime, but that climate did: hot climates produced high levels of crimes against the person; "severe [i.e., cold] climates, which give rise to the greatest number of wants, also give rise to the greatest number of crimes against property" (p. 95). Quetelet also concluded that relative deprivation and high levels of activity creating many opportunities were responsible for high rates of property crime in the north of France.

English studies of the spatial distribution of offenses across the counties of England and Wales were first undertaken following the formal organization of a judicial-statistics recording system in 1834. Rawson (1839) analyzed the judicial statistics for 1835–1839 in terms of the principal occupational characteristics of the counties. He divided the counties into four groups: agricultural, manufacturing, mining, and metropolitan (i.e., London and its surrounding counties). He concluded that crime was highest in the cities; that, without the effect of the cities, the crime rates were about the same in both agricultural and manufacturing counties; and that crime was very low in the mining counties. In addition, Rawson concluded that crime was very infrequent in Wales and the north of England (Morris, 1958, p. 54). Fletcher (1848, 1849) mapped the county patterns of population density, illiteracy, and several measures of personal wealth and poverty in conjunction with a number of measures of crime, including crimes against the person and crimes against property. He concluded that serious crime was a function of ignorance (Levin and Lindesmith, 1937), but that an extension of schools and "Christian education" would not much affect the crime rate (Morris, 1958, p. 53). He also concluded that crime was produced not by actual economic necessity, but by the disrupting effects of economic change, which were giving males the time to commit offenses by putting their wives and children to work as breadwinners.

Plint (1851) analyzed crime patterns in the counties of England for selected periods between 1801 and 1850 using judicial returns for indictable offenses. His objective was to demonstrate that Fletcher, among others, was wrong in downplaying the importance of education as a control on crime, and to demonstrate further that crime was not associated with economic fluctuations. Figure 10–4 maps serious-crime conviction rates for the forty counties of England, circa 1820, dividing the range into five equal parts. London and Middlesex dominated the crime pattern, with rates 25 percent higher than those of the next highest county, and eight times higher than Westmoreland, the county with the lowest conviction rate. Two urban, industrial counties (Warwickshire, with the cities of Birmingham and Coventry, and Lancashire, with the burgeoning cities of Liverpool and Manchester) had the next highest conviction rates. Seven additional midrange counties marked by urban and industrial characteristics completed the high-crime region of England in this period. This pattern appeared in the data mapped by Henry Mayhew (1861) for mid-century, a great cruciform of high-crime, urban, industrial counties surrounded by thirty small-town agricultural and mining counties. Figure 10–5 presents a modified version of Mayhew's map of "criminal intensity," with the range divided into quartiles.

The nineteenth-century studies of regional crime patterns in France and England established a number of important points. First, these studies established the utility of the spatial analysis of crime: mapping crime patterns is a powerful way to identify patterns in crime and to associate those patterns with the patterns formed by other social, economic, and physical variables. The regional patterns of crime were compared, for instance, with the regional patterns of literacy to test the idea that criminal behavior was precipitated by ignorance and that expanded general

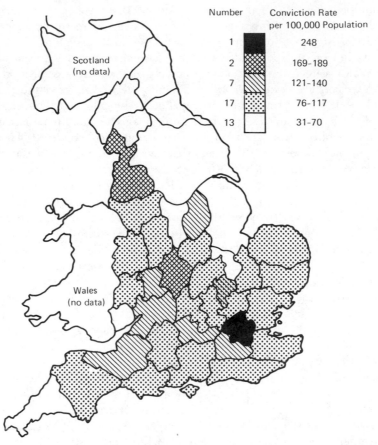

Number		Conviction Rate per 100,000 Population
1		248
2		169-189
7		121-140
17		76-117
13		31-70

Figure 10-4. Conviction rates in England, circa 1820. [Source: Calculated from data in T. Plint, *Crime in England*. London: Charles Gilpin, 1851.]

education of the populace would reduce the crime rate. The regional crime patterns suggested that very different mechanisms might be important in the genesis of crimes against the person and crimes against property: the first might be a product of forces that affected emotional states (such as climate) or interpersonal relationships; the second might be a product of the myriad opportunities and the relative deprivation facing the poor in urban, industrial areas. Second, these studies established some empirical regularities in the distribution of crime within particular nations. Crime was not smoothly distributed but was spread unevenly. Crime was clustered, high- and low-crime areas tending to form regions. The patterns of property crime and crimes against the person were different. Urban, industrial areas had high property-crime rates, but relatively low personal-crime rates. Small-town and rural areas had much higher personal-crime rates, but low property-crime rates. Third, the nineteenth-century studies established the historical regional pattern of crime in England, against which the current regional pattern can be considered. Finally, and regrettably, these studies set the precedent for the use of spatially

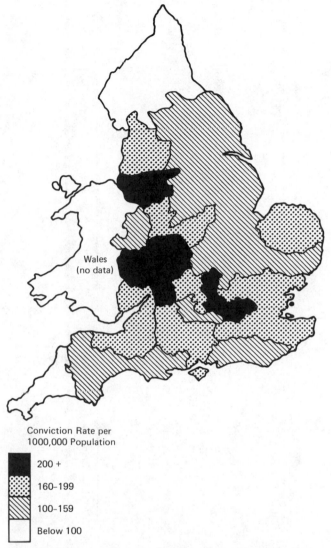

Conviction Rate per
1000,000 Population

200 +

160–199

100–159

Below 100

Figure 10–5. Intensity of criminality in England and Wales, circa 1850. [Source: Calculated from data in H. Mayhew, *London Labour and the London Poor. Vol. 4 Those That Will Not Work, Comprising Prostitutes, Thieves, Swindlers, and Beggars,* (1968 Reprint edition) London: Griffin Bolan, 1861–1862.]

aggregated data in the attempt to understand individual motivations for criminal behavior.

Regional Crime Patterns in England and Wales

The current English crime pattern is dominated by six high-crime regions that each had rates of more than 6,000 indictable offenses known to the police per

265

TABLE 10–6. Highest Ranking Police Areas in England and Wales, Selected Crimes, 1978

Violence			Robbery			Theft		
Area	Rate per 100,000 pop.	Rank	Area	Rate per 100,000 pop.	Rank	Area	Rate per 100,000 pop.	Rank
Nottinghamshire	376	1	London	90	1	London	4,434	1
Humberside	313	2	Merseyside	54	2	Nottinghamshire	4,259	2
West Yorkshire	251	3	West Midlands	40	3	Merseyside	3,921	3
Bedfordshire	250	4	Bedfordshire	29	4	Northumbria	3,626	4
Cleveland	242	5	West Yorkshire	25	5	West Yorkshire	3,420	5
Staffordshire	237	6	Nottinghamshire	23	6	Cleveland	3,299	6
Merseyside	231	7	Greater Manchester	18	7	West Midlands	3,280	7
Durham	212	8	Northumbria	17	8	Cambridgeshire	3,191	9
Gwent	206	9	Hampshire	16	9	Bedfordshire	2,903	10
South Yorkshire	205	10	Humberside	16	9			
West Midlands	203	11						
London	194	12						
Northamptonshire	194	12						
National	177		National	27		National	2,957	

SOURCE: Home Office (Annual) *Criminal Statistics. England and Wales* (London: HMSO, 1978)

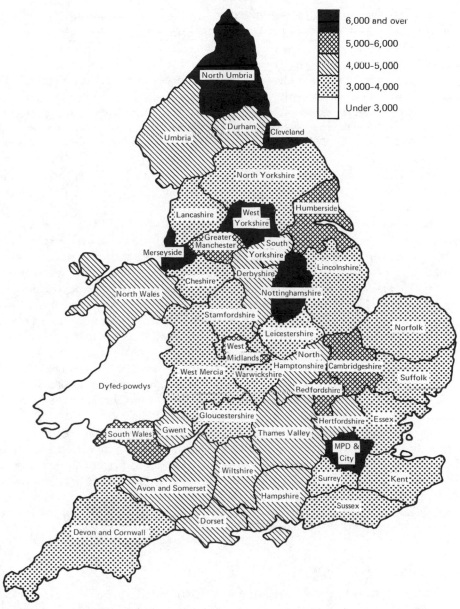

Figure 10–6. Indictable offenses recorded by the police per 100,000 population by police force area in England and Wales, 1978. [Source: Home Office Criminal Statistics: England and Wales. London: HMSO, 1978 (CMND 7670).]

100,000 population in 1978. Two crime regions are particularly notable because they had rates in excess of 7,000 known indictable offenses, and because they have been high-crime regions since at least the early nineteenth century: London; and Merseyside, which is the modern metropolitan region centered on the city of Liverpool. Four high-crime regions are notable because they were not high-crime areas in the nineteenth century, though they were at the core of high-crime regions identified by McClintock and Avison in the mid-1960s. A number of major urban industrial centers with concomitant high crime rates developed in the north of England in the century that passed between Mayhew's mapping of crime regions and the regional analysis undertaken by McClintock and Avison (1968). Two other nineteenth-century high-crime areas, formed around Manchester and around Birmingham, are now independent police areas with very high crime rates: Greater Manchester, which had a 1978 rate of 5,676 known indictable offenses per 100,000 population; and the West Midlands, which had a rate of 5,596 in 1978 (Figure 10–6).

The underlying patterns of offenses that comprised the total crime picture in England and Wales in 1978 differed substantially. Counties with high rates of crimes of violence against the person were widely distributed, though they tended to be in the northern half of England. London ranked twelfth for this category of offenses. Robbery was an urban crime in 1978: London ranked first with a rate more than three times the national average; the West Midlands ranked third. The robbery regions corresponded to the traditional high-crime regions of the nineteenth century. The theft patterns tended to resemble the total crime pattern closely. London again ranked first, with a rate almost 50 percent above the national average. The burglary patterns differed from both the violence pattern and the robbery and theft patterns. Merseyside ranked first in burglary and in combined burglary–theft from a dwelling, and London ranked second (Table 10–6).

The English regional crime pattern in 1978 was far less clustered than it had been in the nineteenth century. Crimes against property were associated with the largest cities, and the connection between crimes of violence and the largest cities was much less pronounced (Figure 10–7). To date, the social dynamics of contemporary regional crime patterns have not been studied. Patterns in population growth, mobility, migration, and race relations; patterns in communication and transport; patterns in industry, occupation, and employment; and patterns in housing, architecture, and environmental policy—all seem likely candidates for examination in conjunction with contemporary regional crime distribution. The convergence of these and many other characteristics of English society may well account for the general dispersion of high-crime-rate areas into many parts of the country.

Regional Crime Patterns in Canada

In 1976, Canadian crime had two distinctive regional patterns: a robbery pattern and a pattern for everything else. The robbery pattern centered on the province of Quebec, which had a rate of 166 per 100,000 population. Other high-rate areas were the Northwest Territories, British Columbia, Alberta, and the Yukon. Manitoba, Ontario, Nova Scotia, and Saskatchewan had intermediate robbery rates in 1976, and the rest of the Maritime Provinces had very low robbery rates. There were two robbery regions: a very high-rate region in the east central part of Canada, and a high-rate region in the northwestern provinces and territories. Breaking-and-entering offenses (burglary-type offenses) followed the second regional pattern: enormously high rates in the Northwest Territories and the Yukon; very high rates in British Columbia, Quebec, and Alberta; a vast region of lower rates

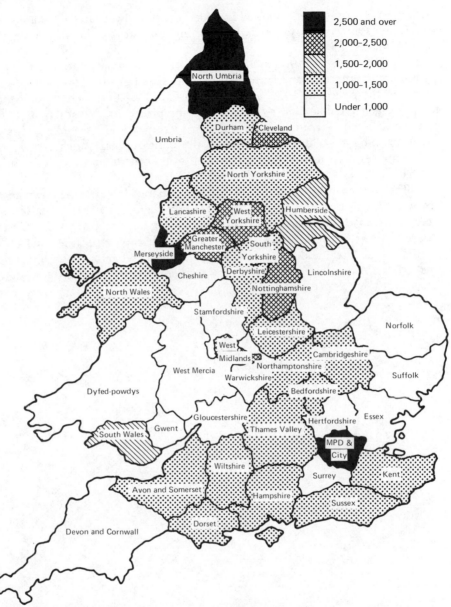

Figure 10–7. Offenses of burglary, aggravated burglary, and theft in a dwelling recorded the police per 100,000 dwellings by police force area in England and Wales, 1978. [Source: Home Office Criminal Statistics: England and Wales. London: HMSO, 1978 (CMND 7670) p.61.]

in Manitoba, Saskatchewan and Ontario; and a region of low rates in the Maritime Provinces. This second regional pattern was also visible in the homicide data for 1976. The Northwest Territories and the Yukon had homicide rates comparable to those found in developing countries, probably as an artifact of very small population bases. Alberta, British Columbia, and Saskatchewan had the highest homicide rates

269

among the ten provinces, followed by Quebec, then lower rates in Manitoba, Nova Scotia, and Ontario. Nova Scotia had the highest rates in the very low-rate Maritime Provinces.

Figures 10–8, 10–9, and 10–10 illustrate the regional patterning of robbery, breaking and entering, and homicide; they are based on the provincial-level crimes known to the police for 1976. A note of caution in reading these figures; they were computer-generated and use a contour-mapping procedure that interpolates patterns between data-entry coordinates. A different picture would have emerged had a different-mapping procedure that followed the political boundaries of the provinces and territories been used. (For a fuller discussion of mapping procedures, refer back to Chapter 6.)

The interprovincial pattern for total criminal-code offenses known to the police was heavily biased toward western Canada (Figure 10–11). Total crime rates were lowest in the Maritime Provinces, with a regional high point in Nova Scotia. Quebec had a total crime rate similar to the Maritimes (because total crime was dominated by theft and other less serious crimes), whereas Ontario's crime rates rose to the national average. Crime rates rose progressively across the western prov-

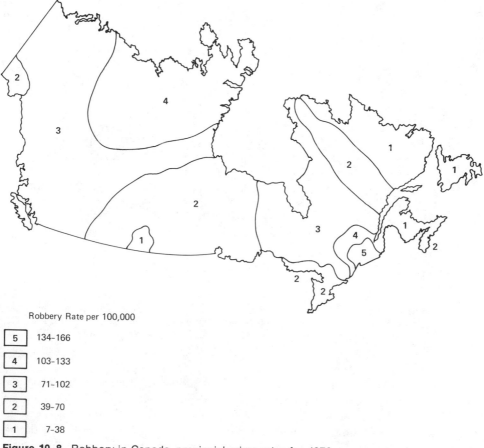

Robbery Rate per 100,000

5	134–166
4	103–133
3	71–102
2	39–70
1	7–38

Figure 10–8. Robbery in Canada, provincial crime rates for 1976.

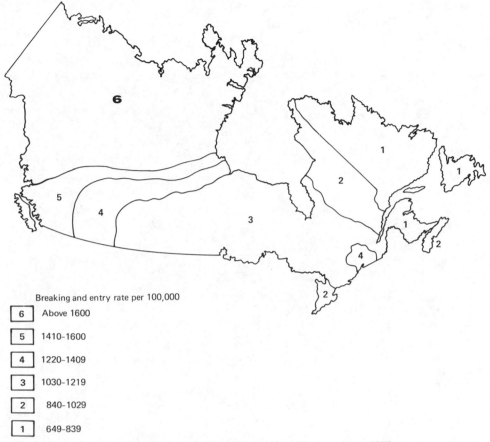

Breaking and entry rate per 100,000

6	Above 1600
5	1410–1600
4	1220–1409
3	1030–1219
2	840–1029
1	649–839

Figure 10–9. Breaking and entering in Canada, provincial crime rates, 1976.

inces of Manitoba, Saskatchewan, Alberta, and British Columbia and were highest in the frontier regions of the Yukon and the Northwest Territories.

The strength of the regional crime patterns in Canada is illustrated in a study by Rae (1981), which analyzed violent crime rates of the forty-eight largest Canadian cities for 1976. Rae used analysis of covariance to test the relative ability of four different variables, singly and in combination, to explain the variation in the violent crime rates observed in those cities: region; city size; population density; and proportion of men without a high-school diploma. He found that all four variables had significant and approximately equal main effects on the violent crime rate, but that no interaction terms were statistically significant. Together, the four variables explained (multiple R^2) 58 percent of the variance in violent crime rates. Rae defined four regions: Ontario; Quebec; Alberta and British Columbia; and a residual region composed of the Maritime Provinces, Manitoba, and Saskatchewan. The unadjusted deviation η showed strong regional differences: Quebec cities were well below the national mean; Ontario cities were at the mean; the residual-region cities were slightly above the national mean; and the western cities were well above the mean. Statistical control of the effects of city size, city population density, and

271

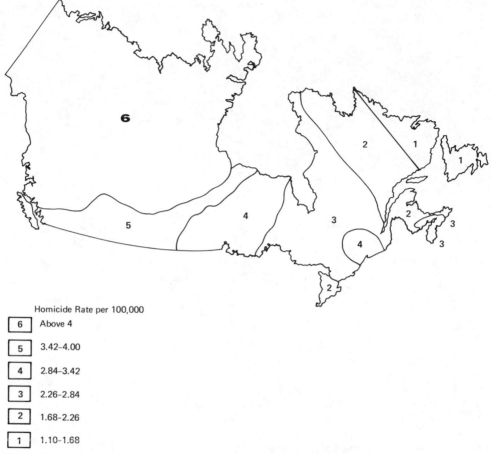

Homicide Rate per 100,000

6	Above 4
5	3.42–4.00
4	2.84–3.42
3	2.26–2.84
2	1.68–2.26
1	1.10–1.68

Figure 10–10. Homicide in Canada, provincial crime rates, 1976.

low education among adult males had a minor impact on the position of Ontario or Quebec cities with respect to the national mean, dropped the residual-region cities below the mean, and substantially increased the location of the western region cities above the mean. Location in the two most western provinces of Canada was, by itself, a powerful predictor of high rates of violent crime. This finding suggests that the social and environmental dynamics of criminal events in western Canada are substantially different from those in other regions.

These patterns have remained relatively stable over the past fifteen years at least, and the general bias toward progressively higher crime rates in the west has been visible in the criminal conviction data for at least sixty years. Bell-Rowbotham and Boydell (1972) found the general western bias, with British Columbia and Alberta dominant, in the known-crime data for 1966 and 1969. They also found Quebec dominant in robbery rates. They found that Nova Scotia had the highest crime rates among the generally low-crime Maritime Provinces. The rank-order correlations between the provinces in the two years were very high for most offense categories: total criminal code, 0.95; homicide, 0.61; robbery, 0.96; breaking and entering, 0.88; and theft, 0.99. Historical data are more restricted (see Chapters 3 and 8), but the interprovincial conviction statistics for indictable offenses for 1921 showed a strong western bias: British Columbia ranked second in conviction rate per 100,000 population, Alberta third, Manitoba fourth, and Saskatchewan fifth. The principal difference between the modern pattern and that of 1921 is that On-

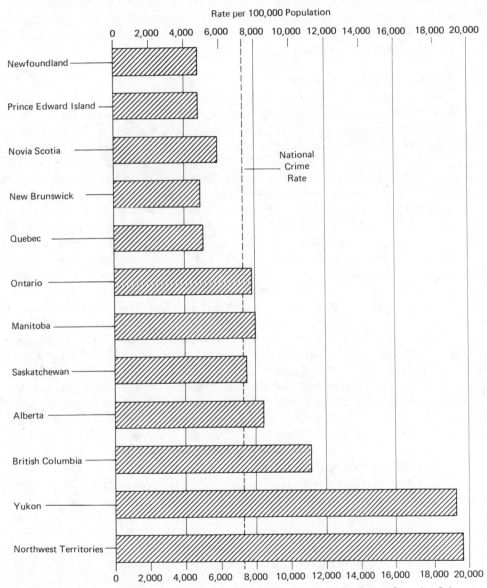

Figure 10–11. Canadian provincial crime rates, 1978. [Source: Statistics Canada, *Crime and Traffic Enforcement Statistics, 1978*. Ottawa: Statistics Canada, 1980.]

tario ranked first in the indictable conviction rate in 1921 but has consistently ranked fifth in known total crime rate in more recent years.[1]

Regional Crime Patterns in the United States

Criminologists have examined regional crime patterns in the United States at two low levels of resolution, using divisions and regions defined by the U.S. Census Bureau for the lowest level of analysis, and using state data for a slightly higher level of resolution. Both levels of analysis show strong regional crime patterns that have persisted over half a century.

Crime in the Census Regions

The Bureau of the Census clusters the fifty American states into four major divisions: the Northeast; the North Central; the South; and the West. Each of these divisions is subdivided into two or more regions. The Northeast is composed of New England and the Middle Atlantic regions. The North Central is composed of the East North Central and the West North Central regions. The South is composed of the South Atlantic, the East South Central, and the West South Central regions. The West is composed of the Mountain region and the Pacific region.

In 1979, the West had the highest crime rates, followed by the Northeast, the South, and the North Central divisions. The West had the highest rates of forcible rape, aggravated assault, burglary, and larceny–theft. The Northeast had the highest rates of robbery and motor vehicle theft. It had the lowest rates of rape, larceny–theft, and murder. The South had the highest murder rate and the lowest rate of motor vehicle theft. The North Central division had the lowest rates for robbery, aggravated assault, and burglary, and it tied the Northeast for the lowest murder rate.

At the higher level of resolution represented by the nine census regions, the underlying structure of the divisional crime pattern is visible. The Pacific region had the highest rates of rape, aggravated assault, burglary, and larceny–theft. The West South Central region had the highest homicide rate. The Middle Atlantic region had the highest robbery rate. New England had the highest rate of motor vehicle theft. Table 10–7 presents the regional crime rates for the seven index offenses for 1979. Figure 10–12 maps the high- and low-rate regions for 1979.

Spatial Distribution of Crime by States

An alternative approach to understanding the regional patterns of crime in the United States is to examine the crime rates of individual states and to cluster together the states with similar crime rates. This approach has been followed repeatedly by criminologists over the past half century. Several stable patterns have emerged.

Lottier (1938a) studied the clustering of state crime rates in the mid-1930s,

---

[1] The different rankings of Ontario in 1921 and 1976 may be a function of different criminal-justice-system measurement points: the correlation between crimes known to the police and convictions is less than unity. See Chapter 3.

274

TABLE 10–7. American Regional Crimes Rates, 1979 (per 100,000 Population)

Region	Murder	Rape	Robbery	Aggravated Assault	Burglary	Theft	Motor Vehicle Theft
Northeast							
New England	3.5	22.1	158.7	233.9	1,515	2,839	834
Middle Atlantic	9.0	27.1	353.2	258.4	1,458	2,554	602
North Central							
East North Central	8.5	32.1	178.0	232.0	1,256	3,026	482
West North Central	5.4	23.1	113.0	170.5	1,133	2,684	317
South							
South Atlantic	11.8	37.0	197.0	364.0	1,551	3,142	355
East South Central	11.1	27.0	116.0	203.0	1,141	1,897	293
West South Central	15.1	41.0	174.0	282.0	1,602	2,860	471
West							
Mountain	7.9	38.0	131.0	275.0	1,623	3,629	409
Pacific	11.0	52.0	282.0	376.0	2,065	3,780	668

SOURCE: Federal Bureau of Investigation (Annual) *Crime in the United States* (Washington, D.C.: Government Printing Office [Uniform Crime Reports], 1979).

using *Uniform Crime Reports* data for 1934 and 1935. He was particularly interested in the idea that the states clustered into sectional regions with different cultural traditions.[2] He reasoned that sectional differences should be reflected in different crime patterns. Lottier mapped murder, robbery, and theft. He found strong sectional clusterings of states with very different crime patterns for all three offenses. The highest rates of murder clustered in the states of the old Confederacy, a sweep of contiguous states from Virginia to Texas, and low-rate regions formed from contiguous states in New England and in the northern Great Plains. Robbery formed a high-rate region of contiguous states in the Midwest and a second high-rate region comprised of Arizona, Nevada, Oregon, and Washington. New England and New York together formed a low-robbery-rate region. Theft was a western problem, with high-rate regions in the Pacific Northwest and in the Southwest connected by Nevada, which had the highest rate of all. Lottier also argued that a smooth gradient of states with successively lower crime rates could be detected by moving outward from the highpoint of a crime region.

Lottier's original study was replicated by Shannon (1954), using data for 1946–1952; by Harries (1971), using data for 1968; and by Kowalski et al. (1980), using data for 1970–1976. Shannon found a cluster of states in the South with high murder and aggravated-assault rates, and a cluster of states in the West that had high rates of burglary, larceny, and auto theft. New England had the lowest crime rates. The crime regions for these crimes were consistent with those found by Lot-

[2] Lottier was actually concerned to demonstrate that sectional regions were constructed from the effects of integrated metropolitan areas. He used state data as a proxy for metropolitan crime data and assumed that he would find crime gradients. The model Lottier had in mind would now be called an *urban field model*. (See Chapter 9.)

275

Patterns in Crime

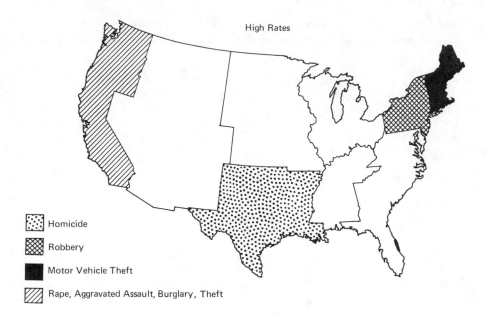

Homicide

Robbery

Motor Vehicle Theft

Rape, Aggravated Assault, Burglary, Theft

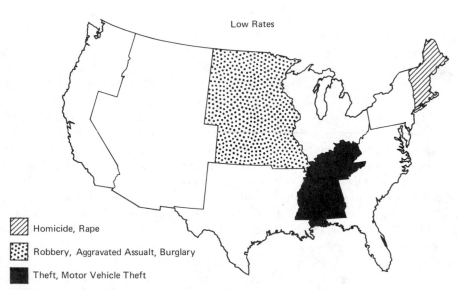

Homicide, Rape

Robbery, Aggravated Assualt, Burglary

Theft, Motor Vehicle Theft

Figure 10–12. Regional crime patterns in the United States, 1979.

tier a decade earlier. The rank-order correlations between states in 1934–1935 and 1946–1952 were murder, 0.94; larceny, 0.86; burglary, 0.77; and aggravated assault, 0.77. Shannon found a different pattern for robbery: Lottier's midwestern cluster was replaced by a western region composed of Nevada, California, Arizona, Colorado, Washington, and Oregon, and by a second high-rate area along the Ohio river, composed of Illinois, Kentucky, Michigan, Missouri, Ohio, Indiana, and West Virginia. Shannon also commented that the relatively low crime rates reported by the State of New York were probably a product of the then-recently-

276

discovered fact that New York City had been sending fraudulently low crime reports to the FBI (see Chapter 3).

Harries's replication (1971), using 1968 data, found a southern murder region; robbery regions in the Far West and in a tier of states running from Missouri along the Great Lakes through New York and down the east coast through New Jersey and Maryland; and a high-burglary region in the far western states and four isolated high-rate states; New York, Michigan, Maryland, and Florida. New England and a cluster of states comprised of the Dakotas, Minnesota, Wisconsin, and Iowa emerged as low-crime-rate regions. Harries found that the regional patterns of violent crimes (murder, rape, and aggravated assault) were strongly similar to each other, and that the regional patterns of property crimes (robbery, burglary, larceny, and auto theft) were strongly similar to each other, but that the violence and property-crime patterns were not similar at all.

Kowalski et al. (1980) replicated the prior studies, using data for 1970–1976. They found patterns very similar to those found by Harries for 1968: the southern-state murder region that appears to be a constant feature of the geography of American crime; robbery regions in the Far West and in the Missouri–New York tier of states; a far western region of high burglary and larceny rates; regions of high rates of motor vehicle theft comprised of California and Nevada, of New York, New Jersey, and the southern New England states, and of Michigan and its contiguous states. Aggravated-assault rates clustered in several groupings of states along all three seaboards, and rape rates were highest in a cluster of western states and in three isolates, Michigan, Maryland, and Florida. Kowalski et al. concluded that, in comparison with the data of earlier studies, there was a marked shift of all types of crime except murder away from the older industrial states of the North and the East toward the Sunbelt states of the South and the West.

The shift of the relative crime problem into the Sunbelt regions can be seen in the 1979 *Uniform Crime Reports* data, as can a second trend that consolidates high crime into three regions: a far western region, a southern region, and an industrial heartland region. Figure 10–13 shows the clusterings of state crime rates, by quintile, for murder, robbery, burglary, and motor vehicle theft. The historical southern murder region is evident: seven of the ten states with the highest murder rates were in the Confederate South; seven of the ten states in the second highest quintile were southern or border states. In 1979, however, there was also a separate far-western murder region composed of Nevada, which ranked first, and California, which ranked sixth. The robbery rate presented a very different pattern. There were three distinctively different regions with high rates: the Nevada–California region; a "New South" region composed of Florida and Georgia; and an industrial heartland region sweeping from Missouri to Massachusetts to Maryland. Eleven of the thirteen states in the industrial heartland had robbery rates in the top two quintiles, five in the top quintile. New York had robbery rates 25 percent higher than the second-ranked state. Burglary emerged with three clusters of high-rate regions, of which two were in the Sunbelt. The western region swept from Texas, along the border and the coast, to Washington, but included Colorado. The New South region of Florida, Georgia, and South Carolina clustered three states from the top two quintiles. The third high-burglary-rate region clustered seven eastern seaboard states from Maryland to Massachusetts. Motor vehicle theft showed a northeastern cluster similar to

277

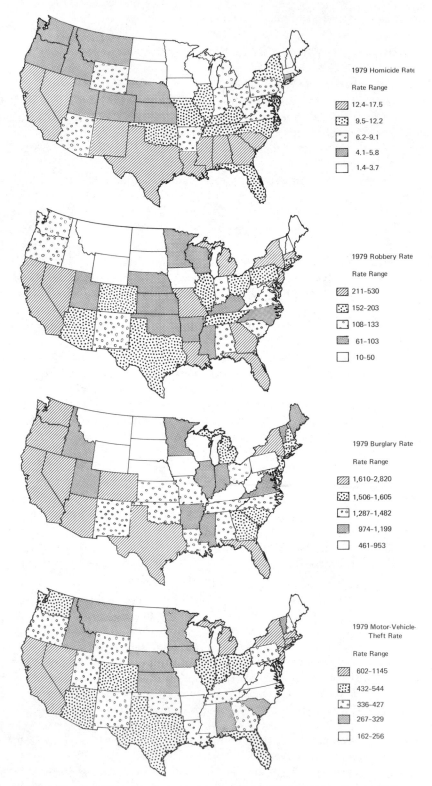

Figure 10–13. Regional crime rates in the United States (State Data), 1979.

278

that of burglary, a Great Lakes cluster centered on Michigan (for obvious reasons), and the Nevada–California cluster. Major low-rate regions were apparent in northern New England and in the northern Great Plains and the Mountain States.

The stable and dynamic components of the regional clusters of high- and low-crime areas are reflected in intercrime correlations in 1934–1935 and 1979. The violent personal crimes tended to correlate highly in both periods. Murder and aggravated-assault rates had interstate correlations of +0.70 in 1934–1935 and +0.60 in 1979. Property crimes also tended to have high interstate correlations in both periods: robbery and burglary had correlations of +0.67 in 1934–1935 and +0.71 in 1979; burglary and larceny had correlations of +0.59 in 1934–1935 and +0.69 in 1979. Property and violent crimes did not have such high interstate correlations. Murder and larceny were correlated at only +0.24 in 1934–1935, and this correlation dropped to +0.08 in 1979. Murder and motor vehicle theft were correlated at only +0.19 in 1979. Burglary and robbery have a much stronger element of implicit violence than theft crimes, and they correlated more highly with crimes of personal violence. In 1979, burglary and murder correlated at +0.46; robbery, which might logically be treated as a crime of violence rather than a property crime for many purposes, correlated more highly still, at +0.55. These relationships were not nearly as strong in the 1930s: burglary correlated with murder at +0.39, and robbery correlated with murder at +0.32.

Explanations for the regional patterns of crime that emerged from clustering together states with similar rates varied. The historical and stable southern murder region has been explained in terms of a regional subculture than condones lethal violence as a proper solution to social problems (Gastil, 1971; Hackney, 1969), and it has been explained in terms of pervasive, structural social and economic inequalities within the region that create conditions conducive to the use of lethal violence (Loftin and Hill, 1974; Erlanger, 1976). The debate between the advocates of these two approaches has been bitter, and remains unresolved (Symposium, 1978). The contemporary clusters of high-crime states in the Far West, the New South, and the industrial heartland might be explained in terms of growing differences in the opportunity patterns of these regions. They are different in terms of net migration patterns, of population density, of employment and occupation patterns, and of transport and mobility patterns. These differences suggest different patterns of property distribution, consumption, and population activity in the different regions, which are conducive to different forms of criminal events. The clusters of low-crime states are basically agricultural, small-city states with very different opportunity patterns from the high-crime states.

Intermetropolitan Crime Patterns

An alternative approach to the analysis of regional crime patterns—one that provides a higher level of geographic resolution—is the study of intermetropolitan crime rates. Cities have dominated the crime patterns of England, Canada, and the United States for a century and more. When urban crime patterns are aggregated by city size, the set of largest cities has the highest crime rates, the set of second largest cities has the second highest crime rates, and so on down to the set of smallest cities, which have the lowest crime rates. The aggregate pattern can be misleading, however. When the crime rates for individual cities and metropolitan areas are examined without being combined, a different clustering of cities with similar crime rates emerge. Some of these clusters are geographic, some are keyed to population size, and some are keyed to social or economic conditions or processes. Intercity or intermetropolitan analyses of crime rates come much closer to the real criminal event than those levels of resolution already examined, and such analyses begin to provide pattern information that can be used by crime-control planners.

City Size and Crime Rates

The difference between aggregate patterns and intercity patterns is apparent in a comparison of large cities' crime rates. Canada's largest cities in 1978 were Toronto, Montreal, Vancouver, Winnipeg, Calgary, Edmonton, Hamilton, and Ottawa. The Canadian cities with the highest crime rates that year, however, were

TABLE 10–8. Top Twenty-five Crime Cities in Canada, 1978

Rank	City	Crime Rate per 100,000 Population	Population (based on 1976 census)
1	Gatineau, Que.	21,290.0	73,479
2	Victoria, B.C.	17,319.1	62,551
3	Prince George, B.C.	15,530.2	59,929
4	Chatham, Ont.	14,141.7	38,685
5	Prince Albert, Sask.	13,834.3	28,631
6	Kamloops, B.C.	13,600.0	58,311
7	Sarnia, Ont.	13,450.9	55,576
8	Belleville, Ont.	12,933.9	35,311
9	Brantford, Ont.	12,843.0	66,950
10	Vancouver, B.C.	12,626.7	410,188
11	Moncton, N.B.	12,517.8	55,934
12	Orillia, Ont.	11,920.3	24,412
13	Brandon, Man.	11,800.0	34,901
14	Halifax, N.S.	11,799.2	117,882
15	Kelowna, B.C.	11,720.0	51,955
16	Edmonton, Alta.	11,712.1	461,361
17	North Vancouver, B.C.	11,677.6	31,934
18	Hamilton-Wentworth, Ont.	11,653.7	312,003
19	Surrey, B.C.	11,458.0	116,497
20	Regina, Sask.	11,448.5	149,593
21	Maple Ridge, B.C.	11,376.1	29,462
22	Nanaimo, B.C.	11,366.0	40,336
23	New Westminster, B.C.	11,178.2	38,393
24	Thunder Bay, Ont.	11,078.8	111,476
25	Peterborough, Ont.	10,695.7	59,683

SOURCE: Statistics Canada, *Crime and Traffic Enforcement Statistics* (Ottawa: Queen's Printer [Catalogue 85-201 annual], 1978).

TABLE 10–9. Twenty-five Largest American SMSA's Ranking by Crime Rates, 1979

Population Rank	SMSA	1979 Estimated Population	Murder Rank	Robbery Bank	Burglary Rank
1	New York	9,175,777	12	1	26
2	Los Angeles	7,208,583	11	5	14
3	Chicago	7,021,758	36	30	—*
4	Philadelphia	4,764,966	—	35	—
5	Detroit	4,395,229	38	15	—
6	Boston	3,309,460	—	26	—
7	San Francisco	3,241,210	—	8	27
8	Washington, D.C.	3,011,183	—	12	—
9	Dallas	2,794,342	20	31	21
10	Long Island	2,674,995	—	—	—
11	Houston	2,669,447	1	10	12
12	St. Louis	2,386,168	29	19	—
13	Baltimore	2,148,562	39	7	—
14	Minneapolis	2,089,467	—	—	—
15	Newark	1,952,632	—	6	—
16	Cleveland	1,935,619	24	14	—
17	Anaheim	1,866,052	—	—	24
18	Atlanta	1,864,689	8	9	22
19	San Diego	1,775,040	—	34	38
20	Denver	1,561,973	—	—	32
21	Seattle	1,527,804	—	—	—
22	Miami	1,500,978	7	3	6
23	Tampa	1,444,091	—	—	—
24	Riverside	1,410,381	—	—	10
25	Cincinnati	1,389,868	—	—	—

—* means not among highest 40 SMSA's

SOURCE: Compiled from data in Federal Bureau of Investigation (Annual) *Crime in the United States* (Washington, D.C.: Printing Office [Uniform Crime Reports], 1979).

smaller places: Gatineau, Quebec; Victoria, British Columbia; Prince George, British Columbia; Chatham, Ontario; and Prince Albert, Saskatchewan. These were all cities with populations between 25,000 and 75,000. Of the very largest cities, Vancouver ranked tenth in overall crime rate, Edmonton ranked sixteenth, and Hamilton ranked eighteenth. None of the other largest cities were among the top twenty-five in terms of highest crime rates (Table 10–8).

A similar pattern emerges from the American crime data for Standard Metropolitan Statistical Areas (SMSAs) for 1979 (Table 10–9). These are large urban areas defined by the U.S. Census Bureau. They are composed of clusters of counties containing a core city and its commuting suburbs, which together have a combined population of at least 50,000. The size range of these urban areas is substantial: the small SMSA of Lawrence, Kansas, had a population of about 66,000 in 1979, and the largest SMSA, New York, had an estimated population of 9,175,777 that year. The ten largest SMSAs in 1979 were New York, Los Angeles, Chicago, Philadelphia, Detroit, Boston, San Francisco, Washington, Dallas, and Long Island. New

York ranked first in robbery, but twelfth in murder and twenty-sixth in burglary. Chicago, third in size, ranked thirty-sixth in murder and thirtieth in robbery and was not among the top forty ranked SMSAs for burglary. Long Island, ranked tenth in total population, was not among the top forty ranked SMSAs for any of these crimes. By way of contrast, Houston, which was ranked eleventh in population, ranked first in murder, tenth in robbery, and twelfth in burglary; Miami, ranked twenty-second in population, ranked seventh in murder, third in robbery, and sixth in burglary; New Orleans, ranked thirty-second in population, ranked second in murder and second in robbery, but thirty-ninth in burglary.

The difference between the patterns of crime seen in the aggregate crime rates of cities in different size categories and the patterns seen in individual crime rankings can be further illustrated by consideration of the SMSAs as rank-ordered by crime rates for 1979 (Table 10–10). For murder, the ten highest-ranked metropolitan areas were Houston; New Orleans; Las Vegas; Pine Bluff, Arkansas; Lubbock, Texas; Columbus, Georgia; Miami; Atlanta; Mobile, Alabama; and Stockton, California. None of these metropolitan areas was among the ten largest. Only five of the ten largest SMSAs had murder rates that ranked them in the top forty. The regional homicide pattern visible at lower levels of resolution is also clearly visible at the intermetropolitan level: eight of the ten highest-ranked SMSAs were in the South; 73 percent of the forty SMSAs with the highest known homicide rates were in the South.

The robbery pattern was different. New York had the highest robbery rate, almost twice as high as the second-ranked city, New Orleans. Three of the ten SMSAs with the highest robbery rates were also among the nation's ten largest metropolitan areas; nine of the ten largest SMSAs had robbery rates that placed them among the forty highest ranked. This finding is more consistent with the pattern found in data aggregated into sets based on city size and with the popular conception of crime as a big-city problem than is the intermetropolitan murder pattern. The regional distribution of the 40 metropolitan areas with the highest robbery rates looks rather more like the murder pattern, however. The Sunbelt region (the South and the West) contained 60 percent of the forty highest-robbery-rate SMSAs; the industrial heartland (the Northeast and the Midwest) had 40 percent of the high-rate metropolitan areas. The Sunbelt region had 55 percent of the SMSAs in 1979, and the industrial heartland had 38 percent, so that the regional distribution of the forty highest-ranking metropolitan areas by robbery rates was roughly consistent with the regional distribution of large cities.

The burglary pattern was strikingly tied to new, automobile-oriented metropolitan areas in the South and the West. Of the ten SMSAs with the highest burglary rates, five were in California and Nevada and four were in Florida. Of the forty SMSAs with the highest burglary rates in 1979, 48 percent were located in California, Nevada, or Florida; 45 percent in the West; and 48 percent in the South. The Sunbelt region, containing 55 percent of the 264 SMSAs had 93 percent of the forty highest-ranking SMSAs. Only four of the ten largest SMSAs were among the forty with the highest burglary rates, and three of these were Sunbelt cities: Los Angeles, San Francisco, and Dallas.

Although there is some annual fluctuation in this sort of rank ordering, through changing local circumstance and through chance, the general intermetropolitan pat-

TABLE 10–10. Twenty-five American SMSA's with Highest Rates on Selected Crimes, 1979 (per 100,000 Population)

Murder		Robbery		Burglary	
City	Rate	City	Rate	City	Rate
Houston, Tx.	30.0	New York, NY.	926.7	Las Vegas, Nv.	3,368.2
New Orleans, La.	26.6	New Orleans, La.	561.1	Springfield, Oh.	3,050.6
Las Vegas, Nv.	22.4	Miami, Fl.	545.4	Reno, Nv.	2,764.9
Pine Bluff, Ar.	22.2	Las Vegas, Nv.	530.2	Daytona, Fl.	2,751.0
Lubbock, Tx.	22.0	Los Angeles, Ca.	529.2	West Palm Beach, Fl.	2,743.6
Columbus, Ga.	21.8	Newark, NJ.	484.5	Miami, Fl.	2,636.5
Miami, Fl.	21.3	Baltimore, Md.	470.3	Fresno, Ca.	2,615.1
Atlanta, Ga.	20.2	San Francisco, Ca.	426.1	Orlando, Fl.	2,537.3
Mobile, Al.	20.1	Atlanta, Ga.	404.9	Stockton, Ca.	2,503.9
Stockton, Ca.	20.1	Houston, Tx.	394.4	Riverside, Ca.	2,493.6
Los Angeles, Ca.	20.0	Memphis, Tn.	392.6	Wilmington, NC.	2,470.3
New York, NY.	19.8	Washington, DC.	390.6	Houston, Tx.	2,450.0
Jackson, Ms.	19.4	Reno, Nv.	369.0	Sacramento, Ca.	2,388.7
Lake Charles, La.	19.4	Cleveland, Oh.	356.3	Los Angeles, Ca.	2,387.8
Longview, Tx.	19.1	Detroit, Mi.	351.5	Fayettville, NC.	2,340.7
Shreveport, La.	19.1	Jersey City, NJ.	337.1	Phoenix, Az.	2,319.8
Augusta, Ga.	18.4	Dayton, Oh.	328.4	Fort Lauderdale, Fl.	2,318.7
Gary, In.	18.4	Fort Lauderdale, Fl.	322.1	Oklahoma City, Ok.	2,313.3
Odessa, Tx.	18.4	St. Louis, Mo.	319.5	Lubbock, Tx.	2,286.6
Dallas, Tx.	18.3	Trenton, NJ.	317.2	Atlantic City, NJ.	2,270.0
Albany, Ga.	17.9	Fresno, Ca.	310.3	Dallas, Tx.	2,245.1
San Antonio, Tx.	17.9	Atlantic City, NJ.	307.7	Atlanta, Ga.	2,244.2
Texarkana, Tx./Ar.	17.4	Sacramento, Ca.	303.4	Bakersfield, Ca.	2,243.7
Cleveland, Oh.	16.7	Gary, In.	301.4	Anaheim, Ca.	2,229.6
Birmingham, Al.	16.6	Savannah, Ga.	295.5	Tallahassee, Fl.	2,218.9

SOURCE: Compiled from data in Federal Bureau of Investigation (Annual) *Crime in the United States* (Washington, D.C.: Printing Office [Uniform Crime Reports], 1979).

tern has been stable over a number of years. Inciardi (1978) found similar regional and size-dependent patterns for these crimes for the period 1971–1975, with rankings for property crimes dominated by Sunbelt SMSAs, robbery rankings dominated by the largest SMSAs, and homicide rankings dominated by southern SMSAs. Harries (1974) analyzed the clusterings of the 134 SMSAs with populations of 200,000 or more in 1970 (Figure 10–14). He factor-analyzed the reported rates for the seven *Uniform Crime Reports* index crimes and found that they clustered into two independent vectors. Murder and assault clustered together into a vector that Harries called "violent" crime. Burglary, auto theft, larceny, robbery, and rape clustered together into a vector that he called "general" crime. When metropolitan areas with similar scores on these two crime vectors are mapped, clear geographic clusterings become apparent. The SMSAs with high scores for violent crime were clustered in the South. Metropolitan areas with low scores on both violent and general crime vectors were clustered in the industrial heartland. SMSAs with high general-crime scores seemed less clustered, despite some minor patterns in California and along the northeastern Atlantic seaboard. This latter distribution is not surprising, given the

SMSA's with Both Low Violence and Low General Crime

Boundary of "Industrial Heartland"

High Violence SMSA's

Boundary of "South"

High General Crime SMSA's

Figure 10–14. Clusterings of SMSAs with similar crime scores, United States, 1970. [Source: Adapted from K. D. Harries, *The Geography of Crime and Justice*. New York: McGraw-Hill, 1974, pp. 53–54.]

very different spatial patterning of such crimes as robbery, auto theft, and burglary. Normandeau and Schwartz (1971) found similar patterns among 164 SMSAs in 1960, 1963, and 1966.

Taken together, the 1979 SMSA crime-rate rankings, the patterns found by Inciardi for the first half of the 1970s, the intermetropolitan crime clusterings mapped by Harries for 1970, and the stable intermetropolitan patterns charted by Normandeau and Schwartz for the early 1960s demonstrate persisting spatial variations and clusterings in crime levels and mixtures from city to city. The existence

284

of such patterns led many criminologists to consider the intermetropolitan variation in social and economic characteristics of American cities in a search for an explanation.

Socioeconomic Predictors of Intermetropolitan Crime Patterns

Classic Studies

Ogburn (1935) collected information on crimes known to the police in sixty-two American cities in 1930. He also gathered information on twenty social, economic, and demographic characteristics of these cities. He divided the cities into three size classes. Large cities—sixteen of them, including Milwaukee, Buffalo, Cincinnati, Minneapolis, Newark, and Seattle—ranged in size from 250,000 to 578,000 population. Middle-sized cities—twenty-four, including Springfield, Massachusetts; Bridgeport, Connecticut; Scranton, Pennsylvania; Des Moines, and Salt Lake City—ranged from 100,000 to 168,000 population in 1930. Small cities—twenty-two, including Fresno, Stockton, and San Jose in California; Pueblo, Colorado; Aurora and Decatur, Illinois; and Pittsfield, Massachusetts—ranged in size from 36,000 to 58,000. Ogburn excluded from the study very large cities, such as New York, Chicago, and San Francisco, and he also excluded all cities from southern states "because of the Negro population, to reduce further heterogeneity." He correlated crime rates with socioeconomic and demographic measures for the three city-size groups separately.

Ogburn found no correlation stronger than 0.55, and he found more inverse correlations than direct correlations. For large cities, stronger positive correlations were with the percentage of black population, 0.51; the percentage of males and percentage of native whites born of native parents, both at 0.44; the percentage of small families, 0.32; and wages (a measure of payroll per capita for nonsalaried employees in retail trade and in manufacturing employment), 0.23. Stronger negative correlations were the percentage of offspring of foreign-born parents, −0.54; increasing city growth rate, −0.31; increase in average manufacturing wages in 1929 over 1919, −0.29; and the percentage of the work force employed in manufacturing, −0.20. Middle-sized cities had only one positive correlation of even moderate strength, the percentage of native whites, 0.31. There was a substantial number of relatively strong inverse correlations: police officers per capita, −0.52; the percentage of offspring of foreign-born parents, −0.51; the percentage of foreign-born population, −0.41, the percentage employed in manufacturing, −0.41; average rent, −0.38; the percentage of blacks, −0.36; average value of dwellings, −0.34; increase in average wages in 1929 over 1919, −0.33; and city size, −0.32. Crime rates in the small cities correlated positively with the percentage of male population, 0.55; the percentage of small families, 0.53; and city size, 0.36. Inverse correlations were increasing growth rate, −0.53; the percentage of young children, −0.50; average value of dwellings, −0.39; percentage employed in manufacturing and increase in wages 1929 over 1919, both at −0.38; and the percentage of offspring of foreign-born parents, −0.34.

Across the sets of cities, the strongest positive associations with crime were the percentage of males; the percentage of small families; and the percentage of

285

native whites born of native parents. The strongest negative associations were the percentage of offspring of foreign-born parents; increasing growth rate; increase in wages, 1929 over 1919; and the percentage employed in manufacturing. The picture that emerged was one of two very different types of cities: a large, stable city with relatively high wages, a high proportion of native American males, and high crime rates; and a smaller, growing city of prosperous immigrant industrial workers with low crime rates.

Some correlations were mixed across the city sets and have interesting implications: city size was negatively correlated with crime for the larger and middle-sized city sets and about equally strongly positively correlated with crime rates for small cities; the percentage of blacks was strongly positively correlated with crime rates for large cities but was negatively correlated with crime rates for middle and small cities; finally, the number of police per capita was strongly negatively correlated with crime rates in middle cities, weakly negatively correlated in small cities, and weakly positively correlated with crime rates in large cities. The correlations suggest that city size interacts with growth, with racial composition, and with police-force strength to affect crime rates.

Ogburn also performed a primitive cluster analysis. He concluded that high crime rates clustered with high rates of growth, with rising wages, with higher monthly rental costs, and with an increasing proportion of males in the population. He concluded that low crime rates clustered with larger numbers of children, with more immigrants, with larger family size, with increasing percentages of the work force employed in manufacturing, and with increasing church membership. Two very different types of cities, with distinctively different characteristics, again emerged.

Schuessler (1962) and Schuessler and Slatin (1964) used the technique of factor analysis to assess the patterns of relationship between *Uniform Crime Reports* index-crime rates and a large number of social, economic, and demographic characteristics of cities of 100,000 or more population in 1950 (101) and 1960 (133). Factor analysis clusters relationships within a correlation matrix into sets of similar relationships called *factors*. The hope of researchers using this technique in the 1950s and the 1960s was that the patterns of relationships found in particular factors would yield empirical insight into theoretically defined relationships between crime and social conditions in cities. Essentially similar patterns emerged in both of these analyses for both years: one factor clustered murder and aggravated-assault rates with a number of social and demographic measures; a second factor clustered five property crimes together with the suicide and divorce rates. The patterns of these factors are shown in Table 10–11. Murder and aggravated assault rates co-varied with crowding, with the percent of the population that was non-white, and with the percent of the population that was aged 15 to 35; and varied inversely with the percent of the school age population that was in school. Property crime rates co-varied with one another, and with the suicide and divorce rates. Crime rates did not intercorrelate strongly with such plausible social and economic variables as police per capita or the unemployment rate.

Eberts and Schwirian (1968) advanced the approach taken by Ogburn and by Schuessler and Slatin in two significant ways. First, they used data for SMSAs rather than for individual cities. They recognized that urban areas and the action fields of

286

TABLE 10–11. Intermetropolitan Crime Factors, 1960

Factor 1 "Minority"

Factor Loading	Variable
+0.80	Crowding (% dwelling units with more than 1.5 persons per room)
+0.76	Murder Rate
+0.71	% Nonwhite population
+0.59	Aggravated-assault rate
+0.51	% Aged 15–25
−0.60	% Enrolled in school, age 16–17
−0.60	Uncrowded (% dwelling units with fewer than 1.5 persons per room)
−0.67	% Enrolled in school, age 5–24

Factor 2 "Anomie"

+0.75	Robbery rate
+0.74	Burglary rate
+0.74	% Divorced
+0.65	Grand larceny rate
+0.59	Petty larceny rate
+0.59	Suicide rate
+0.58	Auto theft rate

Factor 3 "Conformity"

+0.76	% Foreign-born
+0.64	Police per capita
+0.50	% Engaged in manufacturing
−0.53	% married
−0.56	Median schooling, male population aged 15 or older
−0.67	% Owner occupied
−0.86	% Native white

Factor 4 "Economic"

+0.57	Very uncrowded (% dwelling units with fewer than 0.5 persons per room)
−0.53	Average value of single dwelling unit
−0.56	Median schooling
−0.61	% Families, 1 or more under age 6
−0.61	Crowding
−0.62	% Male
−0.67	% Age 15–34
−0.70	% Population increase, 1950–1960

Factor 5 "Family"

+0.89	% Individuals in families
+0.66	% Female population aged 14 years +, not in labor force
+0.65	% Married
+0.16	% Owner occupied

SOURCE: Adapted from K. Schuessler and G. Slatin, "Sources of Variation in U.S. City Crime, 1950 and 1960," *Journal of Research in Crime and Delinquency* 1(1964), pp. 127–148.

urban residents, both law-abiding and criminal, extend beyond city limits. The use of central or core-city data on crime inevitably distorts the crime patterns under analysis. The point had been made thirty years earlier by Lottier (1938b), and it was made more recently by Gibbs and Erickson (1976). The SMSA, as defined by the U.S. Bureau of Census, provides statistical information for an approximation of a city's full urban field: its core city, its satellite towns, its suburbs, and part of its hinterland. SMSA data for crime and for other social, demographic, and economic

287

characteristics of the "city" more closely approximate the urban areas in which people live than do data for individual municipal governmental areas. Second, Eberts and Schwirian began to use intermetropolitian crime analysis to test for the existence of specific patterns of association between crime rates and particular social and economic conditions.

Eberts and Schwirian analyzed the 1961 crime patterns for 200 of the 212 SMSAs identified by the Census Bureau in 1960. Factor analysis of the crime rates for the seven index offenses clustered them into two mathematically independent factors: a violent-personal-attack factor composed of murder and aggravated assault, and a general-crime factor composed of rape, robbery, burglary, theft, and auto theft.[3] On the basis of these results, they used the *Uniform Crime Reports* total crime index (a sum of the rates for all seven crimes) and a violent-personal-attack index (the sum of murder and aggravated-assault rates) as the dependent variables in a study intended to test the hypothesis that cities in which lower-class people were faced with high relative deprivation would have high crime rates.

Relative deprivation refers to the range of deprivations existing in a metropolitan area: the extent to which one segment of the population feels disadvantaged in its socioeconomic position relative to other segments of the population in the same community. Criminal events are not, in this approach, seen as the product of simply Malthusian want or Marxian reaction to absolute economic deprivation. Instead, criminal events are the product of relative deprivations in economic and social status, gaps between the most and least advantaged members of a community, even when none of the members of that community are in absolute want. In this approach, lower-class people are assumed to be short-run hedonists, committed to immediate gratification and concerned with their economic and social situations relative to others only in the immediate present and only in the immediate community, making comparisons with other times and places meaningless. A substantial present and local gap between the socioeconomic situations of rich and poor should raise the relative economic aspirations of the lower classes so that frustrations should be more keenly felt by them. These frustrations should produce reactions in the form of aggressive behavior. The net result is that metropolitan areas with greater structural relative deprivations should have higher crime rates (Eberts and Schwirian, 1968, pp. 45–46; compare, Banfield, 1974; Chester, 1976).

Eberts and Schwirian measured relative deprivation in two ways. First, they constructed an economic deprivation index for each of the 200 SMSAs by calculating the ratio between the number of persons earning more than $10,000 per annum and the number of persons earning less than $3,000. The resulting index scores were divided into three groups: 59 SMSAs with index scores of 1.25 or more were classified as having a relatively large upper class; 40 SMSAs with scores of 0.86–1.24 were classified as having a balanced class structure; and 101 SMSAs with scores of 0.85 or less were classified as having relatively large lower classes. To be consistent with relative deprivation theory, the crime rates of the three classes of metropolitan areas should be highest in the upper-class SMSAs and lowest in the balanced-class SMSAs. Second, relative deprivation was measured in terms of the proportions

---

[3] Note that this two-factor pattern is the same as that obtained by Harries a decade later.

288

TABLE 10–12. Relative Deprivation and Crime Rates, SMSA's, 1961

Economic Class Structure	Crime Rates	Occupation/Race Structure	Crime Rates
Large Upper Class	1,268	High white, low black	1,420
Balanced	895	High white, high black	1,250
Large Lower Class	1,160	Low white, high black	970
		Low white, low black	960

SOURCE: Adapted from P. Eberts and K. P. Schwirian, "Metropolitan Crime Rates and Relative Deprivation," *Criminologica* 5(1968), pp. 43–52.

of white and black white-collar workers in each SMSA relative to the pattern for all SMSAs combined. Using the overall pattern as a cut point for a high–low dichotomy, Eberts and Schwirian identified four categories of metropolitan areas: 62 SMSAs with high proportions of both white and black white-collar workers; 37 SMSAs with relatively low-white, high-black status; 22 with relatively high-white, low-black status; and 45 with relatively low white and black status. To be consistent with relative deprivation theory, the high-white, low-black metropolitan areas should have the highest crime rates, followed by SMSAs with high proportions of both white and black white-collar workers. The other two categories of cities should have lower crime rates because the relative deprivation between high and low status, by race, would be lower. Table 10–12 shows Eberts and Schwirian's general results. The crime rates of the SMSAs were consistent with theoretical expectations and generally remained consistent when statistical controls for population size, for percentage of nonwhite population, and for region were introduced.[4]

Recent Intermetropolitan Studies

A substantial number of metropolitan crime-rate analyses were conducted during the 1970s in attempts by a number of researchers to understand the social, demographic, economic, and environmental correlates of crime. The patterns that emerged from these analyses were fairly stable, and they form the base from which explanations for the geographical patterns of crime must be constructed.

Pressman and Carol (1971) analyzed the crime rates of ninety-five SMSAs for 1965 with respect to the number of police per capita, net immigration, racial composition, family income levels, education levels, unemployment rates, population density (measured as SMSA population divided by SMSA area), and unemployment rates. Police per capita, net immigration rates, and racial composition (nonwhite population/total population) were strongly correlated with nonviolent crimes, and racial composition and police per capita were strongly correlated with violent

---

[4] For the economic-class-structure measure, the model did not hold for small SMSAs, but it did hold for the large SMSAs. For SMSAs with a low percentage of nonwhite population, and for those outside the South, the pattern became linear, with the highest crime rates in the upper-class cities, then in the balanced-class cities, and the lowest crime rates in the lower-class cities. The model held for all control cases for the racial occupational-status measure.

crime rates. Net immigration rates were strongly correlated with burglary and larceny rates, but not with auto theft rates. Racial composition was the most important correlate of both violent and nonviolent crime rates for 1965.

Marlin (1973) analyzed the 1971 crime rates for the thirty largest cities in a study by the Council on Municipal Performance. Robbery and the property crimes had different patterns. Robbery was strongly correlated with racial composition (black population/total population), population density, net emigration of whites from the city between 1960 and 1970, a Gini index of income inequality, the percentages of families earning more than $15,000 and more than $50,000 per year, and police per capita. Nonviolent property crimes were strongly correlated with income inequality, mean family income, and the percentages of families earning more than $15,000 and $50,000 per year. Neither robbery nor the property crimes were significantly correlated with police salary or police expenditure, mean per capita income, the percentage of families with poverty income levels, the net immigration rates of blacks 1960–1970, 1970 unemployment rates, 1970 population, or mean annual temperature. A clear pattern of relative deprivation was visible for property crimes, and a pattern keyed to the development of central cities as impoverished ethnic enclaves was visible in the robbery rate data.

Spector (1975) analyzed the violent crime rates of 103 large SMSAs ranging in size from 104,000 to 11,572,000 population using the 1970 *Uniform Crime Reports* violent-crime index rates (the sum of the murder, rape, robbery, and aggravated-assault rates). Using linear regression techniques, he compared the crime rates with SMSA data for 1970 from the U.S. Census Bureau's *City and County Data Book* for 1972: population per square mile; unemployment rate; the percentage of homes with more than 1.01 persons per room (crowding); total population; and region (Northeast, South, Midwest, and West). He concluded that "there is no significant relationship between population density and violence, or unemployment and violence in the American city. However, there is a strong relationship between city size and violence, and a relationship between area of country and violence" (p. 401). The beta weights of the independent variables in his best regression equation were: total population, $+0.62$; region, $+0.23$; population per square mile, -0.05; crowding, -0.36; and unemployment -0.35.

Flango and Sherbenou (1976) used factor analysis and regression analysis to compare the 1970 crime rates of 840 incorporated cities with 59 social, economic, and demographic variables. They factored the 59 variables into socioeconomic factors that were independent of one another. "Urban affluence" included such variables as the percentage of high-income families, the percentage of the population in professional and managerial occupations, and the percentage of high-value homes and high-rent apartments. "Stage in life cycle" included measures of population age, family age, family size, and family residence. "Economic specialization" measured major employment patterns. "Government expenditure policy" factored data on government expenditure categories and levels. "Urbanization" included data on density, public transit usage, dwelling density, and the proportion of immigrants in the population. "Poverty culture" included the percentage of black population, the percentage of female heads of households, the percentage of low-income families, overcrowded and substandard housing, and employment in service or repair businesses. Flango and Sherbenou used the factor scores for each city as the independent variables in stepwise regression analyses in which the dependent variables were total index-crime rates, robbery rates, aggravated-assault rates, burglary rates, and rates of motor vehicle theft.

The regression modeling produced rather different results for different crimes. The best fit was for robbery, explaining 49 percent of the variance with four variables: urbanization (39 percent of variance explained); stage in life cycle (an additional 5 percent of variance explained); government expenditure (an additional 2 percent); economic specialization (an additional 3 percent). Of the variance in rates of motor vehicle theft, 33 percent was explained by two factors: urbanization (30 percent) and stage in life cycle (3 percent). Of the variance in burglary rates, 27 percent was explained by three factors: urbanization (14 percent); stage in life cycle (9 percent); and poverty culture (4 percent). Urbanization (20 percent) and stage in life cycle (8 percent) together explained 28 percent of the intermetropolitan variation in total index-crime rates. Poverty, stage in life cycle, expenditures policy, and urbanization, taken together, explained a mere 9 percent of the variation in the aggravated-assault rate.

Flango and Sherbenou ran separate analyses for the 153 cities of 100,000 population or larger and for the 687 cities with populations of less than 100,000. The patterns differed for the sets of large and small cities. The factored variables explained substantial amounts of variance for the rates of robbery, aggravated assault, motor vehicle theft, and burglary in the large cities but did less well in explaining the variance across the smaller cities. Poverty culture, urbanization, and affluence explained 24 percent of the large-city aggravated-assault rates, and urbanization and poverty culture explained 45 percent of the large-city robbery rate.

Harries (1976) used canonical correlation analysis to analyze the 1970 crime rates of 726 cities with population of 25,000 or more. Canonical correlation combines the elements of a factor analysis and a regression analysis into a single statistical technique that separately factors a set of criterion variables (e.g., crime rates for several different crimes) and a set of predictor variables (e.g., social, demographic, and economic measures) and then finds the best correlation between a criterion vector and a predictor vector, repeating the process with the next best correlation between the remaining criterion and predictor vectors until the data are exhausted. Harries's criterion variables were total index-crime rates, robbery rates, aggravated-assault rates, burglary rates, and auto theft rates. He had twenty-five predictor variables measuring population and density, population change rates, age, racial and ethnic mix, employment patterns, family structure, income and wealth, housing character and quality, education, government expenditure patterns, and police per capita.

Harries's principal findings are shown in Table 10–13. The first canonical vector had a correlation of +0.82 between the criterion set and the predictor set. The criterion set was a high-crime set led by robbery. The predictor set loaded heavily on the percentage of female household heads, the percentage of black population, police per capita, and density, and negatively on single-family-dwelling patterns. It identified high crime rates with the dense, poor, black-ghetto central cities created by the metropolitan migration patterns of the 1950s and 1960s. The second canonical vector related burglary and the total crime index to a predictor set marked by residential stability, employment in manufacturing, population density,

TABLE 10–13. Intercity Canonical Correlations, 1970

Canonical Vector 1: Robbery and High Crime

Robbery +.97
Total Index +.84
Burglary +.79
Auto Theft +.78
Assault +.63
	+.82	Percentage Female
		   Household Heads
		Percentage Black
		Police per Capita
		Single Family
		   Dwellings
		Density
			+.75
			+.75
			+.68
			
			−.46
			+.44

Canonical Vector 2: Burglary and High Total Crime Index

Burglary +.49
Total Index +.46
	−.56	Percentage in Same Residence
		   Five Years Ago
		Percentage Employed in
		   Manufacturing
		Density
		Median School
		   Years
		Unemployment
			+.67
			
			+.59
			+.51
			
			−.44
			−.35

Canonical Vector 3: Assault

Assault +.62
Auto Theft +.45
	+.51	Percentage Foreign
		   Stock
		Low Income
		Property Tax
		Home Value
		Single-Family
		   Dwellings
			−.76
			+.56
			−.56
			−.49
			
			+.46

SOURCE: Adapted from K. D. Harries, "Cities and Crime: A Geographical Model" *Criminology,* 14(1976), pp. 369–386.

median education levels, and unemployment levels. Because of the direction of the vector, the crime rates varied directly, though relatively weakly, with education and unemployment, and inversely with residential stability, employment in manufacturing, and density. This finding seems to separate industrial heartland cities with low burglary rates from new, growing cities in the Sunbelt with high burglary rates. The third canonical vector tied aggravated-assault rates directly to low-income families and the percentage of single-family dwellings, and inversely to the percentage of foreign stock, property tax levels, and home values. This finding clearly connected high aggravated-assault rates with poor cities.

Worden (1980) analyzed crime rates for 120 SMSAs for 1960 and 1970, using correlation and stepwise regression analysis. Because his dependent-variable sets were substantially different for the two years, his results are not comparable. For 1960, it was possible to explain 37 percent of the variance in property crime rates with three variables: the percentage of population increase between 1950 and 1960, crowding, and SMSA population rank. It was possible to explain 41 percent of the violent crime rate by the percentage of the population that was black, the SMSA population rank, and population increase from 1950 to 1960. For 1970, 36 percent of the property crime rate was explained by the percentage of the population that was Spanish-speaking, by the SMSA population change from 1960 to 1970, and by the percentage of black and Spanish-speaking students in the central-city high schools. It was possible to explain 61 percent of the intermetropolitan variation in the violent crime rate by the percentage of black and Spanish-speaking students in the central-city high schools, by central-city population, and by the percentage of the SMSA population within the central city. In 1970, SMSA murder rates correlated strongly with the percentage of black and Spanish-speaking high-school students in the central-city (+0.72) and with crowded housing (+0.55), and robbery rates correlated strongly with SMSA nonwhite population (+0.76), with unemployment rates (+0.68), with central-city density (+0.59), and with population rank (−0.53).[5]

The Brantinghams (1980) analyzed 1970 crime rates for the SMSAs with 250,000 or more population against a set of employment, occupational, and sociodemographic variables. Prior work by Ogburn (1935), Schuessler and Slatin (1964), Flango and Sherbenou (1976), and Harries (1976) suggested that employment and occupational variables might have a strong effect on crime rates from city to city. Employment patterns indicate the percentage of the metropolitan work force employed in specific industrial and service sectors: manufacturing; government; retail and wholesale trade, finance, insurance, and real estate; entertainment; health; and education. Employment patterns suggest different criminal opportunities created by different mixtures and concentrations of goods and services, and by different daily activity patterns. Occupational patterns suggest the proportions of the work force that hold high-status/high-paying jobs as professional, technical, and managerial workers; medium-status jobs as white-collar or skilled industrial workers; and low-status jobs such as household services or unskilled labor. These patterns measure a range of potential motivations for crime and also suggest something about criminal opportunity. Sociodemographic variables, such as racial mix, migration and urban growth, income levels and unemployment, education, total population, and the percentage of males in the fifteen to thirty-four age range, are known correlates of intermetropolitan crime rates.

In the Brantinghams' 1980 study, murder and assault had similar patterns across the large SMSAs. Stepwise regression explained 84 percent of the variation in murder and 23 percent of the variation in assault rates. The variables that appeared in these regression equations depict the stereotypical urban-slum situation: ethnicity, ignorance, recent immigration, poverty, and employment in menial and low-status occupations. The interaction between a high proportion of black population and low black educational attainment explains almost half of the intermetropolitan murder rate by itself. Murder rates correlated highly with the percentage of black population (+0.67), with poverty (+0.53), and with a high proportion of the work force in household service occupations (+0.69). They correlated inversely with black educational attainment (−0.70). Assault rates correlated relatively highly

---

[5] Worden ranked the largest SMSA 1 and the smallest SMSA 120, so the inverse correlation here actually means that robbery rates rise with city size.

293

with the percentage of black population (+0.35), with the percentage in household service occupations (+0.36), and with black females in the labor force (+0.34). They correlated inversely with blacks in manufacturing employment (−0.34) and black income (−0.33).

Burglary and larceny rates had similar patterns. The rates of these crimes varied with economic specialization. SMSAs that had high levels of employment in entertainment, in finance, insurance and real estate, and in government had high levels for both crimes. Metropolitan areas that specialized in manufacturing had low rates for these crimes in 1970, just as they had in the 1930s, the 1950s, and the 1960s. Residential mobility contributed to high rates of both types of crime. Unemployment contributed to larceny rates, but not to burglary rates. Stepwise regression explained 64 percent of the burglary-rate variation and 58 percent of the larceny-rate variation. Burglary correlations were entertainment employment specialization (+0.56); entertainment, finance, insurance, and real-estate specialization (+0.59); manufacturing specialization (−0.52); percentage of blacks in manufacturing employment (−0.55); and the interaction of migration and poverty (+0.51). Larceny correlations were entertainment specializations (+0.51), unemployment (+0.48), and manufacturing specialization (−0.52).

Rates of robbery and motor vehicle theft were associated with the crudest of opportunity measures: target density. Robbery was the only index offense that fit the popular notion that crime rates rise with city size. By itself, the log of the population explained 42 percent of the intermetropolitan variation in robbery rate. Black unemployment rates explained another 8 percent of the robbery-rate variation. Simple correlations with robbery were the log of the population (+0.64), the percentage of blacks in clerical and sales occupations (+0.41), black unemployment (+0.34), and income (+0.34). Auto theft was correlated with the log of the population (+0.45), with the percentage of people in clerical occupations (+0.36), and with income (+0.31).

Rape rates varied with demographic, employment, and occupational variables. Stepwise regression explained 53 percent of the variation of rape rates across the large SMSAs in 1970. Economic specialization in entertainment, finance, insurance, and real estate accounted for 22 percent of the variation, the percentage of blacks accounted for 8 percent, transportation specialization accounted for 4 percent; and the log of the population and the proportion of males aged fifteen to thirty-four each accounted for 3 percent.

Intercity Victimization Rates

An alternative to the use of police statistics for intermetropolitan crime analysis is the use of victimization survey data. To date, only one set of intercity victimization statistics has been collected. Between 1973 and 1975, the Law Enforcement Assistance Administration conducted victimization surveys in twenty-six large central cities: Boston, Buffalo, Cincinnati, Houston, Miami, Milwaukee, Minneapolis, New Orleans, Oakland, Pittsburgh, San Diego, San Francisco, and Washington (1973); Chicago, Detroit, Los Angeles, New York, and Philadelphia (1974); and Atlanta, Baltimore, Cleveland, Dallas, Denver, Newark, Portland, and St. Louis (1974–1975).

Shichor et al. (1979, 1980) compared the victimization-rate variation across these twenty-six cities for several crime categories with the variation in density and police per capita. They found property crimes with contact (robbery and pocket picking) positively correlated with police per capita and strongly correlated with population density. Property crimes without contact (burglary and larceny), assault, and rape were strongly correlated with both police per capita and population density. This research suggests that the intermetropolitan correlations of crime with variables of opportunity and motivation are consistent, whether crimes known to the police or victimization-survey crime rates are used as the measure of crime.

Chapter Summary

Geographic patterns in crime are apparent at the world, intranational, and intermetropolitan levels of resolution. These patterns persist over relatively long periods of time and are, in some respects, consistent with one another.

At the world level of resolution, clearly different patterns emerge for crimes of violence against the person and for crimes against property. The highest overall crime rates were experienced by the nations of the Caribbean region during the mid-1970s, followed by the nations of Western Europe, North America, and Oceania. The highest levels of violent crimes against the person were experienced in the Caribbean, in North Africa and the Middle East, in sub–Saharan Africa, and in Latin America. Property crimes were highest in Western Europe, North America, and Oceania. Crime patterns appear to be closely associated with economic development and with income inequality: high rates of property crime are associated with high economic development and with low levels of income inequality; and high levels of violent crimes against the person are associated with lack of economic development and with high income inequality. Modernization and urbanization are both associated with higher levels of property crime and lower levels of violent crime.

Regional studies of crime within particular nations have long shown that crime rates vary substantially from one part of a country to another. The English regional crime pattern in 1978 was marked by several clusters tied to major conurbations and industrial cities. When these patterns are compared with English crime regions of a century or more ago, a process of national crime-rate convergence appears to be taking place. Canadian regional crime patterns are marked by a western tilt. The lowest crime rates are in the extreme eastern Maritime Provinces, higher rates are found in central Canada, and the highest rates in the two westernmost provinces, Alberta and British Columbia. The two northern frontier territories, the Yukon and the Northwest Territories, have very high crime rates. Regional crime patterns in the United States are especially striking. There is a southern homicide region that has persisted for at least half a century. There is a Sunbelt region of high general crime and high property crime that stretches from Florida to California. New England has the highest auto theft rates, and the industrial heartland that stretches along the Great Lakes from New York to Illinois forms a region that has high robbery rates, but low rates for most other crimes. All of these patterns, except the southern homicide region, appear to be related to demographic trends and opportunity variables.

Intermetropolitan crime-rate analysis provides a finer-grained resolution of the patterns apparent at the regional level. Cities with similar crime patterns cluster geographically. Different crime patterns are associated with different demographic, economic, and social profiles. Homicide and assault are associated with high proportions of minority population, with poverty and low income, with low-status jobs and low education, and with income inequality. Robbery is highest in large, dense cities that rely on public transit and have high levels of pedestrian traffic. Burglary and theft rates are highest in cities with growing populations, with growing suburbs, and with low density.

11
Crime Within Cities

Introduction

The patterns of crime within cities have been studied for more than a century. The distributions of criminal events, of offenders' residences, of victim and target locations, and of the pathways between them have long formed the basis for police crime-prevention strategy and have served as the information from which most twentieth-century theories of crime and criminality have been constructed. Microlevel crime analysis is the most common study of the geographic patterns in crime and is the best understood by most criminologists. Microlevel analyses of the geographic patterns of crime within cities are subject to some of the most troublesome conceptual and methodological problems in criminology. On balance, however, study of the intraurban patterns in crime is extremely valuable because the patterns are very close to the individual criminal events.

Historical Intraurban Crime Patterns

Spatial variability is one of the key characteristics of crime patterns. Different regions of the world, different regions within particular countries, and different cities have radically different crime rates. The American cone of resolution presented in Chapter 9 made the point clearly, beginning with a national crime map, then moving to successively higher levels of resolution, in presenting the crime map for the counties of Florida, the crime map for the city of Tallahassee based on the crime rates of census tracts, the crime map of one Tallahassee census tract-based on data for one census-block group, and the crime map of one Tallahassee block group based on the crime data for individual city blocks. The patterns visible at different levels of resolution in Chapter 10 also make the point.

The differentiation of crime rates in the neighborhoods of a city is the most easily observed of crime patterns, and characteristic patterns in this differentiation persist over long periods of time. Studies conducted in the nineteenth century—and more recently, using nineteenth-century crime and social data—exhibit three of the major characteristics of intracity crime patterns: the existence of criminal areas; the existence of crime areas; and the connection between both kinds of areas and the social and physical structure of cities.

Criminal areas are areas in which large numbers of criminals reside. They have distinctive social and physical characteristics that set them apart from other neighborhoods by reputation and that support criminal life styles. In the 19th century, they were called "rookeries." Crime areas are places where large proportions of a city's crimes are committed. Crime areas sometimes coincide with criminal areas, but often they do not. Crime areas appear to be tied to specific physical and social environments that are conducive to particular criminal behaviors: robbery areas are keyed to the distributions of pedestrians and shops; burglary areas are keyed to the distributions of homes and shops; and assault areas are keyed to the distributions of taverns and liquor shops.

The Rookeries of London

London and other nineteenth-century English cities were marked by notorious criminal areas, some of which had been in place for centuries. These *rookeries* were slum criminal quarters, known to public and police alike as neighborhoods in which the homes of prostitutes, beggars, thieves, and killers were intermixed with those of the desperate urban poor. They were mazes of squalid hovels and houses carved into warrens of tiny rooms connected by secret doors, tunnels, catwalks, dark passages, and dank lanes. The rookeries sustained criminal social systems that provided schooling in crime for the young or the newcomers, fencing systems to purchase and resell stolen goods, and a protective code of silence in the face of police inquiries. Fagin and Bill Sykes in *Oliver Twist* were based on real characters observed by Dickens on journalistic perambulations with police into the rookeries, and Whitechapel was a real rookery (Chesney, 1972; Tobias, 1972a, 1972b; Mayhew, 1861; Dickens, 1838).

The spatial distribution of London's principal rookeries is shown in Figure 11–1. All of the major criminal areas were located on the perimeter of the historical boundary of the City of London. By the nineteenth-century the boundaries of the imperial metropolis lay far beyond the ancient City limits: the City was just one of a number of municipalities that together formed Greater London. Differences in the quality and character of public administration and the jealous way in which the different municipal constitutents of the metropolis guarded their prerogatives and liberties from encroachment by any of the others go far toward explaining this pattern.

Prior to the organization of the London Metropolitan Police in 1829, policing efforts rarely crossed municipal boundaries. The quality of policing within the City of London, with organized day and night watches, was substantially higher than in the outlying municipalities. A residential area for criminals that lay just beyond the City's jurisdiction was particularly advantageous: a thief could travel into the City to steal, then retreat to the rookery outside the City boundary. City watchmen and constables were unlikely to follow him across the boundary; constables for other municipalities, such as Westminster, were unlikely to execute City warrants or pursue the criminal for crimes committed in the City, and if they did, they were far less efficient than the City officers in any case.

298

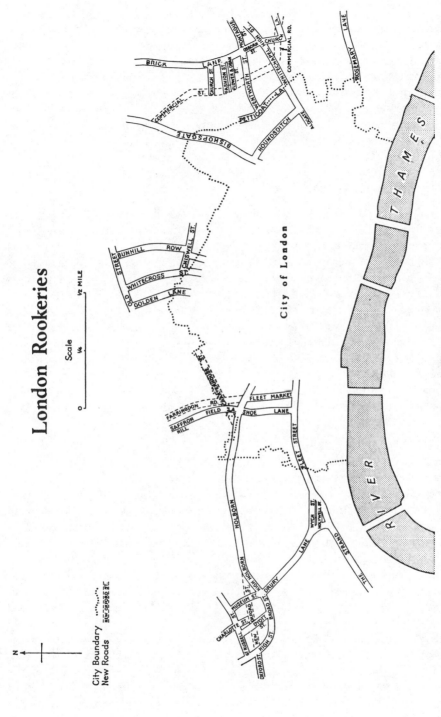

Figure 11-1. London rookeries. [Source: J. J. Tobias, *Crime and Industrial Society in the 19th Century*. London: B. T. Batsford Limited, 1967, p. 133.]

The St. Giles rookery, in the parish of St. Giles-in-the-Fields, was strategically located on the pathways between the City boundary and Oxford Street, one of the major shopping streets of nineteenth century (and modern) London. Mayhew (1861) and his associate, John Binny compared Oxford Street with New York City's fashionable, famous, and expensive Fifth Avenue: both were filled with expensive shops frequented by the wealthy. The St. Giles rookery was connected by Drury Lane to the meeting points of the Strand and Fleet Street. It was notorious as a residential neighborhood for sneak thieves, robbers, burglars, pickpockets, and fences. From its location, criminals could move out into Oxford Street, into the Strand, and into the City. All of these prime target areas were within half a mile, or less. As described by Mayhew and Binny, St. Giles' had been the foremost rookery of London in the 1840's:

> The ground covered by the Rookery was enclosed by Great Russell Street, Charlotte Street, Broad Street, and High Street. . . . Within this space were George Street (once Dyott Street), Carrier Street, Maynard Street, and Church Street, which ran from north to south, and were intersected by Church Lane, Ivy Lane, Buckeridge Street, Bainbridge Street, and New Street. These, with an almost endless intricacy of courts and yards crossing each other, rendered the place like a rabbit warren. . . . The most notorious of these was Jones Court, inhabited by coiners, utterers of base coin, and thieves. . . . The houses in Jones Court were connected by roof, yard, and cellar with those in Bainbridge and Buckeridge Streets, and with each other in such a manner that the apprehension of an inmate or refugee in one of them was almost a task of impossibility to a stranger, and difficult to those well acquainted with the interior of the dwellings. In one of the cellars was a large cess-pool, covered in such a way that a stranger would likely step in it. In the same cellar was a hole about two feet square, leading to the next cellar, and thence by a similar hole into the cellar of a house in Scott's Court, Buckeridge Street. (pp. 299–300)

The Golden Lane rookery in Hoxton, to the north of the City boundary, has a long-documented history as a criminal neighborhood. A witness testifying before the Select Committee on Police in 1817 described the area as one in which nine tenths of the residents earned their livings by "improper practices" as thieves, pickpockets, and prostitutes. Mayhew (1861) described it as one of the principal criminal rookeries of London. Charles Booth described the area as the "leading criminal quarter of London, and indeed of all England" in 1918. Cyril Burt (1925) considered this area one of the worst in London in his survey of juvenile delinquency residences in the 1920s. This area had among the highest delinquency residence rates of any in London in the 1960s, when Wallis and Maliphant (1967) studied the ecology of crime.

The Whitechapel and Spitalfields rookeries on the eastern boundary of the City of London were also enduring criminal areas. In the early part of the nineteenth century, they were particularly frustrating to City law enforcers as the boundary ran down the middle of rookery streets, particularly Petticoat Lane. Criminals taking up residence on the far side of such streets could identify victims in the City, dash across the street to steal a purse or wallet, and then dash back to safety beyond the jurisdiction of City officers. During the course of the nineteenth century, the Whitechapel rookery grew because of the immigration of criminals from other parts of the metropolis as urban renewal schemes and the construction of new roads to ease traffic congestion pulled other rookeries down. The destruction of a rookery was often cited as an important side benefit of road construction. Whitechapel remained a criminal area in the 1890s when Booth (1891) characterized its worst streets as areas of "vice and crime as depraved as any in London." The Whitechapel area had the second highest delinquency rate in London in 1961, second only to the Golden Lane area (Wallis and Maliphant, 1967, p. 255).

London also had rookeries south of the Thames, and rookeries were not exclusive to the metropolis. Other large English cities had their own rookeries. Liverpool, Bristol, and Bath had criminal areas populated by professional criminals, including juveniles, who earned their livings exclusively through crime. Industrial cities such as Manchester, Birmingham, and Leeds had professional criminals and also had large populations of juveniles who worked at honest jobs, but moonlighted in crime. Manchester had the Angel Meadow rookery, behind the Victoria railway station. It was there in 1826, before the building of the railroad; it was there in 1849; and it was there, still a notorious criminal area, in 1897 (Tobias, 1972b, p. 142).

Criminal Areas and Crime Areas in Nineteenth-Century American Cities

Established crime areas and criminal areas were not, of course, unique to England. Both sorts of areas have been traced in Paris in the eighteenth and nineteenth centuries (Petrovich, 1971; Chevalier, 1958). Crime areas and criminal areas also existed in the nineteenth-century American cities. New York and Philadelphia have both been the subjects of recent research.

The Criminal Patterns of New York City

Inciardi (1978) traced the spatial patterning of crime and criminal areas in New York City in the eighteenth and nineteenth centuries. Neither the criminal areas nor the crime areas were as stable over time as the rookeries and target areas of London. The Battery, at the southern tip of Manhattan, became the first major vice area of the city, an established place of assignation between prostitutes and their customers as early as 1730. By 1774, the area between the Battery and St. Paul's Church was a popularly labeled vice area known as the "Holy Ground" and reputed to have five hundred prostitutes resident. A separate tent city was erected near the site of present-day Washington Square by gamblers and prostitutes to service occupying British troops in late 1776. The pattern of vice areas and criminal areas changed substantially after independence.

Between the end of the Revolutionary War and the onset of the Civil War in 1861, the criminal areas of New York formed around slums that grew through successive waves of immigration: Five Points, near the present-day courthouses and city hall; the Lower East Side; Hell's Kitchen and the Upper West Side; and the Bowery. The areas, predominantly Irish, developed concentrations of illegal saloons, which became the operating headquarters of organized criminal gangs with such names as the Dead Rabbits, the Plug Uglies, the American Guards, the Bowery Boys, the Hudson Dusters, and the Gophers. They specialized in strong-arm robbery, in theft, and in street warfare against other gangs. The Fourth Ward, south of Five Points, once a prosperous residential area, became the residential and operational base for theft from the city's piers and, eventually, piracy. Some of these areas—Hell's Kitchen, the Bowery, and the Lower East Side—remained criminal slums well into the twentieth century. Halpern et al. (1934) mapped arrest and conviction patterns in Manhattan in 1930. They found enormously high crime rates in the Bowery, on the Lower East Side, and in Hell's Kitchen.

After the Civil War, a new criminal area, the Tenderloin, stretching from Fifth to Ninth Avenues and from Madison Square to Forty-eighth Street, developed under corrupt political protection. The Tenderloin was a pleasure district of restaurants and saloons, gambling halls and plush bordellos catering to the wealthy and the would-be wealthy. Gang organization in the older criminal areas became stronger: the Whyos from the old Five Points area dominated New York crime for forty years. Criminal organizations also developed in minority ethnic neighborhoods—in Little Italy, tongs in Chinatown, and Jewish gangs on the Lower East Side—as subsequent immigration waves led to ethnic succession in the worst slums. Migration of southern blacks following the Civil War and particularly between 1900 and 1920 created black ethnic neighborhoods with high crime rates and high criminal residence rates. By 1930, sections of black Harlem were second in criminal arrests and convictions only to the Lower East Side (Halpern et al., 1934).

The Crime Patterns of Philadelphia

The geographic patterns of crime in Philadelphia between 1840 and 1870 have recently been researched and analyzed by Johnson (1979) as part of a larger study on how the patterns of crime affected the development of policing in that city. The patterns of violent crime and property crime were distinctively different. Violent crime areas remained spatially stable over three decades, whereas property crime patterns changed. The locations of both kinds of criminal events in 1850 and 1870 are shown in Figures 9–2 and 11–2.

The city of Philadelphia experienced substantial growth and physical and social change between 1840 and 1870. At the beginning of the period, Phildelphia was a physically small city, bounded by the Schuylkill and Delaware rivers, Vine Street to the north, and South Street to the south. The form of the city was comparable to that found in many modern Third World cities and in preindustrial London (see, e.g., De Fleur, 1967): residences of all classes, shops, and, to a lesser extent, manufacturing establishments tended to be intermixed within the city limits. There was no established shopping and commercial core, no central business district. Wealthy citizens lived in the city center. A small industrial sector, surrounded by working-class homes and immigrant slums, was developing on the southern edge of the city and in the suburbs outside the city's southern boundary.

The three decades after 1840 saw the social and physical structure of the city turned inside out and the development of a central business–commercial district. The development of better roads and the development of the omnibus, which together made commuting to work from a distance practicable, made it possible for the wealthy and the middle class to flee the crowding and noise of the central city for the good life in the northwestern suburbs. Demographic and economic growth led merchants to expand into the downtown areas vacated by suburban emigrants.

302

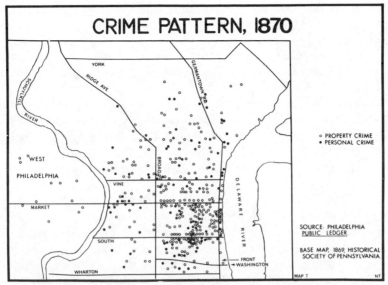

Figure 11–2. Crime areas of Philadelphia, 1870. [Source: D. R. Johnson, *Policing the Urban Underworld: The Impact of Crime on the Development of the American Police, 1800–1887*. Philadelphia: Temple University Press, 1979, p. 76.]

The industrial–immigrant slum area of South Philadelphia grew slowly and, as suburban growth continued, came to be incorporated into the core city proper. A separate, specialized shopping area selling cheap goods to the poor developed along South Street. By 1870, the city had developed its modern pattern, with a central commercial core, sectors of wealthy and middle-class residences to the northwest, and industrial and poor residential sectors to the south.

The property crime patterns of Philadelphia changed substantially between 1840 and 1870, following changes in the residential and business location patterns of the city. Johnson (1979) maintained that most nineteenth-century property crime was a product of the chance intersection of opportunity and inclination. He reported the theft of a sack of gold coins worth $5,000 from the offices Jay Cooke and Co. at Third and Chestnut as typical of such crime. The thief was present in the Cooke offices on minor business. A clerk dropped a sack of gold coins on the floor, and as the Cooke staff were all engaged in retrieving the spilled coins, the thief noticed a second sack of gold in the back room, casually walked into the back room, and departed with the coins (p. 68). Property crime locations moved with business and residential locations. In 1850, most property crimes (66 percent) occurred within the central city grid formed by Broad and Front streets running north–south, and by Vine and South Streets running east–west. By 1870, only 39 percent of known property crimes occurred in the central city grid, whereas 61 percent of property crimes occurred in the suburban areas. In 1870, the different kinds of property crimes were spatially diverse: the property crimes committed in the suburbs were residential burglary, residential theft, and the occasional robbery; the property crimes committed in the center city were business burglary, business theft, business robbery, and personal robberies on side streets.

Philadelphia's violent-crime pattern exhibited far more spatial stability. In 1850, 25 percent of violent crimes occurred within the central city grid, and another 45 percent occurred in the immigrant and industrial areas south of the city. In 1870, 26 percent of violent crimes occurred within the central city area, and another 27 percent occurred in the poor and slum neighborhoods of South Philadelphia. Much of the violent crime in both years could be related to the behavior of the juvenile gangs that were resident in South Philadelphia and that caused trouble there and in the central business areas of the city. Of the 78 gangs identified between 1840 and 1870, 33 (or 42 percent) were located in the South Philadelphia area, and another 20 (26 percent) were located in the central core area. Moreover, 79 percent of the gangs in South Philadelphia were classified by Johnson as violent-crime or combat gangs, whereas only 64 percent of the gangs in the other suburbs were so classified. The gangs tended to roam freely through their own sections of the city rather than defending particular "turf," but except for occasional forays into the central business core, they tended not to travel into distant parts of the city. Many of the gangs apparently evolved into volunteer fire companies, organizations whose epic battles with one another over the privilege of extinguishing fires plagued many American cities during the first half of the nineteenth century (Johnson, 1979, pp. 84–88; Lane, 1971, pp. 22, 33).

Intracity Crime Patterns in the Nineteenth Century

The spatial patterns of crime within nineteenth-century English and American cities are quite clear. First, all cities developed criminal areas, neighborhoods in which large numbers of the residents were involved in criminal activity of one sort or another. These criminal areas developed in particular locations out of two different dynamics: the broader patterns of economic and social stratification reflected in the housing market, which dictated where the poor and dangerous classes could afford to live; and the distribution of criminal opportunities produced by the economic and residential patterns of the city. Once established, criminal areas tended to persist: the criminal areas of London identified in 1817 could still be identified as criminal areas in 1960; the criminal areas of New York City identified in the 1830s and 1840s could still be identified as criminal areas in 1930. Second, the crime areas of nineteenth-century cities, areas in which substantial numbers of crimes occurred, had two different patterns. Property crime areas were strongly associated with the distribution of criminal opportunities. When the physical and socioeconomic patterns of the city changed, particularly through the development of modern transit and the consequent growth of middle- and upper-class residential suburbs, the patterns of property crime also changed. High rates of residential property crimes moved to the suburbs, along with the populace. Violent crime patterns were far more stable. Slums did not move, they merely grew. Violent crime was tied to the slum population. Areas with high violent-crime rates remained spatially fixed in the nineteenth-century cities.

The spatial patterns of crime eluded nineteenth-century observers. The police tended to fix on the operational utility of crime location information or of the location of criminal hangouts; such information was useful in finding specific people

304

to arrest. This attitude prevailed among many criminologists as well. As recently as 1958, Wolfgang argued that the spatial patterns of homicide in Philadelphia had tactical utility for that city's police force but were not of importance to a more general scientific understanding of crime. Journalists tended to become lost in accounts of the sleazy, or the wicked, or the desperate conditions in which the poor and the criminal lived in the worst sections of the large nineteenth-century cities. Journalistic accounts tended to become editorials, smugly denouncing the moral degeneracy of the "dangerous classes," on one hand, or thundering about the evils created by economic and social exploitation on the other. Journalists had little time for analysis. Nineteenth-century criminologists focused on the problem of individual criminal motivation. The Italian positivists, and most American and British criminologists, placed primary emphasis on defective genetics. For them, criminality was biologically determined: economic, social, and spatial conditions merely triggered or amplified inherent traits. French sociologists and their associates, in contrast, placed emphasis on individual social circumstance, particularly social learning, as the explanation of individual criminality: patterns in crime made sense only as individual life histories. (See, generally, Mannheim, 1972; Fink, 1938.)

The analysis of the spatial patterns of crime within the city did not become important to criminologists until the second quarter of the twentieth century. The criminologists associated with the Chicago School of Sociology used a detailed theoretical scheme, social ecology, for the analysis of spatial patterns in the social structures and events of cities. Their research findings and the explanations they offered for these findings form the dominant current in mainstream twentieth-century criminology.

The Social Ecology of Crime:
The Chicago Model

The department of sociology at the University of Chicago was the first such department at any American university, having been created at the same time that the university itself was founded (1892). The research procedures and theoretical models created by Chicago scholars formed a coherent approach or school that dominated the field—and the sociological approach to criminology—for more than half a century. For criminologists, the most important component of the Chicago School is the study of human ecology.

McKenzie (1925) defined *human ecology* as the study of the spatial and temporal relations of human beings as affected by the selective, distributive, and accommodative forces of the environment. Human ecology was concerned with the effect of position in physical and social space and in time on human institutions and human behavior. Spatial relations were seen as critical and were assumed to be the product of competition between individuals and groups for advantageous position. The growing city was seen as a crucible of social and economic competition, and an ideal site for the study of human ecology.

Burgess (1925a) applied some of the general assumptions of human ecology to the problem of urban form under conditions of rapid growth. He assumed that the form of a city would be shaped by competition for desirable position, largely in terms of land rent and transport accessibility. He defined three dynamics: expansion, metabolism, and mobility.

Expansion is the impact of population growth on the physical and social forms of the city. In the simplest terms, a city is assumed to take the form of a set of concentric rings of land use: a commercial and industrial core; a ring of transition from residential to commercial uses; a ring of working-class homes; a ring of middle-class homes; and an unbounded outer zone of suburbs and wealthy commuter's homes. In this view, urban growth causes an expansion of the commercial and industrial core further into the transitional ring; residents of the transitional ring are forced outward into the working-class residential ring; and so forth. The fundamental model was discussed in Chapter 9.

The process of expansion implies that urban immigrants and those displaced by the outward push of the commercial city center will invade parts of the city in which people of their social class, their culture, or their race have not previously lived. The result of the invasion will be competition or conflict with established groups for the use of the area. Similar invasion and struggle can be seen in the expansion of land uses rather than in the movement of people. Invasions of either kind can be touched off by many aspects of growth and change: immigration; changes in the forms or routes of transportation; the deterioration or obsolescence of buildings; the erection of new buildings, bridges, or institutions that have attractive or repellent characteristics; the introduction of new industry or changes in organization of existing industry; changes in the economic base, causing a redistribution of income that necessitates a change in residence; real-estate development; and so on (McKenzie, 1925, p. 75). Conflicts touched off by invasion are resolved by the withdrawal of the invader, by accommodation between established and invading residents and uses, or by the departure of the established and the succession of the invading people and uses to the area.[1] The resolution of this conflict is often effected by means of the mechanisms that Burgess referred to as "metabolism."

Metabolism was Burgess's analogy for the processes by which competing people, cultures, economic skills, and land uses are sifted by the economic and social forces of the city and allocated positions in social and physical space. The process of urban metabolism puts the individual immigrant through successive states of social organization, followed by social disorganization, followed by reorganization and adjustment to the city. Immigrants come with cultural traditions and economic skills that are socially organized and functional in the society that they have left. The traditions and skills may not be well suited to the behavior patterns and economic skills needed in order to prosper in the new city. Immigrants go through a period during which they must abandon the old ways and skills and learn new attitudes, new skills, and new behavior patterns. This period—when the old ways no longer guide behavior, and before the new ways have been fully learned—is the period of social disorganization. When the individual has adjusted and has learned the new attitudes, new skills, new behaviors, she or he is said to be reorganized.

---

[1] This model of invasion, competition, dominance, and withdrawal or succession is borrowed directly from field botany, particularly the ecology of plant communities. (See McKenzie, 1925, p. 74; Park and Burgess, 1970, pp. 185–235.

The process may run smoothly and quickly for some, it may run roughly or slowly for others, or it may not happen at all. The metabolism of the city assigns people in different states of social organization or disorganization to different areas of the city.

The processes of expansion and metabolism, in concert with the physical characteristics of the city, differentiate and segment the city into many different natural areas. They sift and sort and relocate individuals and groups by residence and occupation. Natural areas with characteristic social, economic, cultural, racial, and behavioral features develop and endure for relatively long periods of time: the commercial and industrial core; plush residential areas for the wealthy; ethnic communities such as Chinatown, Little Italy, or the Black Belt; slums; tidy communities of working-class and middle-class homes; criminal areas; artists' colonies; satellite shopping and business districts; and industrial areas centered on transport paths such as railways and rivers. For Burgess (1925a):

> This differentiation into natural economic and cultural groupings gives form and character to the city. For segregation offers the group, and thereby the individuals who compose the group, a place and a role in the total organization of the city life. Segregation limits development in certain directions, but releases it in others. The areas tend to accentuate certain traits, to attract and develop their kind of individuals, and so to become further differentiated. (p. 56)

Mobility is movement attached to change, to growth, to new experience. The city is controlled by its daily activity patterns: simple movement to work, to school, to the shops. Change is keyed to increasing levels of mobility. Burgess measured mobility by transit volume, by telephone traffic, and by land values. Points of high mobility are also points of high land value. Mobility nodes become social, economic, and cultural nodes. Mobility paths shape the direction and content of urban growth, affect the character of natural areas. Burgess argued (1925a) that

> "areas of mobility are also the regions in which are found juvenile delinquency, boys' gangs, crime, poverty, wife desertion, divorce, abandoned infants, vice. . . . Where mobility is the greatest, and where in consequence primary controls break down completely, as in the zone of deteriorization in the modern city, there develop areas of demoralization, of promiscuity, and of vice. (p. 59)

The Chicago Model Applied to Crime: Shaw and McKay

Though the Chicago model of social ecology was used by a number of students and researchers in an attempt to describe and explain social problems in the modern city (e.g., Reckless, 1933, on vice patterns; Faris and Dunham, 1939, on mental illness), the most important work on the spatial patterning of crime within American cities was done outside the university, at the Illinois Institute for Juvenile Research, by Clifford Shaw and his associate, Henry McKay. In a series of massive studies published between 1929 and 1969, they used the Chicago model as a guide to the mapping and analysis of delinquent neighborhoods in Chicago and many other American cities, including Boston, Philadelphia, Baltimore, Richmond, Birmingham, Little Rock, Minneapolis and St. Paul, Omaha, Denver, Cleveland, Cincinnati, and Seattle. Their findings, and the explanations they advanced for the patterns they found, form the basis, one way or another, for nearly all subsequent American work on the sociology of crime (Gibbons, 1979; p. 45; Finestone, 1976).

Shaw began with the assumption that natural areas of crime should be visible in growing American cities, that these natural areas of crime should be spatially patterned in predictable fashion and in predictable relation to the spatial patterns of the physical and social structures of the city, and that these patterns should be explicable in terms of the social ecology of the city. He took Burgess's ideal model of urban form (the zonal model, see Chapter 9) as the basic organizational framework.

In the initial study of Chicago (1929), he and his associates and assistants gathered data on the home addresses of juvenile delinquents for several different time periods, using several different measures of delinquency: boys brought before the juvenile court in the years 1900–1906 and 1917–1923, and before the Boys' Court of Chicago on felony charges in 1924–1926; girls brought before the juvenile court in 1917–1923; truants brought before the juvenile court between 1917 and 1927; alleged delinquents dealt with by police probation officers in 1926 and 1927; and adult offenders placed in the county jail in 1920. These data, together with census data and some city land-use and social data became the basis for Shaw's analysis of criminal areas in Chicago.

The delinquency residency data were spot-mapped onto Chicago base maps, one spot placed at the home address location of each delinquent or criminal in a particular data base.[2] The maps were superimposed on census-tract and square-mile-area maps, and area delinquency rates were calculated for each census tract and each square-mile area. The square-mile areas were aggregations of census tracts, used because some census tracts had very low populations. The square-mile areas (106 constructed out of the 1910 census tracts, 113 constructed out of the 1920 census tracts) became the spatial basis for all subsequent analyses.

The zonal model of the city suggested several things to Shaw and his associates. First, delinquency residence rates should be highest in the center of the city and should decline with radial distance outward from the center. This assumption follows from the argument about the distribution of land uses and social classes in the city according to the zonal model. Second, when the areas of a city are clustered into broad zones, these areas should have similar rates of delinquency residence. Third, areas with anomalous rates in any zone should be identifiable as natural areas that, because of peculiar geography or powerful established cultural institutions, are able to resist pressures toward conformity with the zonal pattern. Fourth, the criminal residence rates of particular areas should change over time, as the processes of expansion and metabolism modify the social and physical structure of the city.

All four expectations were confirmed by the data. The delinquency rates, truancy rates, and adult crime rates varied directly with proximity to the city center: square-mile areas near the Loop (Chicago's central business district) had the

---

[2] Shaw and his associates called each data base (i.e., each separate set of data about a particular group in a particular time period—say, boys brought before the juvenile court in 1917–1923) a "series."

highest rates; areas on the periphery of the city had the lowest rates; areal rates declined in relatively smooth gradient curves with distance from the Loop. The declining gradient was apparent in rate maps, in radial maps, and in zonal maps. The patterns were very similar for all series: the areal intercorrelation between the 1900–1906 data and the 1924–1926 data was +0.85; the areal correlation between the 1920 adult jail data and the 1917–1923 juvenile court data was +0.89. Recidivism-rate data also followed the declining-gradient pattern: rates of recidivism declined with increasing distance from Chicago's central business district.

The zonal pattern was not quite as tidy as the distance decay pattern, but it still conformed to expectations. When the square-mile areas were aggregated into radial zones a mile wide, it became apparent that there were three separate sectors, sweeping north, west, and south, that were different from one another but that had internally consistent patterns. Some anomalous areas, with low rates in high-rate zones or high rates in low-rate zones, became the subjects of field research. Finally, in comparing the location of high-rate areas for 1900–1906 and for 1917–1923, Shaw and his associates detected the expected outward migration of high-rate areas against the backdrop of a general decline in overall delinquency rates.

The variation of crime and delinquency residence rates across the square-mile areas of Chicago could not be attributed to differential neighborhood definitions of "delinquent" or "criminal" conduct, nor could the differences be attributed to differential levels of policing. Many high-rate areas—especially those near the Loop, the stock yards, and the steel mills of South Chicago—were high-rate areas across all the data in all years, despite high turnover in their ethnic composition. High delinquency and criminal residence rates occurred in areas characterized by physical deterioration and declining populations. Shaw and his associates were not, however, prepared to accept the idea that residence near criminal opportunities or in deteriorated, overcrowded housing could be directly linked with criminal behavior. The findings merely pointed toward an underlying social process.

Shaw's (1929) interpretation of the findings drew directly on the metabolism component of social ecology:

> In short, with the process of growth of the city the invasion of residential communities by business and industry causes a disintegration of the community as a unit of social control. This disorganization is intensified by the influx of foreign national and racial groups whose old cultural and social controls break down in the new cultural and racial situation of the city. In this state of social disorganization, community resistance is low. Delinquent and criminal patterns arise and are transmitted socially just as any other cultural or social pattern is transmitted. In time these delinquent patterns may become dominant and shape the attitudes and behavior of persons living in the area. Thus the section becomes an area of delinquency. (pp. 205–206)

The findings and theoretical explanations of the 1929 study were extended by Shaw and McKay (1931) for the National Commission on Law Observance and Enforcement. They conducted spatial analyses of the delinquent areas of Philadelphia, Richmond, Cleveland, Birmingham, Denver, and Seattle. The distance-decay gradient found in the Chicago delinquency residence data held for five of the six cities. The general geographic distribution of delinquent areas, however, was clearly established: "the greatest concentration of cases occurs in districts in or adjacent to the central business center and the major industrial developments. In the outlying neighborhoods, which are further removed from these commercial and industrial centers, the cases are fewer and much more widely dispersed" (p. 187).

Shaw and McKay (1931) also looked more closely at the characteristics of delinquent areas in Chicago. Areas with high rates of resident delinquents and criminals were included in or adjacent to areas zoned for industrial or commercial uses; had high concentrations of old, delapidated, and dangerous buildings; had declining populations; had high population densities; had low average rents and low average family incomes; had high proportions of families receiving welfare payments from various charities and under various governmental programs; and had high proprotions of foreign-born and/or black populations. Shaw and McKay were careful to point out that high-rate areas had remained high-rate areas over a series of immigration waves in which several different ethnic groups had succeeded one another as the predominant population in the neighborhood.

The main body of Shaw and McKay's work, a synthesis of prior studies with spatial analyses of additional cities conducted by themselves and by a number of University of Chicago students and other researchers and with much-expanded analyses of more recent delinquency, crime, and social data for Chicago, was published as *Juvenile Delinquency and Urban Areas* in 1942. In addition to confirming the delinquency gradient for such cities as Boston, Cincinnati, and Minneapolis—St. Paul, this work found a number of additional areal correlations between delinquency and criminal residence rates and various social indicators. Positive correlations with delinquency residence rates included the percentage of families on relief in 1934; the percentage of domestic and service workers in 1930; the percentage of black and foreign-born people; the rates of private character-building institutions; the infant mortality rate; the tuberculosis rate; and the mental disorder rate. Inverse correlations with delinquency residence rates included the population increase from 1920 to 1930; the median rental in 1930 and 1934; and the percentage of families owning their own homes in 1930.

The clustering of square-mile areas with similar delinquency residence rates, based on older boys who appeared in the Boys' Court of Chicago on felony charges in 1938, is shown in Figure 11–3. The radial distance-decay pattern is evident. Overall, delinquency rates are highest in the areas immediately surrounding the central business district. Rates generally decline as proximity from the central business district increases in all directions.

The zonal model of the city predicts that the *actual* form of a city, and the distribution of neighborhoods with different characteristics, will involve complex variations of detail set against the general zonal backcloth. This is clearly the case in Figure 11–3. Two obvious variants on the zonal distribution of delinquent neighborhoods sweep north and south of the central business district. To the north is a sector of neighborhoods with low delinquency rates. It corresponds with Chicago's Gold Coast, a sector of expensive high rise apartments and townhouses. To the south lies a sector of high delinquency neighborhoods extending for miles. It corresponds with the poor neighborhoods of Chicago's black belt and some adjoining ethnic areas.

The final version of the Shaw and McKay research, prepared by McKay for the 1969 revision of *Juvenile Delinquency and Urban Areas,* contained additional

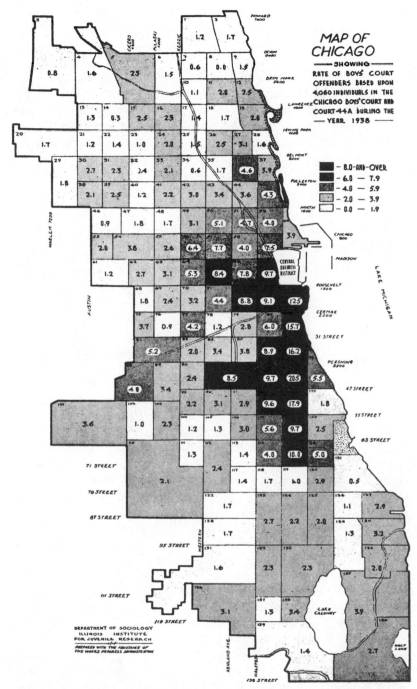

Figure 11-3. Rates of Boys' Court offenders, Chicago, 1938. [Source: Reprinted by special permission from C. R. Shaw and H. D. McKay, *Juvenile Delinquency and Urban Areas* (rev. ed.). Copyright 1969 The University of Chicago Press.]

311

chapters tracing the spatial patterns of delinquency residence in Chicago intermittently from 1934 through 1966. The patterns of delinquency remained relatively constant across this thirty-two-year period. The high-rate sector south of the Loop was as apparent in 1965 as it had been in the 1930s. Changes in Chicago's growth pattern, the development of immigrant-receiving neighborhoods throughout the city, and the growth of suburban cities, however, reduced the stark zonal patterning of the earlier period. McKay presented no zonal analyses, relying instead on neighborhood area-rate maps. The delinquency residence rates in the suburban cities of Cook County were spatially scattered. The analysis presented by McKay in 1969 is much more consistent with Harris and Ullman's (1945) multiple-nuclei model of the city, or the complicated mosaic model of factorial ecologists such as Timms (1971).

Erosion of the Zonal Model of Criminal Area Distribution

The spatial distribution of criminal areas according to the predictions of Burgess's zonal model, together with the social-psychological explanations for this distribution advanced by Shaw and McKay, formed one of the accepted wisdoms of criminology from the early 1930s until the late 1950s. Criminologists apparently ceased to read the literature on urban form. Burgess's zonal model was supplemented by Hoyt's (1939) sector model of residential differentiation and Harris and Ullman's (1945) multiple nuclei of metropolitan form in the late 1930s and early 1940s (see Chapter 9). As it became clear to urban planners and geographers that the zonal model predicted only some urban patterns, and then only when the data had been forced to high levels of aggregation, criminologists continued to arrange their data in zonal patterns. Even Shaw and McKay had been forced to abandon the zonal model and move to much smaller spatial units in formulating delinquency prevention programs. Yet, the zonal pattern is striking, and it dominated criminological thinking about the spatial patterning of crime. The use of large areal aggregates obscured many of the most interesting of intraurban patterns in crime and criminality.

Shaw and McKay followed the tradition of nineteenth-century researchers such as Guerry, Quetelet, or Mayhew in trying to use spatially aggregated data to explain individual motivation to engage in criminal behavior. The data used in their studies told us that square-mile areas with certain gross characteristics, such as a high proportion of dilapidated housing and a high proportion of foreign-born immigrants were likely to have a high number of delinquents resident. This finding was interpreted to mean that individuals subjected to these conditions (i.e., foreign immigrants living in dilapidated housing) were subjected to social pressures that made them delinquent.[3] In a parallel line of analysis, the fact that delinquency rates remained high in some areas while the ethnic composition of these areas changed was accepted as proof that criminality is not an ethnic or racial trait but is learned.

---

[3] To be fair, Shaw and McKay did not fall so deeply into the traps of the ecological fallacy as their detractors often claim, and as many of their followers have. They buttressed their ecological conclusions with extensive numbers of case studies with individuals.

Although the first conclusion might seem common sense, and the second conclusion might be one we all applaud, neither can be demonstrated with areal data. The imputation of areal correlates to individuals is known as the *ecological fallacy.* Any number of patterns among the individuals within the area might produce the areal correlations. Delinquency rates might be high in areas with high rates of foreign immigrants and high rates of dilapidated housing because (1) foreign immigrants living in dilapidated housing steal; (2) natives living in sound housing prey on the foreign immigrants living in dilapidated housing; (3) natives living in dilapidated housing prey on foreigners living in sound housing; or (4) foreigners living in sound housing prey on natives living in dilapidated housing. The aggregate pattern would be the same in all cases, and there is no way to estimate, from the aggregate data alone, which is the true underlying pattern. This point has been made repeatedly, and trenchantly. It is often given lip service, then ignored in the process of ecological analysis. (See, Jonassen, 1949; Robinson, 1950.)

The final analytic problem with the Shaw and McKay studies and with many other ecological studies is the confusion between criminal areas and crime areas. Most of these studies assume that they are functionally identical, that knowing where delinquents live also tells us where those delinquents commit their crimes. Such an assumption is both theoretically and empirically erroneous. Burgess's theory predicted that areas of high mobility would be areas of high crime and that crime site and residence need not be spatially coincident. Criminals and delinquents might well use public transit to commute from the home to the crime site. Shaw and Moore's classic case study, *The Natural History of a Delinquent Career* (1931) made clear that the delinquent under study had traveled into the Loop, away from home, to commit the bulk of his early crimes. Lind's (1930) study of delinquency in Honolulu utilized Burgess's (1925b) concept of the mobility triangle to analyze the movement patterns from home to crime site. More recent studies have consistently shown that crime site and criminal residence are often different, and that analyses and conclusions based on the assumption that they are spatially identical can be badly misleading.

The analytic problems were of sufficient magnitude to cause many scholars to sneer at intraurban crime-pattern analysis. Lady Barbara Wootton (1959) was savage, but representative, when she observed that "even the most unprejudiced sociological eyebrows will hardly be raised at the discovery that delinquency tends to be concentrated in particular areas, and that in general those are the slummy ones" (p. 65).

Baltimore and Croydon: Two Key Studies. Erosion of the classical Chicago approach to intraurban crime analysis was hastened by two studies published in the 1950s. Lander (1954) analyzed the spatial patterns of delinquency residence in Baltimore. Morris (1958) studied the spatial patterns of crime and criminal residence in Croydon, a suburban city of 250,000 on the southeastern edge of Metropolitan London. Neither study found strong support for the Chicago tradition.

Baltimore, 1940. Lander (1954) analyzed the delinquency patterns within the city of Baltimore, Maryland, using data from the juvenile court, from the United States census, and from city agencies for the year 1940 (Figure 11–4). His spatial units were census tracts, 155 small areas of about 5,200 population each. In addi-

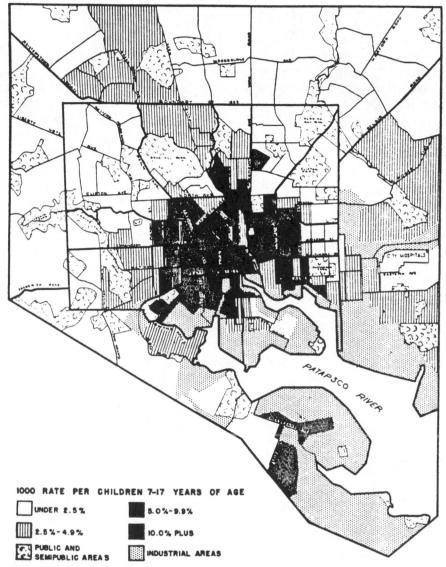

1000 RATE PER CHILDREN 7-17 YEARS OF AGE

☐ UNDER 2.5 %   ■ 5.0 %-9.9%

▥ 2.5 %-4.9 %   ■ 10.0% PLUS

▨ PUBLIC AND
  SEMIPUBLIC AREAS   ▦ INDUSTRIAL AREAS

Figure 11-4. Delinquency residence, Baltimore, 1939–1942. [Source: B. Lander, *Towards an Understanding of Juvenile Delinquency*. New York: Columbia University Press, 1954.]

tion to the delinquency residence rate of each tract, Lander looked at land use patterns and at five socioeconomic variables collected by the census: (1) the median years of school completed by all persons aged twenty-five years over for each census tract; (2) the median monthly residential rent for each census tract; (3) the percentage of persons living in dwellings with more than 1.5 persons per room in each census tract; (4) the percentage of substandard housing in each census tract; and (5) the percentage of nonwhite and the percentage foreign-born population in each census tract. His analyses included mapping, linear and curvilinear correlation anal-

314

ysis, and factor analysis. His findings suggested that the Chicago model of the relationship between delinquency residence and urban form was an oversimplification.

The zonal model and the distance gradient received qualified support from Lander (1954): "An examination of the distribution of delinquency rates by census tracts shows that the zonal hypothesis oversimplifies the actual pattern of delinquency distribution. Each zone includes high and low delinquency rate areas" (p. 86). When census tracts were clustered into concentric zones one mile wide, the central zone had the highest delinquency rates (10.2 per 100 resident juveniles), Zone 2 had the next highest rates (6.1), Zone 3 the next highest rate (2.7), and four succeeding zones had similar low rates (ranged between 2.1 and 1.5). The gradient was steep, but not smooth. The zonal pattern was a product of aggregation effects that masked wide variation in delinquency rates among the census tracts within each zone. The range of delinquency rates in the census tracts of Zone 1, for instance, was from a high of 20.1 delinquents per 100 juveniles resident to a low of 1.1 delinquents per 100 juveniles.

Lander found that his socioeconomic variables could explain almost four fifths of the variance in delinquency rates across the 155 census tracts ($R^2 = 0.79$) of Baltimore. He found that Baltimore's land-use patterns were not consistent with the Chicago model, since much industry was located on the outskirts of the city. Heavy industrial land-use was not a powerful predictor of high delinquency rates, but heavy commercial zoning in a census tract was. There was no single zone in transition from residential to commercial or industrial use; instead, there were many zones in transition in many different parts of the city. Baltimore was not structured around a single, dominant central business district and a few satellite shopping areas; instead, it had a smaller central business district and several other major commercial and industrial nuclei.

In the most controversial part of the study, Lander found that a number of delinquency rate predictors found by Chicago School researchers had curvilinear relationships with delinquency rates in Baltimore (the percentage of blacks), had a relationship inverse to the Chicago pattern (the percentage of foreign-born people), or were unimportant (median rent). His use of factor analysis touched off a series of replication studies and has been subjected to savage criticism (Bordua, 1958–1959; Chilton, 1964; Rosen and Turner, 1967; Gordon, 1967). The factor analysis literature led to the complete abandonment of space and location as variables in ecological analysis; instead, ecological analysts spent a number of years trying to assess the patterns of urban crime in "social space," using one or another system of "social area analysis." This latter line of research provided little useful additional information about criminals or about crime patterns and has been largely abandoned in the face of telling criticism. (See, Schmid, 1960a; Quinney, 1964; Timms, 1965; Polk, 1967. Baldwin, 1974b wrote the standard critique.)

Lander's analysis of the delinquency patterns of Baltimore eroded confidence in the Chicago model of crime and urban form in two ways. First, it showed that the areal patterns found in large-area intracity analysis masked too many underlying differences to permit further use for either research or policy purposes. Second, it suggested that the relationships between delinquency residence rates and the social characteristics of neighborhoods were not constant in time and space.

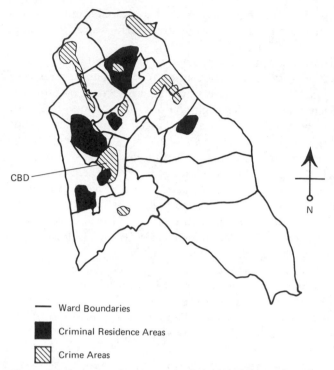

CBD

N

— Ward Boundaries

■ Criminal Residence Areas

▨ Crime Areas

Figure 11–5. Areas of crime and criminal residence, Croyden England, 1952. [Source: Adapted from T. Morris, *The Criminal Area: A Study in Social Ecology.* London: Routledge and Kegan Paul, 1958.]

Croydon, 1952. English areal studies of crime were never strongly influenced by the ecological models of the Chicago school. Instead, they followed the traditions of Mayhew (1861) and Booth (1891) in mapping the patterns of criminal residence and crime on a street-by-street basis. (See, Burt, 1925; Mannheim, 1948; Carter and Jephcott, 1954.) Morris (1958) sought specifically to test the utility of Chicago ecological models in the English situation in his study of the distribution of criminal areas and crime areas in Croydon for 1952. (Figure 11–5).

Croydon is a suburb of Greater London, a county borough with a census population of almost a quarter of a million people in 1951. It served as a bedroom community for people working in London and as a regional governmental and administrative center. Croydon's middle-class character is emphasized by the fact that 25 percent of the occupied and retired males fell into the top two socioeconomic classes (as defined by the Registrar General's classification of occupations), whereas only 18 percent fell into the bottom two classes in 1951.[4] Croydon constituted the bulk of the "Z" Division of the London Metropolitan Police Force.

---

[4] At another level of analysis, Croydon might be seen as having an "unbalanced" socioeconomic class structure and substantial relative deprivation, and it therefore might be expected to have high delinquency rates. See Chapter 10.

Morris mapped crime locations and criminal residence locations at the ward level. Wards are small political areas with about 17,000 population each. He had access to social, demographic, and land use data at this geographic level. For crime areas, he mapped all indictable and some nonindictable offenses known to the police in 1952. He found that most crimes occurred in the central shopping district or in several satellite shopping areas. Incidents of indecent exposure or assault, though widely scattered, occurred on poorly lit or tree-shaded streets or on streets with few passersby on the eastern edge of the central business district. These patterns were attributed to spatial–temporal patterns in the distribution of the "opportunities afforded for crime." Criminal residence areas were mapped on the basis of adult convictions and juvenile delinquency or probation findings for 1952. Only two of the seven highest areas of criminal residence corresponded to areas with high crime rates. Offenders traveled from home to crime sites. Figure 11–5 maps the crime areas and criminal residence areas of Croydon against the background of ward boundaries.

Morris reached several very important conclusions about intraurban crime patterns. First, the zonal model did not do a good job of predicting the location of land uses or criminal residence areas in Croydon, but it did a reasonable job of predicting crime areas because crime is tied to the distribution of opportunities. Second, the zonal model probably did not work well because it assumes that land uses and residential patterns are determined by unfettered market forces. In cities in which the free market has been controlled through use zoning, and particularly in Britain, where government has entered the housing market in a major way, the zonal model is a poor predictor. Shaw and McKay's models are not applicable to post–World War II British cities. Third, there was no exact correspondence between areas of criminal residence and areas in which most offenders committed their crimes. Crime site selection and the journey to crime should be major areas of criminological concern. Finally, all criminological research that assumes geographic correspondence between natural areas of criminal residence or natural areas of crime and administrative–political geographic areas such as census tracts or political wards should be viewed with great caution: there is no necessary correspondence between them.

Morris (1958) made the latter point as follows: "there are variations in social class between adjacent streets, and within individual streets and from an ecological point of view there are very few wards which can be said to constitute 'natural areas' in a cultural sense" (p. 115). His point is also true for American cities. Figure 11–6 shows Calvin Schmid's (1960b) analysis of the natural areas and the census tracts of central Seattle. Schmid concluded that the areal correspondence between census tracts and natural areas was so high that census tracts could easily be treated as functionally identical to the natural areas for analytic purposes. Yet on the basis of the census tract/natural area map he presented, his conclusion was clearly optimistic. Only five of twenty-three natural areas were wholly contained within a single census tract; no census tract was composed of parts of fewer than two natural areas and some tracts were composed of bits of as many as six natural areas. The central business district, a natural area, sprawled across seven different census tracts.

The problem derives from the fact that census tracts, ward broundaries, and the like follow major urban edges, such as roads and rivers. Edge effects are very

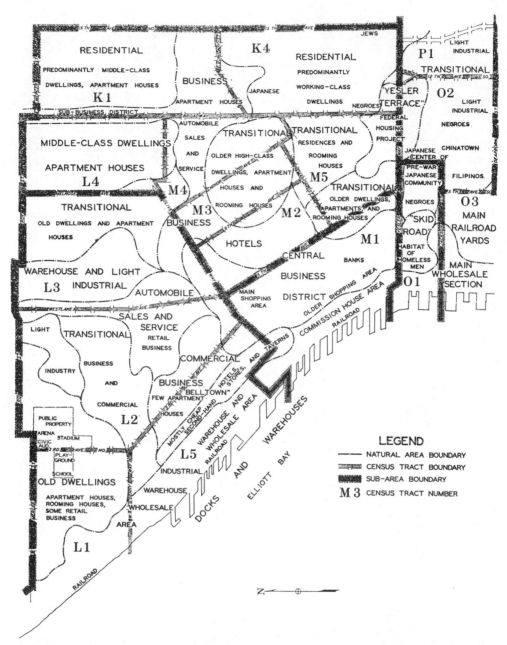

Figure 11–6. Natural areas and census tracts, central segment, Seattle, 1957. [Source: C. F. Schmid, "Urban Crime Areas, Part II," *American Sociological Review* Vol. 25, 1960, p. 656.]

powerful. Sometimes edges form social barriers with different kinds of land uses, residences and behavior patterns found on opposite sides of the barrier. When a census tract (or other social or political boundary) coincides with an urban edge that forms a social barrier, the tract boundary neatly demarcates a natural area boundary

318

as well. This happens only infrequently, as Figure 11–6 illustrates. Even when this occurs, however, there is a further problem. Roads often form edges on which interesting social events or conditions cluster. People and activities seem to be drawn to urban edges, the places at which sharply different lifestyles make contact. As described in detail in Chapter 9, areal crime rates can be singularly misleading when calculated for census tracts which have boundaries running down the middle of roads on which criminal events cluster.

Another reason that census tracts or other such units are problematic is that the social and physical patterns of cities change over time. Most American census tracts were originally defined in an effort to create homogeneous natural areas of approximately similar size. In order to make areally-arrayed census data comparable over time, census-tract boundaries have remained fixed from one decennial census to another. The land uses and populations within a tract may change over time: gentrification, for instance, has converted areas of Philadelphia that were dilapidated slums into some of the most expensive areas in the city; the development of shopping malls in Tallahassee moved virtually all commercial activity out of the central business district, changing the character of both the central-city census tracts and several residential census tracts drastically between the 1970 and 1980 censuses. This pattern, of course, is implicit in Burgess's model of urban growth: areas change over time.

Recent Intraurban Crime Patterns

England and Wales

London, 1961

Wallis and Maliphant analyzed the patterns of delinquency residence in the twenty-nine metropolitan boroughs of the county of London for the year 1961. The distribution of delinquent residence rates is shown in Figure 11–7. The highest rates were in Finsbury (immediately north of the City of London, and containing what was once the Golden Lane rookery) and in North Kensington. Very high delinquent residency rates occurred in Stepney, in Shoreditch, and in southwest Islington. Very low rates were obvious in the central urban core, composed of the City of London and Westminster. The patterns clearly did not correspond to the zonal model of the Chicago School.

Wallis and Maliphant (1967) correlated delinquency residence rates with a number of other physical, social, and demographic characteristics of the county boroughs. They found that areas with high delinquency residence rates were "distinguished by overcrowded houses deficient in basic amenities, by concentration of industry and commerce, with the latter tending to increase, and by a poverty of parks and open spaces" (p. 264). Delinquency rates tended to be high in areas with declining populations, and also to be high in areas receiving a rapid influx of immigrants. Delinquent areas had low divorce and suicide rates; high proportions of populations with low educational levels; high proportions of manual workers; and high proportions of the male working population "out of work." The authors con-

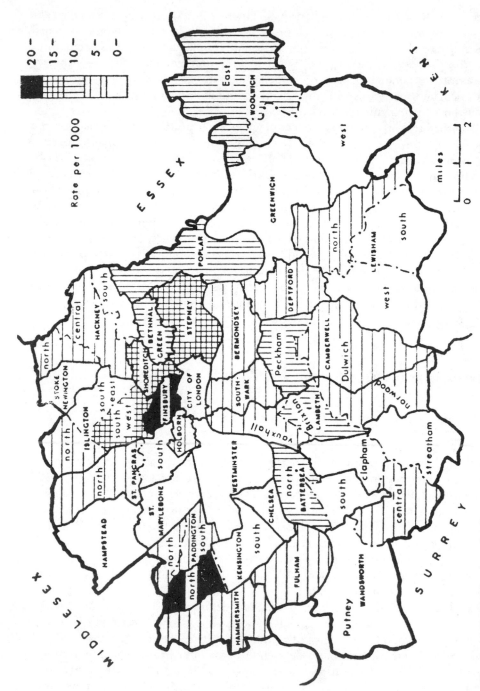

Figure 11-7. Distribution of delinquent rates in London: 1961 estimated annual rate of committals to three types of penal institution of young offenders aged seventeen to twenty years. [Source: C. P. Wallis and R. Maliphant, "Delinquent Areas in the County of London: Ecological Factors," *British Journal of Criminology* 7/1967:250–284.]

cluded that the spatial and social patterns of 1961 were consistent with those found by Burt (1925) forty years earlier, despite significant social and economic changes over the period.

Sheffield, 1966

In Sheffield, Baldwin and Bottoms (1976) conducted one of the most massive ecological analyses of crime and criminal residence within a city since Shaw and McKay's analyses of Chicago (Figure 11–8). They mapped the distribution of criminal events and the distribution of criminal residence, locating both crime areas and criminal areas.

The distribution of criminal offenses known to the police in Sheffield followed a strong distance-decay gradient outward from the central business district (Table

Figure 11–8. Distribution of all types of indictable offenses in Sheffield in 1966 (one spot = 8 offenses). [Source: J. Baldwin and A. E. Bottoms, *The Urban Criminal: A Study in Sheffield.* London: Tavistock Publications, 1976, p. 58.]

321

TABLE 11–1. Distance of Offenses and Offenders from City Center

Distance	Offenses (%)	Offenders (%)
Within ½ Mile of Center	23.7	1.6
½–1 Mile from Center	14.3	14.6
1–3 Miles from Center	50.9	68.6
Over 3 Miles from Center	11.1	15.2

SOURCE: J. Baldwin and A. E. Bottoms, *The Urban Criminal: A Study in Sheffield* (London: Tavistock Publications, 1976), p. 77. Reprinted by permission.

11–1). High incidences and high rates of crimes were recorded in the two wards that comprised the central business district. Incidence and rates of crimes declined with distance from the central business district when adjustments are made for the size of areas. This pattern was consistent with that found by Morris in Croydon. The crime patterns were strongly tied to the distribution of opportunities for crime, with the proviso that the city center appeared to attract far more crime than could be accounted for by a simple opportunity base.

The patterns of offender residence were studied on the basis of the home addresses for all offenders convicted for crimes reported in January, April, July, and October 1966. A few offenders had no fixed abode. They tended to be older than average, to have long records of prior convictions, and to commit more breaking and entering offenses than offenders with homes. A larger number of offenders had homes outside Sheffield, but 75 percent of these were from the city's natural hinterland: nearby villages and towns for which Sheffield was the logical commercial center. These offenders committed more frauds, auto thefts, and shoplifting offenses than Sheffield residents, and fewer violent and breaking-and-entering offenses.

The residency rates for adult and young male offenders for the more than two hundred census enumeration districts of Sheffield are shown in Figure 11–9. Three things are immediately apparent. First, the adult and young male patterns were different from one another. The areal correlation of the two distributions was only 0.26. Thus, Sheffield's patterns may have been substantially different from those found by Shaw and McKay in Chicago. Second, it is clear that no tidy zonal model can account for either of these patterns: areas with high and low offender residence rates were distributed throughout the city in apparently haphazard fashion. Third, it is clear that the distribution of criminal areas was very different from the distribution of crime areas.

In general, offenders tended to concentrate in three identifiable types of areas: areas with relatively high proportions of Irish and/or Commonwealth immigrants; areas adjacent to main locations of heavy industry; and in certain parts of some public housing estates, particularly those built in the interwar period. Low rates of offenders were found in the southwest part of the city, the main middle-class residential areas.

Baldwin and Bottoms turned to an analysis of distance from residence to crime in a effort to put these two sets of patterns together. Their general findings were

322

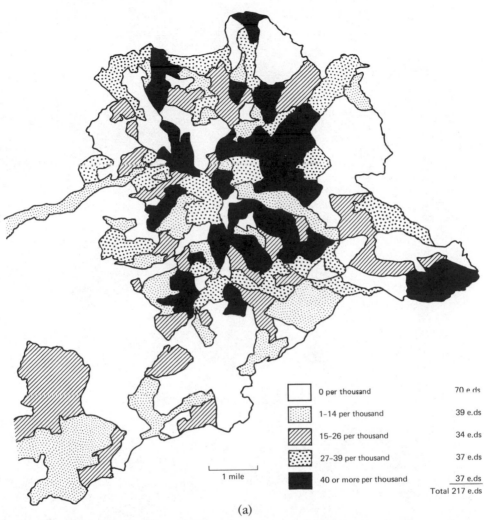

	0 per thousand	70 e.ds
	1–14 per thousand	39 e.ds
	15–26 per thousand	34 e.ds
	27–39 per thousand	37 e.ds
	40 or more per thousand	37 e.ds
		Total 217 e.ds

1 mile

(a)

Figure 11–9(a). Patterns of Male Offender Residence in Sheffield: Adult residence rate (per 1,000 males aged 90 and over) N.B.: rates are mapped by census enumeration district boundaries. [Source: J. Baldwin and A. E. Bottoms, *The Urban Criminal: A Study in Sheffield.* London: Tavistock Publications, 1976, pp. 75–76.]

that violent offenses involved the shortest crime trips, whereas theft, burglary, auto theft, and fraud involved successively longer trips. Offenders under age sixteen committed more offenses close to home and made fewer long journeys to crime than did offenders aged sixteen to twenty-five. Offenders living outside the city were of higher social class than offenders resident within the city. Among offenders resident in the city, social class had no important effect in determining the length of the journey to the crime. The higher the rate of delinquent residence in any ward, the shorter the distance offenders who lived in that ward traveled to commit their offenses. Older offenders tended to travel further as the value of stolen property increased.

323

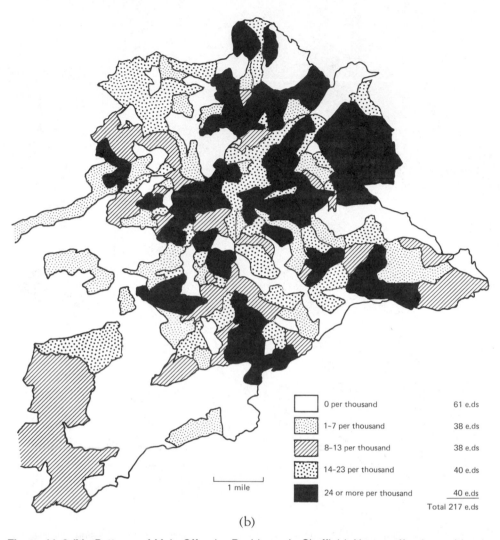

(b)

Figure 11–9 (b). Patterns of Male Offender Residence in Sheffield: Young offender residence rate (per 1,000 males aged 10–19) N.B.: rates are mapped by census enumeration district boundaries. [Source: J. Baldwin and A. E. Bottoms, *The Urban Criminal: A Study in Sheffield.* London: Tavistock Publications, 1976, pp. 75–76.]

Finally, Baldwin and Bottoms examined the patterns of criminal residence according to housing type. Four types of housing were identified: enumeration districts in which more than 50 percent of households were owner-occupied; enumeration districts in which more than 50 percent of the households rented from the council (i.e., publicly owned housing); enumeration districts in which more than 50 percent of the households were privately rented; and mixed property areas. Three patterns emerged. At the simplest level of analysis, owner-occupied areas had much lower criminal residence rates than either private rental areas or council housing areas. At a more complex level, the interaction between council housing areas and social class was important: lower-class council housing areas had high offender-

324

residence rates. Private rental areas with high offender-residence rates exhibited the classic pattern of social disorganization described by Burgess, Shaw and McKay, and many others over the years. This analysis ultimately led Baldwin and Bottoms to conclude that knowledge of the housing market—and particularly governmental housing policy—was critical to an understanding of the patterns of offender residence in England and Wales.

Cardiff, 1971

Herbert (1977) analyzed the patterns of delinquency residence in the census enumeration districts of Cardiff for 1966 and 1971 (Figure 11–10). The basic pattern that emerged for 1971 is the now-familiar distribution of criminal areas throughout the city. High-rate areas near the city center were nineteenth-century terrace houses awaiting urban renewal. High-rate areas in other parts of the city were council housing estates to which residents of previously cleared center-city slums had been moved.

Herbert tried to explain the patterns of delinquency in terms of the social and economic characteristics of the various enumeration districts. Regression analysis explained 44 percent of the variance. The percentage of unemployed males ac-

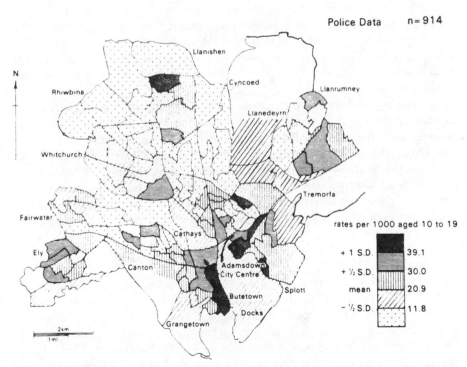

Figure 11–10. Delinquency residence areas in Cardiff, Wales, 1971. [Source: D. T. Herbert, "An Areal and Ecological Analysis of Delinquency Residence: Cardiff 1966 and 1971," *Tijdschrift Voor Economic En Social Geografie* 68/1977: p. 87.]

counted for 31 percent of the variance and lone-parent households for another 6 percent. Social class did not enter into the explanatory equation for 1971. Factor analysis and canonical analysis led him to conclude that high delinquency-residence rates are consistently related to qualities of the environment and particularly to poor social environments. The patterns of Cardiff in 1971 were very consistent with postwar English patterns.

Changes in the distribution of delinquent areas between 1966 and 1971 were principally related to the effect of local-government slum clearance and public-housing activities. Delinquent populations were moved from dilapidated slums in the center of the city to new, sound housing on the periphery. Housing policy clearly plays an important role in the patterns of crime within English and Welsh cities.

Canada

London, Ontario, 1965

Jarvis (1972) analyzed the delinquency residence patterns of London, Ontario, a university city midway between Toronto and Detroit. He calculated the delinquency residence rates for each of the thirty-five census tracts in the city. The pattern shown in Figure 11–11 is different from the patterns commonly observed in either English or American cities. Canadian cities remain far more downtown-oriented than cities in either of the other countries. Nine of the ten highest-rate tracts clustered together in a contiguous grouping in the city center. The zonal model applies nicely to the London data. Mean delinquency rates per 1,000 population aged 10–15 years, by zone, were as follows: Zone 1, 6.2; Zone 2, 3.5; Zone 3, 2.7; Zone 4, 1.2; and Zone 5, 0.7. The Chicago School declining gradient was clearly present.

Correlations between tract delinquency rates and nine commonly used social, economic, and physical variables were consistent with Shaw and McKay's findings in American cities. Delinquency rates were strongly positively correlated with the percentage of families living in poverty ($+0.81$), with the percentage of old housing ($+0.75$), with the percentage in low-status occupations ($+0.56$), and with the percentage of immigrants ($+0.41$). Strong negative correlations were with the percentage of owner-occupied housing (-0.72), with the percentage of residents having high-school education (-0.70), and with the percentage of Protestants (-0.59).

Vancouver, 1976

The patterns of crime in metropolitan Vancouver are shown in Figures 11–12 and 11–13. The city of Vancouver and the small city of New Westminster had the highest rates of both property and violent crimes in 1976. Both cities are major industrial and port centers. Relatively high rates of property crime occurred in Surrey, a major suburban growth area, and in North Vancouver. These patterns are not consistent with the patterns of most ecological studies. They are binodal. Few studies of crime and criminal residence patterns in metropolitan areas have been conducted in North America.

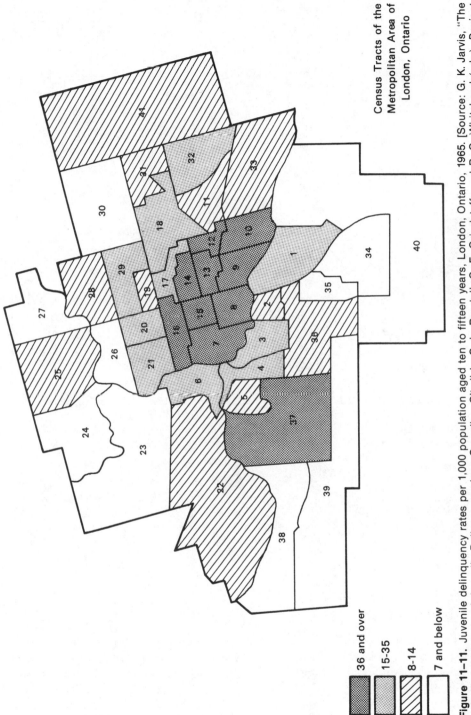

Figure 11–11. Juvenile delinquency rates per 1,000 population aged ten to fifteen years, London, Ontario, 1965. [Source: G. K. Jarvis, "The Ecological Analysis of Juvenile Delinquency in a Canadian City." In C. L. Boydell, C. F. Grindstaff, and P. C. Whitehead (eds.), *Deviant Behavior and Societal Reaction*. Toronto: Holt, Rinehart and Winston, 1972, p. 202.]

Census Tracts of the
Metropolitan Area of
London, Ontario

36 and over
15-35
8-14
7 and below

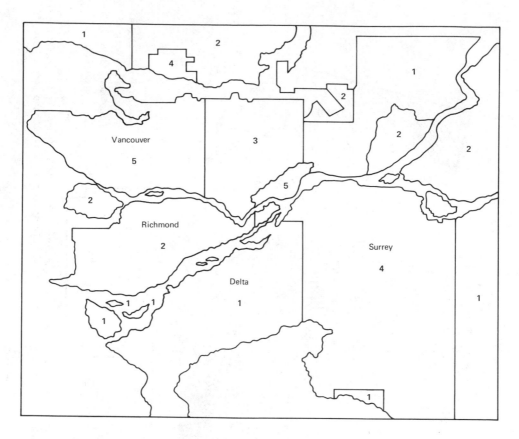

Rate per 100,000

5	7598–8533
4	6663–7597
3	5728–6662
2	4793–5728
1	3858–4792

Figure 11–12. Property crime rates, metropolitan Vancouver, 1976.

United States

The ecological patterns of crime within urban areas have not been much studied in recent years in the United States. Research has moved into more detailed and more sophisticated small-area and mobility analysis. Patterns are available for some cities, however.

Atlanta, 1967

Using isopleth mapping, Curtis (1974) analyzed the spatial patterns of violent crimes in five large cities (Boston, Philadelphia, Atlanta, Chicago, and San Fran-

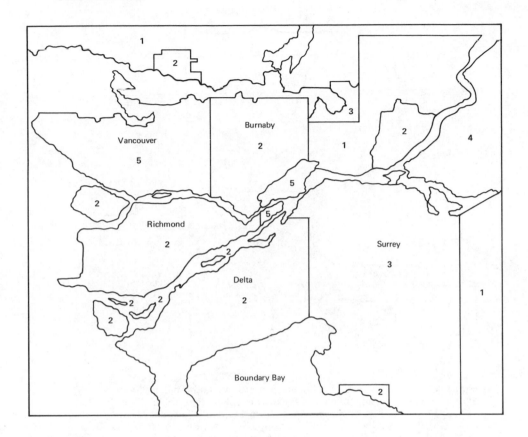

Rate per 100,000

5	1045–1240
4	850–1044
3	655–849
2	460–654
1	265–459

Figure 11–13. Violent crime rates, metropolitan Vancouver, 1976.

cisco) for the National Commission on the Causes and Prevention of Violence. Isopeth mapping produces maps that look like weather maps: contour lines connect points with similar values, enclosing areas with similar levels of criminal violence. Figures 11–14 and 11–15 show the isopleth maps for violent assaultive crimes (murder, rape, and aggravated assault) by crime location and by offender residence. The shaded area on each map covers those census tracts that were officially labeled as "poverty areas" by the U.S. Office of Economic Opportunity using a Census Bureau poverty index that measures the percentage of low-income families, the percentage of children under age eighteen not living with both parents, the per-

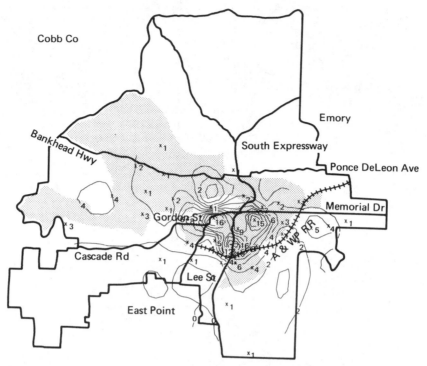

Figure 11–14. Crime location isopleth map of criminal homicide, forcible rape and aggravated assault rates known to the police of Atlanta. [Source: Reprinted by permission of the publisher from *Criminal Violence: National Patterns and Behavior* by Lynn Curtis. Lexington, Mass: Lexington Books, D. C. Heath and Company. Copyright 1974, D. C. Heath and Company.]

centage of males aged twenty-five or over with less than eight years of schooling completed, the percentage of unskilled males employed in the civilian labor force, and the percentage of substandard housing.

Chapter Summary

Intraurban crime studies have been conducted since the mid-nineteenth century. Criminal areas, parts of the city in which many criminals are resident, exist in most cities and persist over relatively long periods of time. Criminal areas are also areas of low income, of rundown housing, of poverty, and of ethnicity. In cities with a free housing market, criminal areas tend to be located near the central business district. In cities with zoning and extensive public-housing programs, criminal areas

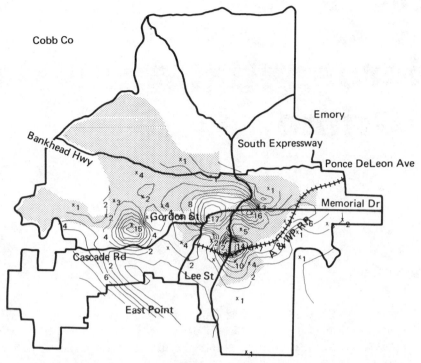

Figure 11–15. Offender location isopleth map of criminal homicide, forcible rape and aggravated assault rates known to the police of Atlanta. [Source: Reprinted by permission of the publisher from *Criminal Violence: National Patterns and Behavior* by Lynn Curtis. Lexington, Mass: Lexington Books, D. C. Heath and Company. Copyright 1974, D. C. Heath and Company.

may be located anywhere. The urban models developed by the Chicago School of sociology worked reasonably well in predicting crime areas during the 1920s and 1930s, but they are less effective now. Multiple-nuclei models of urban form seem to do a better job of predicting criminal area patterns in post–World War II cities.

12

Microspatial Analysis of Crime

Introduction

As demonstrated in Chapter 11, the ecological tradition in criminology is strong. Crime is not uniformly distributed across urban space. This variability calls for explanation. Studies in the ecological tradition primarily describe the socioeconomic conditions of people and relate variability in these conditions to spatial irregularities in crime ocurrence or in the residence of criminals. Spatial concepts within ecological criminology are used to describe the interaction of various social groups, if they are used at all. Ecological criminology looks at *objective space*. Space exists as a fixed quantity, and people or groups are located in this fixed space. Criminal behavior, however, can be viewed from the perspective of *subjective space*. Subjective space is the space perceived by individuals, not an objective quantity. Criminal behavior can be viewed as a complex form of subjective spatial behavior in which movement patterns depend on underlying spatial mobility biases, knowledge, and experience. This chapter explores how criminals move about in urban space, why they pick the targets they do, and, generally, how subjective perceptions influence crime patterns.

Environment

One begins ecological and geographical analyses of crime data by locating crime occurrences or criminal residences in space, that is, locating them on a map or assigning spatial coordinates such as longitude and latitude, and correlating the locations with other urban or social characteristics. As discussed in Chapter 9, the crime occurrence data are usually aggregated to an areal base, often an administratively defined unit such as a census tract. Ecological analysis assumes a fixed spatial or geographic coordinate system where points can be located and which can be used to compare relative locations. Objective space or objective social space is used to form a coordinate reference system for analysis of relative locations.

Space, however, can be viewed from other perspectives. For any individual, the space around him or her exists not in an objective form but as it is perceived.[1] Individuals, because of their varying backgrounds and experiences, perceive differently the space around them, the urban area they live in, and even the country they live in. As an extreme example, a city is quite different for a child of three and for a thirty-five-year-old who owns a store in the core business district. They clearly have different perceptions of the city based on past knowledge and current experiences. Examples need not be so extreme: teenagers, retired persons, housewives, laborers, and managers all have different experiential bases and different potentials for learning about an urban area. Their "perceived" cities vary, even if the objective city does not. There is a unique *subjective space* for every individual. Subjective space tends to be similar for people in similar circumstances but is never identical.

There is no reason to assume that people with highly varied subjective perceptual outlooks would commit crimes at identical locations. If crime occurrence is looked at from the point of view of subjective space, then the analysis of crime patterns becomes more complex. Absolute geographic arrangements cannot be used in analysis without being transformed into subjective coordinates. Knowledge of a city by a criminal cannot be assumed. Crimes occur where they do, not just because targets are located there (targets are located in many places), but because from a subjective perspective the place where the crime occurs is a "good" place to commit a crime. Crimes cannot be analyzed against social or economic spatial data without an understanding of how potential criminals "see" and move about in the city.

To begin a subjective space analysis of crime, it is necessary first to define and describe the environment of a crime. For any individual the *environment* is the totality of objects—people, places and things—that he or she comes in contact with and the relationships that influence his or her behavior. The environment of a criminal act is the totality of objects and relationships that influence the commission of that criminal act.

The environment is potentially a welter of people, objects, and relationships with which an individual interacts and which influence actions or behaviors. If one is to understand the environment, and consequently behavior, space must be categorized or subdivided into categories that are manageable and that help understanding.

An early categorization of the environment was made by Koffka in his *Principles of Gestalt Psychology* (1935). He argued that the environment is perceived as a whole and that any categorization or fragmentation is artificial, a conceptual convenience. However, he divided the total environment into two categories:

1. The Geographic Environment, which is made up of actual physical structures and relationships.
2. The Behavioral Environment, which is an individual's perception of the geographic environment.

---

[1] *Perception* is used in this context to include both the physical mechanism of perception and cognition.

333

Because of similarities in perception, people hold certain *behavioral environments* in common. In 1936, Lewin added the influence of personality to that of perception and proposed that behavior is the result of the interaction of personality with the perceived environment.

Along a slightly different line, Gans (1972) divided the environment into the *potential environment* and the *effective environment*. The potential environment is the physical reality composed of non-manipulatable elements, such as climate and topography, and the manipulatable environment, made up of buildings, roads, and other physical structures created or formed by humans. The potential environment is selectively interpreted through social systems or cultural norms to form an effective environment that influences behavior (Figure 12-1). Human behavior or actions can, in turn, alter the manipulatable physical environment by building or changing the infrastructure. These changes then influence future behavior, so an endless loop is formed between the potential and the effective environments.

Sonnenfeld (1972) provided an overarching categorization of the environment, a categorization that can subsume most other definitions. For Sonnenfeld, the environment can be broken into the following:

1. *Geographical Environment.* The geographical environment includes the totality of all things in the universe. It is the objective reality external to any particular person.

2. *Operational Environment.* The operational environment is the part of the geographical environment that has an impact on a person—whether that person is aware of it or not.

3. *Perceptual Environment.* The subpart of the operational environment that an individual is aware of is the perceptual environment. Awareness may be centered on current events, past experiences, or even indirect experiences, such as those gained through reading or through listening to others.

4. *Behavioral Environment.* The behavioral environment is the portion of the perceptual environment that triggers actions or responses, or the part of the environment toward which actions are directed. (Porteus, 1977, p. 139)

These definitions of the environment, and the associated implied definitions of behavior, are just a few of the many variants found in the literature. Although they are technically different, they do have a common base: people react and act within a world they know, not the world that *exists* in any objective sense. Koffka (1935) provided the classic illustration of this distinction:

> On a winter evening amidst a driving snow storm a man on horseback arrived at an inn, happy to have reached a shelter after hours of riding over the wind-swept plain on which the blanket of snow had covered all paths and landmarks. The landlord who came to the door viewed the stranger with surprise and asked him whence he came. The man pointed in the direction straight away from the inn, whereupon the landlord, in a tone of awe and wonder, said, "Do you know that you have ridden across Lake Constance?" At which the rider dropped stone dead at his feet. (p. 27)

334

Gans's (1972) Representation

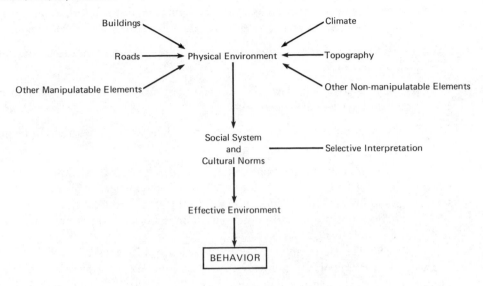

Sonnenfeld's (1972) Representation

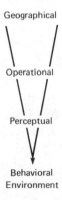

Figure 12–1. The relationship between environment and behavior. Gan's representation and Sonnefeld's Representation.

Behavior

Although people can perceive without action, it is the study of behavior that is of primary interest. Behavior is influenced by many things that can be lumped together into Sonnenfeld's "behavioral environment." The behavioral environment for crime is broken down into:

1. *Physical Setting.* The physical structure, buildings, roads, climate—what Gans (1972) called the potential environment.

335

2. *Social Setting.* The social and economic conditions, the group structures, and the friendship networks that form the social backcloth for action. The social setting has been the traditional area of research for criminologists.

3. *Psychological Setting.* The psychological and physical conditions that predispose some to crime.

4. *Legal Setting.* The laws and the enforcement patterns that result in an action's being labeled *criminal*.

5. *Cultural Setting.* The belief systems and general values that influence actions.

This division of the environment is similar to Talcott Parsons's enumeration of subsystems of behavior. For Parsons (1966), behavior was influenced by (1) the social subsystem; (2) the cultural subsystem; (3) the physiological subsystem; (4) the personality subsystem; and (5) the environmental subsystem, which provides a template for the other subsystems.

Whether the environment is viewed as a Gestalt or as a set of independent subsystems, the important point is that it is complex and includes physical and nonphysical objects mediated by perception. Perception or cognition is, in turn, influenced by past and current experiences and knowledge. Past and current experience and knowledge are influenced by social, psychological, and cultural conditions.

Spatial Behavior

Much behavior involves a decision to move or a decison that results in the movement of some goods. Shopping, working, and seeing a movie (until quite recently, with first-run movies on television cables) all involve moving from one place to another. Most criminal behavior also involves movement and choice in locating a target or victim. As described in Chapter 9, robbery in Miami, Florida, was found to exhibit spatial patterning similar to shopping. Understanding criminal behavior requires not only uncovering the social, cultural, and psychological precursors of crime, but also understanding microspatial decision-making. Microspatial decision-making relates directly to the perceptual and behavioral environments: How does a person find her or his way and why does the person go where she or he goes?

Microanalysis of criminal behavior ties criminology to geography, particularly behavioral geography. The tie to behavioral geography is well illustrated by a list of geographic concerns presented by Golledge and Rushton in their introduction to *Spatial Choice and Spatial Behavior* (1976):

> Much past geographical research supports the contention that information about man's external environment is filtered and distorted in the minds of people and thus decisions should be studied in relation to "imaged" rather than "objective" worlds. Pursuit of this train of thought has focused some studies in "behavioural" geography on the perceived components of environments (or the "cognized" environments). The argument set forth to justify this emphasis is that, if we can understand *how* human

minds process information from external environments and if we can determine *what* they process and use then we can investigate how and why choices concerning those environments are made. Questions that are raised by this argument include: Does *what* is extracted from the environment depend on the type of exposure to it? Are there rules that guide the filtering process such that common decisions can be made by many humans? Are these rules capable of generalization across different environments, or are they place specific? If the acquisition of environmental knowledge is a learning process, which are the positive and which are the negative signals that affect the chance of an environmental element being noticed and used or eliminated from consideration? In short, the questions investigated revolve around the extraction and use of spatial information from external environments. (p. viii)

How do criminals pick their targets? Why do they go to certain areas of the city to find a target or a victim? Are there perceptual environments in which crime is unlikely?

The problems and questions in microspatial criminology or *environmental criminology,* as it is called, are similar to many current concerns in environmental psychology as well as behavioral geography. Environmental psychology addresses questions of how people perceive (cognize) the external environments, what cues are used to conceptualize or work in an environment, and how people process information from the external world. These questions are similar to the list presented by Golledge and Rushton for geography. In fact, the border between these two areas of study is fuzzy. Environmental criminology draws on research and theory in both fields, as well as on architecture and planning, in trying to unravel the microspatial behavior of criminals.

Basic Model of Target Selection

Previous chapters in this book have explored the socioeconomic and demographic factors that seem likely to influence the amount of crime or, looking at it from an individual level, the predisposing or motivating factors underlying criminal behavior. In exploring the microspatial analysis of crime or environmental criminology, it is not necessary to repeat these arguments. It is assumed, without any risk of refutation, that people exist who are motivated to commit crimes. The causes of motivation vary, and the strength of the motivation varies. Given that people motivated to commit crimes exist, it is possible to look at the process of searching out a target or victim as a sequence or series of spatial decisions in which the objective environment is perceived (cognized) and evaluated. This process can be described by the following model presented as propositions (Brantingham and Brantingham, 1978):

> I. Given the motivation of an individual to commit an offense, the actual commission of an offense is the end result of a multi-staged decision process which seeks out and identifies, within the general environment, a target or victim positioned in time and space.

In the case of high-affect motivation (high emotional involvement), the decision process will probably involve a minimal number of stages.

In the case of high-instrumental motivation (low emotional involvement), the decision process locating a target or victim may include many stages and much careful searching

II. The environment emits many signals, or cues, about its physical, spatial, cultural, legal and psychological characteristics.

These cues can vary from generalized to detailed.

III. An individual motivated to commit a crime uses cues (either learned through experience or learned through social transmission) from the environment to locate and identify targets or victims.

IV. As experiential knowledge grows, an individual motivated to commit an offense learns which individual cues are associated with "good" victims or targets. These cues, cue clusters, and cue sequences (spatial, physical, social, temporal, and so on) can be considered a template which is used in victim or target selection. Potential victims or targets are compared to the template and either rejected or accepted, depending on the consequence.

The process of template construction may be consciously conducted, or these processes may occur in an unconscious, cybernetic fashion so that the individual cannot articulate how they are done.

V. Once the template is established, it becomes relatively fixed and influences future searching behaviour, thereby becoming self-reinforcing.

VI. Because of the multiplicity of targets and victims, many potential crime selection templates could be constructed. But because the spatial and temporal distribution of targets and victims is not regular, but clustered or patterned, and because human environmental perception has some universal properties, individual templates have similarities which can be identified. (pp. 107–108)

Each of these propositions is described here separately.

Proposition I: Multistaged Search Behavior

Moving about in urban space is obviously the result of decisions: when to start, where to turn, where to stop. Habitual movement patterns, such as going to work or school, lose their conscious quality. Most people have experienced the sensation of "the car's driving itself" over familiar roads. Whether conscious or not, whether novel or habitual, spatial decisions must be made.

Trying to model individual movement is fascinating and difficult. Spatial behavior is purposeful or goal-directed. Decisions about how to travel and where to travel are based on knowledge of the area, previous experience (which is tied to knowledge), and expectations about the result of traveling. People will travel further to buy furniture than to buy a loaf of bread; some people will travel along aesthetically pleasing roads even if the resulting trip is longer; most people experience "novel" or "first-time trips" as perceptually "longer" than repetitive trips; trips back toward home are usually perceived as "shorter" than trips away from home; people perceive trips with interruptions (e.g., stoplights or turns) as longer than objectively equal distances without interruptions. These are just a few of the behavioral and perceptual regularities that have been uncovered in behavioral geography and environmental psychology. These background empirical regularities, along with others, help to form the perceptual environment for making decisions.

As mentioned before, the spatial choices made are often unconscious, being based on habitual travel patterns. Searching behavior, such as looking for a house to break into, may have an added dimension. A burglar may, in beginning a crime trip, have a particular target in mind and consequently may make spatial decisions in locating the target that are analogous to those of a person seeking out a known store or restaurant. A burglar, however, may not have a particular target in mind and consequently engages in active searching behavior. This searching behavior is analogous to the searching behavior of a motorist looking for a gas station in an unknown or poorly known area of a city or a shopper looking for a coffee shop in an area of a city where he or she has only a vague knowledge of potential locations. The searcher has a general idea where there may be attractive houses to burglarize (the coffee shop or gas station, in the other examples), but some conscious looking or checking must be done. This searching and checking process can be modeled by means of the concept of *mixed scanning*. Mixed scanning employs hierarchical, sequential decisions that move from a broad scanning of all possibilities to a detailed investigation of a limited number of possibilities. The hierarchy may have many tiers, depending on the complexity of the task (Brantingham and Brantingham, 1978, p. 108).

The classic example of mixed scanning is a soldier scanning for the enemy. All areas within the soldier's visual field are given a cursory glance. The soldier, however, looks a little more closely at areas where, by experience, enemy soldiers might be expected to be. If anything unusual catches the attention, the soldier then explores this more restricted subarea in greater detail, possibly homing in on a still smaller subunit. The whole area is not inspected in detail (this is not possible); only selected subareas are given full checking (Etzioni, 1968).

Mixed scanning, as a decision-making process, fits empirically known patterns of target selection. For example, a house burglar may first locate a general area of the city where potential targets may exist—say, older multifamily housing areas (Reppetto, 1974; P. J. Brantingham and P. L. Brantingham, 1975, 1977, 1978; Pyle, 1974). Then, within that general area, the burglar may locate subareas that offer more anonymity (P. L. Brantingham and P. J. Brantingham, 1975, P. J. Brantingham and P. L. Brantingham, 1977; Newman, 1972; Reppetto, 1974), or that exhibit generally useful characteristics, such as poor street lighting or lots of bushes (Phelan, 1977), or that provide easy entry and exit by the street (Bevis and Nutter, 1977; Molumby, 1976). Finally, once the burglar is within the subarea, a specific housing unit or target is selected. In areas with a high degree of architectural homogeneity, the detailed target choice may be random, or it may be keyed to specifics such as locks and dogs (Molumby, 1976; Scarr, 1973). In areas with architectural variety, individual architectural cues may be used. This process is outlined in Letkemann's (1973, pp. 137–157) chapter on "casing" by burglars and robbers (also see Brantingham and Brantingham, 1978, pp. 109–110).

The searching process may be minimal—and is minimal in most assaultive crimes. Assaultive crimes are usually the end product of highly emotional interactions. The victim and the assailant have usually had a precipitating, emotionally charged verbal exchange (and often a history of verbally or physically assaultive exchanges). Once the assaultive behavior is triggered, the search for the victim is usually short, looking across the room, following someone into another room or out of a building. Movement and searching go on, but in a geographically constrained area.

Proposition II: Cue-Emitting Potential of the Environment

The perceptual or behavioral environment is not identical with objective reality. What is perceived is selectively remembered or imbued with meaning. It is impossible to remember everything that is seen, heard, or experienced. As with the mixed-scanning model of decision making, it is not possible to give equal attention to all objects and relations in the objective environment. People act as information processors organizing and structuring what is perceived. The ability to form perceptual patterns is impressive. People learn to judge distances (humans are not born with this ability), to judge the friendliness of the people whom they meet or even the potential threat of dogs, and to judge height and temperature. People learn how to manage within complex cultures norms that even govern how far apart people should stand when talking, how much touching should go on, how loudly people should talk, and the relative importance of time (Hall, 1966; Ashcraft and Scheflen, 1976). Such behaviors are learned and vary from culture to culture, between the sexes, and between people of different ages.

Environmental cues may be perceived at many levels. When one is traveling in an unfamiliar city, some things seem similar to places in cities one knows well: central business districts are easy to identify, as are residential areas; ethnic areas stand out. Once someone has lived in a city, all cities seem somewhat understandable and predictable. There are cues—signs, traffic, intensity of use, and road networks—that one can use to understand a new environment by comparing it with known environments.

Within known environments, cues are perceived at different levels. When driving through an area, a person is not aware of every detail, only possibly the general land use (whether the area is residential, business, or commercial), the socioeconomic characteristics of general areas, and landmark buildings, signs, parks, and so on, which orient the driver and provide a context for the trip. The driver is generally unaware of detail. A person walking along a street, however, can take in detail. He or she sees plantings, building design, signs in stores (Lynch and Rivkin, 1959; Appleyard, 1969). What is seen (the cues) depends on what is there and the characteristics of the perceiver.

Proposition III: Crime Cues

People interpret information from the environment or process information that aids them in moving about or functioning. Cues are used information. As a special case of the general information-processing and interpretation that people do, criminals use cues to help them locate targets in time and space. Indirect evidence of such cues can be found in the correlations reported between crime occurrence data and the physical and nonphysical characteristics of crime sites (Brantingham and Brantingham, 1977; Pyle, 1974; Newman, 1972). More direct evidence can be found in research that looks specifically at how criminals pick targets (Letkemann, 1973; Phelan, 1977; Reppetto, 1974) or perceive the physical environment (McConnell, 1976).

Studies that correlate physical cues and crime occurrence are primarily done at an ecological or areal level, and consequently, they potentially suffer from aggregation biases or interpretively from the ecological fallacy (see Chapter 9). Both an ecologically incorrect argument and the multistaged decision process of crime site location can be illustrated by a burglary example: Residential burglary rates computed at a block level have been found to be positively correlated to the percentage of the housing units within the block that are in small apartment buildings, that is, two to nine units per building (Brantingham and Brantingham, 1977). Ecologically, this is a strong correlation, but what does it mean? Are apartments within smaller apartment complexes more at risk for burglary than larger apartments or single-family dwellings? It would be tempting to draw this conclusion, and in fact, it probably is a valid conclusion. But if all one knows is that there is a correlation between a block's crime rate and the proportion of small apartments in that block, then all one can validly say is that criminals seem attracted (in a positive linear way) to areas with small apartment buildings. One does not know, with block data, whether small apartment buildings or single-family homes or large apartment buildings, which might all be in the same block, are the buildings being broken into. Looking at it from the perspective of a multistaged decision process, the burglar may like areas with small apartment buildings because of a perceived anonymity (Brantingham and Brantingham, 1977), but once within a small apartment area, the burglar might pick single-family homes as targets because of a belief there will be more goods to steal in such homes. The burglar might also home in on apartment units in large buildings while trying to maximize perceived anonymity. With block-level data, the multistaged decision question cannot be completely answered.

It is worth repeating at this point that predisposing or motivational factors do matter in criminal behavior, and that target selection is the end stage of a search process that involves the motivated individual's moving about in a perceptual environment. The social and cultural background and the physiological and psychological makeup of a criminal influences his or her motivation, his or her perceptions of the objective environment, and his or her behavior.

Proposition IV: Template Construction

Individual cues can be associated with "safe" or "good" targets just as they can be associated with "unsafe" or "bad" targets. A hundred-dollar bill lying on a counter in a store is a "good" cue to a potential thief. A clerk standing there is a "bad" cue. Similarly, a convenience store (a small grocery store that may stay open late at night) has been found to be a "good" target for robbers (Capone and Nichols,

341

1976; Duffala, 1976). But if the convenience store is located next to a police station, it may not be such a "good" target.

"Good" and "bad" targets for a criminal are objects (people, buildings, cars, and so on) situated within a perceptual environment that is favorable to crime, an environment that emits many cues supporting the commission of a crime. In Tallahassee, Florida, for example, a convenience store is a "good" target late at night, if it is located near a major highway, but not on the highway, and if it is near open land (Duffala, 1976). These characteristics form a *cluster of cues* that helps identify a "good" target. Cues may also exist in sequence. A convenience store may be an attractive target if it has the above characteristics, if it is located by the robber after a period of "casings," and if it has not been robbed recently.

Cues, cue clusters, and cue sequences, of course, need not be derived exclusively from the physical components of the perceptual environment. Social situations, such as arguments before assaults (Curtis, 1974), illicit sexual relations before robbery (Conklin, 1972, p. 92), or a group gathering of teenagers before a theft (Hindlelang, 1976b), form environmental cues about the appropriateness of a specific setting for a crime. The cue clusters and cue sequences associated with a specific offense can be considered a perceptual "template."

In interpreting the objective environment, people tend to categorize and generalize. They take a new situation and put it into categories of situations known from previous experience. Thus, people can recognize a city: it has tall buildings, dense development, and heavy traffic relative to the surrounding areas. Kaplan (1976) described three capacities that are necessary if one is to function within perpetually varying environments. First, a person must be able to *recognize*. Objects with great individual variety must be categorized and labeled. Many largely varying structures with tops and supporting sides are called *tables*. But when can any particular object be called a *table?* When is a table a counter? People learn to categorize diverse objects into limited categories and/or multileveled categories. Situations (complexes of people, objects, relations, and associated contextual meanings) must also be recognized. People must be able to recognize emergencies, work, entertainment, and play, for example.

Second, and tied to recognition, is the ability to *anticipate* or predict future events. Given an object, a group of objects, or a situation, a person must be able to anticipate what will happen next. This is the essence of intelligent choice. Decisions are often made based on expectations of future states. Such decisions are good if the expectation turns out to be close to what really occurs. People must "look ahead."

Third, when past experience and knowledge make it difficult to anticipate (that is, an object or a situation varies greatly from what has previously been experienced), a person must be able to make *responsible innovations* in order to work out what should be done from partial or incomplete information. Through recognition, anticipation, and responsible innovation people are able to work with and in unique environments.

The pattern of categories and experiences that makes it possible to *recognize* and *anticipate* or *innovate* during the search for a target and the commission of an offense is the *crime template*. Criminals learn to recognize potential crime sites and situations, or they learn to recognize potentially poor crime sites or situations and

342

to refrain from criminal behavior in such settings. Consistent failure to refrain from criminal behavior in inappropriate settings may lead to diagnosis of mental illness or psychopathy. The generally accepted inappropriateness of criminal behavior in most environments may explain the difficult criminological problem of why even the most committed, hard-core criminals behave very much like noncriminals, engaging in nondeviant, legal, inoffensive behavior most of the time.

Proposition V: Relative Endurance of a Crime Template

Once a crime template develops, it tends to endure. The endurance of a template can be justified by the use of a reinforcing schema. By experience in the commission of crimes and/or through social transmission, a template of a "good" target, victim, or setting is constructed. When this template is used to guide criminal activities, and those activities succeed, then the template is reinforced.

It should be noted once again that the process of template construction need not be, and most likely is not, conscious. The matching of a particular crime site or situation probably consists of locating a place where the would-be criminal feels comfortable, that is, feels that her or his action will not be interrupted in any serious fashion.

Proposition VI: Limited Number of Templates

Templates are individual constructions. When descriptions are carried to the extreme, it is clear that each criminal's template with respect to his or her behavior set is unique. But people, although unique, are also similar. Perceptual patterns are also similar, and therefore, cognitive representations follow patterns.

At a behavioral level, Barker (1968) has defined what he called "behavior settings." Barker—and later, LeCompte (1972), Wicker (1972), and Gump (1971)—tried to identify the sets of behaviors that occur in specific settings. We all know that we act differently in a church and at a football game; we act differently at work and relaxing with friends. There are certain patterns of behavior that we learn are appropriate in certain situations. Our behavior is patterned even if not totally predictable.

Tied, of course, to behavioral similarities are perceptual similarities. The existence of patterns can be seen best in the research of people who study "mental maps," or cognitive representations of the objective environment (Lynch, 1960; DeJonge, 1962; Orleans, 1973; Downs and Stea, 1973; Golledge et al., 1976). All have uncovered patterns and group variability. Patterns vary by broad sociodemographic characteristics: knowledge and complexity of images increase with age; are generally more complex for people who work outside the home; vary by social class, generally covering a smaller area for the less mobile, lower socioeconomic groups; and vary directly by length of residence.

With patterned perceptions come a limited number of templates. Individual templates vary but fall into clusters. In research on the "fear-of-crime" templates of residents in New Westminster, British Columbia (Brantingham et al., 1979), strong

343

patterning was found. The residents were generally concerned about the same areas of town, even though "fear" areas ranged from single buildings within the general area to the whole area. The residents were concerned about the same problems: youths, noise, and drunks. Variability exists, but within discernible patterns.

Summary of the Target Selection Model

Criminals do not move randomly through space. Clear patterning does exist. The microanalysis of this patterning can be understood through an information-processing model of crime site selection. The objective world is interpreted, and cues are selectively used and structured into images or templates of "good" and "bad" crime sites. Templates are formed by experience and social transmission of information. These templates are then used predictively to help select targets. Outcomes of potential crimes are projected or anticipated, and decisions are made accordingly. Criminally motivated individuals try to find targets or victims that match their perceptual generalizations or templates. When a match occurs, a crime is highly likely to happen.

Criminal Spatial Behavior

It has been posited that target selection is a spatial information-processing phenomenon. The model just presented is operationally aspatial: no attempt was made to place spatial constraints on the process of target selection. However, to study the pattern of crime in any particular city, it is necessary to understand how people, particularly criminals, move about in space.

Crime Trips

There is a well established distance-decay pattern in human spatial behavior (see Chapter 9). People interact more with people and things that are close to their home location than with people or things that are far away. Interactions decrease as distance increases (distance decay). Some of this decrease in activity as distance increases is the result of the "costs" of overcoming distance. It costs a person money and/or time to travel. As is quite evident in this era of increasing gasoline prices, there is a nonnegligible cost associated with travel. At an individual level, it costs relatively more money now to travel a fixed distance than several years ago. Trips to nearby cities or distant shopping centers cost more; journeys to work or recreation areas cost more. Within a fixed pricing scheme, it makes no sense to travel far for goods or services that are available closeby. Why travel ten miles for a loaf of bread if the same bread is available closer for the same amount of money (or any amount less than the price at the distant location plus the travel costs)? There are logical financial reasons for constraining individual mobility. These financial reasons hold for businesses, too. If two firms producing the same goods at the same price are located outside a city, the firm closer to the city (with lower transportation costs) will have the competitive financial edge.

The bias of greater density of interaction close to home is also the result of biased spatial knowledge. People have more experience of and are more aware of what exists around them. Most people who live in a single-family housing area can identify the houses around them; most people would be able to recognize many of the houses within several blocks of their home, but few people can recognize individual houses a half mile or a mile away unless the house is unusual. If someone needs to buy a loaf of bread, the reasonable thing to do is go to a "known" store that sells food staples. It is more likely that the "known" store will be close to home than far away. If someone is looking for a type of store—say a dry cleaner—and does not know exactly where one is, she or he is most likely to start looking in store areas close to home where a dry cleaning store might be. Searching behavior starts from home and first covers likely areas that are "known".

Criminals probably follow a similar searching pattern. Although specific studies have not been done on the spatial searching patterns of criminals, the results of other studies show strong traces of such patterns. Crimes generally occur close to the home of the criminal. The operational definition of *close* varies by offense, but the distance-decay gradient is evident in all offenses. In a study of homicide, Bullock (1955) found that 40 percent of all murders in Houston, Texas, between 1945 and 1949 occurred within one block of the offerder's residence; 74 percent occurred within two miles. These patterns were found again in Houston in 1958–1961 (Pokorny, 1965). Baldwin and Bottoms (1976) found a distance-decay pattern for property offenses in Sheffield, England. Amir (1971) found the pattern for rape. Capone and Nichols (1976) found it for robbery. Phillips (1980) found it for juvenile offenders. The pattern is persistent overall, but variation exists by offense. Generally, violent offenses have a high concentration close to home, with many assaults and murders actually occurring in the home. The search pattern is a little broader for property offenses, but these are still clustered close to home.

The distribution of offenses around the home base of the criminal would look like a bull's-eye with many "hits" close to the center (Figure 12-2). If there are no conditions to distort the pattern, the offenses should be spatially dense close to the

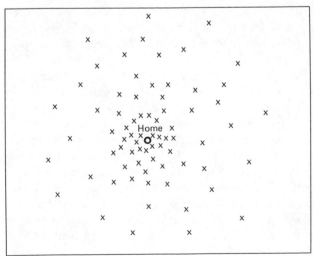

Figure 12–2. Distribution of offenses around a criminal's home.

x - Location of a Crime

home location and should gradually decline in frequency as distance away from home increases.

There are, however, many conditions that distort this basic pattern. One is the criminal's risk of apprehension. Search for targets may be spatially biased toward home, but there is a limited space near the criminal's home where crimes become more risky. Targets close to home are generally "bad" targets. The difference between a "good" and "bad" target is often just a judgment about the relative payoff that the target might yield and the risk of confrontation or apprehension (Reppetto, 1974, pp. 14–17; Letkemann, 1973, pp. 137–157; Waller and Okihiro, 1978). Very close to home, potential targets are well known, but the potential criminal is also likely to be well known. Risk of recognition or confrontation increases close to home. In a study of delinquent behavior in Philadelphia, Turner (1969) found a reduction in offenses close to home. There was very little delinquent behavior within one block of home locations: the pattern of offenses peaked outside this localized safe zone.

Turner looked at property offenses, which are considered instrumental, that is goal directed or planned (even if the search process if fairly unconscious). Violent offenses also cluster close to home. Many violent offenses occur between people who know each other or are related to each other or are living together. Social interactions between people decrease with distance from home. Violent offenses are, however, high-affect crimes. An instrumental assessment of risk that would decrease criminal activity near home is unlikely to occur. An overall pattern of violent crime occurrences in relation to home locations does not show a crime-free zone immediately adjacent to the home. In fact, many violent offenses occur in the home. It should be noted, however, that violent crimes, particularly homicide, have a high clearance rate, a rate consistent with "high-risk" crimes.

Distance Perception

The discussion about distance and crime occurrence was couched in "objective" space terminology. Patterns of movements away from home depend on the perception of distance, not the actual distance in miles or kilometers. Research has shown that although there is a relationship between actual distance and perceived distance, the relationship is not necessarily simple.

Throughout this chapter, the terms *perceived* and *perception* have been used quite loosely. In a description of distance research, a more careful distinction must be made. *Perception* technically refers to the physiological mechanisms of hearing, seeing, touching, and so on, that is, how the brain transforms external impulses, and how impulses are interpreted by the brain. *Distance perception* is the process by which someone sees objects and judges their distance away. Immediate movement depends on distance perception. One must perceive distances accurately to move across a room. The movement of people in a city—and therefore, criminals—depends on distance perception, but it also depends on conceptions or beliefs about how far away or how far apart locations are. The process of deciding where to go within a city involves a memory of what is there, images of what is there, and beliefs about relative locations.

Distance estimations made from memory, as opposed to estimations made while one is looking at what is being estimated, are called *cognitive distance estimations*. The careful distinction between perceptual distance and cognitive distance estimation is not maintained in the literature. The term *perceptual distance estimation* is used for both types of judgments. In understanding a criminal's spatial behavior, cognitive distance estimation is more important. To conform to terminology already used in the chapter, the broader definition of *perceived distance* is used here. Cognitive distance estimation is subsumed under the term *perceptual distance estimation.*

The distance between two locations is not the same as the perceived distance. People are usually inaccurate estimators of measured distance. Many factors appear to influence perceived distance. Although it is not possible at this stage in the development of cognitive science to make definitive statements, the research that has been done points to some interesting relationships. Lee (1970) explored distance estimation within cities—in his case, Dundee, Scotland—and found that people overestimated distances to locations away from the city center; that is, given two locations actually an equal distance away from a base point (home), the location toward the center of the city was thought to be closer than the location away from the city center. Locations that are toward the center of the city are better known and better known locations are estimated as closer. In a study done in Columbus, Ohio, Cox and Zannaras (1973) found that university students underestimated locations *away* from the city center, the opposite of Lee's finding. Thompson (1965), as reported in Briggs (1973), found that "used" stores were seen as closer than "nonused" stores.

Distance cognition also seems to be associated with the complexity or type of distance being estimated. Distance can be measured as point-to-point, shortest-line distances. Shortest-line, or "as-the-crow-flies," measurements do not take into account how a person might actually travel, with all the curving roads and nondirect paths. Shortest-line distances resemble airplane routes between cities. Within a city, there is often no travel analogue to shortest-line distances.

Distance can also be measured in actual travel distance: How many miles (or kilometers) is it from one point to another along existing travel paths? Actual travel distance often diverges greatly from shortest-line distance. Estimations of actual travel distances would be expected to differ from estimations of short-line distances. One of the problems with research into the estimation of distances is that researchers have used both types of real distances as the base to be estimated (see Lee, 1970; Cox and Zannaras, 1973).

The difference between shortest-line distance and actual travel distance can be seen if one considers two hypothetical cities (Figure 12-3). City X has a fairly typical grid street-network. In cities with such a basic street layout, usually several of the north—south and east—west streets become major arteries, carrying large volumes of traffic. The other grid streets become feeder streets to the main arteries. In City X, there are many ways to get from Point A to Point B. Figure 12-3 depicts one possible route. Although many routes exist, all routes share one characteristic: the path from A to B consists of a series of straight-line movements and right-angle turns. In City Y, some routes exist that cut across the basic grid network. In the example in Figure 12-3, the travel distance between Points A and B is longer in City X than in City Y, although the shortest travel times distances might be identical.

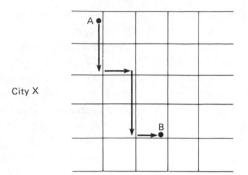

Figure 12–3. Travel paths.

City X

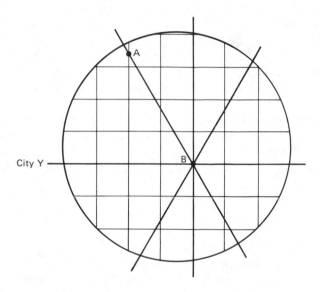

City Y

Distance may also be estimated by travel time. Trips that take a great amount of time seem to cover more distance than trips that take a shorter time. A three-mile walk seems longer than a three-mile drive. Distances along straight routes seem shorter than distances with many turns (Sadalla and Staplin, 1980a; Sadalla and Staplin, 1980b). As the number of turns increases in a route, the perceived length of the route increases.

Stea (1969) summarized the factors that influence an individual's perception of distance:

1. The relative attractiveness of origins and destinations.
2. The number and type of barriers separating points.
3. Familiarity with routes.
4. The actual geographic distance.
5. The attractiveness of routes.

The actual geographic distance is transformed cognitively to yield perceived distances that are often different from the geographic ones.

If we use what is known about the perception of distance, the simple model of crime locations around a criminal's home must be modified. The statement "Crime occurrences decrease as 'distance' increases," must be changed to "Crime occurrences decrease as perceived distance increases." Crime occurrences are likely to decrease at a faster rate in directions where areas are unfamiliar. Crime occurrences are likely to decrease at a slower rate on or near major roads (known routes) leading away from home. Figure 12-4 shows a hypothetical pattern under "perceived-distance" constraints.

Activity Spaces

A criminal's pattern of searching for a target is more complex than shown in Figures 12-2 and 12-4, because mobility or movement in an urban area is more complicated. People have a home base and an associated home range made up of the usual paths taken to and from home. An individual's knowledge of an urban area is greatest around home and on these habitual paths. However, the home base and paths are part of a more general activity space. An activity space for an individual is made up of the locations that the individual most frequently goes to and the paths used to travel from one frequently used location to the next.

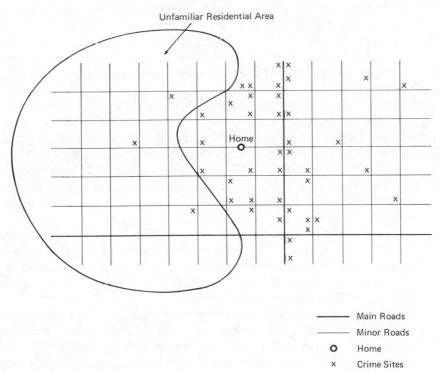

Figure 12-4. Distribution of offenses around a criminal's home, plotted according to the concepts of perceived distance.

Chombart de Lauwe (1965), in describing social space, provided a conceptual base from which to explore the concept of activity spaces. Chombart de Lauwe described five levels of social space:

1. Family Space. The space where family interactions occur.
2. Neighborhood Space. The space in which family space is imbedded; neighborhood space is the locus of daily social interaction.
3. Economic Space. The space that includes frequent economic interaction, such as shopping and working.
4. Urban Regional Space. The space where less frequent monthly or yearly activities take place.
5. World. The generally inaccessible space that people know about but in which they rarely interact or function.

Individuals' activity within a particular space decreases as they move from the familial level to the world level. Most activities take place in familial, neighborhood, or economic space.

Human activities occur at varying frequency. Numerous studies have been done to try to determine how people divide up available time between different activities. Work (for those people who work) and sleep (as might be expected) take up most of the time. In fact, the best-known U.S. study, Chapin and Brail (1969), found that only *five* hours on an average out of a twenty-four-hour day were spent in discretionary activity. Most time was spent at work, eating, shopping, homemaking, or sleeping. The use of discretionary time varied by the sociodemographic characteristics of individuals. The elderly, children, people with young children, people with full-time jobs, and the unemployed spent more discretionary time at home. Young, unattached individuals and part-time workers spent less discretionary time at home. Table 12-1 contains a breakdown of the results of Chapin and Brail's time-budget study.

Activity systems have a spatial analogue. Working, shopping, and socializing involve trips, that is, movements from point to point. As activity patterns change, so do movement patterns. An activity space is the spatial trace of patterns of activities, the geographic identification of locations that are frequent end points of trips, and the paths between end points. At an aggregate level, in a U.S. study of suburban trips, looking at all trips outward bound from home, about 30 percent were to work locations, about 20 percent were recreational, and 20 percent were shopping trips (Table 12-2).

Actual mobility is limited spatially. Schematically, the major components of an individual's activity space can be represented by several major nodes and a limited number of paths between nodes (Figure 12-5a). Trips to and from work (or school) and home, and trips to and from shopping and recreation or entertainment centers dominate an individual's activity space.

Criminals have activity spaces formed by their dominant movement patterns. Most criminals are predominantly noncriminal; that is, they spend most of their time in noncriminal pursuits. Shopping areas, entertainment areas, and home are major nodal points in a criminal's activity space. For school-aged criminals, school is another important nodal point. For adults, there may be additional work nodal points. Although time budgets and travel logs have not been obtained from crimi-

TABLE 12–1. Mean Duration of Time Heads of Households and Spouses of Heads Spend on Weekday Activities, by Work Status, Sex, and Stage in Life Cycle, Washington, 1968

Activity Category	Work Status Differences		Sex-Role Differences		Differences Among Various Stages in Life Cycle				
	Working Full Time (n = 982)	Not Working Full Time (n = 685)	Male (n = 736)	Female (n = 911)	No Children <19 Present, Head <35 (n = 235)	Children <19, Some <13, Head Any Age (n = 730)	Children <19, None <13, Head Any Age (n = 138)	No Children <19 Present, Head 35–65 (n = 404)	No Children <19 Present, Head 65 and Over (n = 160)
Main Job	8.02*	0.82	7.35*	3.26	6.65	4.99	5.37	5.68*	1.26
Eating	1.60*	1.76	1.74*	1.61	1.48*	1.64	1.65	1.72	1.89
Shopping	.39*	0.81	.34*	.73	.45*	.63	.51	.55	.49
Homemaking	1.23*	4.89	.92*	4.16	1.02*	3.41	2.87*	2.18*	3.42
Family Activities	.43*	.63	.41*	.59	.48	.65	.45	.35	.38
Socializing	.60*	.92	.64*	.80	1.09*	.68	.64	.56*	.97
Participation (Ch. and Orgs.)	.09*	.20	.11	.16	.13	.08	.27	.15	.27
Recreation, Other Diversions	.45*	.68	.55	.55	.82*	.41	.63	.51*	.79
Watching TV	1.30*	2.14	1.57	1.71	1.27	1.49	1.60	1.85*	2.44
Rest and Relaxation	.72*	1.25	.93	.94	.71	.79	.85	.98*	1.94
Miscellaneous	3.06*	2.37	3.08*	2.53	3.49*	2.62	2.60	2.68*	2.16
Sleeping	7.19*	7.85	7.32*	7.56	7.44	7.34	7.24	7.56*	7.96
All Forms of Discretionary Activity	5.25*	6.74	5.80	5.91	6.27*	5.41	5.79	5.74*	7.70

* Differences in durations to left and right significant $p \geq 0.05$ in difference-of-means test.

SOURCE: F. S. Chapin, Human Activity Patterns in the City: Things People Do in Time and Space. (New York: John Wiley and Sons, 1974), pp. 114–115. Reprinted by permission.

TABLE 12–2. United States: Suburban Trips
(one-way trips outward from home)

Trip Purpose	Percentage (Chicago Area Transportation)
Work	30
Recreation	22
Shopping	20
School	10
Other	18 *

* Includes personal business, eating, ride, etc.

SOURCE: adapted from J. D. Porteous, *Environment and Behavior: Planning and Everyday Urban Life.* Reading, Mass.: Addison-Wesley, 1977, p. 97.

nals, it is reasonable to assume that their noncriminal activity spaces are formed in a manner similar to the activity spaces of noncriminals.

Awareness Spaces

An activity space consists of those areas and locations where a person actually travels. Any particular activity space is a limited subset of all possible locations and paths within a city. People's knowledge of a city is greater than their habitual paths and frequent destinations. They are aware of the areas surrounding their habitual paths and frequent destinations, even if they do not travel in these areas. The awareness of what is around a familiar path is geographically limited and may not extend beyond "knowing" what is within a block or two on either side of the road. As with patterns of travel distance decay, there is an awareness distance decay away from familiar, habitual paths (Figure 10-5b). Areas close to, or adjacent to, a well-traveled path are visible and are likely to be known by the people using that path. What is actually known about the surrounding areas depends on the characteristics of the observer, the means of transport, and the characteristics of the actual physical environment. The psychological characteristics of the observer are not addressed here: the mode of transport and the characteristics of the physical environment are.

Mode of Transport

The way that a person travels influences what is seen and remembered about the areas close to the travel path. Different things are seen if a person travels by foot, by public transit, or by automobile. Travel by foot is slow, and much detail can be absorbed (Lynch and Rivkin, 1959). Travel by public transit or automobile is faster, and less detail is remembered. In surface public transit, the traveler is similar to a passenger in a car. A surface passenger in a bus can watch the road, the side of the road, or what goes on in the bus. Similarly, an automobile passenger has the same options, possibly with less distraction inside the vehicle, but with better potential view lines.

What is seen while one is traveling, by a car or by bus, depends on the speed

Activity Space

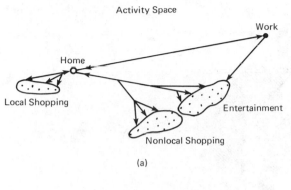

Figure 12–5. Activity and Awareness Space.

(a)

Awareness Space

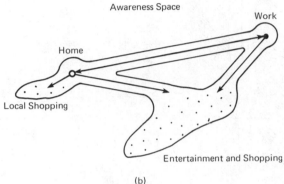

(b)

of the vehicle and on what passes through the visual field. As the speed of a vehicle increases, objects pass through the visual field more quickly and have less chance of being noticed. At 30 miles per hour (50 kilometers per hour) a fair amount of detail can be seen. For example, individual houses pass through the visual field slowly enough so that they can be visually fixed. Road signs can be seen and read. At 50 miles per hour (80 kilometers per hour), individual objects stay within the visual field a shorter length of time and are less likely to be noticed. At all speeds, objects close to the road stay within the visual field of the traveler longer than objects off the road (Figure 12-6).

On public transit, speed varies. At bus stops or transit points, what can be observed increases. Similarly, at major intersections, where cars and buses are stopped by lights or traffic, objects remain in the visual field longer and have a higher probability of being remembered.

The prominent awareness space, the area around habitual paths and destinations, is nonuniform in scope. It narrows along fast transit paths with few stops, and it widens around destinations and delay points.

Physical Environment

The physical environment also directly influences what is seen and remembered. Early research by Appleyard et al. (1964), who worked introspectively with a group of subjects, began an exploration of what it is about the physical environment that makes people notice and remember things. Picking up on the earlier

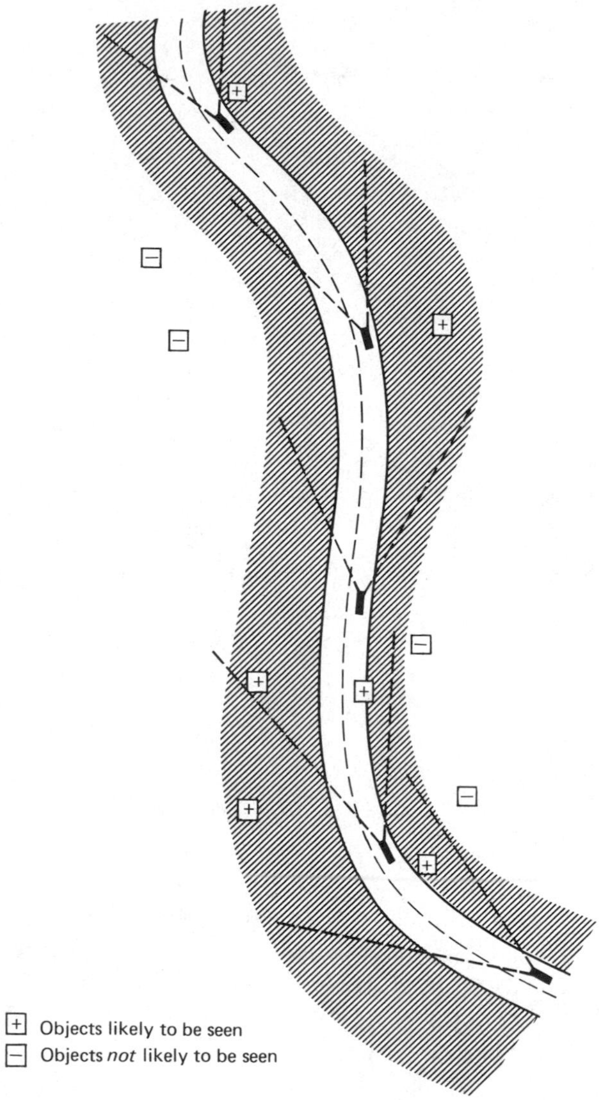

Figure 12–6. Area of visibility: View from a road.

- ⊞ Objects likely to be seen
- ⊟ Objects *not* likely to be seen

work by Appleyard et al. and using more objective and less introspective techniques, Carr and Schissler (1969) found that both the perception and the memory of a city viewed from a highway seem to be determined by the actual physical arrangements. Carr and Schissler used head-mounted devices that tracked where a person looked, what the points of visual fixation were, and how the person turned his or her head. While using such a device, they drove subjects along a strip of highway outside Boston and recorded their eye and head movements. After the trip, the authors checked their subjects' memories of the trip. The researchers found similarities between what was watched (eye fixations) and what was remembered. Although there were obvious dissimilarities in what was remembered and what was watched, there was also a core of buildings and objects recognized by all the sub-

354

jects. The objects that were remembered generally had a known identity, were easy to label, and were unique in size or function. Breaks in continuity helped memorability. If there was a sharp break in land uses, an object marking the break was remembered. Not all objects that were looked at were remembered; for example, factories were not easily remembered. Absorbing and remembering an environment is a complex interaction of the potential of objects to be seen and the attributes of the objects.

Appleyard (1969) reinforced the findings of Carr and Schissler in a study entitled "Why Buildings Are Known." Working in Ciudad Guayana, Venezuela, Appleyard identified two hundred buildings and, using trained personnel, rated the buildings on several major characteristics:

1. *Form Intensity.* Buildings with a high form intensity have much movement about them; have distinctive contours; have unusual size, complexity, or surface; and have distinctive landscaping or signs.

2. *Visibility.* Buildings with high visibility can be seen from the major intersections in a town or the major transportation stops, such as major bus stops; they are near objects that cut across the line of vision.

3. *Use Significance.* Buildings with high use significance are single-use buildings; are singular buildings such as police stations; or buildings that are low use but high in symbolism.

The buildings that were best known in this study had much movement around them and were unique in contour, size, and surfaces. Landscaping and signs had little effect on whether buildings were known. All aspects of high visibility, as defined by Appleyard, were associated with buildings' being remembered. Buildings with high intensity of use and singularity of use were also remembered.

Research shows a link between what *is* and what is *remembered* or *known* about an area. Locations that stand out are those that are visible, that have a high intensity of use, and, in concert with visibility, that are located at breakpoints in or disjunction with the background land uses.

Formation of an Awareness Space

Activity spaces are restricted, and what is remembered within an activity space is also restricted. The awareness space of an individual is limited and potentially predictable. After an initial learning period in a new location, activity and awareness spaces become fairly fixed. Criminals act as other people and function within spatially restricted awareness spaces. Their search areas for targets fall within their awareness spaces and decrease in intensity as distance increases away from their normal activity areas. The distance-decay pattern away from home is a simplification. Distance-decay patterns occur around all major activity nodes and major paths connecting the nodes.

Aggregate Criminal-Spatial-Behavior

Individuals follow fairly fixed patterns when moving about within a city. Although the analysis of individual decisions is of interest within criminology and

355

criminal justice, the analysis of aggregate or composite decision patterns is also of interest. If individual criminals live scattered around a city and travel along diverse and nonoverlapping paths, then aggregate analysis will yield nothing. We know, however, that aggregate patterns of criminal behavior exist.

Criminal Residence

Patterns have been documented as long ago as the eighteenth century. Petrovich (1971, pp. 243–244) described spatially clustered criminal residences in Paris in the last half of the eighteenth century. Criminal districts in New York City were described for the eighteenth and the early nineteenth centuries (Inciardi, 1978, pp. 32–37). In an informative book on Victorian crime, Tobias (1972b, pp. 130–135, 142–144) described clusters of criminal residences in London and Manchester in the nineteenth century. He vividly described "rookeries" and the steps taken by officials to try to break up these criminal areas. In the twentieth century, numerous writers, often with intellectual allegiance to ecological criminology, described criminal areas in the United States and Britain. Shaw and McKay (1969) extensively studied Chicago in the booming growth period of the early twentieth century. Morris (1958) analyzed delinquency areas in Croydon, near London, England. Baldwin and Bottoms performed a similar study in Sheffield in the 1960s. These researchers, and others, found spatial clusterings of criminal residences. Explanations for the spatial clusterings varied, but spatial clusterings were repeatedly found.

The clustering of the home residences of criminals and delinquents should be viewed not as anything unusual but as a special case of the general clustering of human groups in space. The simplest model of the city divides areas into a series of concentric zones made up of similar types of residences and socioeconomically similar people. As discussed in Chapter 9, this model does not hold in detail for actual cities and, in fact, deviates greatly from the urban form of most cities. A more accurate and flexible model of urban areas views a city as a mosaic of homogeneous clusters (Timms, 1971). A city has many subareas that are fairly homogeneous along sociodemographic lines. The norm, in fact, is homogeneous subareas. These homogeneous clusters are held together in a variety of ways, depending on the age of the city, its transportation network, its topography, and just plain accident. Inasmuch as criminal populations can be identified along sociodemographic lines such as age, race, income, and family background, criminal subareas are likely to exist where there is a clustering of people with sociodemographic characteristics similar to those of criminals.

Criminal Mobility

With a clustering of home residences, there will be a concurrent similarity in the paths used to go to and away from home. Starting at the same general base area, people usually travel along the same arteries. In fact, this channeling is a goal of transportation planning. Main arteries are designed to carry the bulk of the traffic. Similarly, people who live in the same base area usually follow similar shopping and urban recreation patterns. Local shops develop for an area; subregional and regional shopping areas develop to serve multiple areas. Local theaters and regional theaters serve local and regional audiences. Local parks and regional parks have different target populations.

Overall, there is a blending of activity spaces for people living in the same base area. Individual patterns are unique, but composite or aggregate patterns exist for areas (or alternatively for varying sociodemographic groups) (Figure 12-7).

The shape of the overall pattern depends on the concentration of housing, shopping, entertainment, and work locations. In cities with dense core areas, where central work and shopping locations dominate the shopping and work locations in the rest of the city, the paths and aggregate activity spaces are highly similar for many groups of people. In more diffuse cities, where shopping and working locations are scattered everywhere, composite activity space is less coherent.

Research into property crime reveals patterns that match aggregate activity spaces. Morris (1958) found that delinquents committed their crimes close to home or in the central shopping area of Croydon, England. Reppetto (1974) found, in interviews with Boston burglars, that most burglars committed their offenses in neighborhoods that they knew from experience rather than in expensive residential areas, even though they perceived that the expected take would be higher in the upper-class neighborhoods. In analyzing crime-trip patterns for male and female burglars in Philadelphia, Rengert (1975) found that crimes were committed either close to home or in the core business area. Rengert speculated that the differences he found between male and female patterns might relate directly to differential activity spaces.

In a European study, Fink (1969) analyzed the location of burglaries in a West German town. He found that out-of-town burglars committed their offenses near major highways, in areas that would be in the limited awareness space of nonresidents. Using direct concepts of activity spaces, Porteous (1977) found that the main activity space of a gang near Victoria, British Columbia, contained most of the gang's delinquent acts. Porteous defined the activity space as areas circumscribed by the homes of the gang members and their school, their work, and the places they frequented in off hours.

Other studies show concentrations of crime along and adjacent to roads that

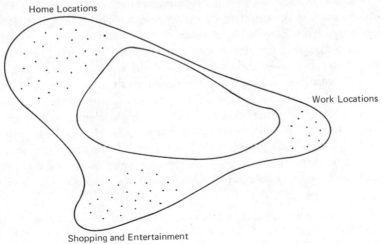

Figure 12–7. Composite activity spaces.

should be major paths in many people's awareness spaces. Studies of robbery in Oakland, California (Wilcox, 1973) and robbery and burglary in Detroit (Luedtke, 1970) showed a mild diffusion pattern of crime reaching one or two blocks into residential areas that abutted shopping and entertainment centers or strip commercial and industrial areas. A study by Rengert and Wasilchick (1980) of burglary in suburbs of Philadelphia found similar matches between usual travel paths and crime. Rengert found that few burglars, when committing offenses, strayed far from their usual path to work or a recreational spot. When they strayed, it was usually along an extension of a normal travel path, just past the usual stopping point.

Cognitive Maps

Direct research knowledge of individuals who commit crimes is limited. It is not easy to develop accurate pictures of the awareness spaces of criminals by working with criminals who are caught. To understand microspatial patterning of crime, it is important, and maybe necessary, to understand how many people in general come to know cities, and to work deductively from this point to see if existing patterns of crime conform to general perceptual patterns. Working in this manner is insufficient in and of itself to uncover all there is to know about microspatial behavior, but it is a conceptual building block.

Cognitive mapping is the general term applied to the processes by which individuals learn about, remember, and use knowledge about an area. The pioneer worker in the field of congitive mapping was Tolman (1948).[2] Tolman found that even rats were able to develop some basic knowledge about the overall shape and design of their environment and that their movements in a maze from a starting point to a food source were not governed just by a learned sequence of left and right turns. People, even more than rats, form conceptual models or "maps" of what an area is like. These maps have many dimensions: color, sounds, and symbols. Of dominant interest in cognitive mapping research is the overall geographic form and complexity of the knowledge of an area.

Most cognitive-mapping research has been done in urban areas. The researcher who has probably had the most influence in the field is Kevin Lynch. In 1960, Lynch published the results of his ingenious explorations of urban images. He asked groups of residents to draw sketch maps of their cities. Using composites of these sketch maps, he uncovered what he considered the basic elements of a person's image of a city. As a physically oriented urban planner, Lynch was looking for the conceptual building blocks that people use to provide an overall structure and form for their experience of living in cities. Some cities are easy to find one's way around; they are distinctive and clearly integrated. Other cities are confusing for both resi-

---

[2] Conceptually, many researchers preceded Tolman, most notably Gulliver (1908), Trowbridge (1913), Lewin (1936), and Piaget and Inhelder (1948), who worked on orientation in space and spatial psychology. The research of Tolman, however, for most people, marks the beginning of formal work on cognitive maps.

dents and visitors. In all cities, however, only limited areas are well known and appear in composite images or cognitive maps.

Lynch (1960) identified five elements of an image (pp. 47–48):

1. *Paths.* Paths are the channels of movement: roads, walkways, and railroads. For many people, paths dominate the image of a city.

2. *Edges.* Edges are linear elements not used as paths. They may be railroads, edges of developments, or shorelines, for example. Although edges are not as important as paths in forming images, they still help to organize cognitive maps.

3. *Districts.* Districts are fairly large subareas of cities that are recognizable by unifying characteristics. People can move in and out of districts. Districts often have well-established cores but fuzzy borders. Financial and industrial districts exist in many large cities. Housing areas may also be districts if they have a unifying element or elements.

4. *Nodes.* Nodes are intense foci of activity in cities. One can enter and leave nodes. Nodes are junctions of major paths, such as intersections or railway terminals, where people leave one type of path and move to another. Nodes may also be just concentrations of activity or interest. The cores of districts are nodes; the corner store may be a node.

5. *Landmarks.* Landmarks are point references that the traveler does not enter, for example, signs, buildings, or mountains. Landmarks are used for orientation and path finding. Distant landmarks help maintain local orientation as paths bend and twist. Local landmarks can be signs, specific trees, and other small-scale objects used in local path-finding (I turn by the Donut Shop) or in generally triggering of familiarity.

The actual form of the city clearly far exceeds the sketch maps in complexity, but the sketch map is like a skeleton showing the basic structure.

Lynch's study was a pioneer effort. He interviewed few people and drew broad conclusions from a limited sample, but subsequent research has supported his insights. Sketch maps have been used to uncover the cognitive maps of people in diverse cultures, and such studies have generally uncovered the same elements as Lynch's (Appleyard, 1970; Milgram, 1976; DeJonge, 1962; Orleans, 1973; Gulick, 1963). Cognitive maps vary with the sociodemographic characteristics of the mappers, just as do activity spaces and awareness spaces. The young, the old, and the poor have more restricted maps. Males tend to have broader maps than females, but these may just be an artifact of differential work patterns.

Paths, nodes, edges, districts, and landmarks stand out in composite or aggregate cognitive maps. Specific paths, nodes, edges, districts, and landmarks appear repeatedly on maps. These elements form major components of individual and composite cognitive maps. Cognitive maps are a representation of awareness space. Elements that stand out on cognitive maps are, tautologically, elements of awareness space. When it is impossible to discover the awareness space of criminals directly, the cognitive maps of residents from similar areas might be used as a subsitute and might give an indication of what is known about a city.

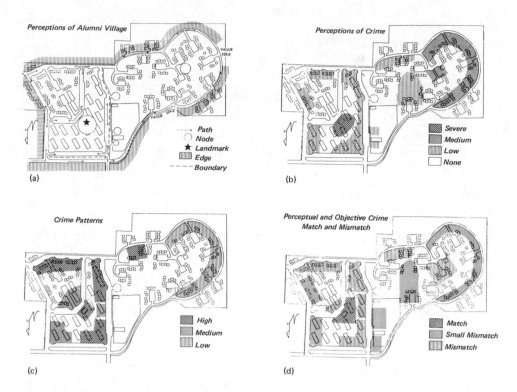

Figure 12–8. Composite perceptual maps of the Florida State University Alumni Village area. [Source: P. J. Brantingham, P. L. Brantingham, and T. Molumby, "Perceptions of Crime in a Dreadful Enclosure," *The Ohio Journal of Science* 77/1977:259.]

Perceived Crime Locations

The link between crime site choice and awareness spaces illustrates an interesting phenomenon in urban crime patterning: crime does not always occur where one might expect. It is generally thought that crimes ought to occur in secluded, out-of-the-way places. However, crimes generally occur near high-awareness locations. This pattern can be seen in any spatial map of crime, and it is well demonstrated in a cognitive mapping study of crime occurrences in a 795-unit housing project in Tallahassee, Florida (Brantingham et al., 1977).

In Tallahassee, property crime is a particular problem in a housing area called Alumni Village, managed by Florida State University. The housing is open to married graduate students. A victimization survey was run, for the study, to enumerate and locate spatially the property crime occurrences within Alumni Village. The survey covered a fifteen-month period, equivalent to five university quarters. During this period, 25 percent of the households had been victimized, a rate that far exceeds even national victimization estimates. Interviewed residents were asked to draw a sketch map of the university housing area and to identify the areas where they considered crime high. The sketch maps produced by the residents were combined and analyzed by means of the "image" elements identified by Kevin Lynch: paths, edges, nodes, landmarks, and districts.

The residents' image of Alumni Village is shown in Figure 12-8a. There were well-defined edges and paths and a node—landmark (the office—main laundry room). Figure 12-8b shows the residents' perceptions of where crime was bad. Crime was perceived to be worst at the node—landmark and in the most remote part of the village, a relatively low-use area that abuts a farm. Crime actually was highest along the major paths in the project and at the major node, the laundry room (Figure 12-8c).

As can be seen by Figure 12-8d, the residents were generally inaccurate in their perceptions despite the excessively high victimization rate. Crime was highest along the major paths and at the major landmark; the perception of crime was highest in deserted areas (fear?) and at the major landmark. The laundry appeared in many images of crime in this project, probably because it was the site of so many thefts that actual knowledge overwhelmed nonexperiential perceptions.

Other research supports an underlying mismatch between perceptions of crime and actual crime-occurrence locations. In studying general social problems in a "problem" housing estate in Glasgow, Damer (1974) found that the residents, who knew generally that crime was high in their housing project, assumed that crime had to be high not where they lived, but somewhere else in the project: they knew that things were not too bad around home. Similarly, the surveys on attitudes toward crime done in the United States have consistently shown that people think crime is going up *but not in their neighborhood.* Crime is thought to occur away from home, either in areas of known "disrepute" or in deserted locations, not in well-known, highly traveled areas.

Target Distribution: Opportunity Space

To this point, the discussion of criminal search behavior has assumed that there is a uniform distribution of targets. This is obviously not the case. Potential targets and victims are unevenly distributed across time and space. Consider the crime of street robbery. Street robbery, as the name implies, involves the robbery of an individual or individuals on a street. Thus, people must be present on the street. In most cities, selective areas have high pedestrian activity; others have no pedestrian activity. In addition, the presence or absence of pedestrians in any part of a city depends on the time of day. A central shopping area has high activity levels when stores are open but is soon deserted after the stores close.

The varying distribution of targets can also be easily seen in the crime of auto theft. Automobiles are driven about the city. During working hours, they are clustered (parked) near work locations. At night, they are scattered (parked) in residential areas and occasionally clustered near entertainment and shopping areas. Sarah Boggs (1964) demonstrated the importance of considering the distribution of targets in analyzing the spatial patterning of crimes, particularly auto theft. The apparent auto-theft pattern changed when crime rates were calculated with autos, not people, as the base. Her position has been reaffirmed by Mayhew et al. (1976) in more general research done for the Home Office in Britain.

Potential targets and victims are not distributed uniformly in space. Neither are potential criminals. The interaction of the locations of potential targets or victims and the awareness and activity spaces of potential criminals produces the patterns of crime occurrence (Figure 12-9).

This interaction of criminals and the spatial distribution of targets has long been noted by criminologists. As early as 1916, Burgess, the conceptual father of much social-ecological work, noted that the delinquency patterns in a city in Kansas conformed to the opportunity structure of the city. He noted that the critical factor determining the delinquency rates of the wards in Lawrence, Kansas, was the "geographical proximity to the business street," an area of high opportunity for minor offenses. He noted that in wards of similar socioeconomic makeup, it was the ward close to the business area that had the highest delinquency rate. Similarly, Thrasher (1927), in his well-known study of gang behavior, argued that the proximity to criminal opportunities was a major factor determining the criminal behavior of a gang.

Shaw and McKay (1929, 1931, 1969) repeatedly reported that areal delinquency rates in Chicago, over sixty years, were associated with proximity to criminal opportunities. Although they found this strong analytic relationship over time, they attributed the cause not to the increased opportunity to commit crimes but to social conditions and the transmission of criminal norms between groups. Lander (1954), another criminal ecologist, found high delinquency rates associated with commercial land-use concentrations.

Burgess, Shaw and McKay, and Lander executed their studies before there was

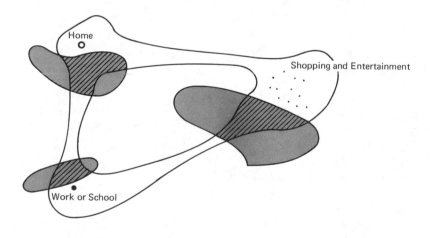

Awareness Space

Opportunities

Areas of Crime Occurrence

Figure 12–9. Intersection of opportunities with awareness space.

concern over the link between opportunity and crime. A recent study by Rhodes et al. (1980, 1981) consciously looked for the link between where criminals are and where targets are. Using data from Washington, D.C., and working at a very fine level of spatial resolution (the block level), Rhodes et al. reported movement from multifamily residential areas to transitional commercial areas for the commission of robberies and burglaries. There was a weaker movement to commit offenses within small business areas and a movement away from single-family housing areas. These movements occurred within a general distance-decay pattern. The movements reported by Rhodes et al. conform to hypothesized patterns.

Crime Occurrence Space

For a crime to occur, a motivated individual must come in contact with a potential target. A criminal is most likely to pick targets in and around his or her awareness space. However, not all potential targets within a person's awareness space are "good" targets. The characteristics of a target that make it "good" or "bad" are probably diverse, but they include at least an assessment of the risk associated with choosing a particular target or the difficulty of actually succeeding. There are irrational criminals—those who commit offenses without regard to risk or in the hopes of being apprehended—but most criminals are psychologically normal. Some offenses are so emotional or affective that consideration of risk does not occur, but in most offenses it is clear that the people committing the offenses take some precautions.

The risk is the probability of being caught. In house burglary, the risk is primarily the probability that the criminal will encounter the resident of a house while committing the crime. In bank robberies, the risk to the robber is the probability that someone in the bank might interfere, or that the police might arrive quickly enough to make an arrest, or, a more remote risk, that the robber might be tracked down through investigation. The risk is primarily the probability of someone's interfering in the completion of a crime or noticing facts that lead to later apprehension.

As well as assessing risk, criminals also assess the payoff of committing an offense. For property crime, the value of the goods that might be stolen in a particular house is the expected payoff. A judgment, either conscious or unconscious, is made about what goods might be stolen and what their value will be if stolen. For example, if a teenager breaks into a house, only some goods in the house are of potential value. A large, heavy television in a cabinet has no immediate value because it cannot be removed. Portable stereos, portable televisions, liquor, and cash all have immediate value and are the usual objects of theft. Sterling silver has high actual value but low immediate value to teenagers who commit crimes, and it is rarely taken by juveniles. Silver, however, is a likely target for more professional thieves, who know how to dispose of it for cash. The decision about whether a target is "good" or "bad" can, in some ways, be thought of as an assessment of the relative payoff and risks.

Some aspects of the attractiveness of a target or a victim have to do with the direct, immediate characteristics of the target. Other aspects relate to the general

363

location of targets or victims in the awareness space of potential criminals. For example, the growth in branch-bank robberies is consistent with an assessment of the relative risk and payoff of the targets within an awareness space. Major highways and roads are common elements of awareness spaces. Branch banks are obviously located near highways and major roads for the convenience of patrons. The banks are also convenient for criminals; escape is easy. Accessibility for customers also means accessibility for criminals.

The recent growth in convenience-store robberies also fits this pattern. Convenience stores are in highly accessible locations, are open late, and often have a limited number of customers in the store at anyone time, and, consequently, few witnesses. Convenience stores should be attractive targets. In a study of convenience-store robbery, Duffala (1976) found that within the general class of convenience stores, those stores that were near major roads, but not on them, and that had no surrounding businesses open in the evening had the highest victimization rates. The nearness to major roads assured that the stores were in the awareness space of many people (a requirement of a successful store). The slight distancing from the major roads and the lack of surrounding nighttime activity lowered the "risk" of interference during a robbery. In a study of arson and vandalism, Rengert (1972) found that opportunities, risks (relative police efficiency), familiarity, and the accessibility of various areas in Philadelphia could explain or describe 73 percent of the variance in the distribution of the crimes studied.

Areal characteristics help identify "safe" areas for crimes. Shlomo Angel (1968) developed a schema describing the interaction of risk, payoff, and awareness-space characteristics that go together to produce high-crime environments. Looking at street crime (armed robberies, strong-arm robberies, and purse snatches), Angel described the boundary conditions of crime:

1. Behavioral Characteristics of Offenders:
    a. *Territoriality*. Offenders and potential offenders cling to areas where they can function inconspicuously and feel secure, and where they have enough knowledge to make a fast and efficient escape.
    b. *Accessibility*. Offenders and potential offenders cling to areas that have easy access from areas of criminal habitation.
2. Behavioral Characteristics of Victims:
    a. *Territoriality and accessibility*. Victims or likely victims frequent or are found in areas with characteristics described in the first set of boundary conditions.
3. Social Deterrents of Crime:
    a. *Police Patrols*. Police patrols act as deterrents for street crimes that are "visible" crimes.
    b. *Community Awareness*. If a community is aware of crime potential, then the potential anonymity of an area for a criminal is reduced.
    c. *Effective Witnesses*. If many witnesses are present, then the risk of committing an offense increases for the potential criminal.

Street crime is a localized phenomenon. Only restricted areas of cities have street crime. Within these areas, the intensity of use influences crime. Crimes are most likely in areas where there are enough potential victims to make the search for a victim worthwhile to the criminal, and where the number of people is not so great that many potential witnesses are around. When there are few or many people around, crime is much less likely than when there are many targets, but few clusters of people. When usage is low, there are few potential victims and few witnesses. When usage is high, there are many potential victims but many potential witnesses. In the medium range of intensity of use, there are enough potential victims, but not enough people for adequate surveillance.

Angel argued that street crime can be reduced by the use of environmental design to influence where people walk and travel and thereby to increase the intensity of use above the critical zone or to reduce use below the critical zone. Underutilized pedestrian paths, such as pedestrian tunnels, should be eliminated. Evening activities in parks should be increased to provide protection. Nighttime businesses should be clustered together. Specialized areas, such as financial districts, should not be used for overflow parking for entertainment districts. Generally, evening pedestrians should be channeled together to provide mutual protection.

Crime occurrence areas are those parts of a city within the awareness space of many potential criminals, and areas that have attractive, low-risk targets. Here, crime will be highly clustered and localized.

Chapter Summary

Crime occurrence within the microenvironment of a city is highly patterned. Potential criminals do not search through a whole city for targets; they look for targets within their more restricted awareness space. In order to understand the spatial patterning of crime within a city, it is necessary to look at the city as a subjective environment. Individual knowledge of a city is limited and is structured by daily activities. Similarly, a criminal's knowledge is limited. Crime clusters, as do criminal residences.

Potential victims and targets are not uniformly distributed throughout an urban area. Crimes are more likely where targets cluster within the awareness space of many potential criminals. Many highly attractive targets are located far away from potential criminals and are therefore fairly safe.

Potential targets that fall within the awareness space of many criminals are not all equally likely to become actual targets. The characteristics of the area or of the target itself may provide immunity. Potential surveillance and actual surveillance are major characteristics of immunity.

The actual pattern of crime within any particular city is the result of the residential patterning of the people motivated to commit offenses, the spatial patterning of the potential targets and victims, and the presence or absence of factors that help criminals to identify targets or victims that will yield a reasonable payoff with little risk.

Bibliography

Abbiateci, A.; Billacois, F.; Bongert, Y.; Castan, N.; Castan, Y.; and **Petrovich, P.** *Crimes et criminalité en France sous l'Ancien Régime: 17e–18e siècles.* Paris: Librarie Armand Colin, 1971.

Akers, R. L. "Socio-Economic Status and Delinquent Behavior: A Retest," *Journal of Research in Crime and Delinquency* 1 (1964):38–46.

Akers, R. L. *Deviant Behavior: A Social Learning Approach.* Belmont, Calif.: Wadsworth, 1973.

Allen, J.; Kelly, D. H.; and Heymann, P. *Assault with a Deadly Weapon: The Autobiography of a Street Criminal.* New York: McGraw-Hill, 1977.

Amadeo, D., and Golledge, R. G. *An Introduction to Scientific Reasoning in Geography.* New York: John Wiley and Sons, 1975.

American Law Institute. *Model Penal Code* (Proposed Official Draft). Philadelphia: American Law Institute, 1962.

Amir, M. *Patterns in Forcible Rape.* Chicago: University of Chicago Press, 1971.

Anderson, R. W. *The Economics of Crime.* London: Macmillan Press, 1976.

Angel, S. *Discouraging Crime Through City Planning.* Berkeley: Centre for Planning and Development Research, University of California at Berkeley, 1968.

Anttila, I., and Jaakkola, R. *Unrecorded Crime in Finland.* Helsinki: Kriminologinen Tutkimuslaitos, 1966.

Appleyard, D. "Why Buildings Are Known," *Environment and Behavior* 1 (1969): 131–156.

Appleyard, D. "Styles and Methods of Structuring a City," *Environment and Behavior* 2 (1970):100–117.

Appleyard, D.; Lynch, K.; and Meyer, J. *The View From the Road.* Cambridge, Mass.: MIT Press, 1964.

Archer, D., and Gartner, R. "Homicide in 110 Nations: The Development of the Comparative Crime Data File." In E. Bittner and S. Messinger (Eds.), *Criminology Review Yearbook.* Vol. 2, pp. 433–463. Beverly Hills, Calif.: Sage Publications, 1980.

Ashcraft, N., and Scheflen, A. E. *People Space: The Making and Breaking of Human Boundaries.* Garden City, New York: Anchor Books, 1976.

Avio, K. L., and Clarke, C. S. *Property Crime in Canada: An Econometric Study.* Toronto: University of Toronto Press, 1976.

Avison, N. *Patterns of Crime in the Lower Mainland.* Vancouver: British Columbia Police Commission, 1977.

Bagley, C. "Juvenile Delinquency in Exeter: An Ecological and Comparative Study," *Urban Studies* 2 (1965):33–50.

Baker, J. H. "Criminal Courts and Procedure at Common Law, 1550–1800." In J. S. Cockburn (Ed.), *Crime in England: 1550–1800,* pp. 5–48. Princeton, N.J.: Princeton University Press, 1977.

Baldwin, J. "The Role of Victim in Certain Property Offences." *Criminal Law Review* 1974a:353–358.

Baldwin, J. "Social Area Analysis and Studies of Delinquency." *Social Science Research* 3 (1974b):151–168.

Baldwin, J. "Ecological and Areal Studies in Great Britain and the United States." In N.

Morris and M. Tonry (Eds.), *Crime and Justice: An Annual Review of Research*, Vol. 1., pp. 29–65. Chicago: University of Chicago Press, 1979.

Baldwin, J., and Bottoms, A. E. *The Urban Criminal: A Study in Sheffield*. London: Tavistock Publications, 1976.

Banfield, E. C. *The Unheavenly City Revisited*. Boston: Little, Brown, 1974.

Barker, R. R. *Ecological Psychology*. Stanford: Stanford University Press, 1968.

Beard, C. *An Economic Interpretation of the Constitution of the United States*. New York: Macmillan, 1935.

Beattie, J. M. "The Pattern of Crime in England, 1660–1800." *Past and Present* 62 (1974):47–95.

Beattie, J. M. "Crime and the Courts in Surrey, 1736–1753." In J. S. Cockburn (Ed.), *Crime in England, 1550–1800*, pp. 155–186. Princeton, N.J.: Princeton University Press, 1977.

Beattie, R. H. "Problems of Criminal Statistics in the United States." *Journal of Criminal Law, Criminology, and Police Science* 46 (1955): 178–186.

Becker, G. "Crime and Punishment: An Economic Approach." *Journal of Political Economy* 76 (1968):169–217.

Becker, H. S. *Outsiders*. New York: Free Press, 1963.

Beier, A. L. "Vagrants and the Social Order in Elizabethan England." *Past and Present* 64 (1974):3–29.

Bell-Robotham, B., and Boydell, C. L. "Crime in Canada: A Distributional Analysis." In C. Boydell, C. F. Grindstaff, and P. Whitehead (Ed.), *Deviant Behavior and Societal Reaction*, pp. 93–116. Toronto: Holt, Rinehart and Winston, 1972.

Bellamy, J. G. "The Coterel Gang: An Anatomy of a Band of Fourteenth Century Criminals." *English Historical Review* 79 (1963): 698–717.

Bellamy, J. G. *Crime and Public Order in the Later Middle Ages*. Toronto: University of Toronto Press, 1973.

Belson, W. A. "The Extent of Stealing by London Boys." *The Advancement of Science* 25 (1968): 171–184.

Belson, W. A. *Juvenile Theft: The Causal Factor*. New York: Harper and Row, 1975.

Bensing, R. C., and Schroeder, O. *Homicide in an Urban Community*. Springfield, Ill.: Charles C. Thomas, 1960.

Bentham, J. *An Introduction to the Principles of Morals and Legislation*. London: T. Payne and Son, 1789.

Berry, B. J. L. "Hierarchical Diffusion: The Basis of Developmental Filtering and Spread in a System of Growth Centers." In N. M. Hansen (Ed.), *Growth Centers in Regional Economic Development*, pp. 108–139. New York: Free Press, 1971.

Berry, B. J. L. *The Human Consequences of Urbanization*. New York: St. Martin's Press, 1973.

Bevis, C., and Nutter, J. B. "Changing Street Layouts to Reduce Residential Burglary." Paper read at American Society of Criminology annual meeting, Atlanta, 1977.

Biderman, A.; Johnson, L.; McIntyre, J.; and Weir, A. *Report on a Pilot Study in the District of Columbia on Victimization and Attitudes Towards Law Enforcement: Field Surveys I*. President's Commission on Law Enforcement and Administration of Justice. Washington: Government Printing Office, 1967.

Black, D. *The Behavior of Law*. New York: Academic Press, 1976.

Blanchard, J., and Cassidy, R. G. *Crime and Criminal Process in Canada: 1880–1970 and Beyond*. Ottawa: Statistics Division, Solicitor General of Canada, 1975. (CANJUS Project Report # 21; Statistics Division Report # 2/75.)

Block, R. *Violent Crimes: Environment, Interaction, and Death*. Lexington, Mass: Lexington Books, 1977.

Blomberg, T. G. "Diversion and Accelerated Social Control." *Journal of Criminal Law and Criminology* 68 (1977):274–282.

Blomberg, T. G. "Diversion from Juvenile Court: A Review of the Evidence." In **F. L. Faust** and **P. J. Brantingham** (Eds.), *Juvenile Justice Philosophy*. (2d ed.), pp. 415–430. St. Paul, Minn.: West Publishing Co., 1979.

Blumstein, A.; Cohen, J; and **Nagin, D. S.** "The Dynamics of a Homeostatic Punishment Process." *Journal of Criminal Law and Criminology* 67 (1977):317–334.

Blumstein, A., and **Nagin, D. S.** "Analysis of Arrest Rates for Trends in Criminality." *Socio-Economic Planning Sciences* 9 (1975):221–227.

Boggs, S. L. "Urban Crime Patterns." *American Sociological Review* 30 (1966):899–908.

Bonger, W. A. *Criminality and Economic Conditions*. Boston: Little, Brown, 1916.

Booth, C. *Life and Labour of the People in London*, vol. 1. London: Macmillan and Co., Ltd., 1891.

Bordua, D. J. "Juvenile Delinquency and 'Anomie': An Attempt at Replication." *Social Problems* 6 (1958–1959):230–238.

Bottomley, A. K., and **Coleman, C. A.** "Criminal Statistics: The Police Role in the Discovery and Detection of Crime." *International Journal of Criminology and Penology* 4 (1976):33–58.

Bottoms, A. E. "On the Decriminalization of English Juvenile Courts." In R. Hood (Ed.), *Crime, Criminology and Public Policy*, pp. 319–345. London: Heinemann, 1974.

Box, G. E. P., and **Jenkins, G. M.** *Time Series Analysis: Forecasting and Control* (rev. ed.). San Francisco: Holden-Day, 1976.

Braithwaite, J., and **Braithwaite, V.** "The Effect of Income Inequality and Social Democracy on Homicide: A Cross-National Comparison." *British Journal of Criminology* 20 (1980): 45–53.

Brana-Shute, R., and **Brana-Shute, G.** *Crime and Punishment in the Caribbean*. Gainesville, Fla.: Center for Latin American Studies, University of Florida, 1980.

Brantingham, P. J. *The Children's Hour: Juvenile Justice in England and America*. Cambridge: Radzinowicz Library, Cambridge University. Unpublished Research Paper, 1970.

Brantingham, P. J. "The Medico-Penal Model of Drug Abuse Control: The English Experience." In **R. L. Rachin** and **E. H. Czajkoski** (Eds.), *Drug Abuse Control: Administration and Politics*, pp. 51–72. Lexington, Mass.: Lexington Books, 1975a.

Brantingham, P. J. "The Southernness Index: Crime and Cultural Diffusion." Paper read at Southern Region Demographic Group annual meeting, Atlanta, 1975b.

Brantingham, P. J. "Juvenile Justice Reforms in California and New York in the Early 1960's." In **F. L. Faust** and **P. J. Brantingham** (Eds.), *Juvenile Justice Philosophy* (2d ed.), pp. 259–268. St. Paul, Minn.: West Publishing Co., 1979.

Brantingham, P. J., and **Brantingham, P. L.** "Spatial Patterning of Burglary." *Howard Journal of Penology and Crime Prevention* 14 (1975):11–24.

Brantingham, P. J., and **Brantingham, P. L.** "Housing Patterns and Burglary in a Medium-Sized American City." In **J. Scott** and **S. Dinitz** (Eds.), *Criminal Justice Planning*, pp. 63–74. New York: Praeger, 1977.

Brantingham, P. J., and **Brantingham, P. L.** "A Theoretical Model of Crime Site Selection." In **M. D. Krohn** and **R. L. Akers** (Eds.), *Crime, Law and Sanctions*, pp. 105–118. Beverly Hills, Calif.: Sage Publications, 1978.

Brantingham, P. J., and **Brantingham, P. L.** "Crime, Occupation, and Economic Specialization: A Consideration of Inter-Metropolitan Patterns." In **D. Georges-Abeyie** and **K. Harries** (Eds.), *Crime: A Spatial Perspective*, pp. 93–108. New York: Columbia University Press, 1980.

Brantingham, P. J., and **Brantingham, P. L.** *Environmental Criminology*. Beverly Hills, Calif.: Sage Publications, 1981.

Brantingham, P. J.; Brantingham, P. L.; and Fister, R. "Mental Maps of Crime in a Canadian City." Paper presented at the Academy of Criminal Justice Sciences, Cincinnati, Ohio, 1979.

Brantingham, P. J.; Brantingham, P. L.; and Molumby, T. "Perceptions of Crime in a Dreadful Enclosure." *Ohio Journal of Science* 77 (1977):256–261.

Brantingham, P. J.; Dyreson, D. A.; and Brantingham, P. L. "Crime Seen Through a Cone of Resolution." *American Behavioral Scientist* 20 (1976):261–273.

Brantingham, P. J., and Kress, J. M. *Structure, Law and Power: Essays in the Sociology of Law.* Beverly Hills, Calif.: Sage Publications, 1979.

Brantingham, P. L. *Dynamic Modelling of the Felony Court System.* Tallahassee: Ph.D. Dissertation, Florida State University, 1977.

Brantingham, P. L., and Brantingham, P. J. "Residential Burglary and Urban Form." *Urban Studies* 12 (1975):273–284.

Brantingham, P. L., and Brantingham, P. J. "A Topological Technique For Regionalization." *Environment and Behavior* 10 (1978):335–353.

Brantingham, P. L., and Brantingham, P. J. "Notes on the Geometry of Crime." In P. J. Brantingham and P. L. Brantingham (Eds.), *Environmental Criminology*, pp. 27–54. Beverly Hills, Calif.: Sage Publications, 1981.

Brearly, H. C. *Homicide in the United States.* Chapel Hill: University of North Carolina Press, 1932.

Bridenbaugh, C. *Cities in Revolt: Urban Life in America, 1743–1776.* New York: Alfred A. Knopf, 1955.

Briggs, R. "Urban Cognitive Distance." In R. M. Downes and D. Stea (Eds.), *Image and Environment*, pp. 361–388. Chicago: Aldine Publishing Co., 1973.

British Columbia Police Commission. *The Public and the Police.* Vancouver: B.C. Police Commission Bulletin No. 6. (April), 1979.

Brosi, K. B. *A Cross-City Comparison of Felony Case Processing.* Washington: National Criminal Justice Information and Statistics Service, 1979.

Bugliosi, V., and Gentry, C. *Helter Skelter.* New York: W.W. Norton, 1974.

Bullock, H. A. "Urban Homicide in Theory and Fact." *Journal of Criminal Law, Criminology and Police Science* 45 (1955): 565–575.

Bureau of Justice Statistics. *Technical Report: Criminal Victimization in the U. S.-1979–80 Changes, 1973–80 Trends.* Washington: U.S. Department of Justice, July, 1982. (SD-NCS-N-21, NCJ-80838).

Burgess, E. W. "Juvenile Delinquency in a Small City." *Journal of the American Institute of Criminal Law and Criminology* 6 (1916):724–728.

Burgess, E. W. "The Growth of the City." In R. E. Park, E. W. Burgess, and R. D. McKenzie (Eds.), *The City*, pp. 47–62. Chicago: University of Chicago Press, 1925a.

Burgess, E. W. "Can Neighborhood Work Have a Scientific Basis?" In R. E. Park., E. W. Burgess, and R. D. McKenzie (Eds.), *The City*, pp. 142–155. Chicago: University of Chicago Press, 1925b.

Burns, A. F., and Mitchell, W. C. *Measuring Business Cycles.* New York: National Bureau of Economic Research, 1946.

Burt, C. *The Young Delinquent.* London: Appleton, 1925.

Campbell, M. F. *Torso.* Toronto: Macmillan of Canada, 1974.

CANJUS # 16. *Flow of Offenders in the Criminal Justice System of British Columbia for 1971.* Ottawa: Statistics Division, Ministry of the Solicitor General, Report # 10/74, 1974.

Cantor, D. and Cohen, L. E. "Comparative Measures of Homicide Trends: Methodological and Substantive Differences in the Vital Statistics and Uniform Crime Reports Time Series (1933–1975)." Paper read at American Society of Criminology annual meeting, Philadelphia, 1979.

Capone, D., and **Nichols, W. J.** "Urban Structure and Criminal Mobility." *American Behavioral Scientist* 20 (1976): 199–213.

Carr, S. and **Schissler, D.** "The City as a Trip: Perceptual Selection and Memory in the View from the Road." *Environment and Behavior* 1 (1969): 7–36.

Carter, H. *The Study of Urban Geography.* London: Edward Arnold, 1972.

Carter, M. P. and **Jephcott, P.** *The Social Background of Delinquency.* Nottingham, England: Unpublished report, University of Nottingham, 1954.

Central Statistical Office. *Social Trends. No. 8-1977 Edition.* London: HMSO, 1977.

Central Statistical Office. *Social Trends. No. 12-1982 Edition.* London: HMSO, 1981.

Chambliss, W. J. "A Sociological Analysis of the Law of Vagrancy." *Social Problems* 12 (1964): 67–77.

Chambliss, W. J. and **Seidman, R. B.** *Law, Order, Power.* Reading, Mass. Addison-Wesley, 1971.

Chapin, F. S. *Human Activity Patterns in the City: Things People Do in Time and Space.* New York: John Wiley and Sons, 1974.

Chapin, F. S., and **Brail, R. K.** "Human Activity Systems in the Metropolitan United States." *Environment and Behavior* 1 (1969): 107–130.

Cheffins, R. I., and **Tucker, R. N.** *The Constitutional Process in Canada* (2d ed.). Toronto: McGraw-Hill Ryerson, 1976.

Chesney, K. *The Victorian Underworld.* Harmondsworth, England: Penguin Books, 1972.

Chester, C. R. "Perceived Relative Deprivation as a Cause of Property Crime." *Crime and Delinquency* 22 (1976): 14–30.

Chevalier, L. *Classes Laborieuses et Classes Dangereuses à Paris Pendant La Première Moitié du 19ème Siècle.* Paris: Librarie Plon, 1958.

Chilton, R. J. "Continuity in Delinquency Area Research: A Comparison of Studies for Baltimore, Detroit and Indianapolis." *American Sociological Review* 29 (1964): 71–83.

Chombart de Lauwe, P. H. *Des Hommes et Des Villes.* Paris: Payot, 1965.

Christie, N.; Andenaes, J.; and **Skirbekk, S.** "A Study of Self-Reported Crime." *Scandinavian Studies in Criminology* 1 (1965): 86–116.

Cipolla, C. M. *The Industrial Revolution.* London: Fontana/Collins, 1973.

Clark, J. P., and **Tifft, L. L.** "Polygraph and Interview Validation of Self-Reported Deviant Behavior." *American Sociological Review* 31 (1966): 516–533.

Clarke, K. L.; Barnhorst, R.; and **Barnhorst, S.** *Criminal Law and the Canadian Criminal Code.* Toronto: McGraw-Hill Ryerson, 1977.

Clarke, R. V. G. *Tackling Vandalism.* Home Office Research Study No. 17. London: HMSO, 1978.

Clarren, S. N., and **Schwartz, A. I.** "Measuring a Program's Impact: A Cautionary Note." In **W. G. Skogan** (Ed.), *Sample Surveys of the Victims of Crime,* pp. 121–134. Cambridge, Mass.: Ballinger, 1976.

Clinard, M. B., and **Abbott, D. J.** *Crime in Developing Countries: A Comparative Perspective.* New York: John Wiley and Sons, 1973.

Cloward, R. A., and **Ohlin, L. E.** *Delinquency and Opportunity: A Theory of Delinquent Gangs.* New York: Free Press, 1960.

Cockburn, J. S. *A History of English Assizes: 1558–1714.* Cambridge: Cambridge University Press, 1972.

Cockburn, J. S. (Ed.). *Crime in England: 1550–1800.* Princeton, N.J.: Princeton University Press, 1977a.

Cockburn, J. S. "The Nature and Incidence of Crime in England, 1559–1625: A Preliminary Survey." In **J. S. Cockburn** (Ed.), *Crime in England: 1550–1800,* pp. 49–71. Princeton, N.J.: Princeton University Press, 1977b.

Cohen, A. K. *Delinquent Boys: The Culture of the Gang.* Glencoe, Ill.: The Free Press, 1955.

Cohen, L. E., and Felson, M. "Social Change and Crime Rate Trends." *American Sociological Review* 44 (1979):588–605.

Cohen, S. *Folk Devils and Moral Panics: The Creation of the Mods and the Rockers.* London: MacGibbon and Kee, 1972.

Cole, E. *Criminal Statistics in Canada: An Overview. Vol. I, 1876–1900.* Ottawa: Statistics Division, Ministry of the Solicitor General. Report # 2/74, 1974 *a*.

Cole, E. *Criminal Statistics in Canada: An Overview, Vol. II, 1901–1925.* Ottawa: Statistics Division, Ministry of the Solicitor General. Report # 11/74, 1974 *b*.

Coleman, J. S. "Problems of Conceptualization and Measurements in Studying Policy Impacts." In K. M. Dolbeare (Ed.), *Public Policy Evaluation,* pp. 19–40. Beverly Hills, Calif.: Sage Publications, 1975.

Conklin, J. E. *Robbery and the Criminal Justice System.* Philadelphia: Lippincott, 1972.

Connidis, I. "Problems in the Use of Official Statistics for Criminal Justice System Research." *Canadian Journal of Criminology* 21 (1979):397–415.

Connor, W. D. *Deviance in Soviet Society: Crime, Delinquency and Alcoholism.* New York: Columbia University Press, 1972.

Courtis, M. C. *Attitudes to Crime and the Police in Toronto: A Report on Some Survey Findings.* Toronto: Centre of Criminology, University of Toronto, 1970.

Courtis, M. C. "Victimization in Toronto." In R. A. Silverman and J. J. Teevan (Eds.), *Crime in Canadian Society,* pp. 119–125. Toronto: Butterworths, 1975.

Cousineau, D. F., and Veevers, J. E. "Juvenile Justice: An Analysis of the Canadian Young Offenders Act." In C. L. Boydell, C. F. Grindstaff, and P. C. Whitehead (Eds.), *Deviant Behavior and Societal Reaction,* pp. 243–261. Toronto: Holt, Rinehart and Winston, 1972.

Cowman, G. E. *Stolen Property and Its Redistribution in the Metropolitan Vancouver Region.* Victoria: Ministry of the Attorney General, Province of British Columbia, 1977.

Cox, K. R., and Zannaras, G. "Designative Perceptions of Macro-Spaces: Concepts, a Methodology, and Applications." In R. M. Downes and D. Stea, *Image and Environment,* pp. 162–181. Chicago: Aldine Publishing Co., 1973.

Cressey, D. R. "The State of Criminal Statistics." *National Probation and Parole Association Journal* 3 (1957):230–241.

Criminal Justice Planning Institute. *Criminal Justice Planning Course.* Los Angeles: University of Southern California, 1976.

Critchley, T. A. *A History of Police in England and Wales* (rev. ed.). London: Constable, 1978.

Curtis, L. A. *Criminal Violence: National Patterns and Behavior.* Lexington, Mass.: D. C. Heath, Lexington Books, 1974.

Damer, S. "Wine Alley: the Sociology of a Dreadful Enclosure." *Sociological Review* (N.S.) 22 (1974):221–248.

Davidovitch, A. "Criminalité et Repression in France Depuis un Siècle (1851–1952)." *Revue Francaise Sociologie* 2 (1961):30–49.

Davis, K. "The Urbanization of the Human Population." In C. Tilly (Ed.), *An Urban World,* pp. 160–177. Boston: Little, Brown, 1974.

DeFleur, L. B. "Ecological Variables in the Cross-Cultural Study of Delinquency." *Social Forces* 45 (1967):556–570.

DeFleur, M. L. and Quinney, R. "A Reformulation of Sutherland's Differential Association Theory and a Strategy for Empirical Verification." *Journal of Research in Crime and Delinquency* 3 (1966):1–22.

DeJonge, D. "Images of Urban Areas: Their Structure and Psychological Foundations." *Journal of the American Institute of Planners* 28 (1962):226–276.

Dentler, R. A., and Monroe, L. J. "Social Correlates of Early Adolescent Delinquency." *American Sociological Review* 26 (1961):733–743.

Departmental Committee on Criminal Statistics [Perks Committee]. *Report* London: HMSO (Cmnd. 3448), 1967.

Dickens, C. *Oliver Twist.* London: Richard Bentley, 1838.

Ditton, J. *Contrology: Beyond Criminology.* London: Macmillan Press, 1979.

Doleschal, E. *Criminal Statistics.* Rockville, Maryland: National Institute of Mental Health, Centre for Studies of Crime and Delinquency, 1972.

Downs, R. M., and Stea, D. (Eds.), *Image and Environment: Cognitive Mapping and Spatial Behavior.* Chicago: Aldine Publishing Co., 1973.

Duffala, D. C. "Convenience Stores, Armed Robbery, and Physical Environmntal Features." *American Behavioral Scientist* 20 (1976): 227–246.

Dugdale, R. L. *The Jukes.* New York: AMS Press (reprint of 1895 edition), 1975.

Dye, T. *Understanding Public Policy.* Englewood Cliffs, N.J.: Prentice Hall, 1972.

Easton, D. *A Framework for Political Analysis.* Englewood Cliffs, N. J.: Prentice Hall, 1965.

Eberts, P. and Schwirian, K. P. "Metropolitan Crime Rates and Relative Deprivation." *Criminologica* 5 (1968): 43–52.

Eck, J. E., and Riccio, L. J. "Relationship Between Reported Crime Rates and Victimization Survey Results: An Empirical and Analytical Study." *Journal of Criminal Justice* 7 (1979):293–308.

Ehrlich, I. "Participation in Illegitimate Activities: A Theoretical and Empirical Investigation." *Journal of Political Economy* 81 (1973):521–565.

Elliott, D. S., and Ageton, S. S. "Reconciling Race and Class Differences in Self-Reported and Official Estimates of Delinquency." *American Sociological Review* 45 (1980):95–110.

Elmhorn, K. "Study in Self-Reported Delinquency Among School Children in Stockholm." *Scandinavian Studies in Criminology* 1 (1965):117–146.

Engstad, P. A. *Perspectives on the Ecology of Crime: An Application and Appraisal.* Edmonton: Unpublished M.A. thesis, University of Alberta, 1971.

Engstad, P. A. "Environmental Opportunities and the Ecology of Crime." In R. A. Silverman and J. J. Teevan, Jr., (Eds.), *Crime in Canadian Society,* pp. 193–211. Toronto: Butterworths, 1975.

Ennis, P. *Criminal Victimization in the United States: A Report of the National Field Surveys II.* President's Commission on Law Enforcement and Administration of Justice. Washington: Government Printing Office, 1967.

Erickson, M. L., and Empey, L. "Court Records, Undetected Delinquency and Decision Making." *Journal of Criminal Law, Criminology and Police Science* 54 (1963):456–469.

Erikson, K. T. *Wayward Puritans.* New York: John Wiley and Sons, 1966.

Erlanger, H. S. "Is There a 'Subculture of Violence' in the South?" *Journal of Criminal Law and Criminology* 66 (1976):483–490.

Etzioni, A. *The Active Society.* New York: The Free Press, 1968.

Faris, R. E. L., and Dunham, H. W. *Mental Disorders in Urban Areas.* Chicago: University of Chicago Press, 1939.

Farrington, D. P. "Self-Reports of Deviant Behavior: Predictive and Stable?" *Journal of Criminal Law and Criminology* 64 (1973):99–110.

Fattah, E.; Bissonnet, F.; and Geoffrion, G. *Etude exploratrice des statistiques de criminologie ecologique,* Vol. I. Montreal: Université de Montreal, 1972.

Fattah, E.; Bissonnet, F.; and Scholtes, A. C. *Etudes de Criminologie Ecologique,* Vol. II, Pt. 1. Montreal: Université de Montreal, 1973.

Fattah, E.; Bissonnet, F.; and Scholtes, A. C. *Etudes de Criminologie Ecologique,* Vol. II, Pt. 2. Montreal: Université de Montreal, 1974.

Fattah, E.; Sturrock, J.; and Rathbone, L. *Studies in Ecological Criminology,* Vol. III. Burnaby: Simon Fraser University, 1978.

Faust, F. L., and Brantingham, P. J. *Juvenile Justice Philosophy* (2d ed.). St. Paul. Minn.: West Publishing Co., 1979.

Federal Bureau of Investigation (Annual). *Crime in the United States.* Washington: Government Printing Office [*Uniform Crime Reports*], 1972, 1975, 1977, 1979, 1980.

Feeney, F., and Weir, A. *The Prevention and Control of Robbery* (5 vols.). Davis: The Center on Administration of Justice, University of California at Davis, 1973.

Ferdinand, T. N. "The Criminal Patterns of Boston Since 1849." *American Journal of Sociology* 73 (1967): 84–99.

Ferdinand, T. N. *Burglary in Auburn, Massachusetts.* Boston: Northeastern University, 1970.

Ferdinand, T. N. "Criminal Justice: From Colonial Intimacy to Bureaucratic Formality." In D. Street (Ed.), *Handbook of Contemporary Urban Life,* pp. 279–281. San Francisco: Jossey-Bass, 1978.

Ferdinand, T. N. "Criminality, the Courts and the Constabulary of Boston: 1702–1967." *Journal of Research in Crime and Delinquency* 17 (1980): 190–208.

Ferri, F. *Criminal Sociology.* Boston: Little, Brown, 1917.

Finestone H. "The Delinquent and Society: the Shaw and McKay Tradition." In J. F. Short (Ed.), *Delinquency, Crime, and Society,* pp. 23–49. Chicago: University of Chicago Press, 1976.

Fink, A. E. *Causes of Crime: Biological Theories in the United States, 1800–1915.* Philadelphia: University of Pennsylvania Press, 1938.

Fink, G. "Einsbruchstatorte Vornehmilch Einfallstassen?" *Kriminalistik* 23 (1969): 358–360.

Firth, M. *Forecasting Methods in Business and Management.* London: Edward Arnold, 1977.

Flango, V. E., and Sherbenou, E. L. "Poverty, Urbanization and Crime." *Criminology* 14 (1976): 331–346.

Fleisher, B. M. *The Economics of Delinquency.* Chicago: Quadrangle Books, 1966.

Florida Department of Criminal Law Enforcement. *1972 Annual Report: Crime in Florida.* Tallahassee: State of Florida, 1973.

Florida Division of Health. *Florida Vital Statistics-1972.* Tallahassee: State of Florida, 1973.

Fox, J. A. *Forecasting Crime Data.* Lexington, Mass.: Lexington Books, 1979.

Friedland, M. C., and Mohr, J. W. "Canadian Criminal Statistics." *Criminal Law Quarterly* 7 (1964): 170–186.

Friedman, L. M. *A History of American Law.* New York: Simon and Schuster, 1973.

Friedman, L. M., and Percival, R. V. *The Roots of Justice: Crime and Punishment in Alameda County, California, 1870–1910.* Chapel Hill: University of North Carolina Press, 1981.

Friedmann, J. R. *Regional Development Policy: A Case Study of Venezuela.* Cambridge, Mass.: MIT Press, 1966.

Fuller, W. A. *Introduction to Statistical Time Series.* New York: John Wiley and Sons, 1976.

Gans, H. *People and Plans.* Harmondsworth, England: Penguin Books, 1972.

Gardiner, J. A. "Problems in the Use of Evaluation in Law Enforcement and Criminal Justice." In K. M. Dolbeare (Ed.), *Public Policy Evaluation,* pp. 177–183. Beverly Hills, Calif.: Sage Publications, 1975.

Gastil, R. D. "Homicide and a Regional Culture of Violence." *American Sociological Review* 36 (1971): 412–417.

Gatrell, V. A. C., and Hadden, T. B. "Criminal Statistics and Their Interpretation." In E. A. Wrigley (Ed.), *Nineteenth Century Society: Essays in Quantitative Methods for the Study of Social Data,* pp. 336–396. Cambridge: Cambridge University Press, 1972.

Gibbons, D. C. *The Criminological Enterprise.* Englewood Cliffs, N.J.: Prentice Hall, 1979.

Gibbs, J. P. *Sociological Theory Construction.* Hinsdale, Ill.: Dryden Press, 1972.

Gibbs, J. P. *Crime, Punishment and Deterrence.* New York: Elsevier, 1975.

Gibbs, J. P., and Erickson, M. L. "Crime Rates of American Cities in an Ecological Context." *American Journal of Sociology* 83 (1976): 605–620.

Giffen, P. J. "Official Rates of Crime and Delinquency." In W. T. McGrath (Ed.), *Crime and Its Treatment in Canada* (2d ed.), pp. 66–110. Toronto: Macmillan of Canada, 1976.

Gilchrist, W. G. *Statistical Forecasting.* London: John Wiley and Sons, 1976.

Given, J. B. *Society and Homicide in Thirteenth-Century England.* Stanford: Stanford University Press, 1977.

Glaser, D. and Rice, K. "Crime, Age, and Employment." *American Sociological Review* 24 (1959):679–686.

Glueck, S. and Glueck, E. *Physique and Delinquency.* New York: Harper and Brothers, 1956.

Goebel, J. N., Jr. and Naughton, T. R. *Law Enforcement in Colonial New York: A Study in Criminal Procedure, 1664–1776.* Montclair, N.J.: Patterson Smith, 1970.

Goddard, H. H. *The Kallikak Family.* New York: Macmillan, 1931.

Goddard, H. H. *Feeble-Mindedness: Its Causes and Consequences.* Freeport, N.Y.: Books for Libraries Press, 1972. (Reprint of 1914 edition.)

Gold, M. "Undetected Delinquent Behavior." *Journal of Research in Crime and Delinquency* 3 (1966):27–46.

Gold, M. *Delinquent Behavior in an American City.* Belmont, Calif.: Brooks/Cole Division of Wadsworth Publishing Co., 1970.

Golledge, R.; Rivizzigno, V. L.; and Spector, A. "Learning About A City: An Analysis of Multi-Dimensional Scaling." In R. Golledge and G. Rushton (Eds.), *Spatial Choice and Spatial Behavior,* pp. 95–116. Columbus, Ohio: Ohio State University Press, 1976.

Golledge, R., and Rushton, G., (Eds.), *Spatial Choice and Spatial Behavior: Geographic Essays on the Analysis of Preferences and Perceptions.* Columbus, Ohio: Ohio State University Press, 1976.

Gordon, R. A. "Issues in the Ecological Study of Delinquency." *American Sociological Review* 32 (1967):927–944.

Gorer, J. "Modification of National Character: The Role of the Police in England." *Journal of Social Issues* 11 (1955):24–32.

Goring, C. *The English Convict.* London: HMSO, 1913.

Gottfredson, M. R. "Treatment Destruction Techniques." *Journal of Research in Crime and Delinquency* 16 (1979): 39–54.

Gould, L. "The Changing Structure of Property Crime in an Affluent Society." *Social Forces* 48 (1969):50–59.

Granger, C. W. J., and Newbold, P. *Forecasting Economic Time Series.* New York: Academic Press, 1977.

Greenaway, W. K., and Brickey, S. L. *Law and Social Control in Canada.* Scarborough, Ontario: Prentice Hall, 1978.

Greenberg, D. *Crime and Law Enforcement in the Colony of New York: 1691–1776.* Ithaca, N.Y.: Cornell University Press, 1976.

Greenberg, D. F. "The Dynamics of Oscillatory Punishment Processes." *Journal of Criminal Law and Criminology* 68 (1977): 643–651.

Greenwood, M. J., and Wadychi, W. J. "Crime Rates and Public Expenditures for Police Protection: Their Interaction." *Review of Social Economy* 31 (1973): 138–151.

Griffiths, C.; Klein, J.; and Verdun-Jones, S. N. *Criminal Justice in Canada.* Vancouver: Butterworths, 1980.

Gross, L. *Symposium on Sociological Theory.* New York: Harper and Row, 1959.

Guerry, A. M. *Essai Sur la Statistique Morale de la France.* Paris: Chez Crochard, 1831.

Gulick, J. "Images of an Arab City." *Journal of the American Institute of Planners* 20 (1963): 179–198.

Gulliver, F. P. "Orientation of Maps." *Journal of Geography* 7 (1908): 55–58.

Gump, P. V. "Mileu, Environment, and Behavior." *Design and Environment* 8 (1971): 48–50.

Gurr, T. R. *Rogues, Rebels and Reformers: A Political History of Urban Crime and Conflict.* Beverly Hills, Calif.: Sage Publications, 1976.

Gurr, T. R. "On the History of Violent Crime in Europe and America." In H. D. Graham and T. R. Gurr, *Violence in America: Historical and Comparative Perspectives* (rev. ed.), pp. 353–374. Beverly Hills, Calif.: Sage Publications, 1979.

Gurr, T. R.; Grabosky, P. N.; and Hula, R. C. *The Politics of Crime and Conflict:' A Comparative History of Four Cities.* Beverly Hills, Calif.: Sage Publications, 1977.

Gusfield, J. R. *Symbolic Crusade: Status Politics and the American Temperance Movement.* Urbana, Ill.: University of Illinois Press, 1963.

Hackney, S. "Southern Violence." *American Historical Review* 74 (1969): 906–925.

Hagan, J. *The Disreputable Pleasures.* Toronto: McGraw-Hill Ryerson, 1977.

Hagan, J.; Gillis, A. R.; and Chan, J. "Explaining Official Delinquency: A Spatial Study of Class, Conflict and Control." *The Sociological Quarterly* 19 (1978): 386–398.

Hagerstrand, T. *The Propagation of Innovation Waves.* Lund Studies in Geography, Series B: Human Geography, no. 4. Lund: C. Wk. Gleerup, 1952.

Haggett, P. *Locational Analysis in Human Geography.* London: Edward Arnold, 1965.

Hall, E. T. *The Hidden Dimension.* Garden City, New York: Doubleday, 1966.

Halpern, I. W.; Stanislas, J. W.; and Botein, B. *The Slum and Crime: A Statistical Study of the Distribution of Adult and Juvenile Delinquents in the Boroughs of Manhattan and Brooklyn, New York.* New York: New York City Housing Authority, 1934.

Hammond, R., and McCullagh, P. S. *Quantitative Techniques in Geography: An Introduction.* Oxford: Clarendon Press, 1974.

Hanawalt, B. A. "Economic Influences on the Pattern of Crime in England, 1300–1348." *American Journal of Legal History* 18 (1974): 281–297.

Hanawalt, B. A. *Crime and Conflict in English Communities: 1300–1348.* Cambridge, Mass.: Harvard University Press, 1979.

Harding, A. *A Social History of English Law.* Harmondsworth, England: Penguin Books, 1966.

Hardt, R. H.; Peterson, S.; and Bodine, G. E. "Neighborhood Status and Delinquency Activity as Indexed by Police Records and a Self-Report Survey." *Criminologica* 6 (1968): 34–47.

Harries, K. D. "The Geography of American Crime, 1968." *Journal of Geography* 70 (1971): 204–213.

Harries, K. D. *The Geography of Crime and Justice.* New York: McGraw-Hill, 1974.

Harries, K. D. "Cities and Crime: A Geographical Model." *Criminology* 14 (1976): 369–386.

Harris, C. D., and Ullman, E. L. "The Nature of Cities." *Annals of the American Academy of Social and Political Science* 242 (1945): 7–17.

Harvey, D. *Social Justice and the City.* London: Edward Arnold, 1974.

Hasenpusch, B. "The Rise and Fall of Crime in Canada: An Attempt at Criminological Forecasting." *Crime and/et Justice* 6 (1978): 108–123.

Hauge, R., and Wolf, P. "Criminal Violence in Three Scandinavian Countries." *Scandinavian Studies in Criminology* 5 (1974):25–33.

Hawley, A. *Human Ecology.* New York: Ronald Press, 1950.

Hay, D. "Property, Authority and the Criminal Law." In D. Hay, P. Linebaugh, J. G. Rule, E. P. Thompson, and C. Winslow (Eds.), *Albion's Fatal Tree: Crime and Society in Eighteenth-Century England,* pp. 17–63. New York: Pantheon Books, 1975.

Hay, D.; Linebaugh, P.; Rule, J. G.; Thompson, E. P.; and Winslow, C. (Eds.). *Albion's Fatal Tree: Crime and Society in Eighteenth-Century English Society.* New York: Pantheon Books, 1975.

Henderson, C. R. *An Introduction to the Study of the Dependent, Defective and Delinquent Classes.* Boston: D. C. Heath, 1893.

Herbert, D. T. "An Areal and Ecological Analysis of Delinquency Residence: Cardiff 1966 and 1971." *Tijdschrift Voor Economic En Social Geografie* 68 (1977):83–99.

Hindelang, M. J. "The Uniform Crime Reports Revisited." *Journal of Criminal Justice* 2 (1974):1–17.

Hindelang, M. J. Criminal Victimization in Eight American Cities: A Descriptive Analysis of Common Theft and Assault. Cambridge, Mass.: Ballinger, 1976*a*.

Hindelang, M. J. "With a Little Help from their Friends: Group Participation in Reported Delinquent Behavior." *British Journal of Criminology* 16 (1976b):190–125.

Hindelang, M. J. "Race and Involvement in Common Law Personal Crimes." *American Sociological Review.* 43 (1978):93–109.

Hindelang, M. J.; Hirschi, T.; and Weis, J. G. *Measuring Delinquency.* Beverly Hills, Calif.: Sage Publications, 1981.

Hindus, M. S. *Prison and Plantation: Crime, Justice, and Authority in Massachusetts and South Carolina, 1767–1878.* Chapel Hill: University of North Carolina Press, 1980.

Hippchen, L., (Ed.), *Ecologic-Biochemical Approaches to Treatment of Delinquents and Criminals.* New York: Van Nostrand Reinhold, 1978.

Hirschi, T. *The Causes of Delinquency.* Berkeley: University of California Press, 1969.

Hirschi, T., and Hindelang, M. J. "Intelligence and Delinquency: A Revisionist Review." *American Sociological Review* 42 (1977):571–587.

Hirschi, T., and Selvin, H. C. *Principles of Survey Research.* New York: The Free Press, 1973.

Hobbs, A. H. "Criminality in Philadelphia: 1790–1810 Compared with 1937." *American Sociological Review* 8 (1943):198–202.

Home Office (Annual). *Criminal Statistics, England and Wales.* London: HMSO, 1975 (Cmnd 6566); 1977 (Cmnd 7289); 1978 (Cmnd 7670); 1979 (Cmnd 8098); 1980 (Cmnd 8376).

Hood, R. (Ed.), *Crime, Criminology and Public Policy.* London: Heinemann, 1974a.

Hood, R. "Criminology and Penal Change: A Case Study of the Nature and Impact of Some Recent Advice to Governments." In R. Hood (Ed.), *Crime, Criminology and Public Policy,* pp. 375–417. London: Heinemann, 1974*b*.

Hood, R., and Sparks, R. *Key Issues in Criminology.* London: Weidenfeld and Nicolson, 1970.

Hooton, E. A. *Crime and the Man.* Cambridge, Mass.: Harvard University Press, 1939.

Howard, M. K. "Police Reports and Victimization Survey Results: An Empirical Study." *Criminology* 12 (1975):433–446.

Howson, G. *Thief-Taker General: The Rise and Fall of Jonathan Wild.* London: Hutchinson, 1970.

Hoyt, H. *The Structure and Growth of Residential Neighborhoods in American Cities.* Washington: Government Printing Office, 1939.

Inciardi, J. A. *Reflections on Crime.* New York: Holt, Rinehart and Winston, 1978.

Inciardi, J. A. "Heroin Use and Street Crime." *Crime and Delinquency* 25 (1979):335–346.

Institute of Public Administration. "Abuses in Crime Reporting." In **M. E. Wolfgang, L. Savitz,** and **N. Johnston** (Eds.), *The Sociology of Crime and Delinquency,* pp. 56–58. New York: John Wiley and Sons, 1962.

International Criminal Police Organization {INTERPOL}. *International Crime Statistics: 1975–1976.* St. Cloud, France: INTERPOL, 1980.

Inter-University Consortium for Political and Social Research {ICPSR}. *National Crime Surveys, Cities Attitude Sub-Sample, 1972–1975.* Ann Arbor, Mich.: ICPSR.

Jarvik, L. F.; Klodin, V.; and Matsuyama, S. S. "Human Aggression and the Extra Y Chromosome." *American Psychologist* 8 (1973):674–682.

Jarvis, G. K. "The Ecological Analysis of Juvenile Delinquency in a Canadian City." In **C. L. Boydell, C. F. Grindstaff,** and **P. C. Whitehead** (Eds.), *Deviant Behavior and Societal Reaction,* pp. 195–211. Toronto: Holt, Rinehart and Winston, 1972.

Jaywardene, C. H. S. "The Nature of Homicide: Canada 1961–1970." In **R. A. Silverman** and **J. J. Teevan** (Eds.), *Crime in Canadian Society,* pp. 279–310. Toronto: Butterworths, 1975.

Jeffery, C. R. "Criminal Behavior and Learning Theory." *Journal of Criminal Law, Criminology and Police Science* 56 (1965): 294–300.

Jeffery, C. R. *Biology and Crime.* Beverly Hills, Calif.: Sage Publications, 1979.

Jenkins, W. I. *Policy Analysis: A Political and Organizational Perspective.* London: Martin Robertson, 1978.

Johnson, D. R. *Policing the Urban Underworld: The Impact of Crime on the Development of the American Police, 1800–1887.* Philadelphia: Temple University Press, 1979.

Johnson, R. E. "Social Class and Delinquent Behavior." *Criminology* 18 (1980):86–93.

Johnson, R. W. "Research Objectives for Policy Analysis." In **K. M. Dolbeare** (Ed.), *Public Policy Evaluation,* pp. 75–92. Beverly Hills, Calif.: Sage Publications, 1975.

Jonassen, C. T. "A Re-Evaluation and Critique of the Logic and Some of the Methods of Shaw and McKay." *American Sociological Review* 14 (1949):600–614.

Juviler, P. D. *Revolutionary Law and Order: Politics and Social Change in the USSR.* New York: The Free Press, 1976.

Kansky, K. *The Structure of Transportation Networks.* Chicago: Department of Geography, University of Chicago {Research Paper No. 84}, 1963.

Kaplan, S. "Adaptation, Structure and Knowledge." In **G. Moore** and **R. Golledge** (Eds.), *Environmental Knowing: Theories, Research and Methods,* pp. 32–45. Stroudsburg, Pa.: Dowden, Hutchinson, and Ross.

Kendall, M. G. *Time Series.* London: Charles Griffen and Co, 1973.

Kirkham, G. *Signal Zero.* Philadelphia: Lippincott, 1976.

Kitsuse, J., and Cicourel, A. V. (1963) "A Note on the Uses of Official Statistics." *Social Problems* 11 (1963): 131–139.

Klein, J. F., and Montague, A.. "Cheque Writing as a Way of Life." In **R. A. Silverman** and **J. J. Teevan, Jr.** (Eds.), *Crime in Canadian Society,* pp. 263–278. Toronto: Butterworths, 1975.

Klein, J. F., and Montague, A. *Check Forgers.* Lexington, Mass.: Lexington Books, 1977.

Klockars, C. B. *The Professional Fence.* New York: The Free Press, 1974.

Koffka, K. *Principles of Gestalt Psychology.* London: Kegan Paul, 1935.

Konig, D. T. *Law and Society in Puritan Massachusetts: Essex County, 1629–1692.* Chapel Hill: University of North Carolina Press, 1979.

Kowalski, G. S.; Dittman, R. L., Jr.; and Bung, W. L. "Spatial Distribution of Criminal Offenses by States, 1970–1976." *Journal of Research in Crime and Delinquency* 17 (1980):4–25.

Kress, J. M. *Pilot Analysis of the Albany County Rape Crisis Center*. Albany: State University of New York at Albany, 1976.

Krohn, M. D. "Inequality, Unemployment and Crime: A Cross-National Analysis." *The Sociological Quarterly* 17 (1976):303–313.

Krohn, M.; Waldo, G. P., and Chiricos, T. G. "Self-Reported Delinquency: A Comparison of Structured Interviews and Self-Administered Checklists." *Journal of Criminal Law and Criminology* 65 (1974):545–553.

Kuhn, T. S. *The Structure of Scientific Revolutions* (2d ed., enlarged). Chicago: University of Chicago Press, 1970.

Kulik, J. A.; Stein, K. B., and Sarbin, T. R. "Disclosure of Delinquent Behavior Under Conditions of Anonymity and Nonanonymity." *Journal of Consulting and Clinical Psychology* 32 (1968):506–509.

Kvalseth, T. O. "A Note on the Effects of Population Density and Unemployment on Urban Crime." *Criminology* 15 (1977):104–109.

Lander, B. *Towards An Understanding of Juvenile Delinquency*. New York: Columbia University Press, 1954.

Lane, R. *Policing the City: Boston, 1822–1885*. New York: Atheneum, 1971.

Lane, R. "Crime and the Industrial Revolution: British and American Views." *Journal of Social History* 7 (1974):287–303.

Lange, J. *Crime and Destiny*. New York: C. Boni, 1930.

Laslett, P. *The World We Have Lost: England Before the Industrial Age*. New York: Charles Scribner's Sons, 1971.

Lasswell, H. D. *A Pre-View of Policy Sciences*. New York: American Elsevier, 1971.

Law Enforcement Assistance Administration, Statistics Division. *Technical Report #1: The San Jose Methods Test of Known Crime Victims*. Washington: U.S. Department of Justice, 1973.

LeBlanc, M. "La Reaction Sociale à la Delinquance Juvénile: Un Analyse Stigmatique." *Acta Criminologica* 4 (1971):113–191.

LeCompte, W. F. "Behavior Settings." In W. J. Mitchell (Ed.), *Environmental Design: Research and Practice*. Los Angeles: University of California at Los Angeles, [EDRA 3], 1972.

Lee, T. "Perceived Distance as a Function of Direction in the City." *Environment and Behavior* 2 (1970):40–51.

Lemert, E. M. *Social Pathology*. New York: McGraw-Hill, 1951.

Lemert, E. M. *Social Action and Legal Change: Revolution Within the Juvenile Court*. Chicago: Aldine, 1970.

Letkemann, P. *Crime as Work*. Englewood Cliffs, N.J.: Prentice-Hall, 1973.

Levin, Y., and Lindesmith, A. C. "English Ecology and Criminology of the Past Century." *Journal of Criminal Law and Criminology* 27 (1937): 801–816.

Levine, J. P. "The Potential for Crime Overreporting in Criminal Victimization Surveys." *Criminology* 14 (1976):307–330.

Levine, J. P. "Reply to Singer." *Criminology* 16 (1978):103–107.

Lewin, K. *Principles of Topological Psychology*. New York: McGraw-Hill, 1936.

Lind, A. W. "Some Ecological Patterns of Community Disorganization in Honolulu." *American Journal of Sociology* 36 (1930):206–220.

Lipton, D.; Martinson, R.; and Wilkes, J. *The Effectiveness of Correctional Treatment*. New York: Praeger, 1975.

Lodhi, A. Q., and Tilly, C. "Urbanization, Crime and Collective Violence in 19th Century France." *American Journal of Sociology* 79 (1973):296–317.

Lofland, J. *Deviance and Identity*. Englewood Cliffs, N.J.: Prentice Hall, 1969.

Lofland, L. *A World of Strangers: Order and Action in Urban Public Space*. New York: Basic Books, 1973.

Loftin, C. and Hill, R. "Regional Subculture and Homicide: An Examination of the Gastil-Hackney Thesis." *American Sociological Review* 39 (1974):714–724.

Lombroso, C. *Crime: Its Causes and Remedies*. Boston: Little, Brown, 1911.

Lottier, S. "The Distribution of Criminal Offenses in Sectional Regions." *Journal of Criminal Law, Criminology, and Police Science* 29 (1938a):329–344.

Lottier, S. "The Distribution of Criminal Offenses in Metropolitan Regions." *Journal of Criminal Law, Criminology, and Police Science* 29 (1938b):37–50.

Lowe, J. C., and Moryadas, S. *The Geography of Movement*. Boston: Houghton Mifflin Company, 1975.

Luedtke, G., and Associates. *Crime and The Physical City: Neighborhood Design Techniques for Crime Prevention*. Springfield, Va.: National Technical Information Service, 1970.

Lynch, K. *The Image of the City*. Cambridge, Mass.: MIT Press, 1960.

Lynch, K., and Rivkin, M. "A Walk Around the Block." *Landscape* 8 (1959):24–34.

MacDonald, J. A. "Juvenile Training Schools and Juvenile Justice Policy in British Columbia." *Canadian Journal of Criminology* 20 (1978): 418–436.

McCarthy, J. D.; Galle, O. R.; and Zimmerman, W. "Population Density, Social Structure, and Interpersonal Violence." *American Behavioral Scientist* 18 (1975): 771–791.

McClintock, F. H. "Facts and Myths About the State of Crime." In R. Hood (Ed.), *Crime, Criminology, and Public Policy*, pp. 33–46. London: Heinemann, 1974.

McClintock, F. H., and Avison, N. H. *Crime in England and Wales*. London: Heinemann, 1968.

McClintock, F. H., and Gibson, E. *Robbery in London*. London: Macmillan and Co., 1961.

McConnell, M. V. "Criminal vs. Non-Criminal Differential Edge Perception." Tallahassee, Fla.: Unpublished paper, Department of Urban and Regional Planning, Florida State University, 1976.

McConville, S. *A History of English Prison Administration, Vol. I: 1750–1877*. London: Routledge and Kegan Paul, 1981.

McDonald, L. *Social Class and Delinquency*. London: Faber and Faber, 1968.

McDonald, L. *The Sociology of Law and Order*. London: Faber and Faber, 1976. [Reprinted, Toronto: Methuen, 1979.]

McEvedy, C., and Jones, R. *Atlas of World Population History*. Harmondsworth, England: Penguin Books, 1978.

McGrath, W. T. *Crime and Its Treatment in Canada*. (2d ed.). Toronto: Macmillan of Canada, 1976.

McKenzie, R. D. "The Ecological Approach to the Study of the Human Community." In R. E. Park, E. W. Burgess, and R. D. McKenzie (Eds.), *The City*, pp. 63–79. Chicago: University of Chicago Press, 1925.

McPheters, L. R., and Stronge, W. B. "Crime as an Environmental Externality of Tourism: Miami, Florida." *Land Economics* 50 (1974a):288–292.

McPheters, L. R., and Stronge, W. B. "Spectral Analysis of Reported Crime Data." *Journal of Criminal Justice* 2 (1974b):329–344.

Maddala, G. S. *Econometrics*. New York: McGraw-Hill, 1977.

Mannheim, H. *Social Aspects of Crime in London Between the Wars*. London: George Allen and Unwin, 1940.

Mannheim, H. *Comparative Criminology*. London: Routledge and Kegan Paul, 1965.

Mannheim, H. *Pioneers in Criminology* (2d ed.). Montclair, N.J.: Patterson Smith, 1972.

Mansfield, R.; Gould, L. C.; and Namenwirth, Z. "A Socioeconomic Model for the Prediction of Societal Rates of Property Theft." *Social Forces* 52 (1974):462–472.

Mark, V. H., and Irvin, F. R. *Violence and the Brain.* New York: Harper and Row, 1970.

Marlin, J. T. "City Crime: Report of the Council on Municipal Performance." *Criminal Law Bulletin* 9 (1973):557–611.

Mawby, R. I. "The Victimization of Juveniles: A Comparative Study of Three Areas of Publicly Owned Housing in Sheffield." *Journal of Research in Crime and Delinquency* 16 (1979):98–113.

Mawby, R. I. "Police Practices and Crime Rates: A Case Study From A British City." In P. J. Brantingham and P. L. Brantingham, (Eds.), *Environmental Criminology,* pp. 135–146. Beverly Hills, Calif.: Sage Publications, 1981.

Mayhew, H. *London Labour and the London Poor. Vol. IV: Those That Will Not Work. Comprising Prostitutes, Thieves, Swindlers, and Beggars.* London: Griffin Bohn, 1861–1862. [Reprinted, New York: Dover Publications, Inc., 1968.]

Mayhew, P.; Clarke, R. V. G.; Sturman, R.; and Hough, J. M. *Crime as Opportunity.* Home Office Research Study No. 34. London: HMSO, 1976.

Mednick, S. A., and Christiansen, K. O. *Biosocial Bases of Criminal Behavior.* New York: Gardner Press, 1977.

Melling, E. (Ed.). *Kentish Sources: Vol. 4. Crime and Punishment.* Maidstone, England: Kent County Council, 1969.

Michael, J., and Adler, M. J. *Crime, Law and Social Science.* Montclair, N.J.: Patterson Smith, 1971.

Milgram, S. "Psychological Maps of Paris." In W. Proshansky, W. Ittelson, and L. Rivlin (Eds.), *Environmental Psychology* (2d ed.), pp. 104–124. New York: Holt, Rinehart and Winston, 1976.

Miller, W. R. *Cops and Bobbies: Police Authority in New York and London, 1830–1870.* Chicago: University of Chicago Press, 1975.

Molumby, T. "Patterns of Crime in a University Housing Project." *American Behavioral Scientist* 20 (1976): 247–259.

Monkkonen, E. H. *The Dangerous Class: Crime and Poverty in Columbus, Ohio, 1860–1885.* Cambridge, Mass.: Harvard University Press, 1977.

Monkkonen, E. H. "Systematic Criminal Justice History: Some Suggestions." *The Journal of Interdisciplinary History* 9 (1979a):451–464.

Monkkonen, E. H. "Toward a Dynamic Theory of Crime and the Police: A Criminal Justice System Perspective." In S. L. Messinger and E. Bittner, *Criminology Review Yearbook, Vol, 1,* pp. 335–343. Beverly Hills, Calif.: Sage Publications, 1979b.

Monkkonen, E. H. *Police in Urban America: 1860–1920.* Cambridge: Cambridge University Press, 1981.

Morris, C. R. "The Children and Young Persons Act: Creating More Institutionalization." *Howard Journal of Penology and Crime Prevention* 16 (1978):154–158.

Morris, T. *The Criminal Area: A Study in Social Ecology.* London: Routledge and Kegan Paul, 1958.

Moynihan, D. P. *Maximum Feasible Misunderstanding.* New York: Free Press, 1969.

Muir, G. "Car Theft Patterns in Burnaby, British Columbia: A Study in Target Accessibility and Crime." Unpublished seminar paper, Department of Criminology, Simon Fraser University, 1978.

Munford, R. S.; Kaser, R. S.; Feldman, R. A.; and Stivers, R. R. "Homicide Trends in Atlanta." *Criminology* 14 (1976): 213–232.

Nagel, E. *The Structure of Science: Problems in the Logic of Scientific Explanation.* New York: Harcourt, Brace and World, Inc., 1961.

National Commission on Law Observance and Enforcement. *Reports* (15 vols.). Washington: Government Printing Office, 1931. [Wickersham Commission.]

National Criminal Justice Information and Statistics Service. *Criminal Victimization in*

Chicago, Detroit, Los Angeles, New York, Philadelphia: A Comparison of 1972 and 1974 Findings. Washington: Government Printing Office (SD-NCS-C-6), 1976a.

National Criminal Justice Information and Statistics Service. *Criminal Victimization in the United States-1976.* Washington: Government Printing Office (SD-NCS-N-9; NCJ-49543), 1976b.

National Criminal Justice Information and Statistics Service. *Criminal Victimization in the United States: A Comparison of 1973 and 1974 Findings.* Washington: Government Printing Office (SD-NCP-N-3), 1976c.

National Criminal Justice Information and Statistics Service. *Criminal Victimization Surveys in Boston.* Washington: Government Printing Office (SD-NCS-C-7), 1977a.

National Criminal Justice Information and Statistics Service. *Criminal Victimization in the United States: A Comparison of 1974 and 1975 Findings.* Washington: Government Printing Office (SD-NCP-N-5), 1977b.

National Criminal Justice Information and Statistics Service. *Criminal Victimization in the United States-1977.* Washington: Government Printing Office (SD-NCS-N-12; NCJ-58725), 1979a.

National Criminal Justice Information and Statistics Service. *Criminal Victimization in the United States: Summary Findings of 1977–1978—changes in Crime and of Trends Since 1973.* Washington: Government Printing Office (SD-NCS-13-A; NCJ-61368), 1979b.

National Criminal Justice Information and Statistics Service. *Boston: Public Attitudes About Crime.* Washington: Government Printing Office (SD-NCS-C-20; NCJ-46235), 1979c.

Nease, B. "Measuring Juvenile Delinquency in Hamilton." *Canadian Journal of Criminology and Corrections* 8 (1966):133–145.

Nelson, C. R. *Applied Time Series Analysis for Managerial Forecasting.* San Francisco: Holden-Day, 1973.

Nelson, J. F. "Implications for the Ecological Study of Crime: A Research Note." In W. H. Parsonage (Ed.), *Perspectives on Victimiology,* pp. 21–28. Beverly Hills, Calif.: Sage Publications, 1979.

Nelson, J. F. "Alternative Measures of Crime: A Comparison of the Uniform Crime Reports and the National Crime Surveys in Twenty-Six American Cities." in D. Georges-Abeyie and K. D. Harries (Eds.), *Crime: A Spatial Perspective,* pp. 77–92. New York: Columbia University Press, 1980.

Nettler, G. *Explaining Crime.* New York: McGraw-Hill, 1978.

Newman, G. *Comparative Deviance: Perception and Law in Six Cultures.* New York: Elsevier, 1976.

Newman, O. *Defensible Space: Crime Prevention Through Urban Design.* New York: Macmillan, 1972.

Normandeau, A. "International Bibliography on Criminal Statistics: 1945–1968." *Canadian Journal of Corrections* 11 (1969):108–120.

Normandeau, A. "Canadian Criminal Statistics—Not Again!" *Canadian Journal of Corrections* 12 (1970):198–206.

Normandeau, A., and Schwartz, B. "A Crime Classification of American Metropolitan Areas." *Criminology* 9 (1971):228–247.

Nye, F. I., and Short, J. F., Jr. "Scaling Delinquent Behavior." *American Sociological Review* 22 (1957):326–341.

Ogburn, W. F. "Factors in the Variation of Crime Among Cities." *Journal of the American Statistical Association* 30 (1935): 12–34.

Oosthoek, A. *The Utilization of Official Crime Data.* Ottawa: Solicitor General of Canada, 1978.

Orleans, P. "Differential Cognition of Urban Residents: Effects of Social Scale on Mapping." In **R. Downs** and **D. Stea** (Eds.), *Image and Environment,* pp. 115–130. Chicago: Aldine, 1973.

Packer, H. L. *The Limits of Criminal Sanction.* Stanford: Stanford University Press, 1968.

Pahl, R. E. *Patterns in Urban Life: The Social Structure of Modern Britain.* London: Longman, 1970.

Parisi, N.; Gottfredson, M. R.; Hindelang, M. J.; and **Flanagan, T. J.** (Eds.) *Sourcebook of Criminal Justice Statistics.* Washington: U.S. Department of Justice, 1979.

Park, R. E., and **Burgess, E. W.** *Introduction to the Science of Sociology* (Student edition). Chicago: University of Chicago Press, 1970

Park, R. E.; Burgess, E. W.; and **McKenzie, R. D.** *The City.* Chicago: University of Chicago Press, 1925.

Parker, T., and **Allerton, R.** *The Courage of His Convictions: The True Story of a Professional Criminal.* London: Arrow Books, 1969.

Parsons, T. *Societies.* Englewood Cliffs, N.J.: Prentice Hall, 1966.

Penick, B. K. E., and **Owens, M. B., III.** *Surveying Crime.* Washington: National Academy of Sciences, 1976.

Pepinsky, H. "The Growth of Crime in the United States." *Annals of the American Academy of Political and Social Sciences* 423 (1976): 23–30.

Perroux, F. "Economic Space: Theory and Applications." *Quarterly Journal of Economics* 64 (1950): 89–104.

Petrovich, P. "Recherces sur la criminalité à Paris dans la seconde moitié du XVIII siècle." In **Abbiateci, A.; Billacois, F.; Bongert, Y.; Castan, N.; Castan, Y.;** and **Petrovich, P.** (Eds.). *Crimes et Criminalité en France sous l'Ancien Régime: 17–18 siècles,* pp. 187–261. Paris: Librarie Armand Colin, 1971.

Phelan, G. F. "Testing 'Academic' Notions of Architectural Design for Burglary Prevention: How Burglars Perceive Cues of Vulnerability in Suburban Housing Complexes." Paper read at American Society of Criminology annual meeting, Atlanta, 1977.

Phillips, L.; Votey, H. L., Jr.; and **Maxwell, D.** "Crime, Youth and the Labor Market." *Journal of Political Economy* 80 (1972):491–503.

Phillips, P. "Characteristics and Typology of the Journey to Crime." In **D. Georges-Abeyie** and **K. D. Harries** (Eds.), *Crime: A Spatial Perspective,* pp. 167–180. New York: Columbia University Press, 1980.

Piaget, J., and **Inhelder, B.** *The Child's Conception of Space.* New York: Norton, 1948.

Pike, L. O. *A History of Crime in England.* London: 1873. [Reprint Montclair, N.J.: Patterson Smith.]

Plint, T. *Crime in England.* London: Charles Gilpin, 1851.

Plucknett, T. F. T. *Edward I and the Criminal Law.* Cambridge: Cambridge University Press, 1960.

Pokorny, A. D. "A Comparison of Homicide in Two Cities." *Journal of Criminal Law, Criminology and Police Science* 56 (1965):479–487.

Polk, K. "Urban Social Areas and Delinquency." *Social Problems* 14 (1967):320–225.

Polk, K., and **Schafer, W. E.** *Schools and Delinquency.* Englewood Cliffs, N.J.: Prentice Hall, 1972.

Popham, R. E., and **Schmidt, W.** *Statistics of Alcohol Use and Alcoholism in Canada: 1871–1956.* Toronto: University of Toronto Press, 1958.

Porteous, J. D. *Environment and Behavior: Planning and Everyday Urban Life.* Reading, Mass.: Addison-Wesley, 1977.

Porterfield, A. L. *Youth in Trouble.* Fort Worth, Texas: The Leo Pottisham Foundation, 1946.

Postalan, L. A., and **Carson, D.** *Spatial Behavior of Older People.* Ann Arbor, Mich.: Institute of Gerontology, University of Michigan, 1970.

383

Pound, R., and Frankfurter, F. *Criminal Justice in Cleveland.* Cleveland: The Cleveland Foundation, 1922.

Powell, E. H. "Crime as a Function of Anomie." *Journal of Criminal Law, Criminology and Police Science* 57 (1966):161–171.

Powell, E. H. *The Design of Discord: Studies of Anomie.* New York: Oxford University Press, 1970.

Powell, R. R. *Compromises of Conflicting Claims: A Century of California Law, 1760–1860.* Dobbs Ferry, N.Y.: Oceana Publications, 1977.

President's Commission on Law Enforcement and Administration of Justice. *Task Force Report: The Courts.* Washington: Government Printing Office, 1967a.

President's Commission on Law Enforcement and Administration of Justice. *Task Force Report: Crime and Its Impact—An Assessment.* Washington: Government Printing Office, 1967b.

Pressman, I., and Carol, A. "Crime as a Diseconomy of Scale." *Review of Social Economy* 29 (1971):227–236.

Pyle, G. F. *The Spatial Dynamics of Crime.* Chicago: Department of Geography, University of Chicago [Research Paper No. 159], 1974.

Pyle, G. F. "Spatial Aspects of Crime in Cleveland, Ohio." *American Behavioral Scientist* 20 (1976):175–198.

Pyle, G. F. "Systematic Sociospatial Variation in Perceptions of Crime Location and Severity." In D. E. Georges-Abeyie and K. D. Harries (Eds.), *Crime: A Spatial Perspective,* pp. 219–245. New York: Columbia University Press, 1980.

Quetelet, L. A. J. *A Treatise on Man and the Development of His Faculties.* Edinburgh: W. and R. Chambers, 1842.

Quinney, R. "Crime, Delinquency, and Social Areas." *Journal of Research in Crime and Delinquency* 1 (1964):149–154.

Quinney, R. "Suicide, Homicide, and Economic Development." *Social Forces* 43 (1965):401–406.

Quinney, R. *The Social Reality of Crime.* Boston: Little, Brown, 1970.

Radin, M. *Handbook of Anglo-American Legal History.* St. Paul, Minn.: West Publishing Co., 1936.

Radzinowicz, L. *A History of English Criminal Law from 1750: Vol. I. The Movement for Reform.* London: Stevens, 1948.

Radzinowicz, L. "English Criminal Statistics: A Critical Appraisal." In L. Radzinowicz and J. W. C. Turner (Eds.), *The Modern Approach to Criminal Law,* pp. 174–194. London: Macmillan, 1945.

Rae, R. "Canadian Crime Patterns: An Analysis of Provincial Data." Unpublished paper, Department of Criminology, Simon Fraser University, 1981.

Rawson, R. W. "An Inquiry into the Statistics of Crime in England and Wales." *Journal of the Statistical Society of London* 2 (1839): 316–334.

Reckless, W. C. *Vice in Chicago.* Chicago: University of Chicago Press, 1933.

Reiss, A. J., Jr. *Studies in Crime and Law Enforcement in Major Metropolitan Areas, Vol. 1, Field Surveys III.* President's Commission on Law Enforcement and Administration of Justice. Washington: Government Printing Office, 1967.

Reiss, A. J., Jr., and Rhodes, A. L. "The Distribution of Juvenile Delinquency in the Social Class Structure." *American Sociological Review* 26 (1961):720–732.

Rengert, G. F. "Spatial Aspects of Criminal Behavior: A Suggested Approach." Paper read at East Lakes Division, Association of American Geographers annual meeting, 1972.

Rengert, G. F. "Journey to Crime: An Empirical Analysis of Spatially Constrained Female Mobility." Paper read at Association of American Geographers annual meeting, Milwaukee, 1975.

Rengert, G. F., and **Wasilchick, J.** "Residential Burglary: The Awareness and Use of Extended Space." Paper read at American Society of Criminology annual meeting, San Francisco, 1980.

Reppetto, T. A. *Residential Crime.* Cambridge, Mass.: Ballinger, 1974.

Rex, J. A., and **Moore, R.** *Race, Community and Conflict.* Oxford: Oxford University Press, 1967.

Rhodes, W. M., and **Conly, C.** "Crime and Mobility: An Empirical Study." In **P. J. Brantingham** and **P. L. Brantingham** (Eds.), *Environmental Criminology,* pp. 167–188. Beverly Hills, Calif.: Sage Publications, 1981.

Rhodes, W. M., Conly, C., and **Schachter, C.** *The Criminal Commute: A Study of the Geography of Crime and Justice in the District of Columbia.* Washington: Institute for Law and Social Research, 1980.

Robinson v. *California.* 370 U.S. 660; 82 S.Ct. 1417; 8 L. Ed. 2d 758, 1962.

Robinson, A. H. "The Necessity of Weighting Values in Correlation of Areal Data." *Annals of the Association of American Geographers* 46 (1956):233–236.

Robinson, W. S. "Ecological Correlations and the Behavior of Individuals." *American Sociological Review* 15 (1950):351–357.

Rosen, L., and **Turner, S. H.** "An Evaluation of the Lander Approach to Ecology of Delinquency." *Social Problems* 15 (1967):189–200.

Rusche, G., and **Kirchheimer, O.** *Punishment and Social Structure.* New York: Russell and Russell, 1968.

Sadalla, E. K., and **Staplin, L. J.** "The Perception of Traversed Distance." *Environment and Behavior* 12 (1980):167–182.

Sadalla, E. K., and **Staplin, L. J.** "An Information Storage Model for Distance Cognition." *Environment and Behavior* 12 (1980):183–193.

Sagi, P. C., and **Wellford, C. F.** "Age Composition and Patterns of Change in Criminal Statistics." *Journal of Criminal Law, Criminology and Police Science* 59 (1968):29–36.

Salas, L. *Social Control and Deviance in Cuba.* New York: Praeger, 1979.

Samaha, J. *Law and Order in Historical Perspective: The Case of Elizabethan Essex.* New York: Academic Press, 1974.

Scarr, H. A. *Patterns in Burglary* (2d ed.). Washington: U.S. Dept. of Justice, 1973.

Schlapp, M., and **Smith, E. H.** *The New Criminology.* New York: Boni and Liverwright, 1928.

Schmid, C. F. "Urban Crime Areas, Part I." *American Sociological Review* 25 (1960a):527–543.

Schmid, C. F. "Urban Crime Areas, Part II." *American Sociological Review* 25 (1960b):655–678.

Schneider, A. L. "Victimization Surveys and Criminal Justice System Evaluation." In **W. G. Skogan,** *Sample Surveys of the Victims of Crime,* pp. 135–150. Cambridge, Mass.: Ballinger, 1976.

Schuessler, K. "Components of Variation in U.S. City Crime." *Social Problems* 9 (1962):314–321.

Schuessler, K., and **Slatin, G.** "Sources of Variation in U.S. City Crime, 1950 and 1960." *Journal of Research in Crime and Delinquency* 1 (1964): 127–148.

Schur, E. *Crimes Without Victims.* Englewood Cliffs, N.J.: Prentice Hall, 1965.

Scioli, F. P., Jr., and **Cook, T. J.** *Methodologies for Analyzing Public Policies.* Lexington, Mass.: Lexington Books, 1975.

Seidman, D., and **Couzens, M.** "Getting the Crime Rate Down: Political Pressure and Crime Reporting." *Law and Society Review* 8 (1974): 457–493.

Sellin, T. "The Basis of A Crime Index." *Journal of the American Institute of Criminal Law and Criminology* 22 (1931):335–356.

385

Sellin, T. *Research Memorandum on Crime in the Depression*. New York: Social Science Research Council, 1937.

Sellin, T. *Culture Conflicts and Crime*. New York: Social Science Research Council, 1938.

Sellin, T. "The Significance of Records of Crime." *The Law Quarterly Review* 67 (1951):489–504.

Semmes, R. *Crime and Punishment in Early Maryland*. Baltimore: Johns Hopkins Press, 1938.

Shannon, L. W. "The Spatial Distribution of Criminal Offenses by States." *Journal of Criminal Law, Criminology and Police Science* 45 (1954):264–273.

Shannon, L. W. *A Cohort Study of the Relationship of Adult Criminal Careers to Juvenile Careers*. Iowa City: Iowa Urban Community Research Center, University of Iowa, 1978a.

Shannon, L. W. *The Relationship of Juvenile Delinquency and Adult Crime to the Changing Ecological Structure of the City*. Iowa City: Iowa Urban Community Research Center, University of Iowa, 1978b.

Shaw, C. R. *Delinquency Areas*. Chicago: University of Chicago Press, 1929.

Shaw, C. R., and McKay, H. D. *Social Factors in Juvenile Delinquency* [National Commission on Law Observance and Enforcement, Report on the Causes of Crime, Vol. 2.]. Washington: Government Printing Office, 1931.

Shaw, C. R., and McKay, H. D. *Juvenile Delinquency and Urban Areas*. Chicago: University of Chicago Press, 1942.

Shaw, C. R., and McKay, H. D. *Juvenile Delinquency and Urban Areas* (rev. ed.). Chicago: University of Chicago Press, 1969.

Shaw, C. R., and Moore, M. E. *The Natural History of a Delinquent Career*. Chicago: University of Chicago Press, 1931.

Sheldon, W. H.; Hartl, E. M.; and McDermott, E. *Varieties of Delinquent Behavior: An Introduction to Constitutional Psychiatry*. New York: Harper and Brothers, 1949.

Shelley, L. I. *Crime and Modernization: The Impact of Industrialization on Crime*. Carbondale, Ill.: Southern Illinois University Press, 1981.

Shichor, D.; Decker, D. L.; and O'Brien, R. M. "Population Density and Criminal Victimization: Some Unexpected Findings in Central Cities." *Criminology* 17 (1979):184–193.

Shichor, D.; Decker, D. L.; and O'Brien, R. M. "The Relationship of Criminal Victimization, Police Per Capita, and Population Density in Twenty-Six Cities." *Journal of Criminal Justice* 8 (1980):309–316.

Short, J. F., and Nye, F. I. "Extent of Unrecorded Juvenile Delinquency." *Journal of Criminal Law, Criminology and Police Science* 49 (1958):296–302.

Short, J. F., and Strodtbeck, F. L. *Group Process and Gang Delinquency*. Chicago: University of Chicago Press, 1965.

Silver, A. "The Demand for Order in Civil Society: A Review of Some Themes in the History of Urban Crime, Police, and Riot." In D. Bordua (Ed.), *The Police: Six Sociological Essays*, pp. 1–24. New York: John Wiley and Sons, 1967.

Silverman, R. A., and Teevan, J. J., Jr. *Crime in Canadian Society*. Toronto: Butterworths, 1975.

Skogan, W. G. *Sample Surveys of the Victims of Crime*. Cambridge, Mass.: Ballinger, 1976.

Skogan, W. G. "The Changing Distribution of Big City Crime: A Multi-City Time Series Analysis." *Urban Affairs Quarterly* 13 (1977a): 33–48.

Skogan, W. G. "Dimensions of the Dark Figure of Unreported Crime." *Crime and Delinquency* 23 (1977b):41–50.

Skogan, W. G. Public Lecture on Victimization Survey Research, Simon Fraser University, May, 1980.

Slocum, W. L., and Stone, C. L. "Family Culture Patterns and Delinquent Type Behavior." *Marriage and Family Living* 25 (1963):202–208.

Small, S. J. "Canadian Narcotics Legislation, 1908–1923: A Conflict Model Interpretation." In W. K. Greenaway and S. L. Brickey, *Law and Social Control in Canada,* pp. 28–42. Scarborough, Ontario: Prentice Hall, 1978.

Smith, D. M. *Patterns in Human Geography.* Harmondsworth, England: Penguin Books, 1975.

Smith, J. C., and Hogan, B. *Criminal Law* (2d ed.). London: Butterworths, 1969.

Smith, T. S. "Inverse Distance Variations for the Flow of Crime in Urban Areas." *Social Forces.* 54 (1976):804–815.

Solicitor General Canada. *Statistics Handbook: Canadian Criminal Justice—1977.* Ottawa: Information Systems and Statistics Division, Research and Systems Development Branch, Solicitor General Canada, 1977.

Sommer, D. *Personal Space: The Behavioral Basis of Design.* Englewood Cliffs, N.J.: Prentice Hall, 1969.

Sonnenfeld, J. "Geography, Perception and the Behavioral Environment." In P. W. English and R. C. Mayfield, *Man, Space and the Environment,* pp. 244–251. New York: Oxford University Press, 1972.

Sparks, R. F. "Crimes and Victims in London." In W. G. Skogan, (Ed.), *Sample Surveys of the Victims of Crime,* pp. 43–71. Cambridge, Mass.: Ballinger, 1976.

Sparks, R. F.; Genn, H. G.; and Dodd, D. J. *Surveying Victims: A Study of the Measurement of Criminal Victimizations, Perceptions of Crime and Attitudes to Criminal Justice.* London: John Wiley and Sons, 1977.

Spector, P. "Population Density and Unemployment: The Effects on the Incidence of Violent Crime in the American City." *Criminology* 12 (1975):399–401.

Spergel, I. *Racketville, Slumtown, Haulberg: An Exploratory Study of Delinquent Subcultures.* Chicago: University of Chicago Press, 1964.

Statistics Canada. *Crime and Traffic Enforcement Statistics.* Ottawa: Queen's Printer (Catalogue 85-205 annual), 1972, 1977, 1978, 1979, 1980.

Stea, D. "The Measurement of Mental Maps: An Experimental Model for Studying Conceptual Spaces." In K. R. Cox and R. G. Golledge, (Eds.), *Behavioral Problems in Geography,* pp. 228–253. Evanston, Ill.: Northwestern University Press, 1969.

Stewart, J. A. "Demographic Gravitation." *Sociometry* 11 (1948):31–58.

Stott, D. H. *Troublesome Children.* London: National Childrens Home, 1966.

Stouffer, S. *Social Research to Test Ideas.* New York: The Free Press, 1959.

Stuart, D. *Canadian Criminal Law: A Treatise.* Toronto: Carswell, 1982.

Sudnow, D. "Normal Crimes: Sociological Features of the Penal Code in a Public Defender Office." *Social Problems* 12 (1965):255–276.

Sutherland, E. H. "Mental Deficiency and Crime." In K. Young, *Social Attitudes,* pp. 357–375. New York: Holt, 1931.

Sutherland, E. H. *Principles of Criminology* (4th ed.). Philadelphia: Lippincott, 1947.

Sutherland, E. H. *White Collar Crime.* New York: Dryden Press, 1949.

Sutherland, E. H. *The Professional Thief.* Chicago: University of Chicago Press, 1956.

Sveri, K. *Crime and Industrialization.* Stockholm: Scandinavian Research Council for Criminology, 1976.

Symposium. "Violence and Southernness: Three Views." *Criminology* 16 (1978):47–67.

Tappan, P. "Who is the Criminal?" *American Sociological Review* 12 (1947):96–102.

Tarde, G. *Penal Philosophy.* Montclair, N.J.: Patterson Smith, 1968.

Tardif, G. "Les delit de violence à Montreal." Paper read at the 5th Research Conference on Delinquency and Criminality, Societé de Criminologie du Quebec, Montreal, 1967.

Tarnopolsky, W. S. *The Canadian Bill of Rights* (2d rev. ed.). Toronto: McClelland and Stewart, 1975.

Taylor, I.; Walton, P.; and Young, J. *The New Criminology.* London: Routledge and Kegan Paul, 1973.

Taylor, I.; Walton, P., and Young, J. *Critical Criminology,* London: Routledge and Kegan Paul, 1975.

Tepperman, L. *Crime Control: The Urge Toward Authority.* Toronto: McGraw-Hill Ryerson, 1977.

Thompson, D. L. "New Concept: Subjective Distance." *Journal of Retailing* 39 (1965):1–6.

Thompson, E. P. *The Making of the English Working Class* (rev. ed.) Harmondsworth, England: Penguin Books, 1968.

Thompson, E. P. *Whigs and Hunters: The Origin of the Black Act.* New York: Pantheon Books, 1975.

Tilly, C. "Race and Migration to the American City." In J. Q. Wilson (Ed.), *The Metropolitan Enigma,* pp. 144–169. Garden City, New York: Anchor Books, 1970.

Timms, D. W. G. "The Spatial Distribution of Deviants in Luton, England." *Australian and New Zealand Journal of Criminology* 1 (1965):38–52.

Timms, D. W. G. *The Urban Mosaic: Towards a Theory of Residential Differentiation.* Cambridge: Cambridge University Press, 1971.

Tittle, C. R., and Villemez, W. J. "Social Class and Criminality." *Social Forces* 56 (1977):474–502.

Tobias, J. J. *Nineteenth Century Crime: Prevention and Punishment.* Newton Abbot, England: David and Charles, 1972a.

Tobias, J. J. *Urban Crime in Victorian England.* New York: Schocken Books, 1972b.

Tolman, E. C. "Cognitive Maps in Rats and Man." *Psychological Review* 55 (1948):189–208.

Trasler, G. *The Explanation of Criminality.* London: Routledge and Kegan Paul, 1962.

Tribble, S. "Socio-Economic Status and Self-Reported Juvenile Delinquency." *Canadian Journal of Criminology and Corrections* 14 (1972):409–415.

Trowbridge, C. C. "Fundamental Methods of Orientation and Imaginary Maps." *Science* 39 (1913):1–6.

Tuchfarber, A. J., and Klecka, W. R. *Measuring Criminal Victimization: An Efficient Method.* Washington: The Police Foundation, 1976.

Tuchman, B. *A Distant Mirror: The Calamitous Fourteenth Century.* New York: Alfred A. Knopf, 1978.

Turk, A. *Criminality and Legal Order.* Chicago: Rand-McNally, 1969.

Turner, S. "Delinquency and Distance." In T. Sellin and M. E. Wolfgang, *Delinquency: Selected Studies,* pp. 11–26. New York: John Wiley and Sons, 1969.

United Nations. *Crime Prevention and Control: Report to the Secretary General.* New York: United Nations (22 Sept. 1977), (A/32/150) 77-17605, 1977.

Urquhart, M. C., and Buckley, K. A. H. *Historical Statistics of Canada.* Toronto: Macmillan of Canada, 1965.

Vaz, E. W. "Self-Reported Delinquency and Socio/Economic Status." *Canadian Journal of Corrections* 8 (1966):20–27.

Vetter, H. J., and Silverman, I. J. *The Nature of Crime.* Philadelphia: W. B. Saunders, 1978.

Viccica, A. D. D. "Toward the First World Crime Survey." *LAE: Journal of the American Criminal Justice Association* 42 (1979):1–10.

Vigderhous, G. "Cyclical Variations of Monthly and Yearly Homicide Rates in the United States and Their Relationship to Changes in the Unemployment Rate." In C. Wellford (Ed.), *Quantitative Studies in Criminology,* pp. 100–120. Beverly Hills, Calif.: Sage Publications, 1978.

Vold, G. B. *Theoretical Criminology.* New York: Oxford University Press, 1958.

Vold, G. B. *Theoretical Criminology* (2d ed.). New York: Oxford University Press, 1979.

Voss, H. L. "Socio-Economic Status and Reported Delinquent Behavior." *Social Problems* 13 (1968):314–324.

Voss, H. L., and Hepburn, J. "Patterns in Criminal Homicide." *Journal of Criminal Law, Criminology and Police Science* 59 (1968):449–508.

Voss, H. L., and Petersen, D. M. *Ecology, Crime and Delinquency.* New York: Appleton-Century-Crofts, 1971.

Waldo, G. P., and Chiricos, T. G. "Perceived Penal Sanction and Self-Reported Criminality—A Neglected Approach to Deterrence Research." *Social Problems* 19 (1972): 522–540.

Walker, N. *Crimes, Courts and Figures: An Introduction to Criminal Statistics.* Harmondsworth, England: Penguin Books, 1971.

Waller, I., and Okihiro, N. *Burglary: The Victim and the Public.* Toronto: University of Toronto Press, 1978.

Wallerstein, I. *The Modern World System* (Text ed.). New York: Academic Press, 1976.

Wallerstein, J. S., and Wyle, C. J. "Our Law-Abiding Law Breakers." *Probation* 25 (1947):107–112.

Wallis, C. P., and Maliphant, R. "Delinquent Areas in the County of London: Ecological Factors." *British Journal of Criminology* 7 (1967):250–284.

Wambaugh, J. *The Onion Field.* New York: Delacorte Press, 1973.

Warner S. B. *Crime and Criminal Statistics in Boston.* Cambridge, Mass.: Harvard University Press, 1934.

Wattenberg, B. J. (Ed.). *The Statistical History of the United States From Colonial Times to the Present.* New York: Basic Books, 1976.

Wellford, C. F. "Age Composition and the Increase in Recorded Crime." *Criminology* 11 (1973):61–70.

Wellford, C. F. "Crime and the Dimensions of Nations." *International Journal of Criminology and Penology* 2 (1974):1–10.

West, D. J. *Present Conduct and Future Delinquency.* London: Heinemann, 1969.

West, D. J., and Farrington, D. P. *Who Becomes Delinquent?* London: Heinemann, 1973.

West, D. J., and Farrington, D. P. *The Delinquent Way of Life.* London: Heinemann, 1977.

Whyte, W. F. *Street Corner Society: The Social Structure of an Italian Slum* (2d ed.). Chicago: University of Chicago Press, 1955.

Wicker, A. W. "Mediating Behavior-Environment Congruence." *Behavioral Science* 17 (1972): 265–278.

Wilcox, S. *The Geography of Robbery* [The Prevention and Control of Robbery, Vol. 3]. Davis: The Center of Administration of Criminal Justice, University of California at Davis, 1973.

Wiles, P. "Criminal Statistics and Sociological Explanations of Crime." In W. G. Carson and P. Wiles, (Eds.), *Crime and Delinquency in Britain,* pp. 174–192. London: Martin Robertson.

Wilkins, L. *Social Deviance.* London: Tavistock, 1964.

Willbach, H. "The Trends of Crime in New York City." *Journal of Criminal Law and Criminology* 29 (1938):62–73.

Willbach, H. "The Trend of Crime in Chicago." *Journal of Criminal Law and Criminology* 31 (1940): 720–727.

Williams, J. R., and Gold, M. "From Delinquent Behavior to Official Delinquency." *Social Problems* 20 (1972):209–229.

Willmer, M. A. P. *Crime and Information Theory*. Edinburgh: Edinburgh University Press, 1970.

Wilson, J. Q. *The Metropolitan Enigma*. Garden City, New York: Anchor Books, 1970.

Wilson, J. Q. *Thinking About Crime*. New York: Basic Books, 1975.

Wirth, L. "Urbanism as a Way of Life." *American Journal of Sociology* 44 (1938):1–24.

Wirth, L. *On Cities and Social Life*. Chicago: University of Chicago Press, 1964.

Wolf, P. "Crime and Development: An International Comparison of Crime Rates." *Scandinavian Studies in Criminology* 3 (1971):107–120.

Wolfgang, M. E. *Patterns of Criminal Homicide*. Philadelphia: University of Pennsylvania Press, 1958.

Wolfgang, M. E. "Uniform Crime Reports: A Critical Appraisal." *University of Pennsylvania Law Review* 111 (1963):708–738.

Wolfgang, M. E. *Patterns in Criminal Homicide*. New York: John Wiley and Sons, 1966.

Wolfgang, M. E. "Urban Crime." In J. Q. Wilson, *The Metropolitan Enigma*, pp. 270–311. Garden City, New York: Anchor Books, 1970.

Wolfgang, M. E., and Ferracuti, F. *The Subculture of Violence*. London: Tavistock, 1967.

Wolpin, K. I. "An Economic Analysis of Crime and Punishment in England and Wales, 1894–1967." *Journal of Political Economy* 86 (1976):815–840.

Wootton, B. *Social Science and Social Pathology*. London: George Allen and Unwin, 1959.

Worden, M. A. "Criminogenic Correlates of Intermetropolitan Crime Rates, 1960 and 1970." In D. Georges-Abeyie and K. D. Harries (Eds.), *Crime: A Spatial Perspective*, pp. 109–126. New York: Columbia University Press, 1980.

Wrigley, E. A. *Population and History*. New York: McGraw-Hill, 1969.

Wrigley, E. A. *Nineteenth-Century Society: Essays in the Use of Quantitative Methods for the Study of Social Data*. Cambridge: Cambridge University Press, 1972.

Yablonsky, L. *The Violent Gang* (rev. ed.). Baltimore: Penguin Books, 1970.

Young, J. *The Drugtakers: The Social Meaning of Drug Use*. London: Paladin, 1971.

Zay, N. "Gaps in Available Statistics on Crime and Delinquency in Canada." *Canadian Journal of Economics and Political Science*. 29 (1963):75–89.

Zehr, H. *Crime and The Development of Modern Society: Patterns of Criminality in Nineteenth Century Germany and France*. Totowa, N.J.: Rowman and Littlefield, 1976.

Zipf, G. K. "P1P2/D Hypothesis: On the Intercity Movement of Persons." *American Sociological Review* 11 (1946):677–686.

Index

DATE DUE
